THE IMMORTAL IRON FIST

THE BOOK OF THE IRON FIST

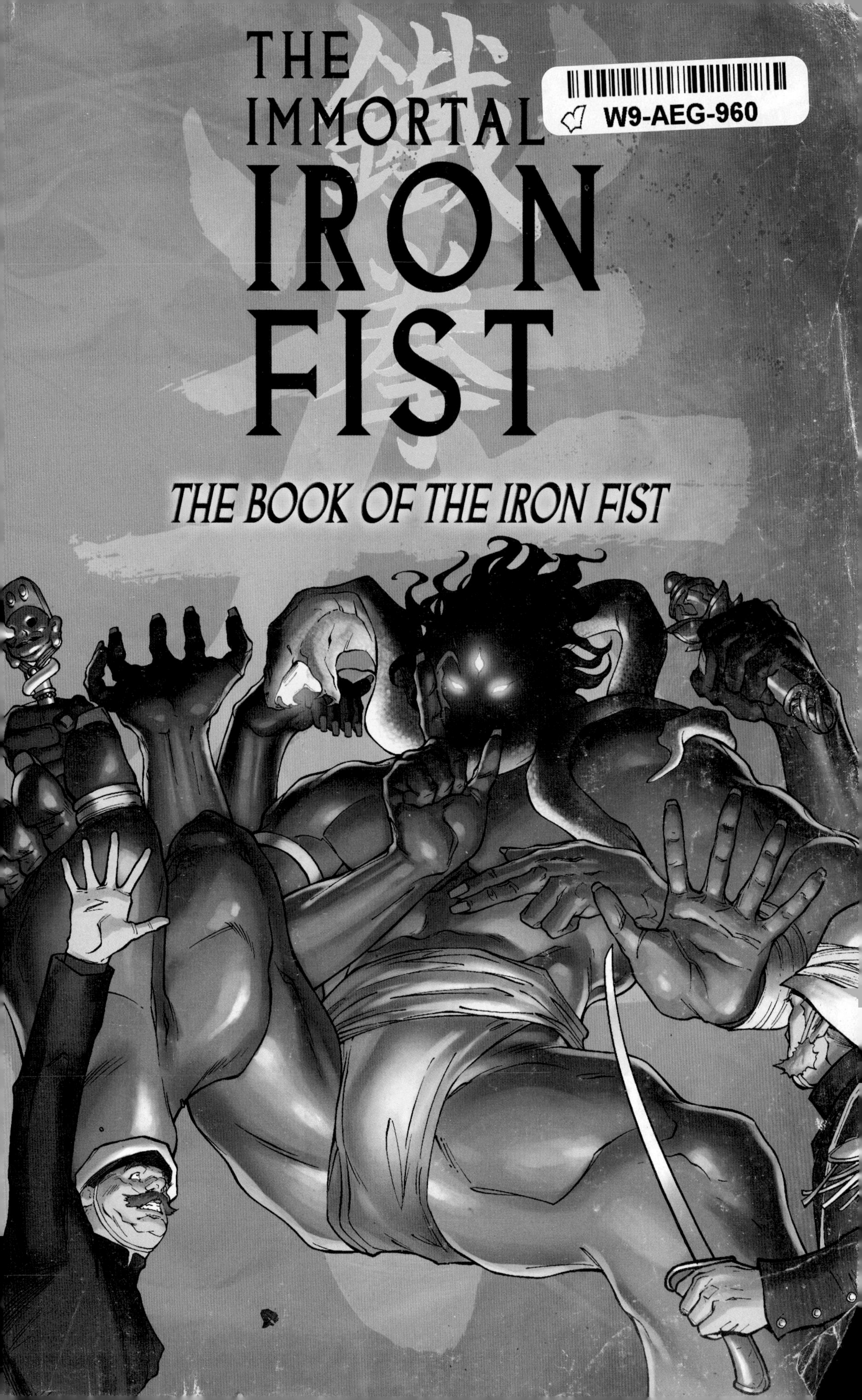

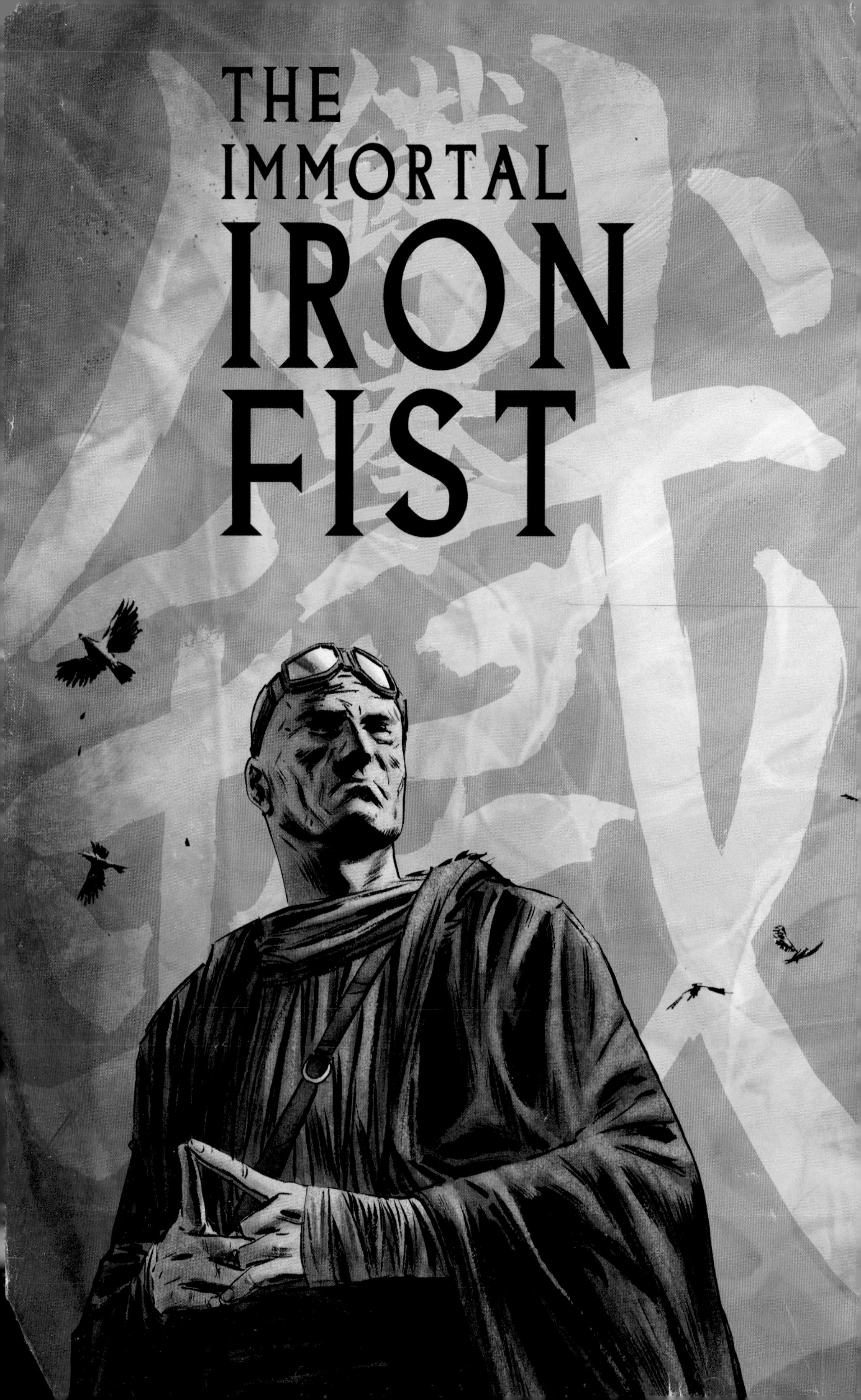
THE
IMMORTAL
IRON
FIST

THE BOOK OF THE IRON FIST

Writers: Matt Fraction
with Ed Brubaker (Issue #7)

ISSUE #7
Artists: Travel Foreman & Derek Fridolfs, Leandro Fernandez
& Francisco Paronzini and Khari Evans & Victor Olazaba
Colorist: Dan Brown • Cover Art: Travel Foreman & Len O'Grady

ISSUE #15
Artists: Khari Evans & Victor Olazaba
Colorists: Jelena Kevic Djurdjevic & Paul Mounts
Cover Art: Khari Evans, Victor Olazaba & Matt Hollingsworth

ORSON RANDALL & THE GREEN MIST OF DEATH
Artists: Nick Dragotta, Mike Allred, Russ Heath, Lewis LaRosa &
Stefano Gaudiano and Mitch Breitweiser
Colorists: Laura Allred, Russ Heath & Matt Hollingsworth
Cover Art: Kaare Andrews

ISSUE #16
Artist: David Aja • Colorist: Matt Hollingsworth • Cover Art: David Aja

Letterers: Dave Lanphear & Artmonkeys Studios
Assistant Editor: Alejandro Arbona • Editor: Warren Simons

THE ORIGIN OF DANNY RAND
Writers: Roy Thomas, Len Wein & Matt Fraction
Pencilers: Gil Kane, Larry Hama & Kano
Inkers: Dick Giordano & Kano
Colorists: Sotocolor's A. Crossley & Kano
Letterers: L.P. Gregory & Dave Lanphear
Cover Artists: Gil Kane, Larry Hama & Rain Beredo

Collection Editor: Jennifer Grünwald
Assistant Editors: Alex Starbuck & Nelson Ribeiro
Editor, Special Projects: Mark D. Beazley
Senior Editor, Special Projects: Jeff Youngquist
Senior Vice President of Sales: David Gabriel
SVP of Brand Planning & Communications: Michael Pasciullo

Editor in Chief: Axel Alonso • Chief Creative Officer: Joe Quesada
Publisher: Dan Buckley • Executive Producer: Alan Fine

IMMORTAL IRON FIST VOL. 3: THE BOOK OF THE IRON FIST. Contains material originally published in magazine form as IMMORTAL IRON FIST #7 and #15-16, IMMORTAL IRON FIST: ORSON RANDALL AND THE GREEN MIST OF DEATH and IMMORTAL IRON FIST: THE ORIGIN OF DANNY RAND. Second printing 2011. ISBN# 978-0-7851-2536-5. Published by MARVEL WORLDWIDE, INC., a subsidiary of MARVEL ENTERTAINMENT, LLC. OFFICE OF PUBLICATION: 135 West 50th Street, New York, NY 10020. Copyright © 2007 and 2008 Marvel Characters, Inc. All rights reserved. $16.99 per copy in the U.S. and $18.99 in Canada (GST #R127032852); Canadian Agreement #40668537. All characters featured in this issue and the distinctive names and likenesses thereof, and all related indicia are trademarks of Marvel Characters, Inc. No similarity between any of the names, characters, persons, and/or institutions in this magazine with those of any living or dead person or institution is intended, and any such similarity which may exist is purely coincidental. **Printed in the U.S.A.** ALAN FINE, EVP - Office of the President, Marvel Worldwide, Inc. and EVP & CMO Marvel Characters B.V.; DAN BUCKLEY, Publisher & President - Print, Animation & Digital Divisions; JOE QUESADA, Chief Creative Officer; JIM SOKOLOWSKI, Chief Operating Officer; DAVID BOGART, SVP of Business Affairs & Talent Management; TOM BREVOORT, SVP of Publishing; C.B. CEBULSKI, SVP of Creator & Content Development; DAVID GABRIEL, SVP of Publishing Sales & Circulation; MICHAEL PASCIULLO, SVP of Brand Planning & Communications; JIM O'KEEFE, VP of Operations & Logistics; DAN CARR, Executive Director of Publishing Technology; SUSAN CRESPI, Editorial Operations Manager; ALEX MORALES, Publishing Operations Manager; STAN LEE, Chairman Emeritus. For information regarding advertising in Marvel Comics or on Marvel.com, please contact John Dokes, SVP Integrated Sales and Marketing, at jdokes@marvel.com. For Marvel subscription inquiries, please call 800-217-9158. **Manufactured between 8/3/11 and 8/22/11** by R.R. DONNELLEY, INC., SALEM, VA, USA.

1 0 9 8 7 6 5 4 3 2

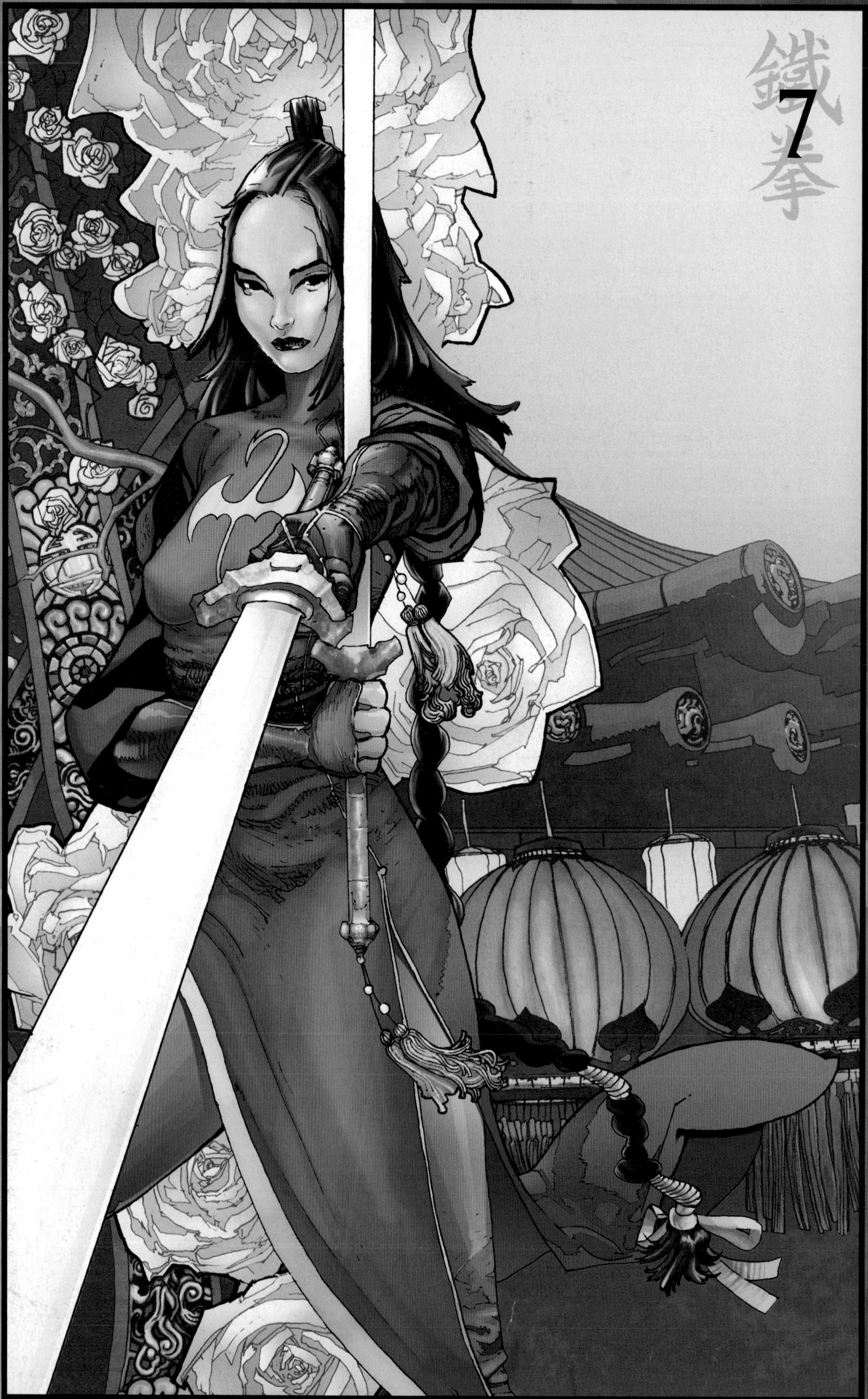
鐵拳
7

There have been sixty-six men and women to carry the mantle of THE IMMORTAL IRON FIST throughout the ages, men and women of great courage, valor, skill, and sacrifice. Sixty-six men and women have stood between man and the unstoppable forces of evil, willing to give all they have to hold back the hordes.

This is the story of one of them, as told in THE BOOK OF THE IRON FIST.

The Story of the Iron Fist Wu Ao-Shi

The Pirate Queen of Pinghai Bay

ED BRUBAKER & MATT FRACTION – WRITERS
TRAVEL FOREMAN – ARTIST 1-6
DEREK FRIDOLFS – INKER 1-6
LEANDRO FERNANDEZ – ARTIST 7-13
FRANCISCO PARONZINI AND LEO FERNANDEZ
– INKERS 7-13
KHARI EVANS – ARTIST 14-22
VICTOR OLAZABA – INKER 14-22
DAN BROWN – COLORIST
DAVE LANPHEAR LETTERER
BRAD JOHANSEN - PRODUCTION
ALEJANDRO ARBONA – ASSISTANT EDITOR
WARREN SIMONS – EDITOR
JOE QUESADA – EDITOR IN CHIEF
DAN BUCKLEY – PUBLISHER

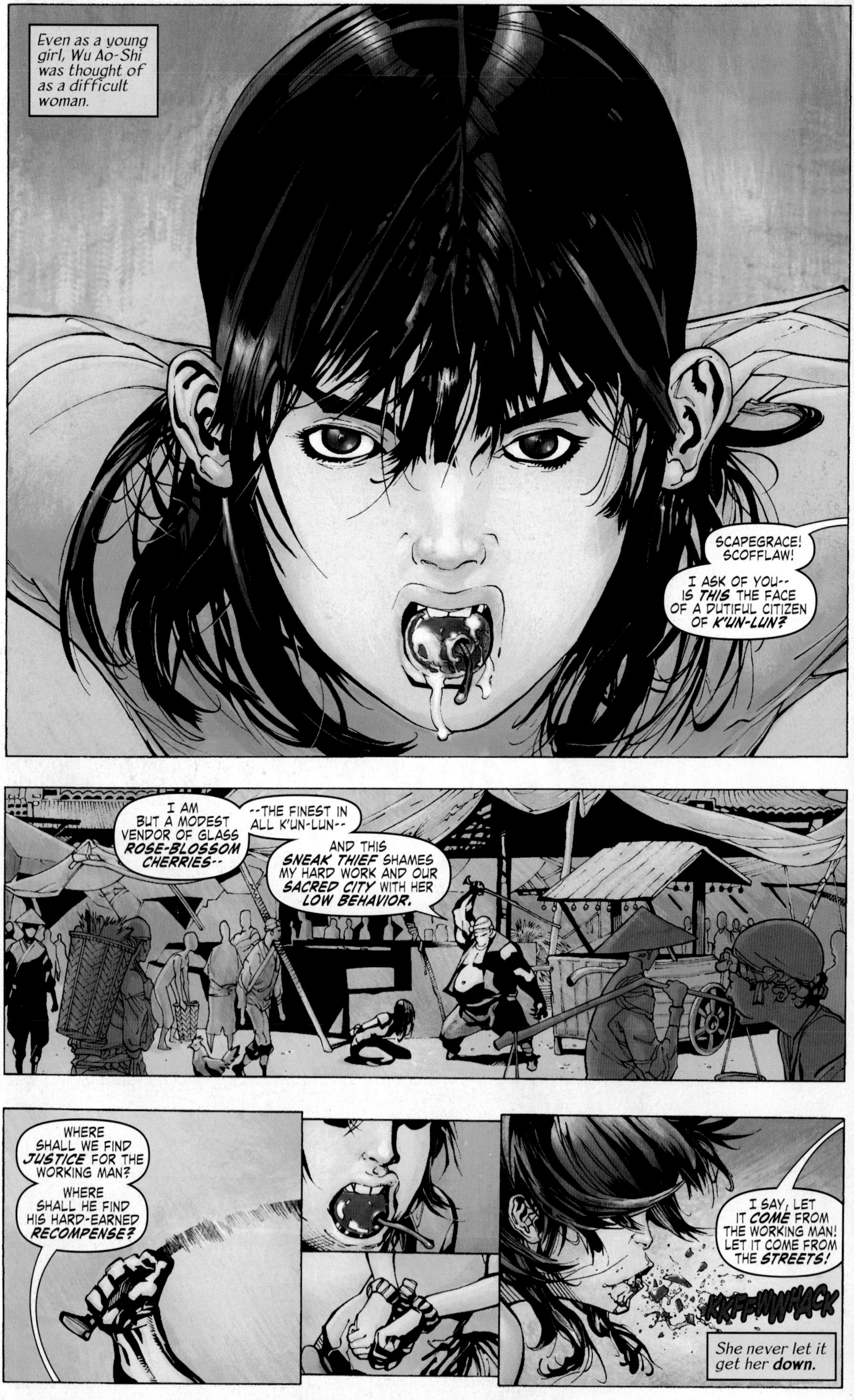
Even as a young girl, Wu Ao-Shi was thought of as a difficult woman.
SCAPEGRACE! SCOFFLAW!
I ASK OF YOU-- IS THIS THE FACE OF A DUTIFUL CITIZEN OF K'UN-LUN?
I AM BUT A MODEST VENDOR OF GLASS ROSE-BLOSSOM CHERRIES--
--THE FINEST IN ALL K'UN-LUN--
AND THIS SNEAK THIEF SHAMES MY HARD WORK AND OUR SACRED CITY WITH HER LOW BEHAVIOR.
WHERE SHALL WE FIND JUSTICE FOR THE WORKING MAN?
WHERE SHALL HE FIND HIS HARD-EARNED RECOMPENSE?
I SAY, LET IT COME FROM THE WORKING MAN! LET IT COME FROM THE STREETS!
KKFFWWHACK
She never let it get her down.

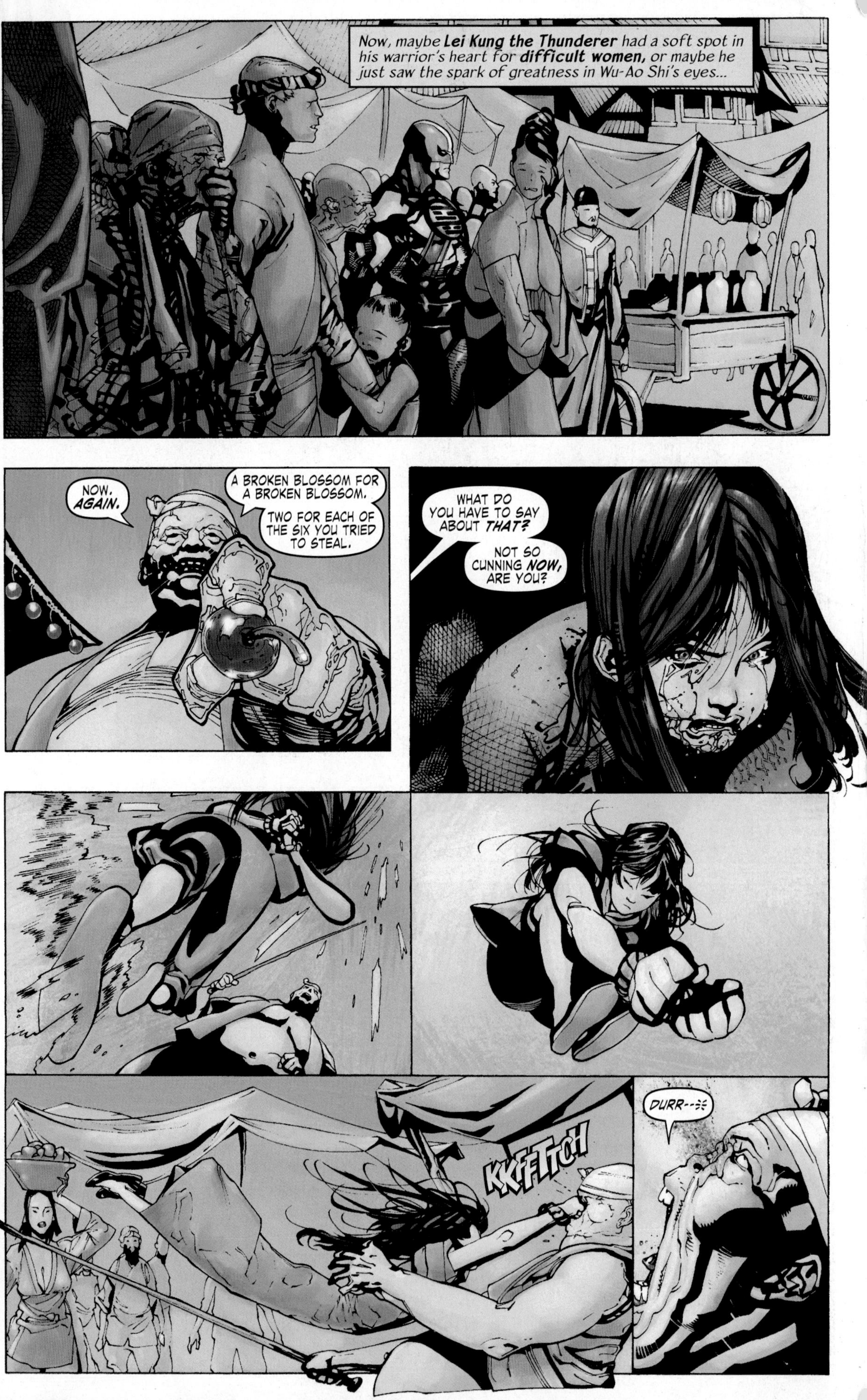
Now, maybe **Lei Kung the Thunderer** had a soft spot in his warrior's heart for **difficult women,** or maybe he just saw the spark of greatness in Wu-Ao Shi's eyes...
NOW. AGAIN.
A BROKEN BLOSSOM FOR A BROKEN BLOSSOM.
TWO FOR EACH OF THE SIX YOU TRIED TO STEAL.
WHAT DO YOU HAVE TO SAY ABOUT THAT?
NOT SO CUNNING NOW, ARE YOU?
KKFTTCH
DURR--

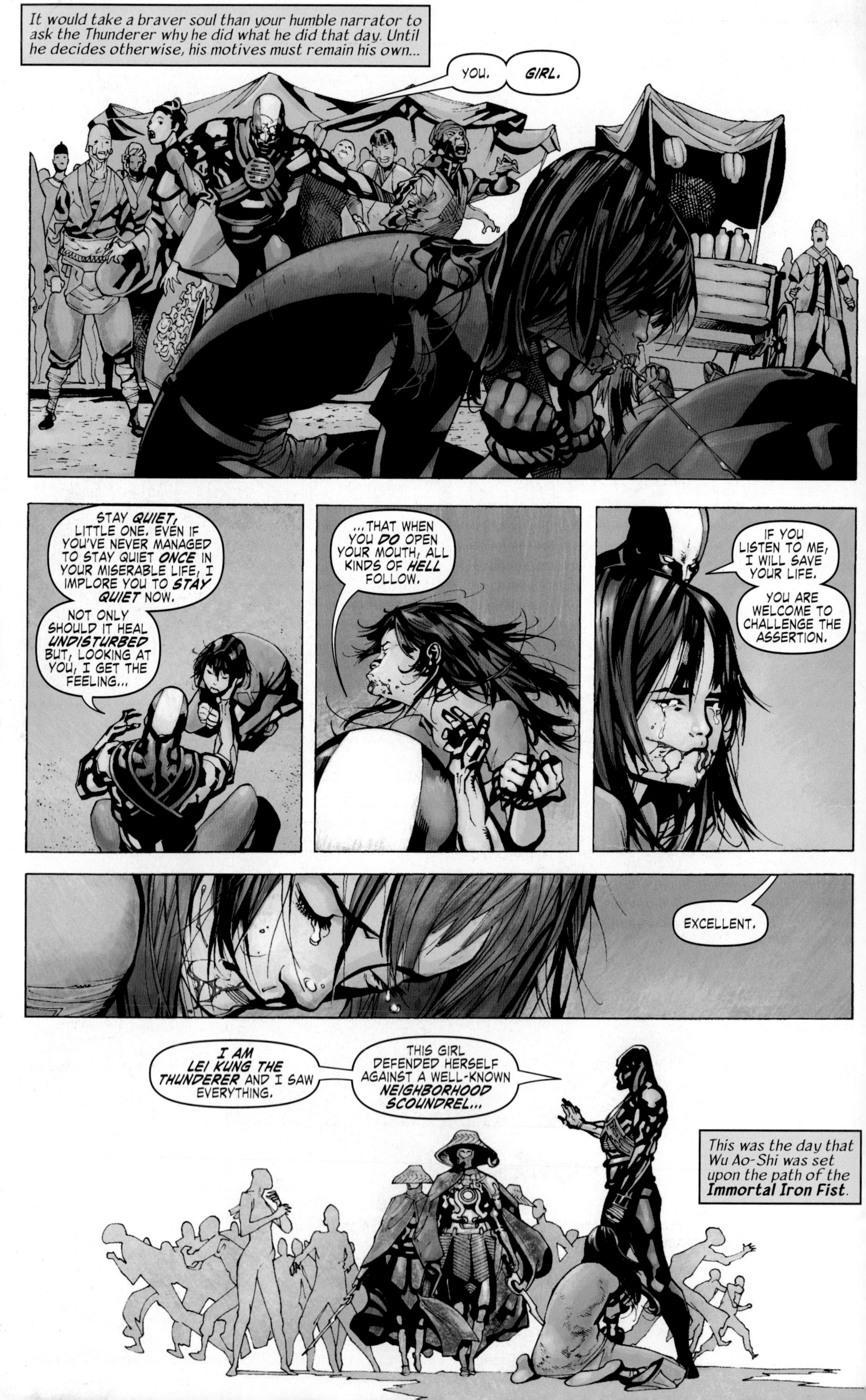
It would take a braver soul than your humble narrator to ask the Thunderer why he did what he did that day. Until he decides otherwise, his motives must remain his own...
YOU.
GIRL.
STAY QUIET, LITTLE ONE. EVEN IF YOU'VE NEVER MANAGED TO STAY QUIET ONCE IN YOUR MISERABLE LIFE, I IMPLORE YOU TO STAY QUIET NOW.
NOT ONLY SHOULD IT HEAL UNDISTURBED BUT, LOOKING AT YOU, I GET THE FEELING...
...THAT WHEN YOU DO OPEN YOUR MOUTH, ALL KINDS OF HELL FOLLOW.
IF YOU LISTEN TO ME, I WILL SAVE YOUR LIFE.
YOU ARE WELCOME TO CHALLENGE THE ASSERTION.
EXCELLENT.
I AM LEI KUNG THE THUNDERER AND I SAW EVERYTHING.
THIS GIRL DEFENDED HERSELF AGAINST A WELL-KNOWN NEIGHBORHOOD SCOUNDREL...
This was the day that Wu Ao-Shi was set upon the path of the Immortal Iron Fist.

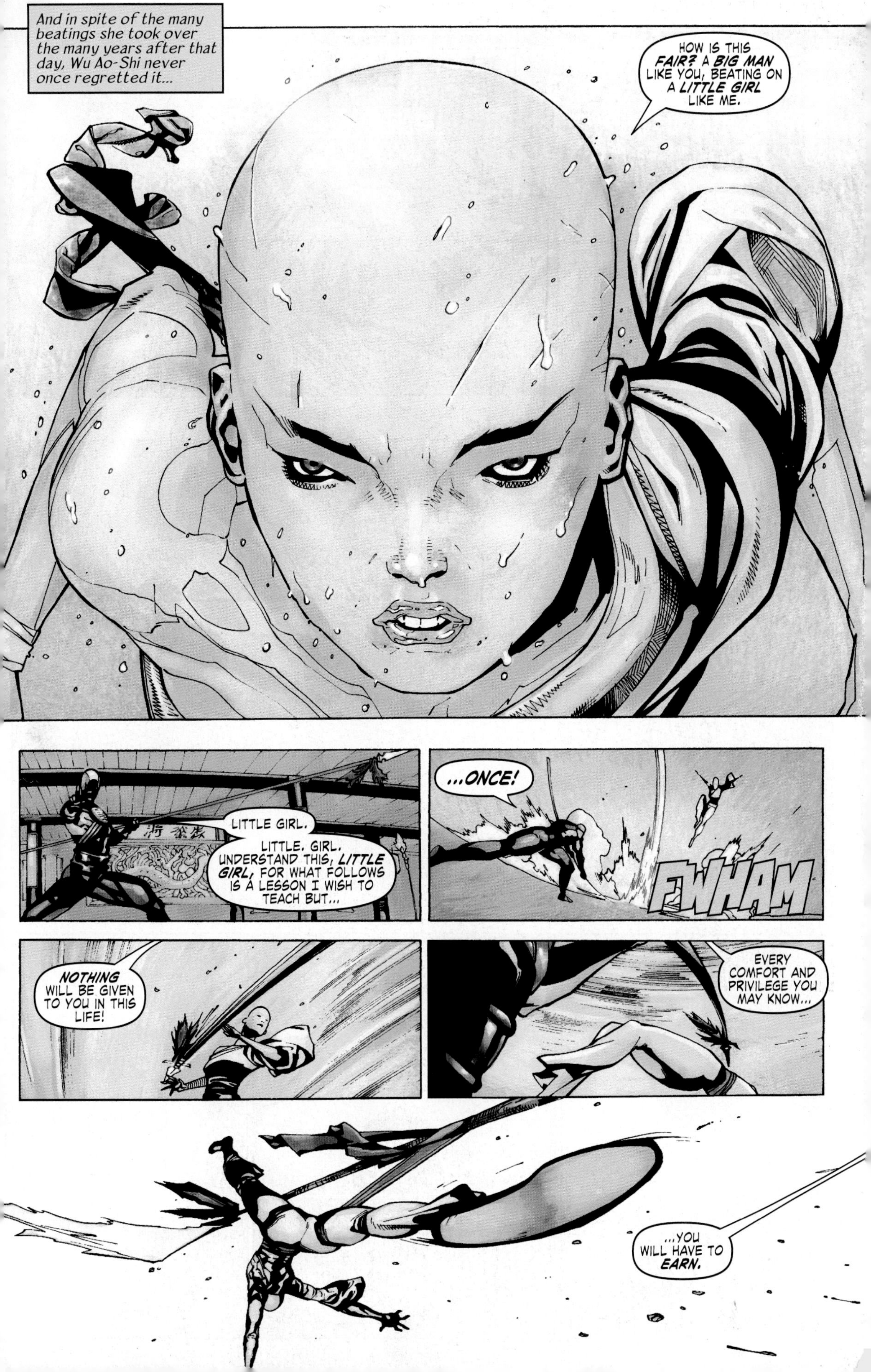
And in spite of the many beatings she took over the many years after that day, Wu Ao-Shi never once regretted it...
HOW IS THIS ***FAIR?*** A ***BIG MAN*** LIKE YOU, BEATING ON A ***LITTLE GIRL*** LIKE ME.
LITTLE GIRL.
LITTLE. GIRL. UNDERSTAND THIS, ***LITTLE GIRL,*** FOR WHAT FOLLOWS IS A LESSON I WISH TO TEACH BUT...
...ONCE!
FWHAM
NOTHING WILL BE GIVEN TO YOU IN THIS LIFE!
EVERY COMFORT AND PRIVILEGE YOU MAY KNOW...
...YOU WILL HAVE TO ***EARN.***

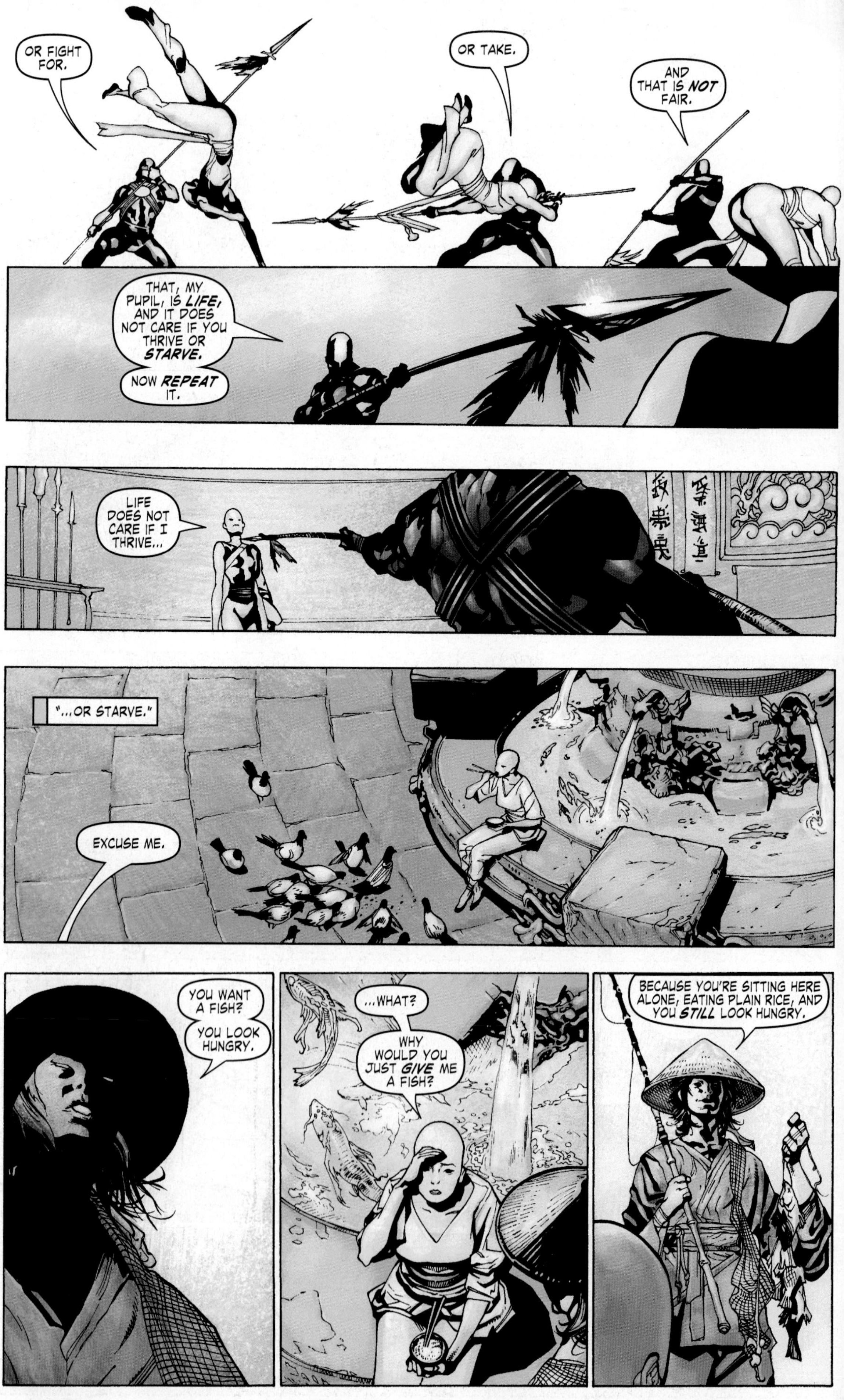
OR FIGHT FOR.
OR TAKE.
AND THAT IS NOT FAIR.
THAT, MY PUPIL, IS LIFE, AND IT DOES NOT CARE IF YOU THRIVE OR STARVE.
NOW REPEAT IT.
LIFE DOES NOT CARE IF I THRIVE...
"...OR STARVE."
EXCUSE ME.
YOU WANT A FISH?
YOU LOOK HUNGRY.
...WHAT?
WHY WOULD YOU JUST GIVE ME A FISH?
BECAUSE YOU'RE SITTING HERE ALONE, EATING PLAIN RICE, AND YOU STILL LOOK HUNGRY.

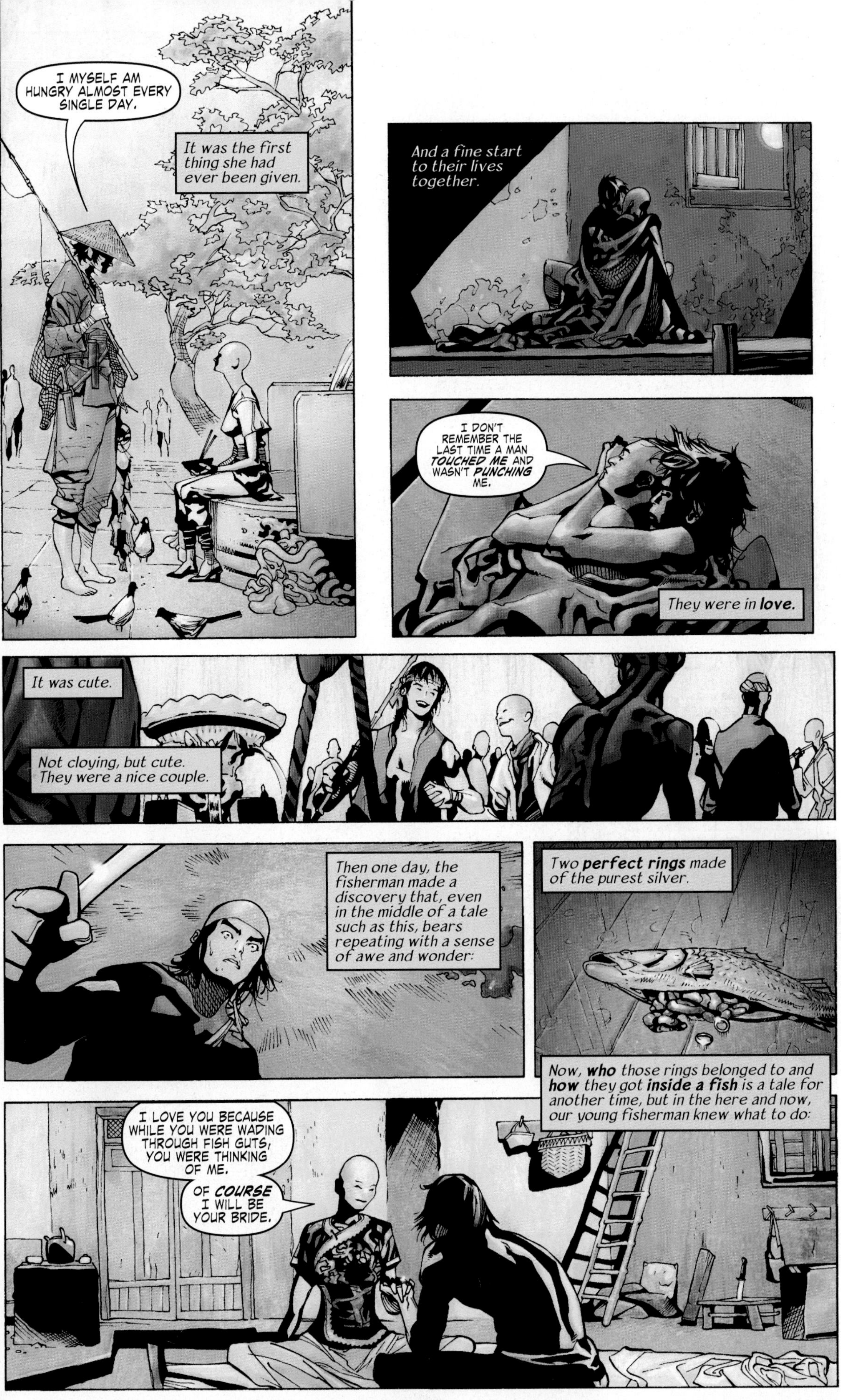
I MYSELF AM HUNGRY ALMOST EVERY SINGLE DAY.
It was the first thing she had ever been given.
And a fine start to their lives together.
I DON'T REMEMBER THE LAST TIME A MAN TOUCHED ME AND WASN'T PUNCHING ME.
They were in love.
It was cute.
Not cloying, but cute. They were a nice couple.
Then one day, the fisherman made a discovery that, even in the middle of a tale such as this, bears repeating with a sense of awe and wonder:
Two perfect rings made of the purest silver.
Now, who those rings belonged to and how they got inside a fish is a tale for another time, but in the here and now, our young fisherman knew what to do:
I LOVE YOU BECAUSE WHILE YOU WERE WADING THROUGH FISH GUTS, YOU WERE THINKING OF ME.
OF COURSE I WILL BE YOUR BRIDE.

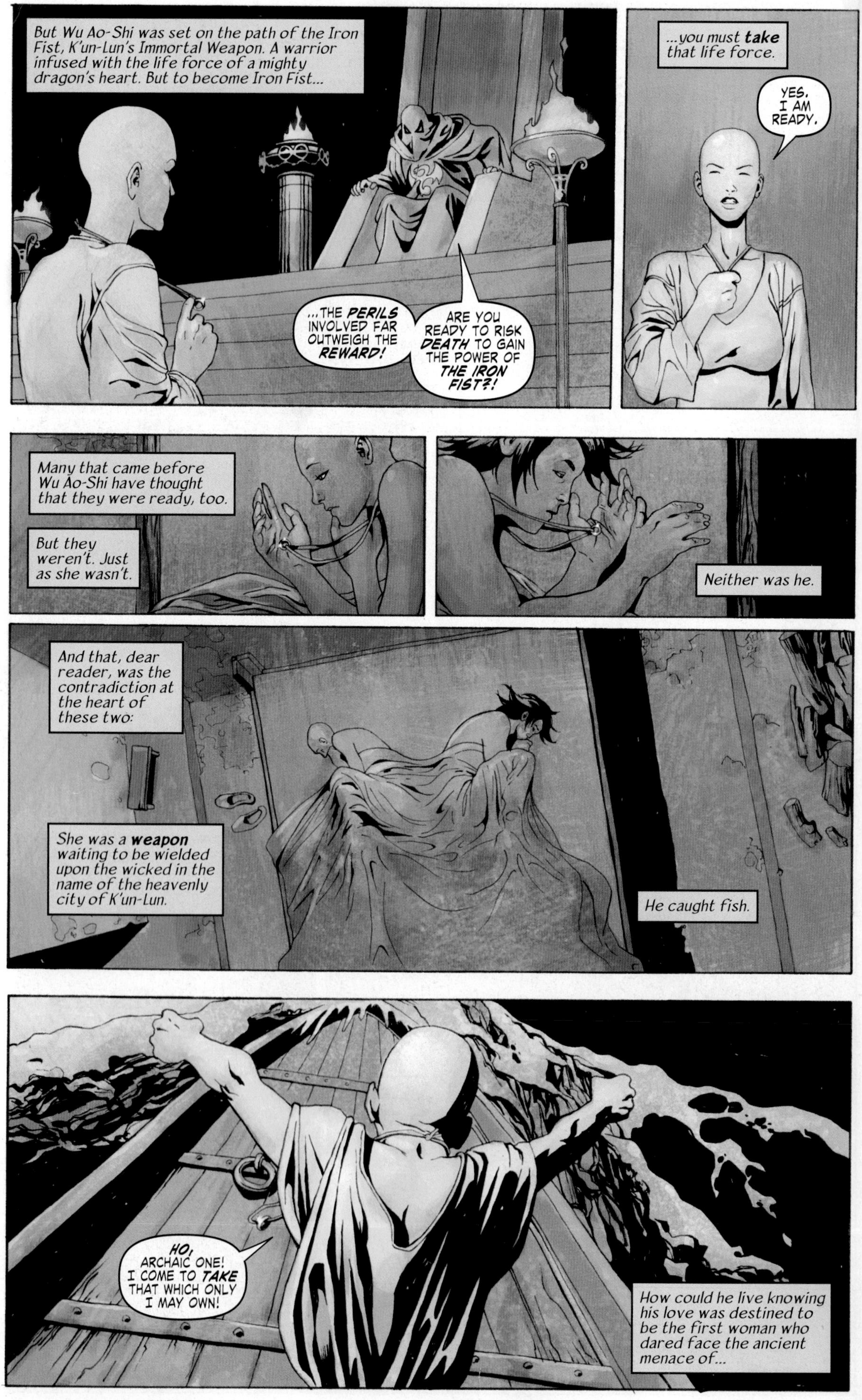
But Wu Ao-Shi was set on the path of the Iron Fist, K'un-Lun's Immortal Weapon. A warrior infused with the life force of a mighty dragon's heart. But to become Iron Fist...
ARE YOU READY TO RISK DEATH TO GAIN THE POWER OF THE IRON FIST?!
...THE PERILS INVOLVED FAR OUTWEIGH THE REWARD!
...you must take that life force.
YES. I AM READY.
Many that came before Wu Ao-Shi have thought that they were ready, too.
But they weren't. Just as she wasn't.
Neither was he.
And that, dear reader, was the contradiction at the heart of these two:
She was a weapon waiting to be wielded upon the wicked in the name of the heavenly city of K'un-Lun.
He caught fish.
HO, ARCHAIC ONE! I COME TO TAKE THAT WHICH ONLY I MAY OWN!
How could he live knowing his love was destined to be the first woman who dared face the ancient menace of...

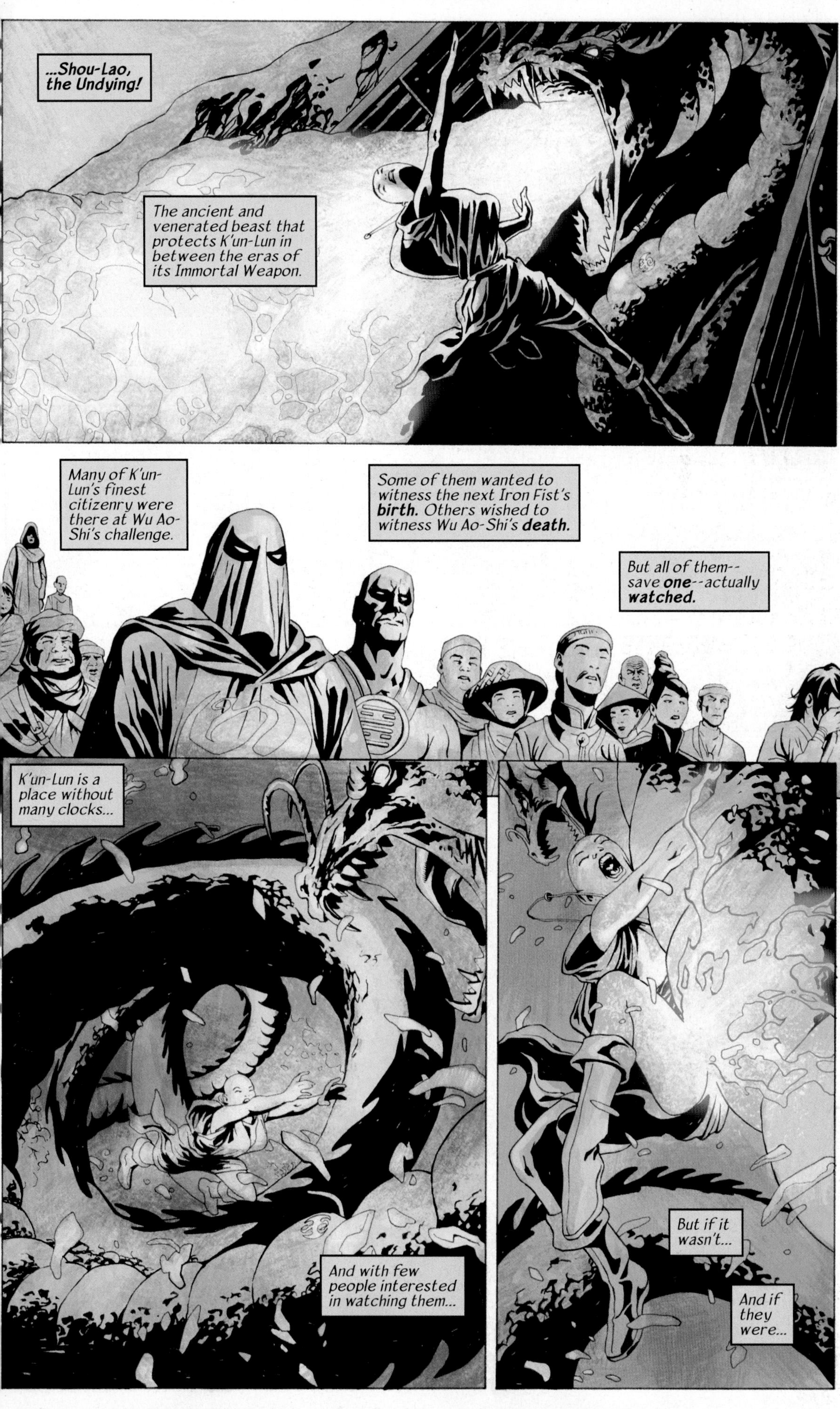
...Shou-Lao, the Undying!
The ancient and venerated beast that protects K'un-Lun in between the eras of its Immortal Weapon.
Many of K'un-Lun's finest citizenry were there at Wu Ao-Shi's challenge.
Some of them wanted to witness the next Iron Fist's **birth**. Others wished to witness Wu Ao-Shi's **death**.
But all of them--save **one**--actually **watched.**
K'un-Lun is a place without many clocks...
And with few people interested in watching them...
But if it wasn't...
And if they were...

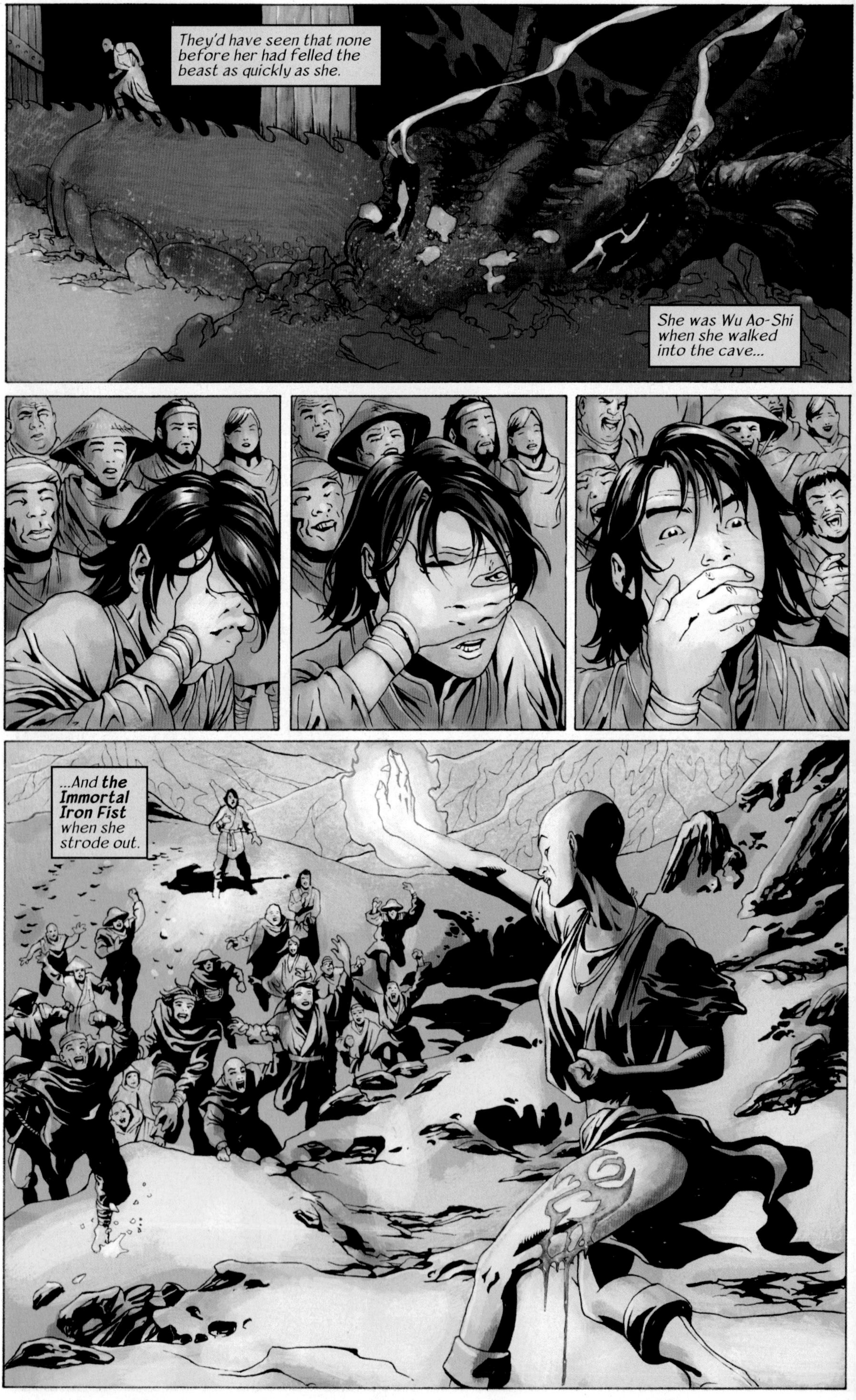
They'd have seen that none before her had felled the beast as quickly as she.
She was Wu Ao-Shi when she walked into the cave...
...And **the Immortal Iron Fist** when she strode out.

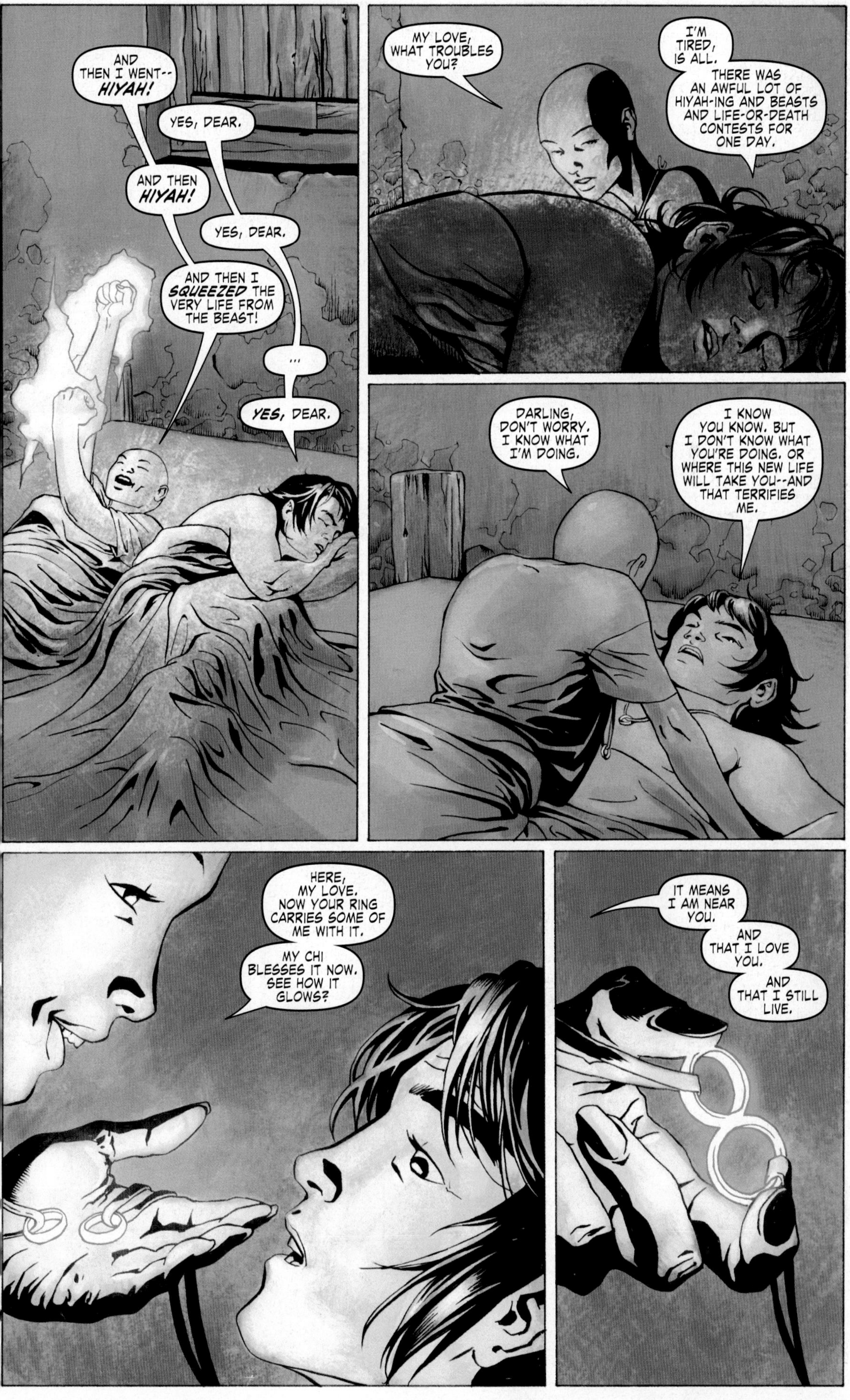
AND THEN I WENT-- *HIYAH!*
YES, DEAR.
AND THEN *HIYAH!*
YES, DEAR.
AND THEN I *SQUEEZED* THE VERY LIFE FROM THE BEAST!
...
YES, DEAR.
MY LOVE, WHAT TROUBLES YOU?
I'M TIRED, IS ALL.
THERE WAS AN AWFUL LOT OF HIYAH-ING AND BEASTS AND LIFE-OR-DEATH CONTESTS FOR ONE DAY.
DARLING, DON'T WORRY. I KNOW WHAT I'M DOING.
I KNOW YOU KNOW. BUT I DON'T KNOW WHAT YOU'RE DOING. OR WHERE THIS NEW LIFE WILL TAKE YOU--AND THAT TERRIFIES ME.
HERE, MY LOVE. NOW YOUR RING CARRIES SOME OF ME WITH IT.
MY CHI BLESSES IT NOW. SEE HOW IT GLOWS?
IT MEANS I AM NEAR YOU.
AND THAT I LOVE YOU.
AND THAT I STILL LIVE.

But the fisherman was still just a fisherman, thinking fisherman thoughts and dreaming dragon-less fisherman dreams.

He would **always** be a fisherman, and she would always be the **Immortal Weapon** of K'un-Lun.

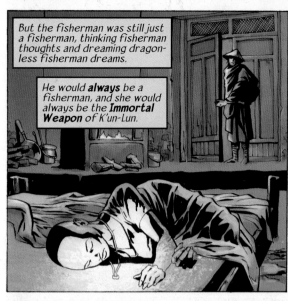

Same **planet,** different **worlds.**

He would never ask her not to be who she was, but he knew in his heart he could not **take** watching her risk her life time and time again.

On that magic day that K'un-Lun intersected with the world of men, the fisherman decided to **leave.**

He could never stand between his true love and her destiny, so he would go fish elsewhere--far away from dragons and kung fu and dying of slow, sick worry.

Wu Ao-Shi found this choice **unacceptable.**

AS YOU KNOW, K'UN-LUN APPEARS IN THE WORLD OF MEN ONCE A DECADE, AND--

I WISH TO **LEAVE.**

Destiny has a way of not really caring **what** you think.

It was well within her rights to leave. It was law; it was allowed; it was her **choice.** But Yu-Ti knew in his old, bitter bones **why** she was leaving:

DO YOU WISH TO TELL ME... THAT YOU WOULD **LEAVE** THE HEAVENLY CITY AND CHOOSE **LOVE** OVER **DUTY?**

And it infuriated him.

But to Wu Ao-Shi, love and duty were one and the same.

Old, bitter men with old, bitter bones have trouble remembering that sometimes.

...WOMEN ARE INFURIATING.

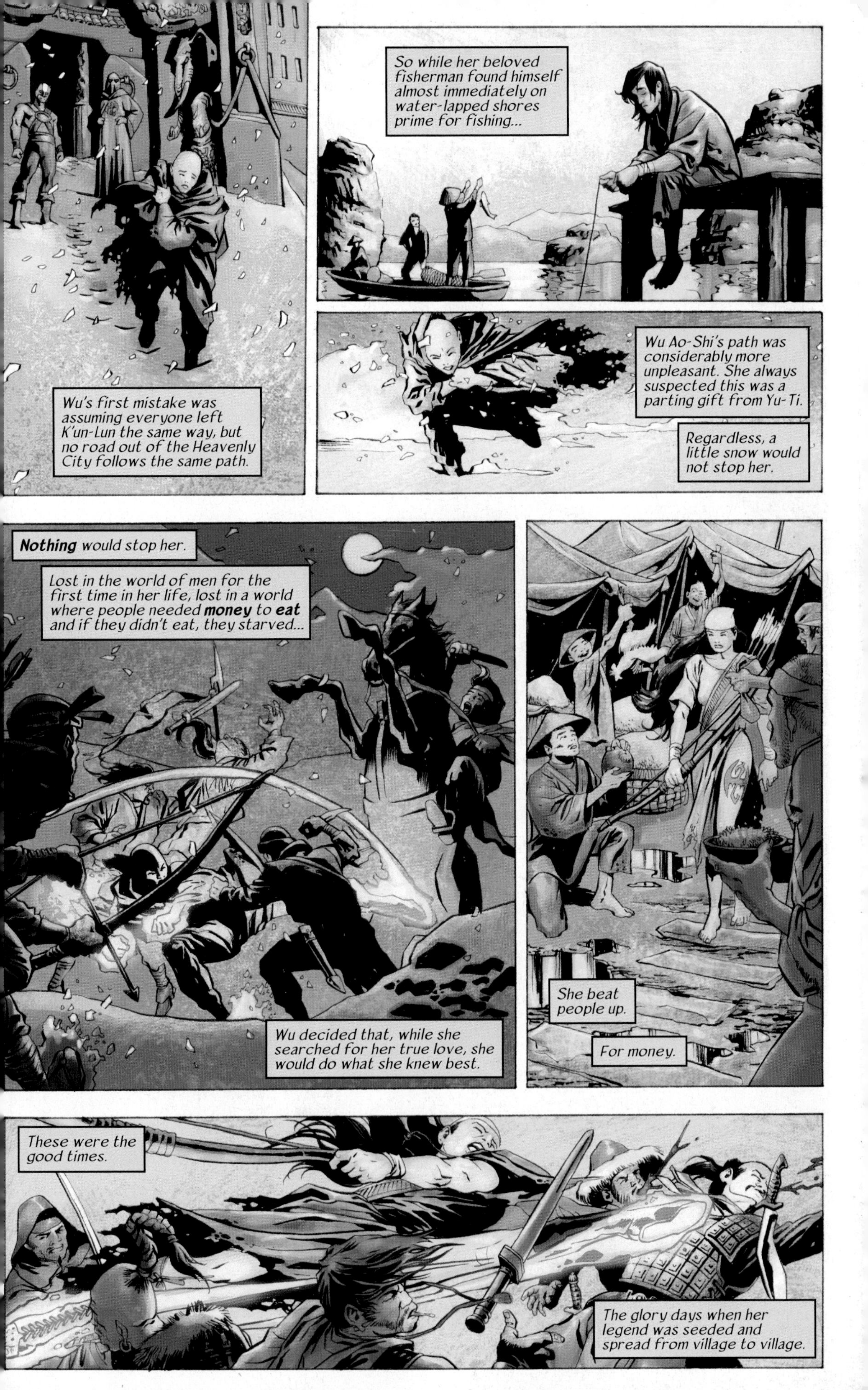

Wu's first mistake was assuming everyone left K'un-Lun the same way, but no road out of the Heavenly City follows the same path.
So while her beloved fisherman found himself almost immediately on water-lapped shores prime for fishing...
Wu Ao-Shi's path was considerably more unpleasant. She always suspected this was a parting gift from Yu-Ti.
Regardless, a little snow would not stop her.
Nothing would stop her.
Lost in the world of men for the first time in her life, lost in a world where people needed **money** to **eat** and if they didn't eat, they starved...
Wu decided that, while she searched for her true love, she would do what she knew best.
She beat people up.
For money.
These were the good times.
The glory days when her legend was seeded and spread from village to village.

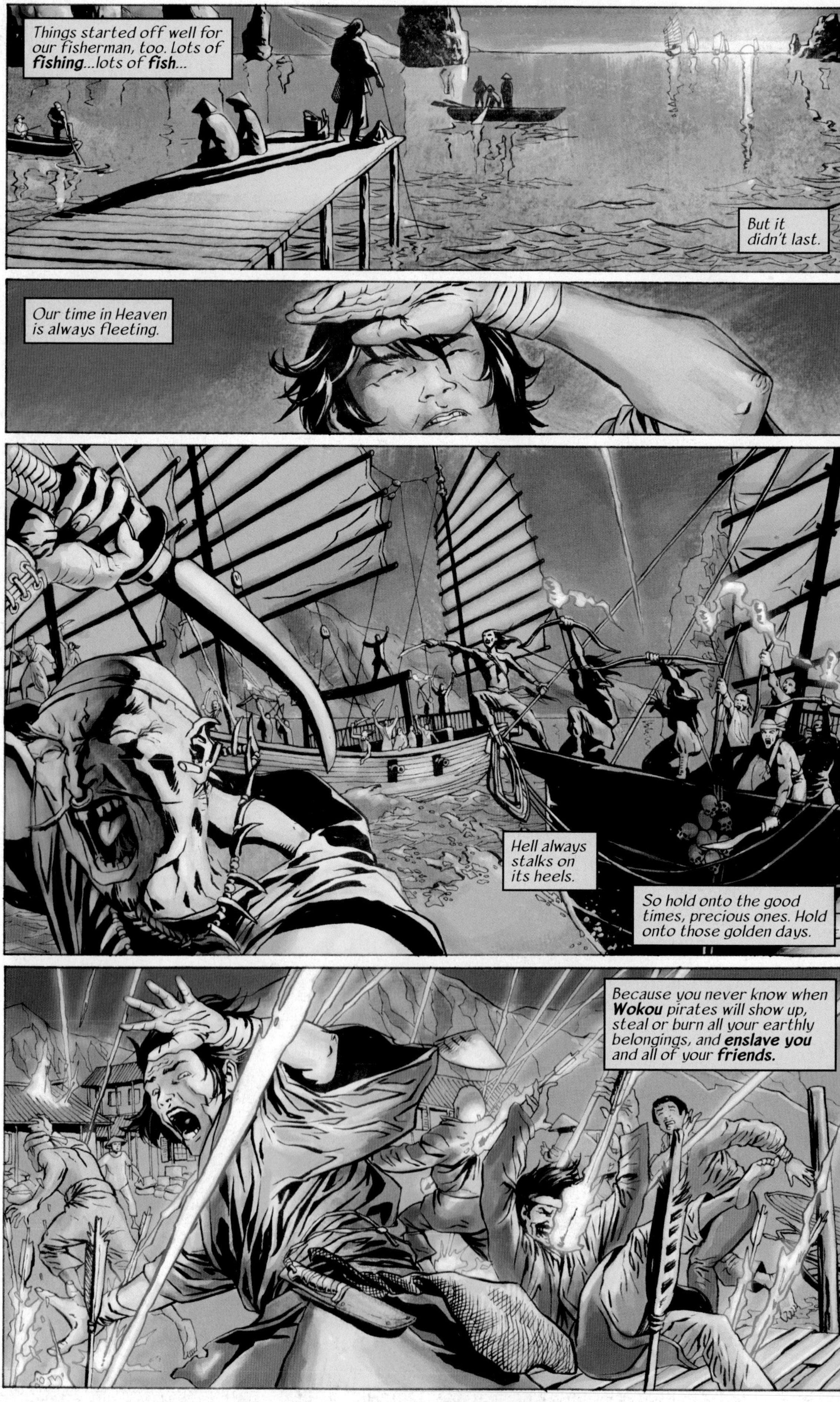
Things started off well for our fisherman, too. Lots of **fishing**...lots of **fish**...
But it didn't last.
Our time in Heaven is always fleeting.
Hell always stalks on its heels.
So hold onto the good times, precious ones. Hold onto those golden days.
Because you never know when **Wokou** pirates will show up, steal or burn all your earthly belongings, and **enslave you** and all of your **friends.**

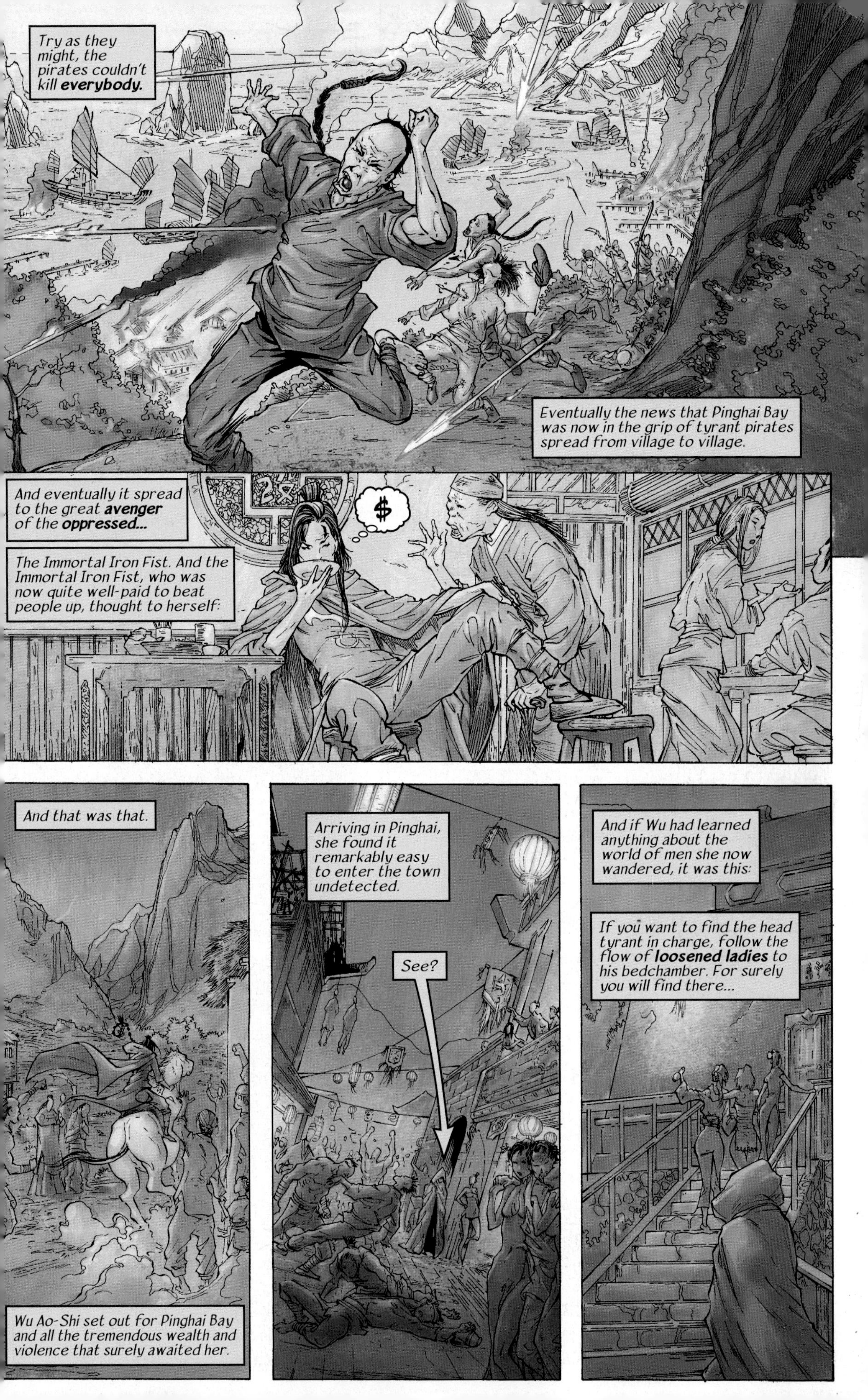
Try as they might, the pirates couldn't kill **everybody.**
Eventually the news that Pinghai Bay was now in the grip of tyrant pirates spread from village to village.
And eventually it spread to the great **avenger** of the **oppressed...**
The Immortal Iron Fist. And the Immortal Iron Fist, who was now quite well-paid to beat people up, thought to herself:
$
And that was that.
Wu Ao-Shi set out for Pinghai Bay and all the tremendous wealth and violence that surely awaited her.
Arriving in Pinghai, she found it remarkably easy to enter the town undetected.
See?
And if Wu had learned anything about the world of men she now wandered, it was this:
If you want to find the head tyrant in charge, follow the flow of **loosened ladies** to his bedchamber. For surely you will find there...

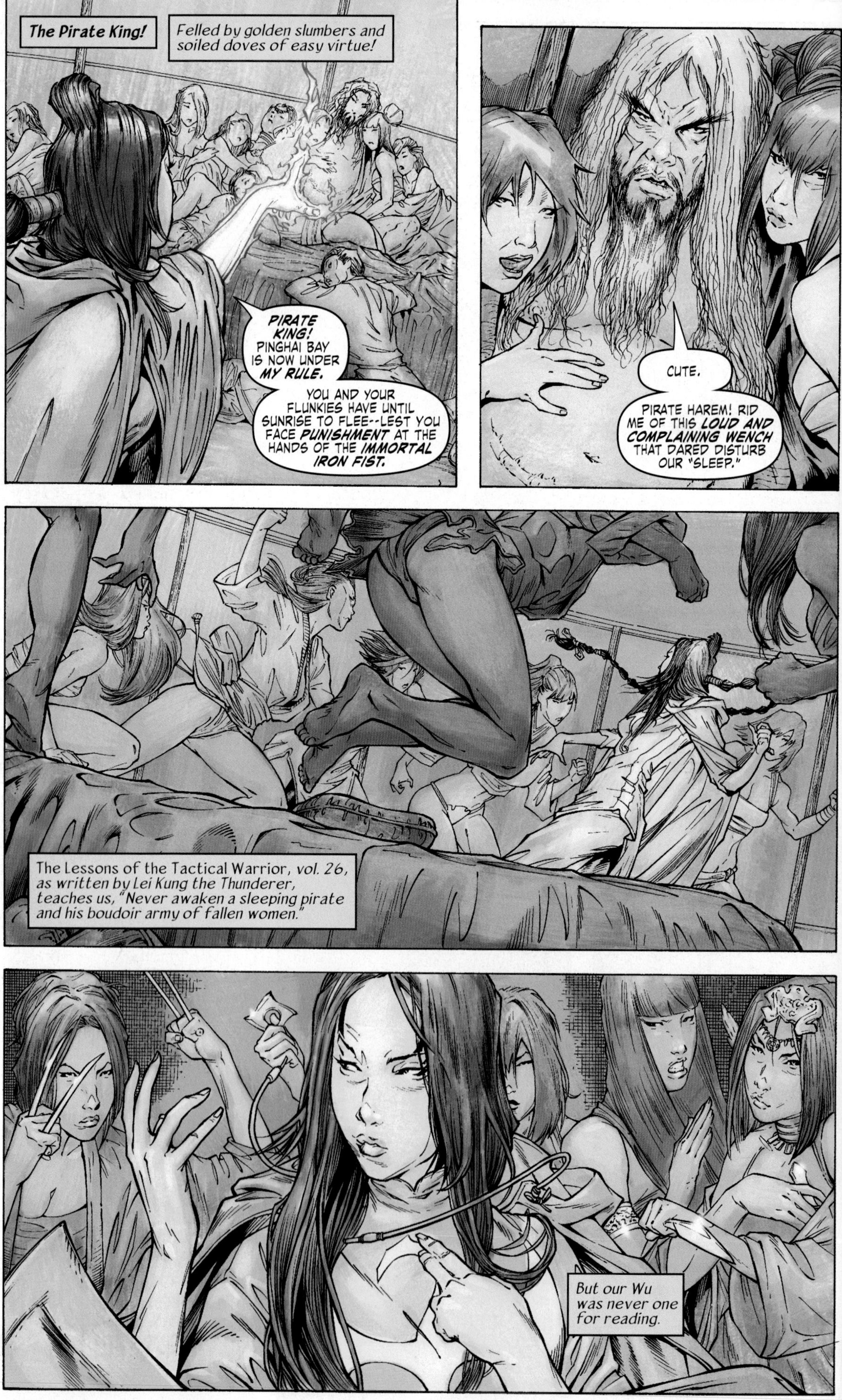

The Pirate King!
Felled by golden slumbers and soiled doves of easy virtue!
PIRATE KING! PINGHAI BAY IS NOW UNDER MY RULE.
YOU AND YOUR FLUNKIES HAVE UNTIL SUNRISE TO FLEE--LEST YOU FACE PUNISHMENT AT THE HANDS OF THE IMMORTAL IRON FIST.
CUTE.
PIRATE HAREM! RID ME OF THIS LOUD AND COMPLAINING WENCH THAT DARED DISTURB OUR "SLEEP."
The Lessons of the Tactical Warrior, vol. 26, as written by Lei Kung the Thunderer, teaches us, "Never awaken a sleeping pirate and his boudoir army of fallen women."
But our Wu was never one for reading.

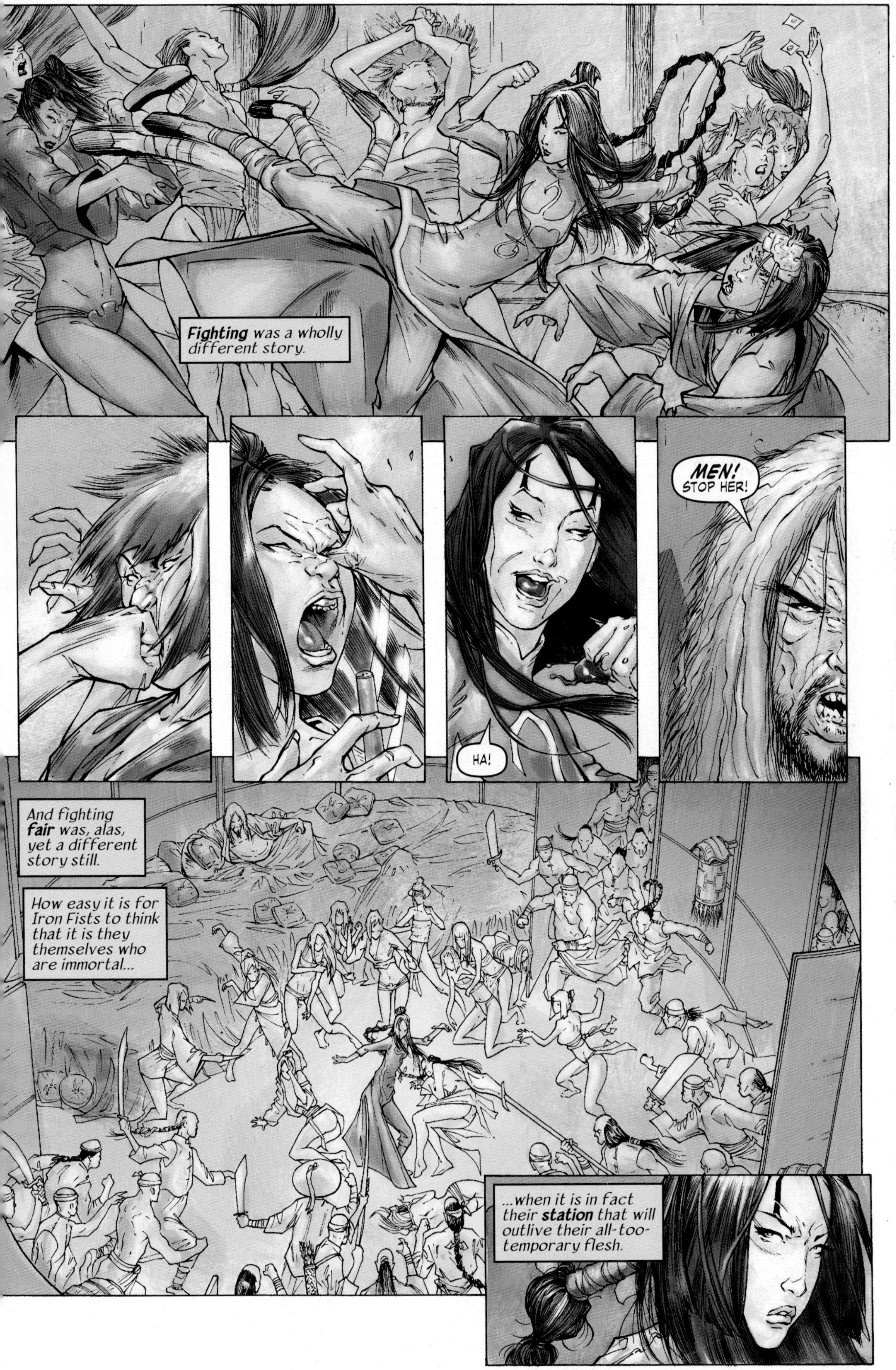
Fighting was a wholly different story.
MEN! STOP HER!
HA!
And fighting fair was, alas, yet a different story still.
How easy it is for Iron Fists to think that it is they themselves who are immortal...
...when it is in fact their station that will outlive their all-too-temporary flesh.

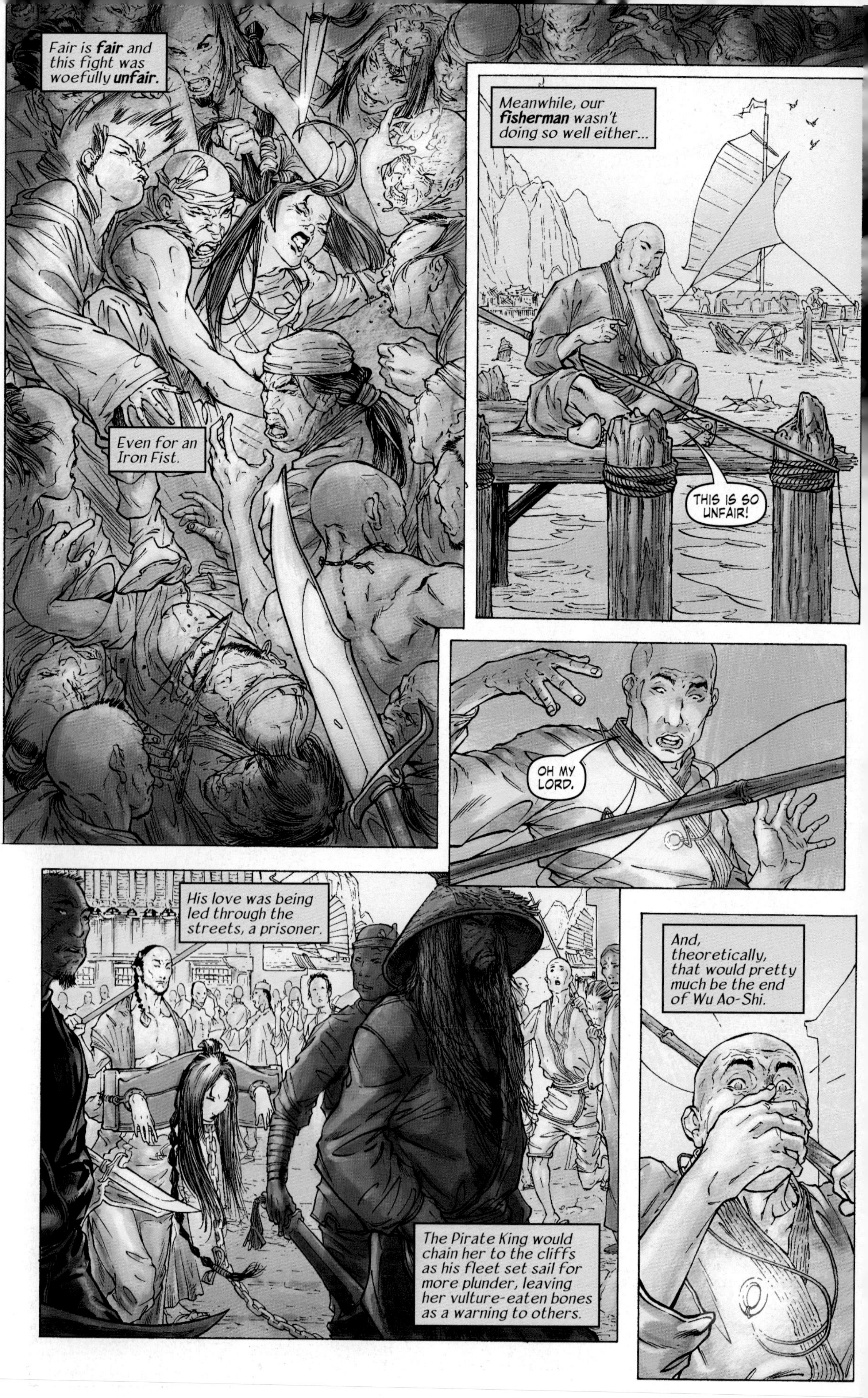
Fair is **fair** and this fight was woefully **unfair**.
Even for an Iron Fist.
Meanwhile, our **fisherman** wasn't doing so well either...
THIS IS SO UNFAIR!
OH MY LORD.
His love was being led through the streets, a prisoner.
The Pirate King would chain her to the cliffs as his fleet set sail for more plunder, leaving her vulture-eaten bones as a warning to others.
And, theoretically, that would pretty much be the end of Wu Ao-Shi.

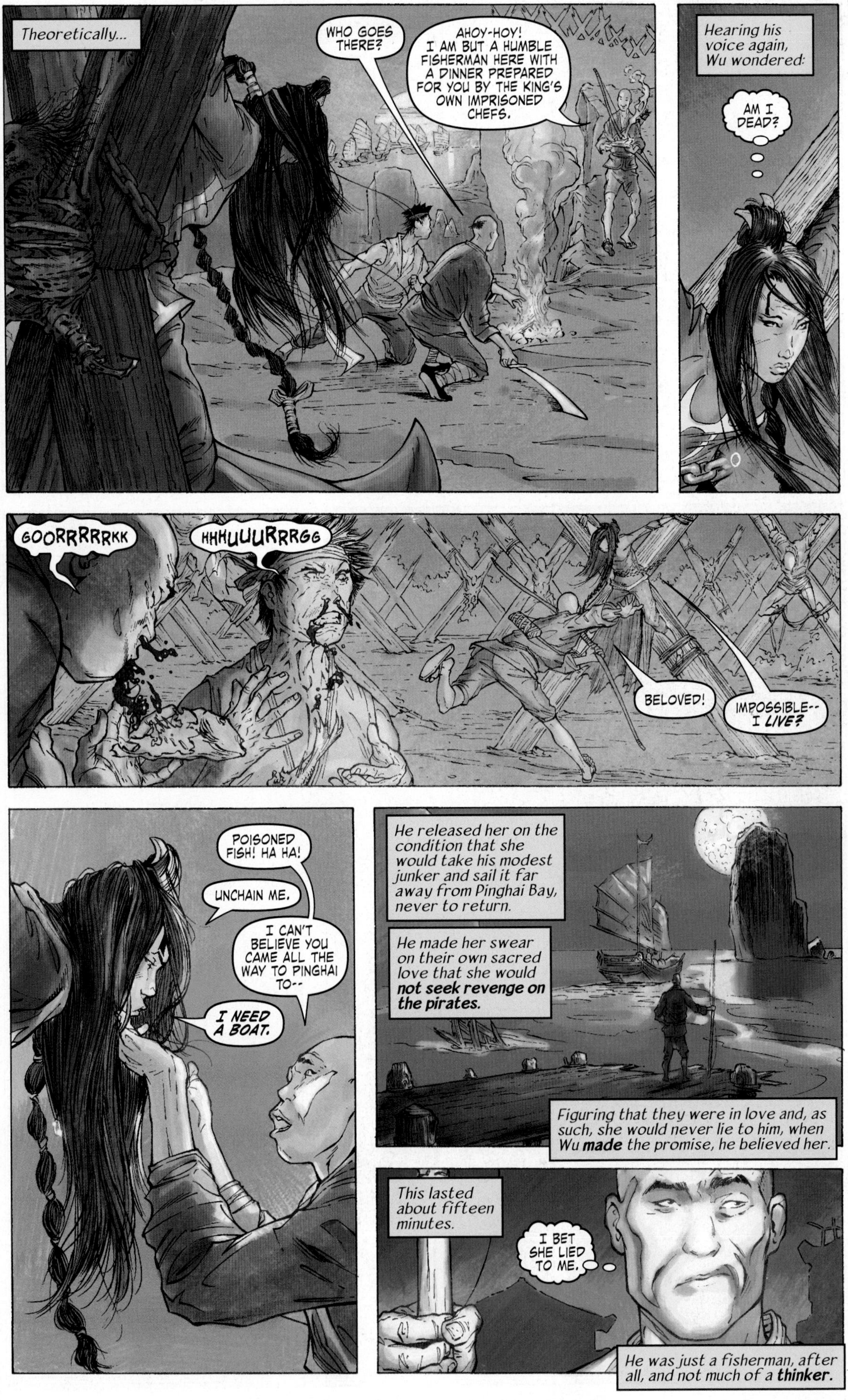
Theoretically...
WHO GOES THERE?
AHOY-HOY! I AM BUT A HUMBLE FISHERMAN HERE WITH A DINNER PREPARED FOR YOU BY THE KING'S OWN IMPRISONED CHEFS.
Hearing his voice again, Wu wondered:
AM I DEAD?
GOORRRRRKK
HHHUUURRRGG
BELOVED!
IMPOSSIBLE-- I LIVE?
POISONED FISH! HA HA!
UNCHAIN ME.
I CAN'T BELIEVE YOU CAME ALL THE WAY TO PINGHAI TO--
I NEED A BOAT.
He released her on the condition that she would take his modest junker and sail it far away from Pinghai Bay, never to return.
He made her swear on their own sacred love that she would not seek revenge on the pirates.
Figuring that they were in love and, as such, she would never lie to him, when Wu made the promise, he believed her.
This lasted about fifteen minutes.
I BET SHE LIED TO ME.
He was just a fisherman, after all, and not much of a thinker.

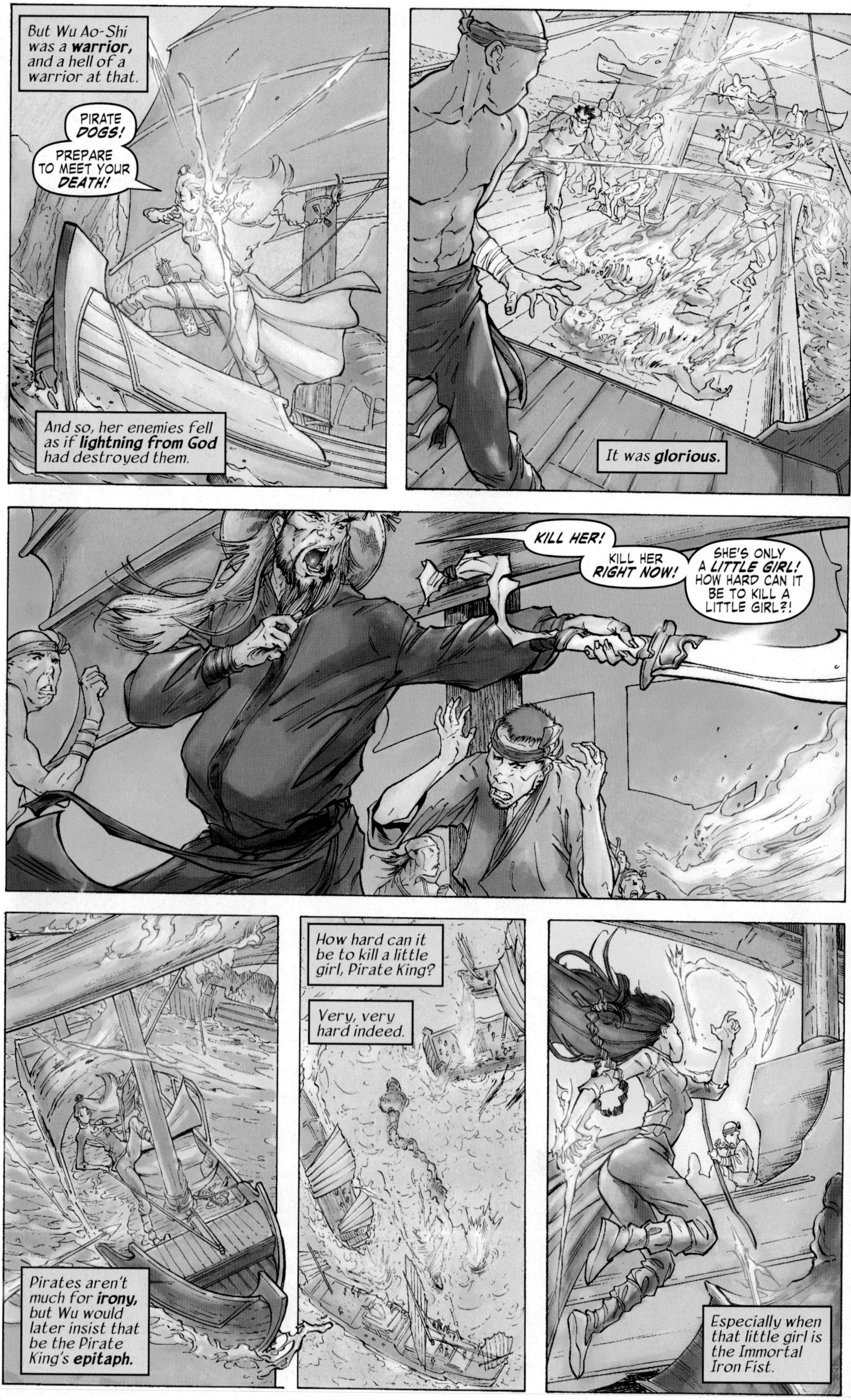

But Wu Ao-Shi was a **warrior,** and a hell of a warrior at that.
PIRATE ***DOGS!***
PREPARE TO MEET YOUR ***DEATH!***
And so, her enemies fell as if **lightning from God** had destroyed them.
It was **glorious.**
KILL HER!
KILL HER ***RIGHT NOW!***
SHE'S ONLY A ***LITTLE GIRL!*** HOW HARD CAN IT BE TO KILL A LITTLE GIRL?!
Pirates aren't much for **irony,** but Wu would later insist that be the Pirate King's **epitaph.**
How hard can it be to kill a little girl, Pirate King?
Very, very hard indeed.
Especially when that little girl is the Immortal Iron Fist.

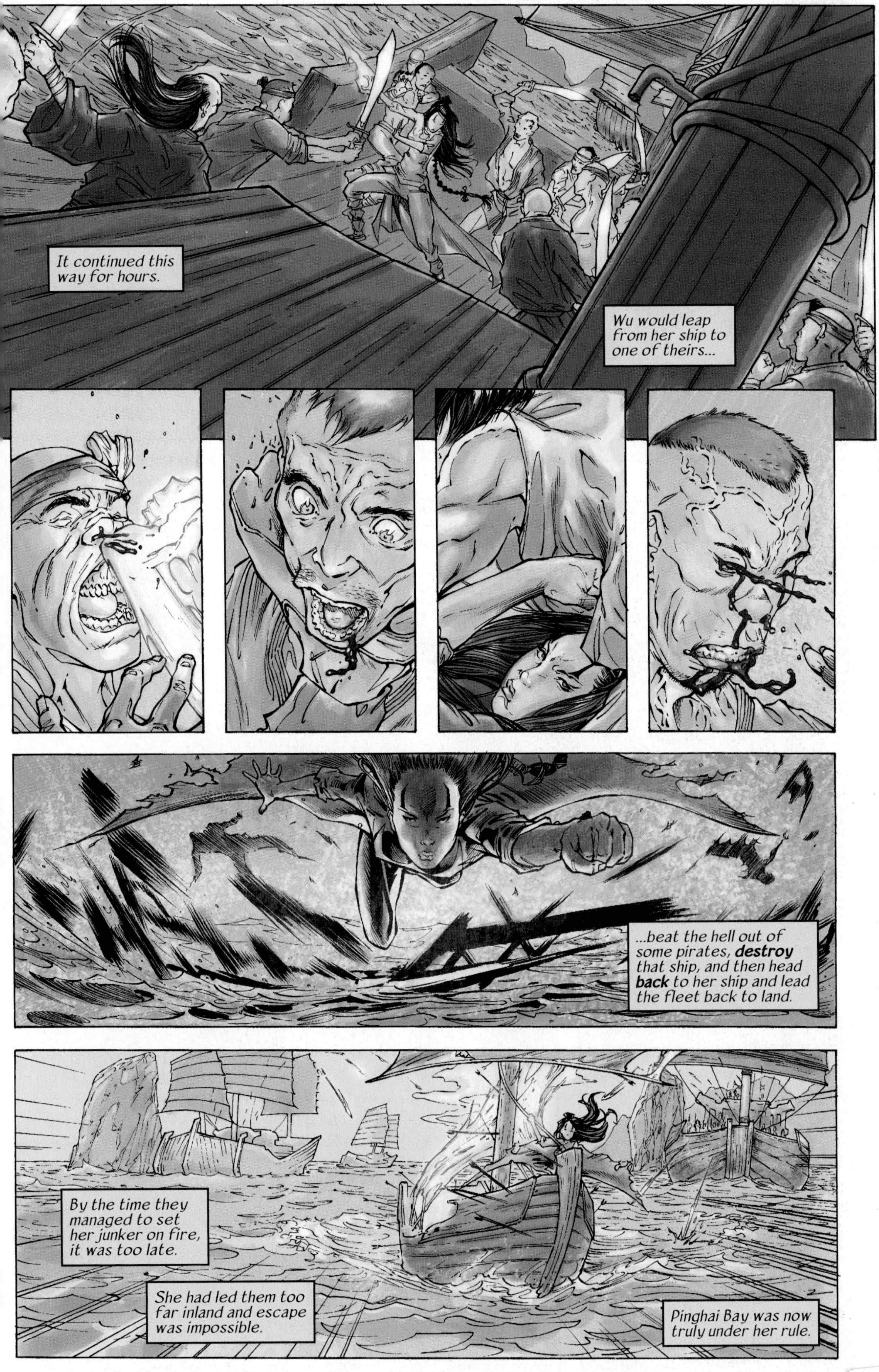
It continued this way for hours.
Wu would leap from her ship to one of theirs...
...beat the hell out of some pirates, **destroy** that ship, and then head **back** to her ship and lead the fleet back to land.
By the time they managed to set her junker on fire, it was too late.
She had led them too far inland and escape was impossible.
Pinghai Bay was now truly under her rule.

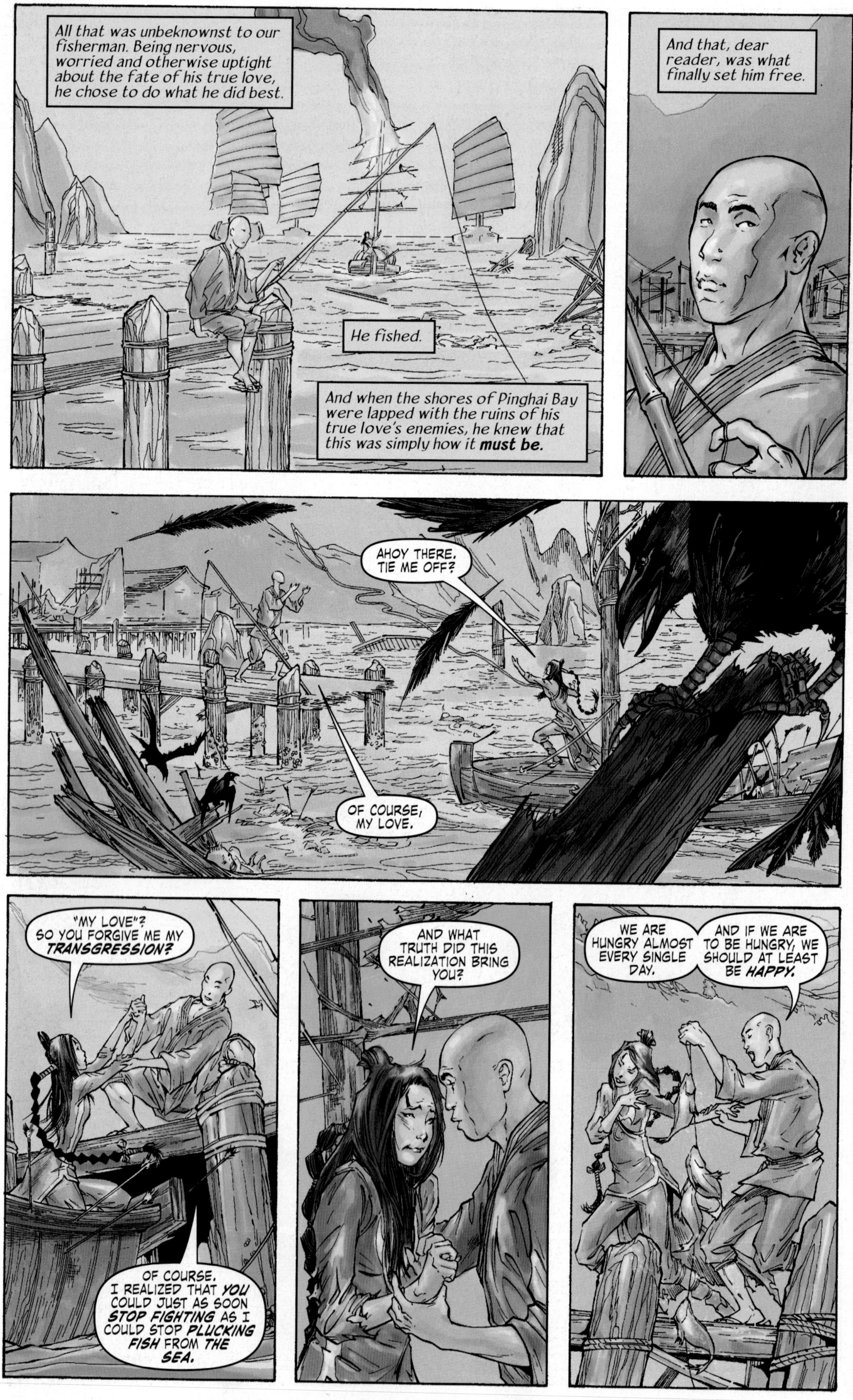
All that was unbeknownst to our fisherman. Being nervous, worried and otherwise uptight about the fate of his true love, he chose to do what he did best.
He fished.
And when the shores of Pinghai Bay were lapped with the ruins of his true love's enemies, he knew that this was simply how it **must be.**
And that, dear reader, was what finally set him free.
AHOY THERE. TIE ME OFF?
OF COURSE, MY LOVE.
"MY LOVE"? SO YOU FORGIVE ME MY ***TRANSGRESSION?***
OF COURSE. I REALIZED THAT ***YOU*** COULD JUST AS SOON ***STOP FIGHTING*** AS I COULD STOP ***PLUCKING FISH*** FROM ***THE SEA.***
AND WHAT TRUTH DID THIS REALIZATION BRING YOU?
WE ARE HUNGRY ALMOST EVERY SINGLE DAY.
AND IF WE ARE TO BE HUNGRY, WE SHOULD AT LEAST BE ***HAPPY.***

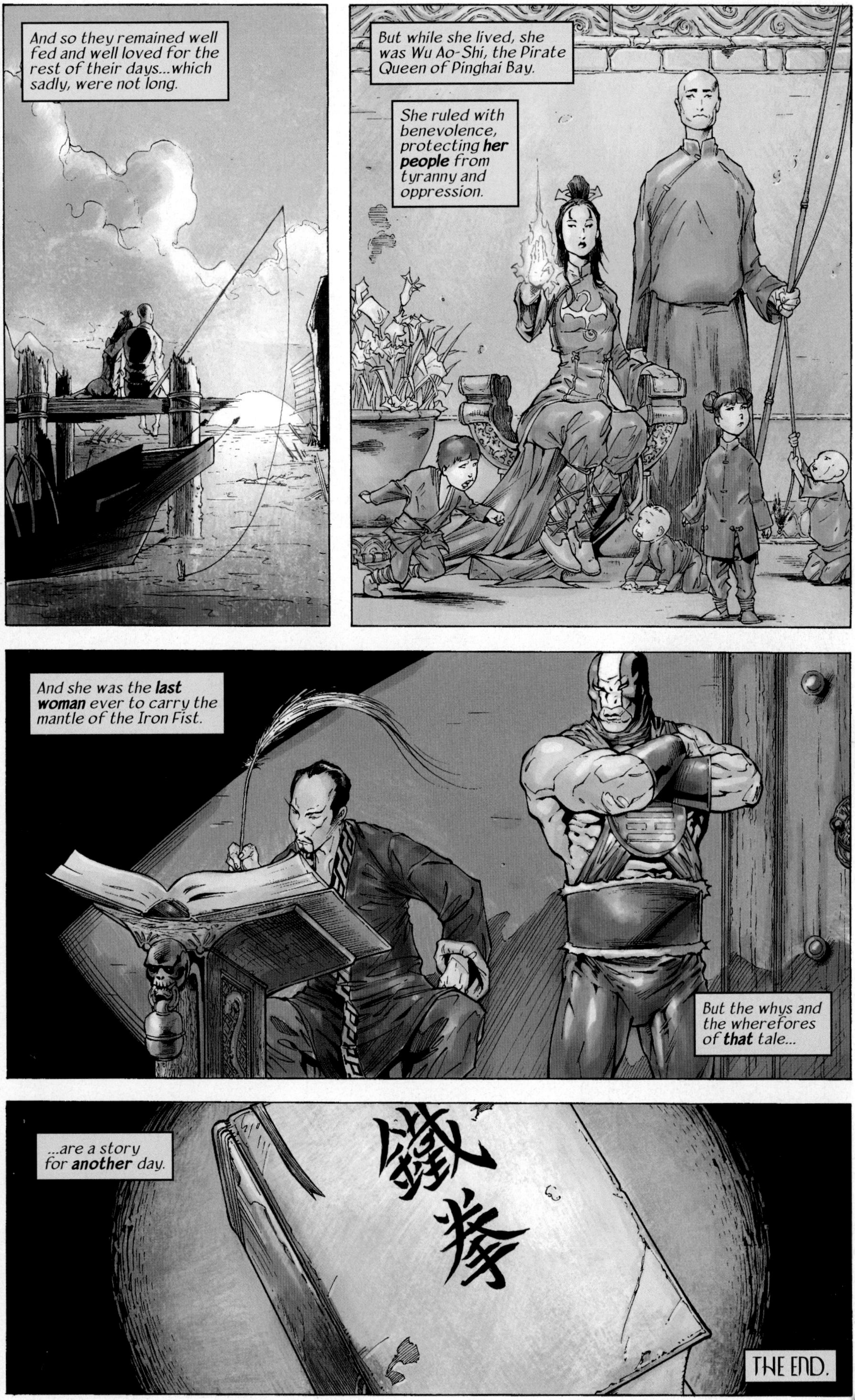
And so they remained well fed and well loved for the rest of their days...which sadly, were not long.
But while she lived, she was Wu Ao-Shi, the Pirate Queen of Pinghai Bay.
She ruled with benevolence, protecting **her people** from tyranny and oppression.
And she was the **last woman** ever to carry the mantle of the Iron Fist.
But the whys and the wherefores of **that** tale...
...are a story for **another** day.
鐵拳
THE END.

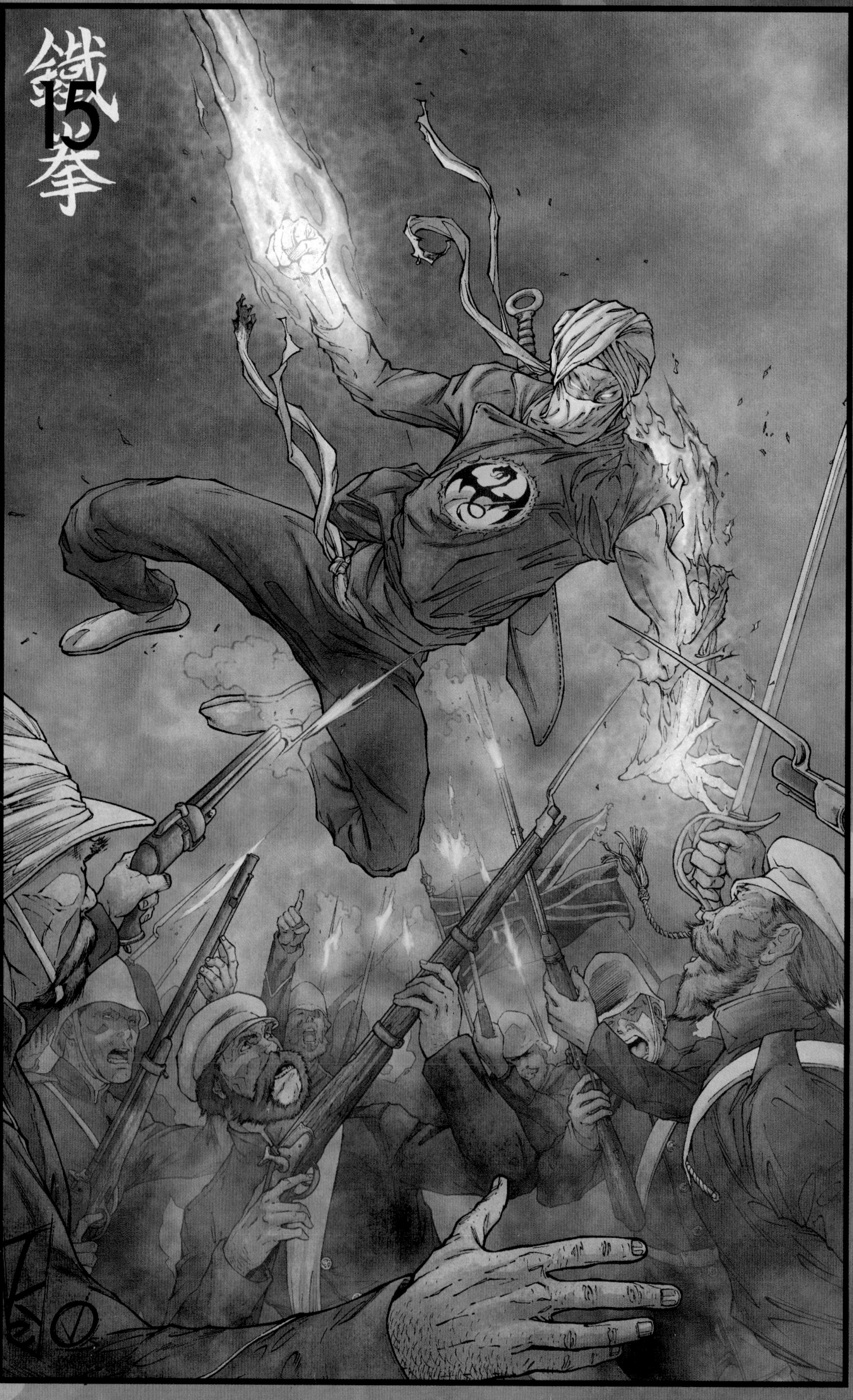
鐵拳
15

There have been sixty-six men and women to carry the mantle of THE IMMORTAL IRON FIST throughout the ages, men and women of great courage, valor, skill, and sacrifice. Sixty-six men and women have stood between man and the unstoppable forces of evil, willing to give all they have to hold back the hordes.

This is the story of one of them, as told in THE BOOK OF THE IRON FIST.

The Story of the Iron Fist Bei Bang-Wen
(1827-1860)

The Perfect Strategy Mind and his Miraculous Travels to the Dark Continent, and what Mysteries of the World and of the Self that He Learned There.

MATT FRACTION – WRITER
KHARI EVANS – PENCILER
VICTOR OLAZABA – INKER
JELENA KEVIC DJURDJEVIC &
PAUL MOUNTS – COLOR ART
DAVE LANPHEAR – LETTERER
IRENE LEE – PRODUCTION
ALEJANDRO ARBONA – ASSISTANT EDITOR
WARREN SIMONS – EDITOR
JOE QUESADA – EDITOR IN CHIEF
DAN BUCKLEY – PUBLISHER

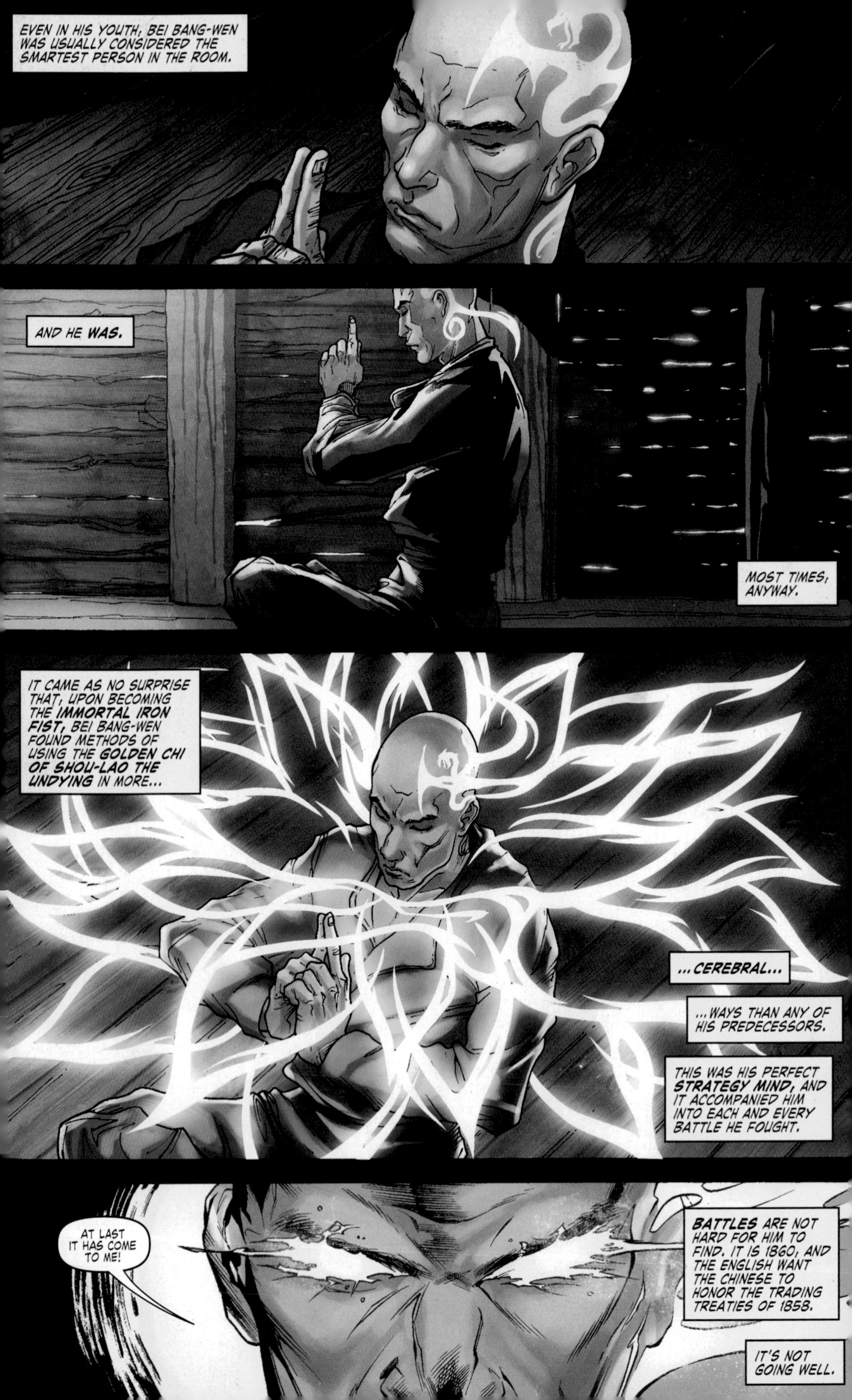
EVEN IN HIS YOUTH, BEI BANG-WEN WAS USUALLY CONSIDERED THE SMARTEST PERSON IN THE ROOM.
AND HE WAS.
MOST TIMES, ANYWAY.
IT CAME AS NO SURPRISE THAT, UPON BECOMING THE IMMORTAL IRON FIST, BEI BANG-WEN FOUND METHODS OF USING THE GOLDEN CHI OF SHOU-LAO THE UNDYING IN MORE...
...CEREBRAL...
...WAYS THAN ANY OF HIS PREDECESSORS.
THIS WAS HIS PERFECT STRATEGY MIND, AND IT ACCOMPANIED HIM INTO EACH AND EVERY BATTLE HE FOUGHT.
AT LAST IT HAS COME TO ME!
BATTLES ARE NOT HARD FOR HIM TO FIND. IT IS 1860, AND THE ENGLISH WANT THE CHINESE TO HONOR THE TRADING TREATIES OF 1858.
IT'S NOT GOING WELL.

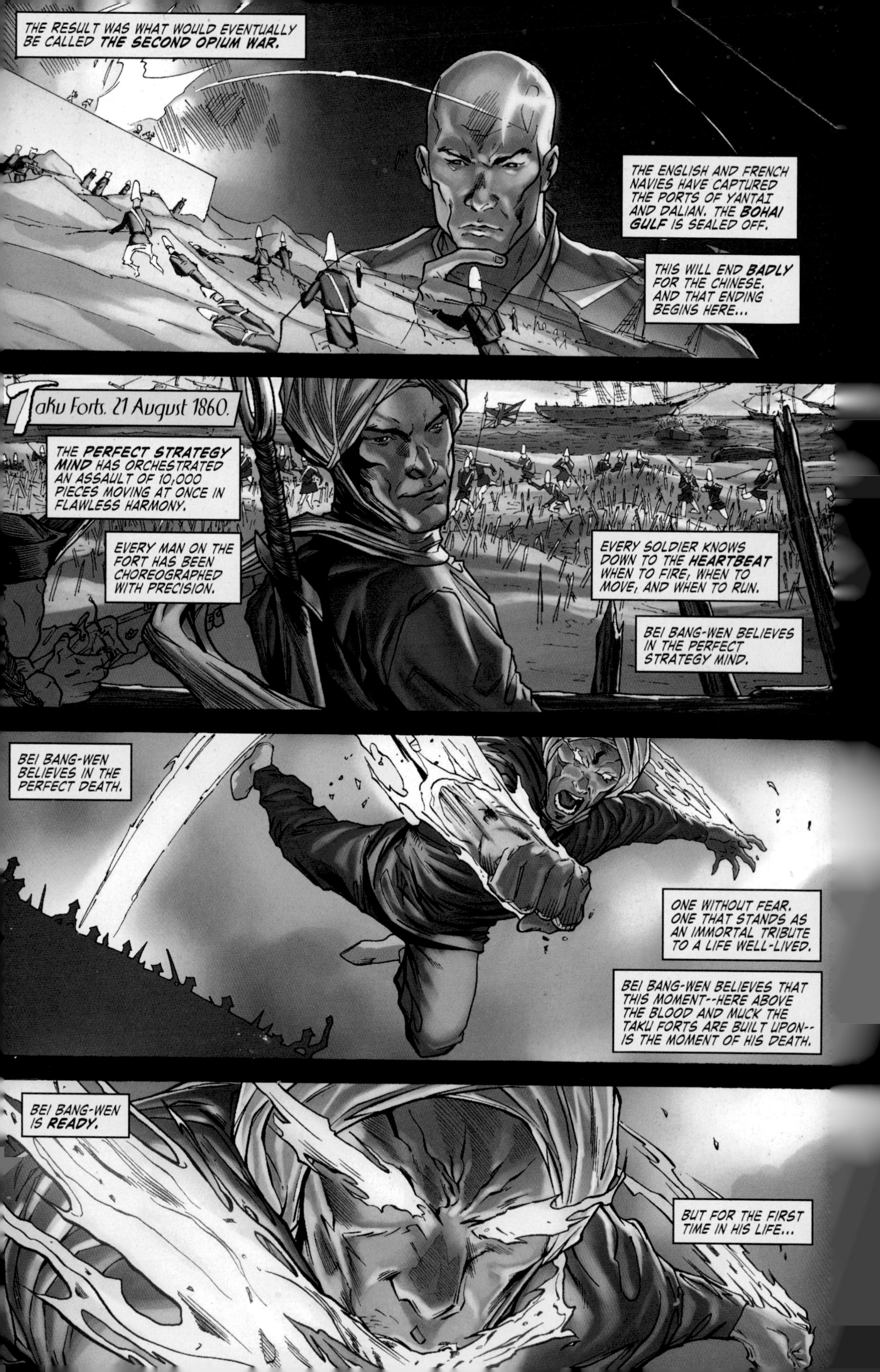
THE RESULT WAS WHAT WOULD EVENTUALLY BE CALLED THE SECOND OPIUM WAR.
THE ENGLISH AND FRENCH NAVIES HAVE CAPTURED THE PORTS OF YANTAI AND DALIAN. THE BOHAI GULF IS SEALED OFF.
THIS WILL END BADLY FOR THE CHINESE. AND THAT ENDING BEGINS HERE...
Taku Forts. 21 August 1860.
THE PERFECT STRATEGY MIND HAS ORCHESTRATED AN ASSAULT OF 10,000 PIECES MOVING AT ONCE IN FLAWLESS HARMONY.
EVERY MAN ON THE FORT HAS BEEN CHOREOGRAPHED WITH PRECISION.
EVERY SOLDIER KNOWS DOWN TO THE HEARTBEAT WHEN TO FIRE, WHEN TO MOVE, AND WHEN TO RUN.
BEI BANG-WEN BELIEVES IN THE PERFECT STRATEGY MIND.
BEI BANG-WEN BELIEVES IN THE PERFECT DEATH.
ONE WITHOUT FEAR. ONE THAT STANDS AS AN IMMORTAL TRIBUTE TO A LIFE WELL-LIVED.
BEI BANG-WEN BELIEVES THAT THIS MOMENT--HERE ABOVE THE BLOOD AND MUCK THE TAKU FORTS ARE BUILT UPON--IS THE MOMENT OF HIS DEATH.
BEI BANG-WEN IS READY.
BUT FOR THE FIRST TIME IN HIS LIFE...

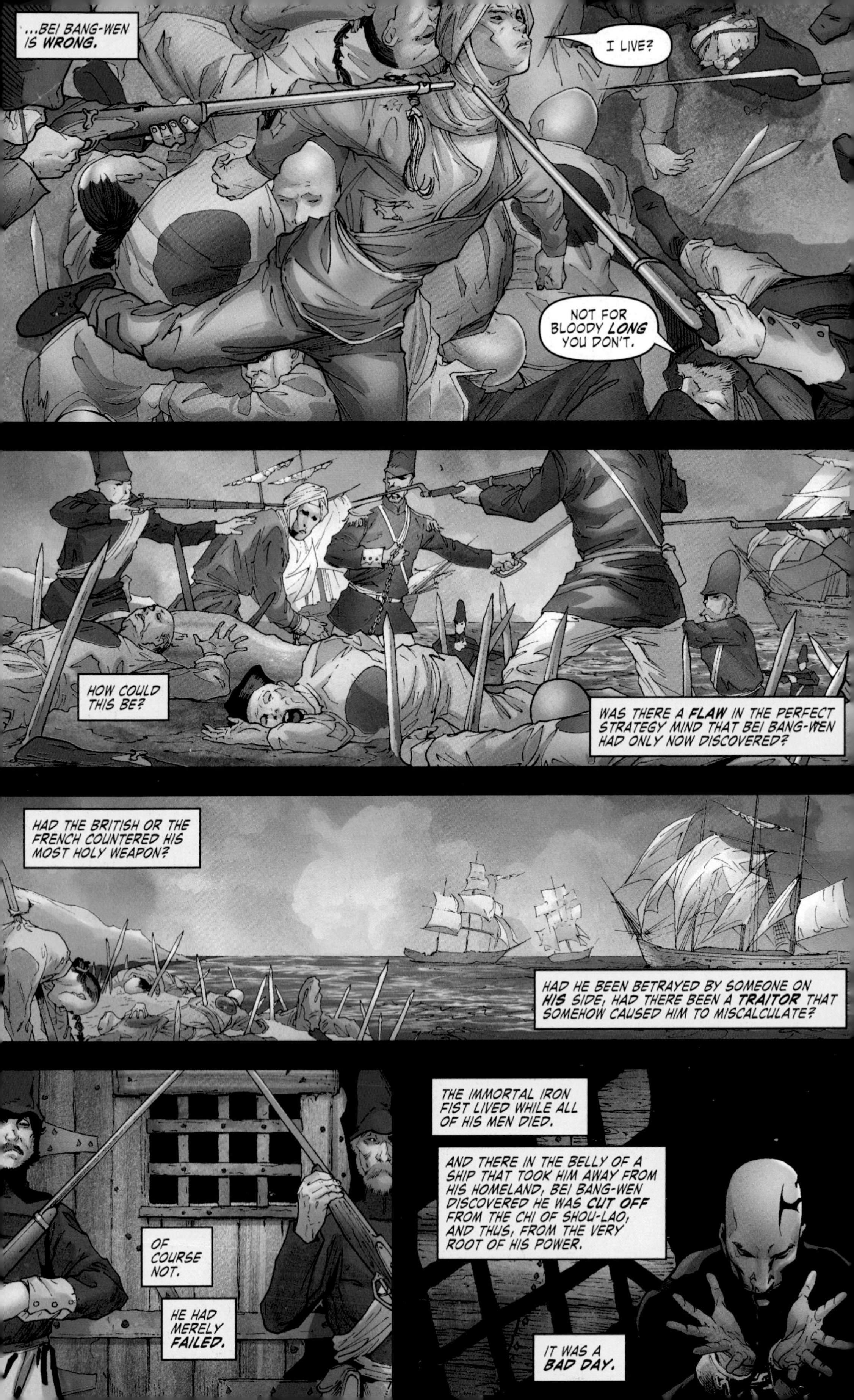
...BEI BANG-WEN IS WRONG.
I LIVE?
NOT FOR BLOODY LONG YOU DON'T.
HOW COULD THIS BE?
WAS THERE A FLAW IN THE PERFECT STRATEGY MIND THAT BEI BANG-WEN HAD ONLY NOW DISCOVERED?
HAD THE BRITISH OR THE FRENCH COUNTERED HIS MOST HOLY WEAPON?
HAD HE BEEN BETRAYED BY SOMEONE ON HIS SIDE, HAD THERE BEEN A TRAITOR THAT SOMEHOW CAUSED HIM TO MISCALCULATE?
OF COURSE NOT.
HE HAD MERELY FAILED.
THE IMMORTAL IRON FIST LIVED WHILE ALL OF HIS MEN DIED.
AND THERE IN THE BELLY OF A SHIP THAT TOOK HIM AWAY FROM HIS HOMELAND, BEI BANG-WEN DISCOVERED HE WAS CUT OFF FROM THE CHI OF SHOU-LAO, AND THUS, FROM THE VERY ROOT OF HIS POWER.
IT WAS A BAD DAY.

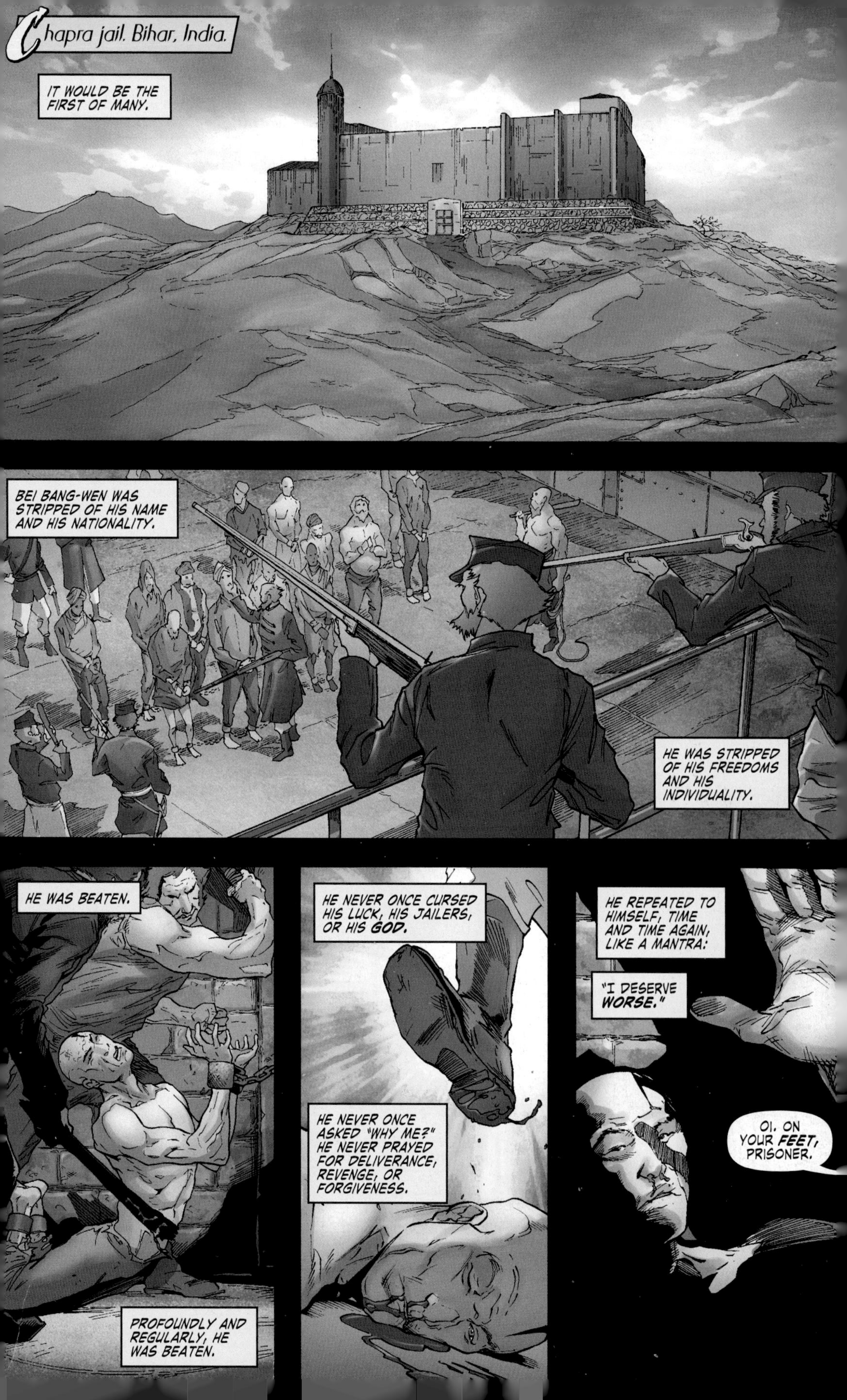
Chapra jail. Bihar, India.
IT WOULD BE THE FIRST OF MANY.
BEI BANG-WEN WAS STRIPPED OF HIS NAME AND HIS NATIONALITY.
HE WAS STRIPPED OF HIS FREEDOMS AND HIS INDIVIDUALITY.
HE WAS BEATEN.
PROFOUNDLY AND REGULARLY, HE WAS BEATEN.
HE NEVER ONCE CURSED HIS LUCK, HIS JAILERS, OR HIS GOD.
HE NEVER ONCE ASKED "WHY ME?" HE NEVER PRAYED FOR DELIVERANCE, REVENGE, OR FORGIVENESS.
HE REPEATED TO HIMSELF, TIME AND TIME AGAIN, LIKE A MANTRA:
"I DESERVE WORSE."
OI. ON YOUR FEET, PRISONER.

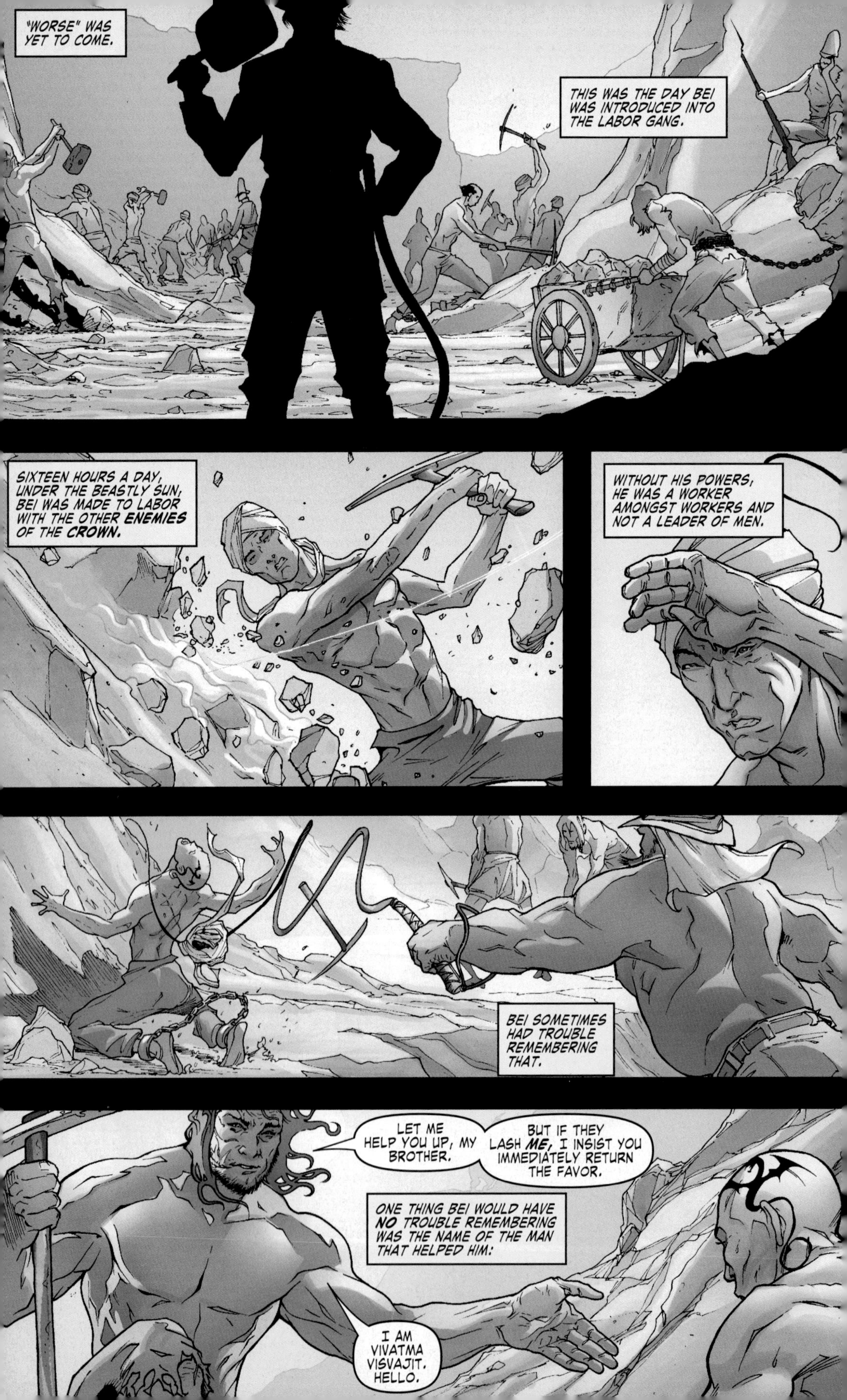
"WORSE" WAS YET TO COME.
THIS WAS THE DAY BEI WAS INTRODUCED INTO THE LABOR GANG.
SIXTEEN HOURS A DAY, UNDER THE BEASTLY SUN, BEI WAS MADE TO LABOR WITH THE OTHER ENEMIES OF THE CROWN.
WITHOUT HIS POWERS, HE WAS A WORKER AMONGST WORKERS AND NOT A LEADER OF MEN.
BEI SOMETIMES HAD TROUBLE REMEMBERING THAT.
LET ME HELP YOU UP, MY BROTHER.
BUT IF THEY LASH ME, I INSIST YOU IMMEDIATELY RETURN THE FAVOR.
ONE THING BEI WOULD HAVE NO TROUBLE REMEMBERING WAS THE NAME OF THE MAN THAT HELPED HIM:
I AM VIVATMA VISVAJIT. HELLO.

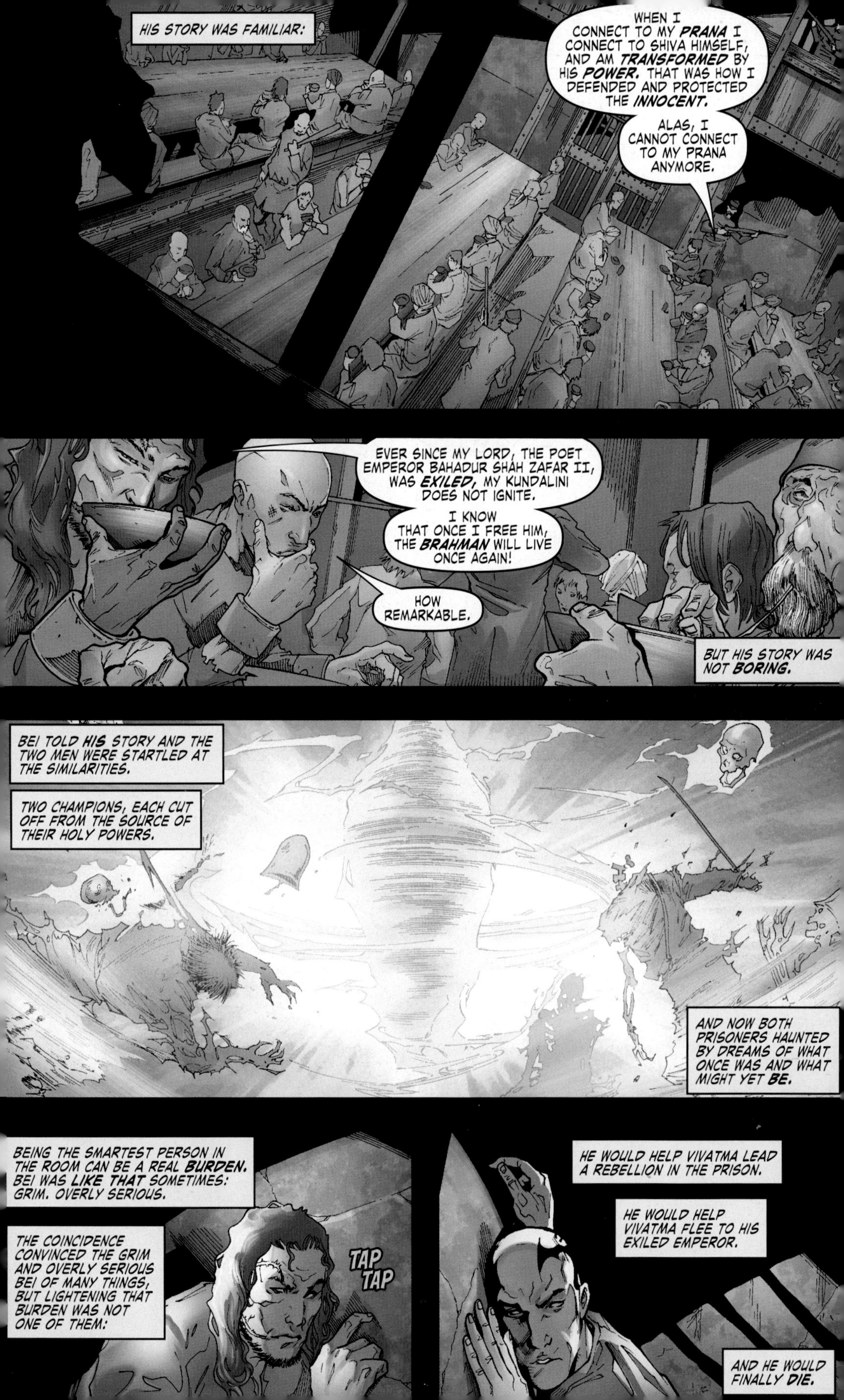

HIS STORY WAS FAMILIAR:
WHEN I CONNECT TO MY PRANA I CONNECT TO SHIVA HIMSELF, AND AM TRANSFORMED BY HIS POWER. THAT WAS HOW I DEFENDED AND PROTECTED THE INNOCENT.
ALAS, I CANNOT CONNECT TO MY PRANA ANYMORE.
EVER SINCE MY LORD, THE POET EMPEROR BAHADUR SHAH ZAFAR II, WAS EXILED, MY KUNDALINI DOES NOT IGNITE.
I KNOW THAT ONCE I FREE HIM, THE BRAHMAN WILL LIVE ONCE AGAIN!
HOW REMARKABLE.
BUT HIS STORY WAS NOT BORING.
BEI TOLD HIS STORY AND THE TWO MEN WERE STARTLED AT THE SIMILARITIES.
TWO CHAMPIONS, EACH CUT OFF FROM THE SOURCE OF THEIR HOLY POWERS.
AND NOW BOTH PRISONERS HAUNTED BY DREAMS OF WHAT ONCE WAS AND WHAT MIGHT YET BE.
BEING THE SMARTEST PERSON IN THE ROOM CAN BE A REAL BURDEN. BEI WAS LIKE THAT SOMETIMES: GRIM. OVERLY SERIOUS.
THE COINCIDENCE CONVINCED THE GRIM AND OVERLY SERIOUS BEI OF MANY THINGS, BUT LIGHTENING THAT BURDEN WAS NOT ONE OF THEM:
TAP TAP
HE WOULD HELP VIVATMA LEAD A REBELLION IN THE PRISON.
HE WOULD HELP VIVATMA FLEE TO HIS EXILED EMPEROR.
AND HE WOULD FINALLY DIE.

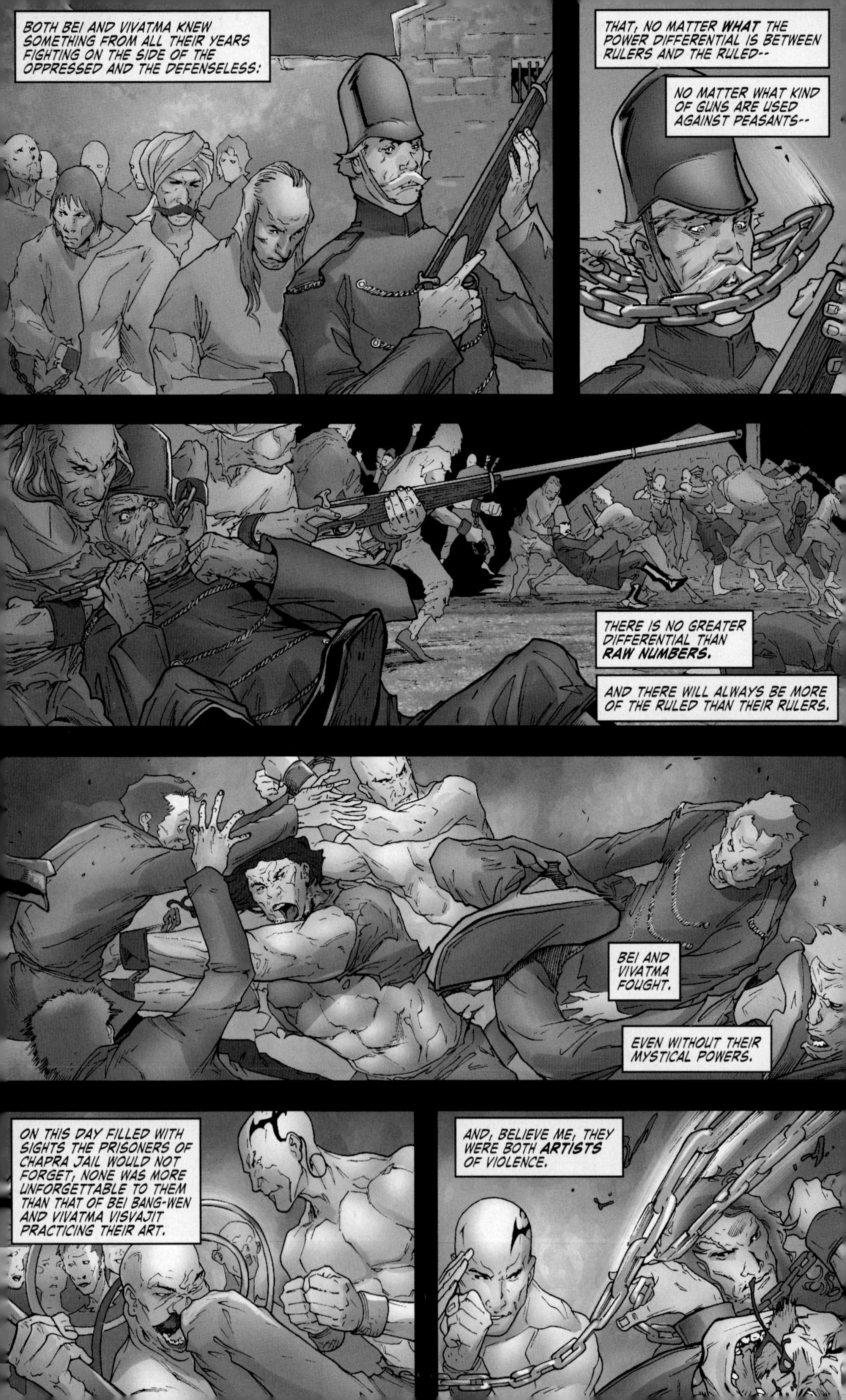
BOTH BEI AND VIVATMA KNEW SOMETHING FROM ALL THEIR YEARS FIGHTING ON THE SIDE OF THE OPPRESSED AND THE DEFENSELESS:
THAT, NO MATTER **WHAT** THE POWER DIFFERENTIAL IS BETWEEN RULERS AND THE RULED--
NO MATTER WHAT KIND OF GUNS ARE USED AGAINST PEASANTS--
THERE IS NO GREATER DIFFERENTIAL THAN **RAW NUMBERS.**
AND THERE WILL ALWAYS BE MORE OF THE RULED THAN THEIR RULERS.
BEI AND VIVATMA FOUGHT.
EVEN WITHOUT THEIR MYSTICAL POWERS.
ON THIS DAY FILLED WITH SIGHTS THE PRISONERS OF CHAPRA JAIL WOULD NOT FORGET, NONE WAS MORE UNFORGETTABLE TO THEM THAN THAT OF BEI BANG-WEN AND VIVATMA VISVAJIT PRACTICING THEIR ART.
AND, BELIEVE ME, THEY WERE BOTH **ARTISTS** OF VIOLENCE.

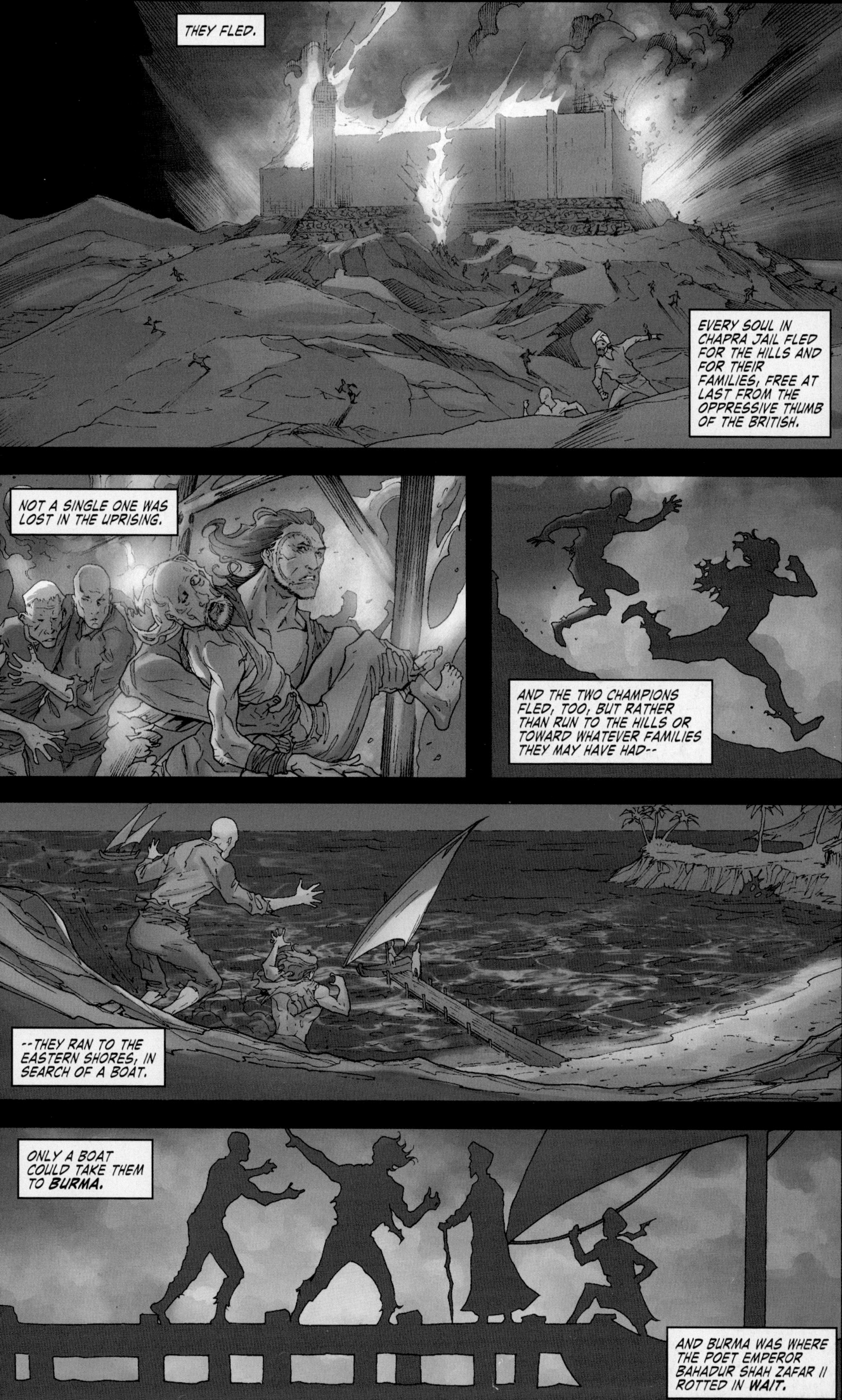
THEY FLED.
EVERY SOUL IN CHAPRA JAIL FLED FOR THE HILLS AND FOR THEIR FAMILIES, FREE AT LAST FROM THE OPPRESSIVE THUMB OF THE BRITISH.
NOT A SINGLE ONE WAS LOST IN THE UPRISING.
AND THE TWO CHAMPIONS FLED, TOO, BUT RATHER THAN RUN TO THE HILLS OR TOWARD WHATEVER FAMILIES THEY MAY HAVE HAD--
--THEY RAN TO THE EASTERN SHORES, IN SEARCH OF A BOAT.
ONLY A BOAT COULD TAKE THEM TO **BURMA.**
AND BURMA WAS WHERE THE POET EMPEROR BAHADUR SHAH ZAFAR II ROTTED IN **WAIT.**

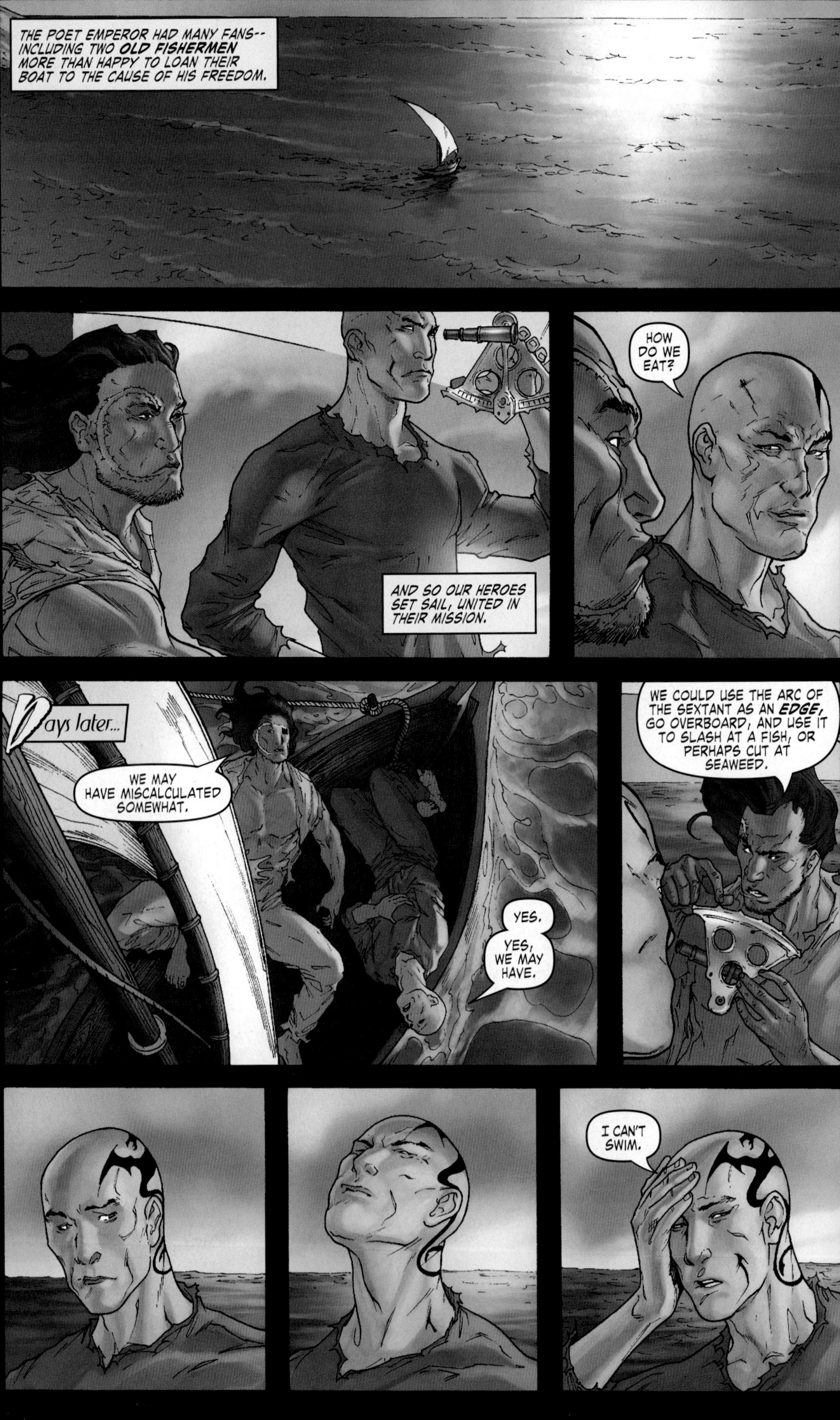
THE POET EMPEROR HAD MANY FANS-- INCLUDING TWO OLD FISHERMEN MORE THAN HAPPY TO LOAN THEIR BOAT TO THE CAUSE OF HIS FREEDOM.
AND SO OUR HEROES SET SAIL, UNITED IN THEIR MISSION.
HOW DO WE EAT?
Days later...
WE MAY HAVE MISCALCULATED SOMEWHAT.
YES.
YES, WE MAY HAVE.
WE COULD USE THE ARC OF THE SEXTANT AS AN EDGE, GO OVERBOARD, AND USE IT TO SLASH AT A FISH, OR PERHAPS CUT AT SEAWEED.
I CAN'T SWIM.

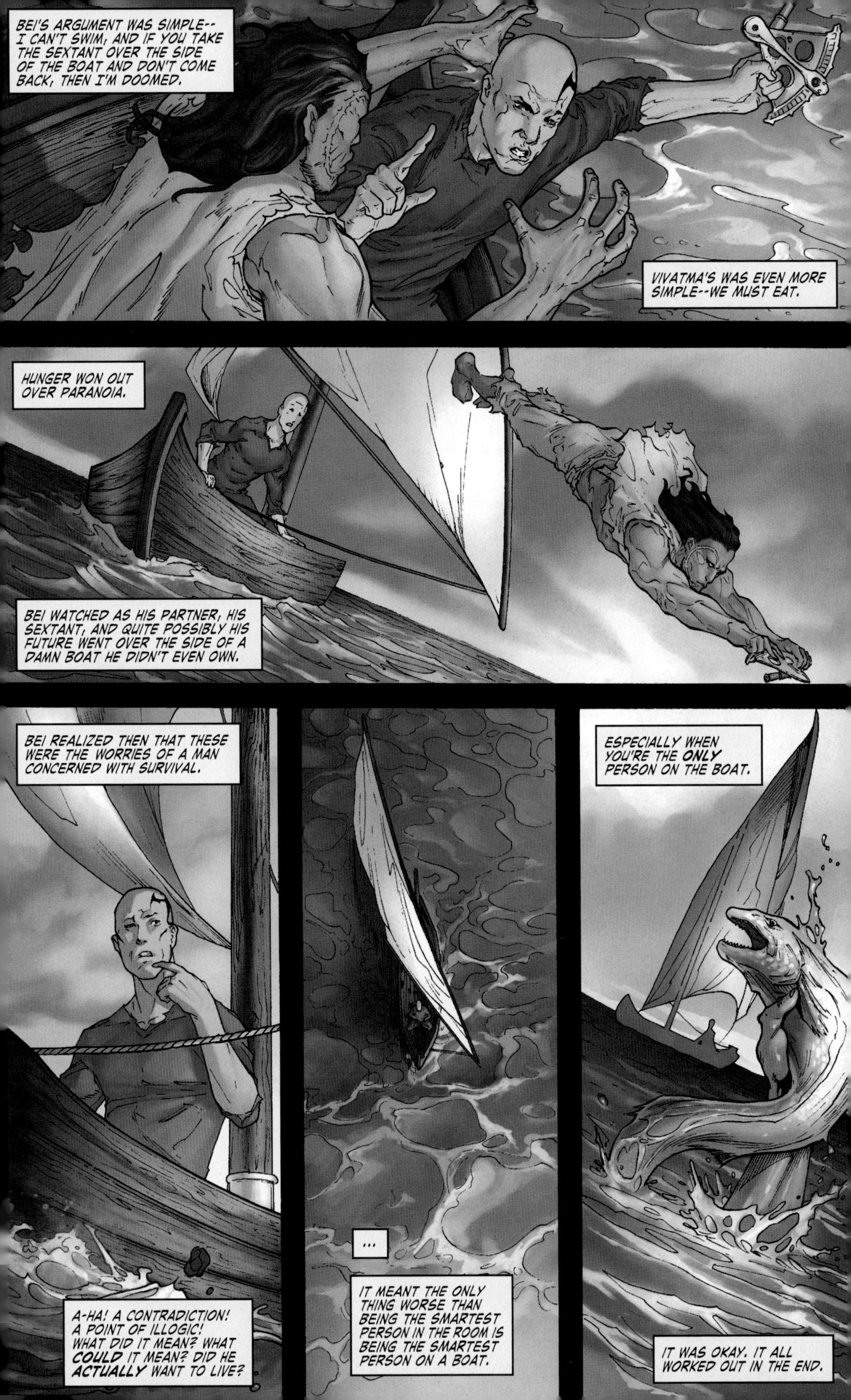
BEI'S ARGUMENT WAS SIMPLE-- I CAN'T SWIM, AND IF YOU TAKE THE SEXTANT OVER THE SIDE OF THE BOAT AND DON'T COME BACK, THEN I'M DOOMED.
VIVATMA'S WAS EVEN MORE SIMPLE--WE MUST EAT.
HUNGER WON OUT OVER PARANOIA.
BEI WATCHED AS HIS PARTNER, HIS SEXTANT, AND QUITE POSSIBLY HIS FUTURE WENT OVER THE SIDE OF A DAMN BOAT HE DIDN'T EVEN OWN.
BEI REALIZED THEN THAT THESE WERE THE WORRIES OF A MAN CONCERNED WITH SURVIVAL.
A-HA! A CONTRADICTION! A POINT OF ILLOGIC! WHAT DID IT MEAN? WHAT **COULD** IT MEAN? DID HE **ACTUALLY** WANT TO LIVE?
...
IT MEANT THE ONLY THING WORSE THAN BEING THE SMARTEST PERSON IN THE ROOM IS BEING THE SMARTEST PERSON ON A BOAT.
ESPECIALLY WHEN YOU'RE THE **ONLY** PERSON ON THE BOAT.
IT WAS OKAY. IT ALL WORKED OUT IN THE END.

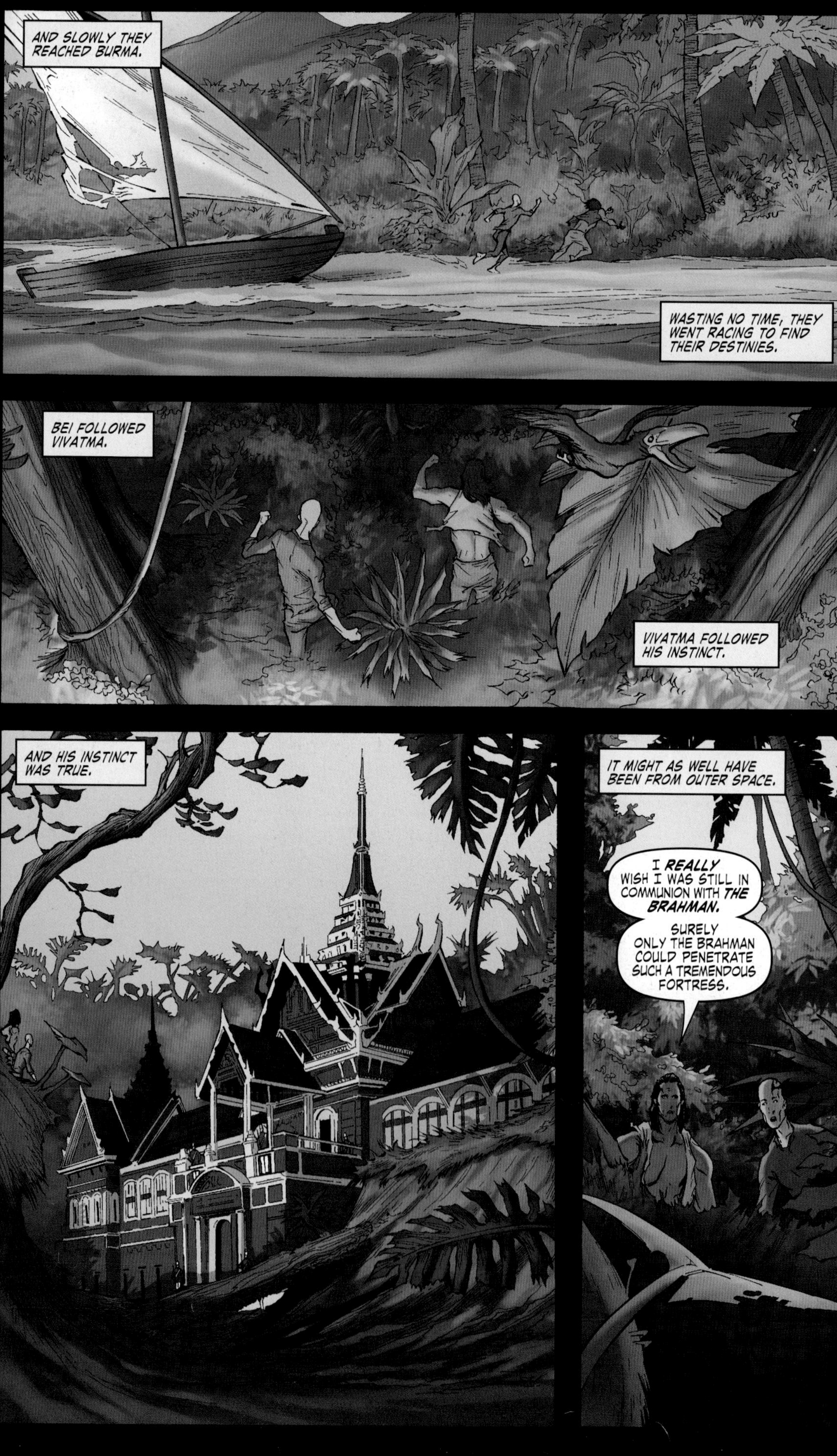
AND SLOWLY THEY REACHED BURMA.
WASTING NO TIME, THEY WENT RACING TO FIND THEIR DESTINIES.
BEI FOLLOWED VIVATMA.
VIVATMA FOLLOWED HIS INSTINCT.
AND HIS INSTINCT WAS TRUE.
IT MIGHT AS WELL HAVE BEEN FROM OUTER SPACE.
I REALLY WISH I WAS STILL IN COMMUNION WITH THE BRAHMAN.
SURELY ONLY THE BRAHMAN COULD PENETRATE SUCH A TREMENDOUS FORTRESS.

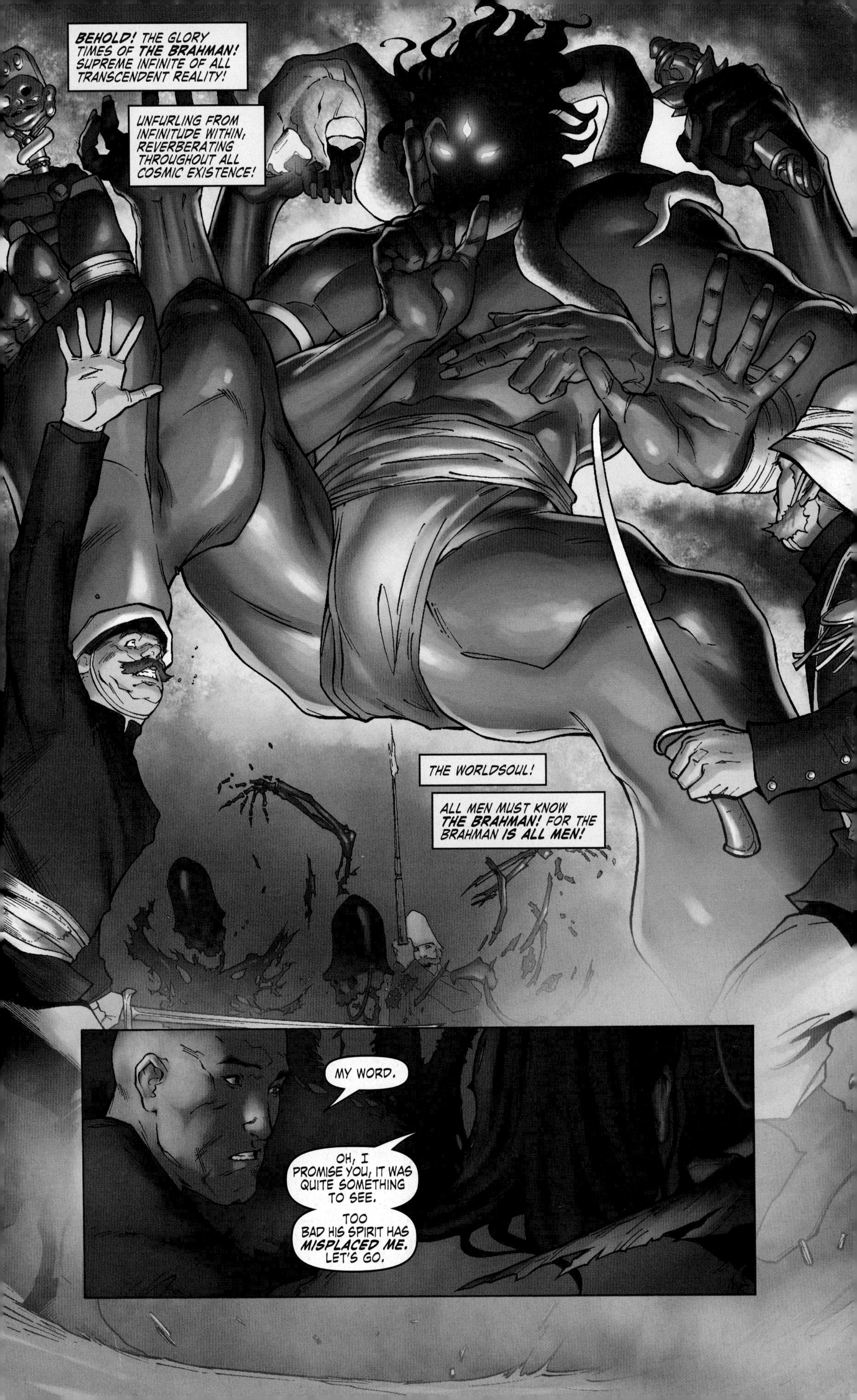
BEHOLD! THE GLORY TIMES OF THE BRAHMAN! SUPREME INFINITE OF ALL TRANSCENDENT REALITY!
UNFURLING FROM INFINITUDE WITHIN, REVERBERATING THROUGHOUT ALL COSMIC EXISTENCE!
THE WORLDSOUL!
ALL MEN MUST KNOW THE BRAHMAN! FOR THE BRAHMAN IS ALL MEN!
MY WORD.
OH, I PROMISE YOU, IT WAS QUITE SOMETHING TO SEE.
TOO BAD HIS SPIRIT HAS MISPLACED ME. LET'S GO.

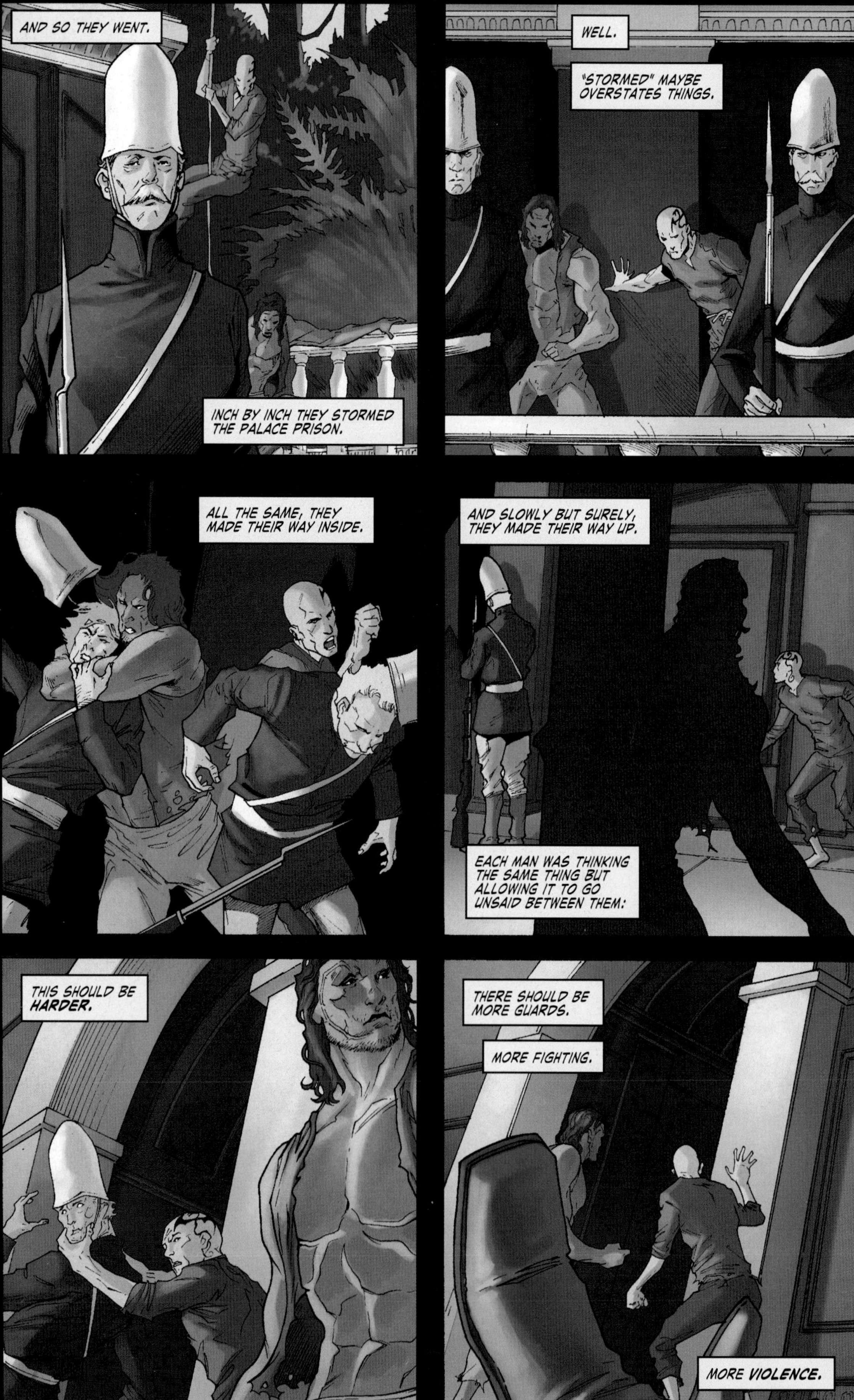
AND SO THEY WENT.
INCH BY INCH THEY STORMED THE PALACE PRISON.
WELL.
"STORMED" MAYBE OVERSTATES THINGS.
ALL THE SAME, THEY MADE THEIR WAY INSIDE.
AND SLOWLY BUT SURELY, THEY MADE THEIR WAY UP.
EACH MAN WAS THINKING THE SAME THING BUT ALLOWING IT TO GO UNSAID BETWEEN THEM:
THIS SHOULD BE **HARDER.**
THERE SHOULD BE MORE GUARDS.
MORE FIGHTING.
MORE **VIOLENCE.**

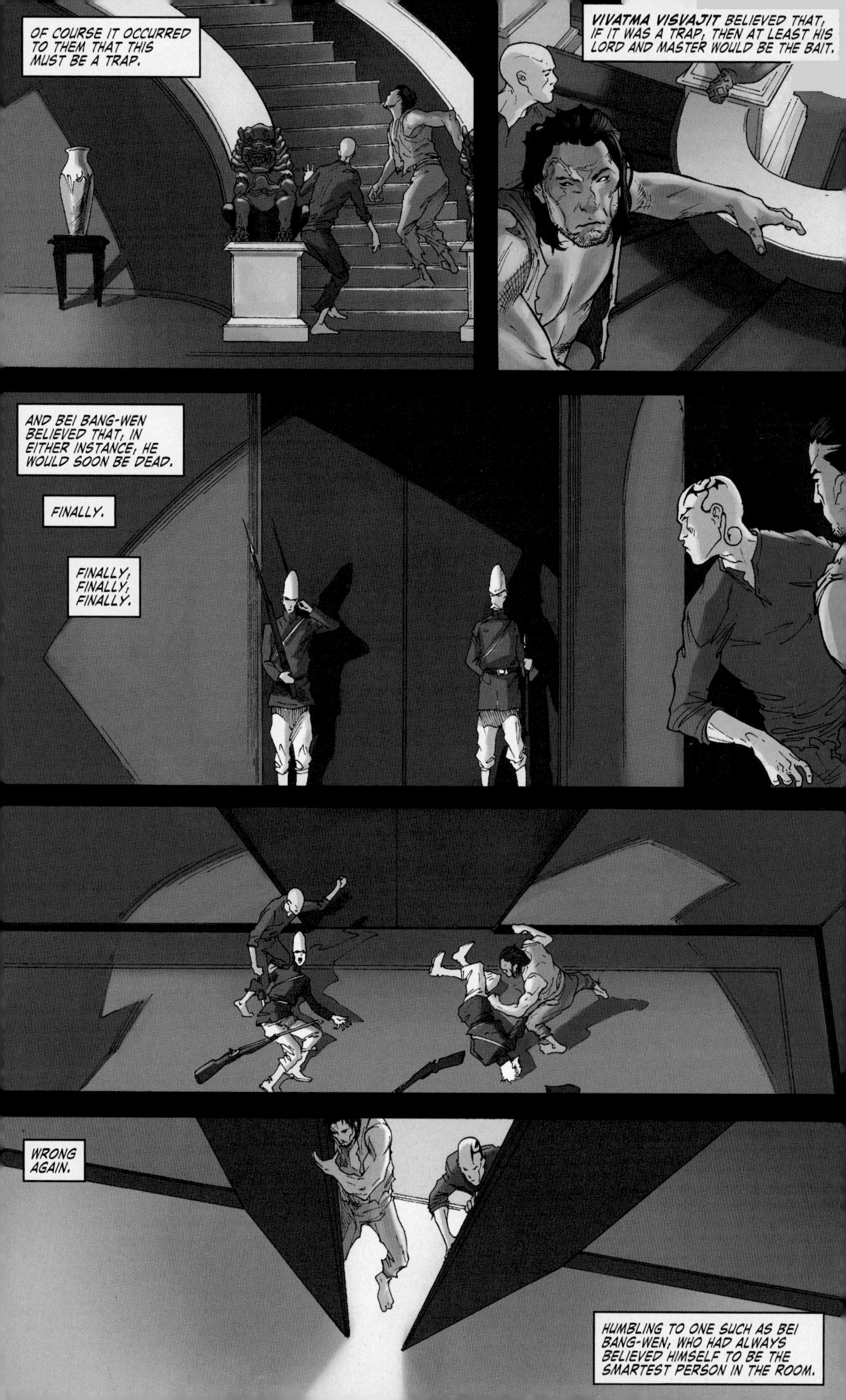
OF COURSE IT OCCURRED TO THEM THAT THIS MUST BE A TRAP.
VIVATMA VISVAJIT BELIEVED THAT, IF IT WAS A TRAP, THEN AT LEAST HIS LORD AND MASTER WOULD BE THE BAIT.
AND BEI BANG-WEN BELIEVED THAT, IN EITHER INSTANCE, HE WOULD SOON BE DEAD.
FINALLY.
FINALLY, FINALLY, FINALLY.
WRONG AGAIN.
HUMBLING TO ONE SUCH AS BEI BANG-WEN, WHO HAD ALWAYS BELIEVED HIMSELF TO BE THE SMARTEST PERSON IN THE ROOM.

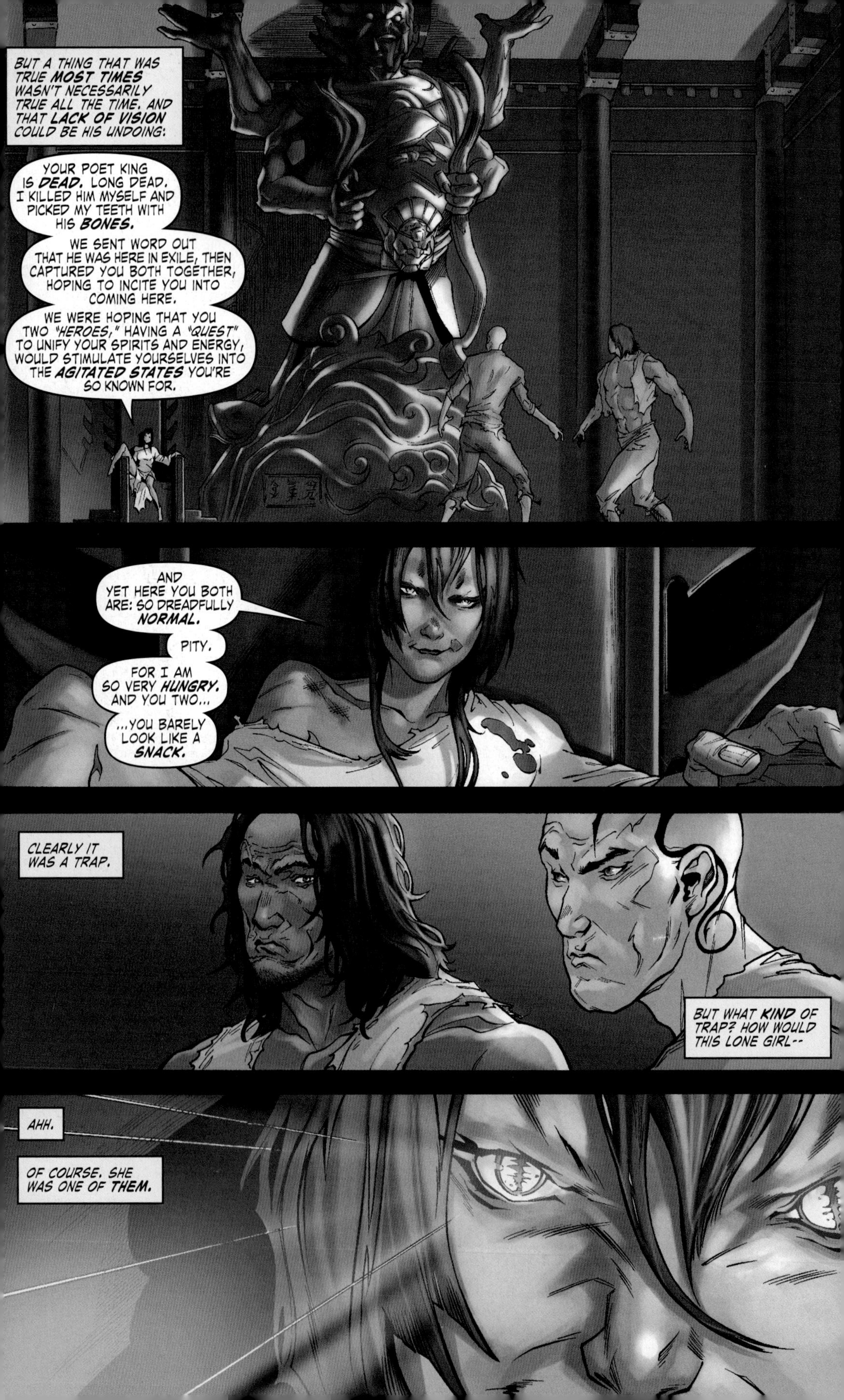
BUT A THING THAT WAS TRUE MOST TIMES WASN'T NECESSARILY TRUE ALL THE TIME. AND THAT LACK OF VISION COULD BE HIS UNDOING:
YOUR POET KING IS DEAD. LONG DEAD. I KILLED HIM MYSELF AND PICKED MY TEETH WITH HIS BONES.
WE SENT WORD OUT THAT HE WAS HERE IN EXILE, THEN CAPTURED YOU BOTH TOGETHER, HOPING TO INCITE YOU INTO COMING HERE.
WE WERE HOPING THAT YOU TWO "HEROES," HAVING A "QUEST" TO UNIFY YOUR SPIRITS AND ENERGY, WOULD STIMULATE YOURSELVES INTO THE AGITATED STATES YOU'RE SO KNOWN FOR.
AND YET HERE YOU BOTH ARE: SO DREADFULLY NORMAL.
PITY.
FOR I AM SO VERY HUNGRY. AND YOU TWO...
...YOU BARELY LOOK LIKE A SNACK.
CLEARLY IT WAS A TRAP.
BUT WHAT KIND OF TRAP? HOW WOULD THIS LONE GIRL--
AHH.
OF COURSE. SHE WAS ONE OF THEM.

TIGER JANI WAS LONG CONSIDERED TO BE A LOCAL GHOST STORY.

A FOLK LEGEND USED BY UGLY OLD WIDOWS TO FRIGHTEN OFF THE WET-EYED DRUNKS THAT INVARIABLY WOULD COME A'COURTIN' AFTER MIDNIGHT.

TIGER JANI IS REAL?

BEI HAD FORGOTTEN WHAT IT FELT LIKE TO **NOT** KNOW EVERYTHING ALL THE TIME.

THAT, AND THE SUDDEN BLOOD LOSS, CREATED IN HIM A FEELING LIKE UNTO EUPHORIA.

SUDDENLY DEATH DIDN'T SEEM LIKE SUCH A GREAT IDEA.

I SHALL FEAST UPON YOUR HOLY SOULS!

OH WELL.

VIVATMA WAS STUNNED. NOT BY THE GIRL'S TRANSFORMATION--

ALTHOUGH IT **WAS** STUNNING--

BUT BY FINDING HIMSELF QUITE SUDDENLY WITHOUT A DIRECTION.

WITHOUT A POET EMPEROR TO SAVE, VIVATMA HAD NO PURPOSE.

WITHOUT A GREAT SIN TO ATONE FOR, VIVATMA HAD NO MORE SHAME.

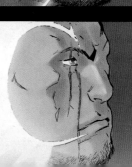

AND FREE OF SHAME, VIVATMA FELT HIS KUNDALINI REALIGNING, HIS PRANA CATCHING THE MOST HOLY FIRE OF GOD IN ALL OF GOD'S GLORY.

HIS AWARENESS WAS AGAIN TRANSFORMED INTO THE INFINITE.

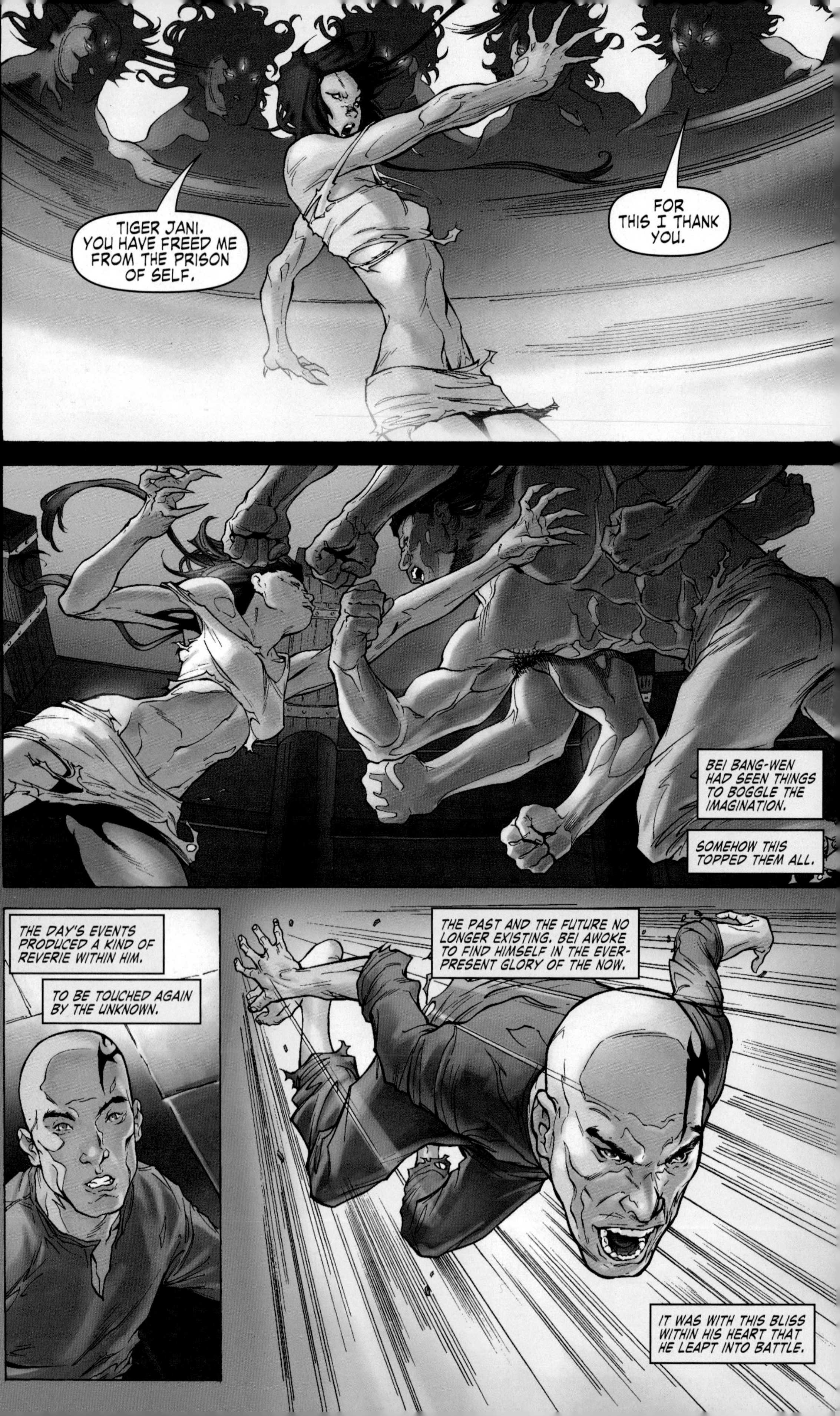
TIGER JANI. YOU HAVE FREED ME FROM THE PRISON OF SELF.
FOR THIS I THANK YOU.
BEI BANG-WEN HAD SEEN THINGS TO BOGGLE THE IMAGINATION.
SOMEHOW THIS TOPPED THEM ALL.
THE DAY'S EVENTS PRODUCED A KIND OF REVERIE WITHIN HIM.
TO BE TOUCHED AGAIN BY THE UNKNOWN.
THE PAST AND THE FUTURE NO LONGER EXISTING. BEI AWOKE TO FIND HIMSELF IN THE EVER-PRESENT GLORY OF THE NOW.
IT WAS WITH THIS BLISS WITHIN HIS HEART THAT HE LEAPT INTO BATTLE.

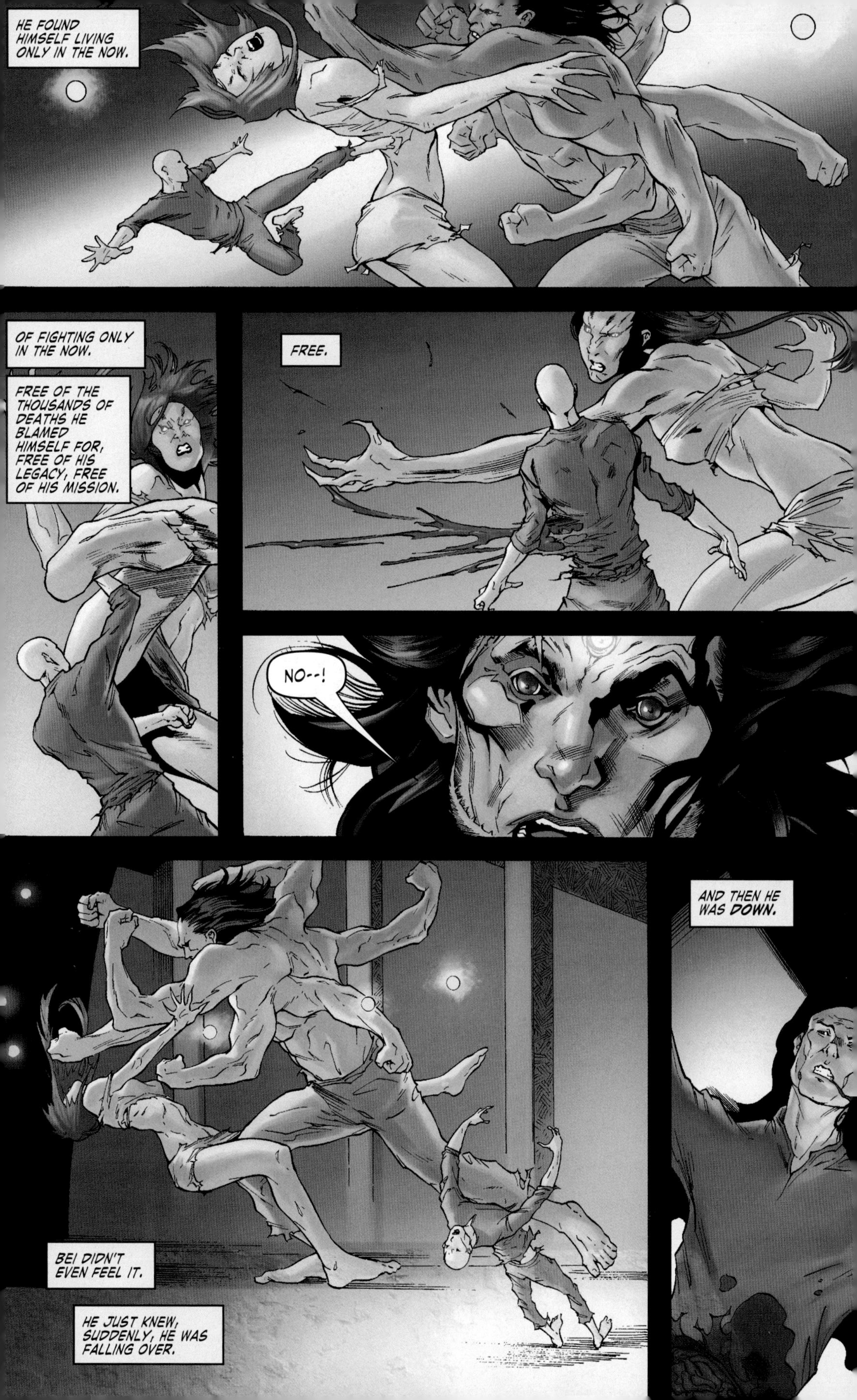
HE FOUND HIMSELF LIVING ONLY IN THE NOW.
OF FIGHTING ONLY IN THE NOW.
FREE OF THE THOUSANDS OF DEATHS HE BLAMED HIMSELF FOR, FREE OF HIS LEGACY, FREE OF HIS MISSION.
FREE.
NO--!
AND THEN HE WAS DOWN.
BEI DIDN'T EVEN FEEL IT.
HE JUST KNEW, SUDDENLY, HE WAS FALLING OVER.

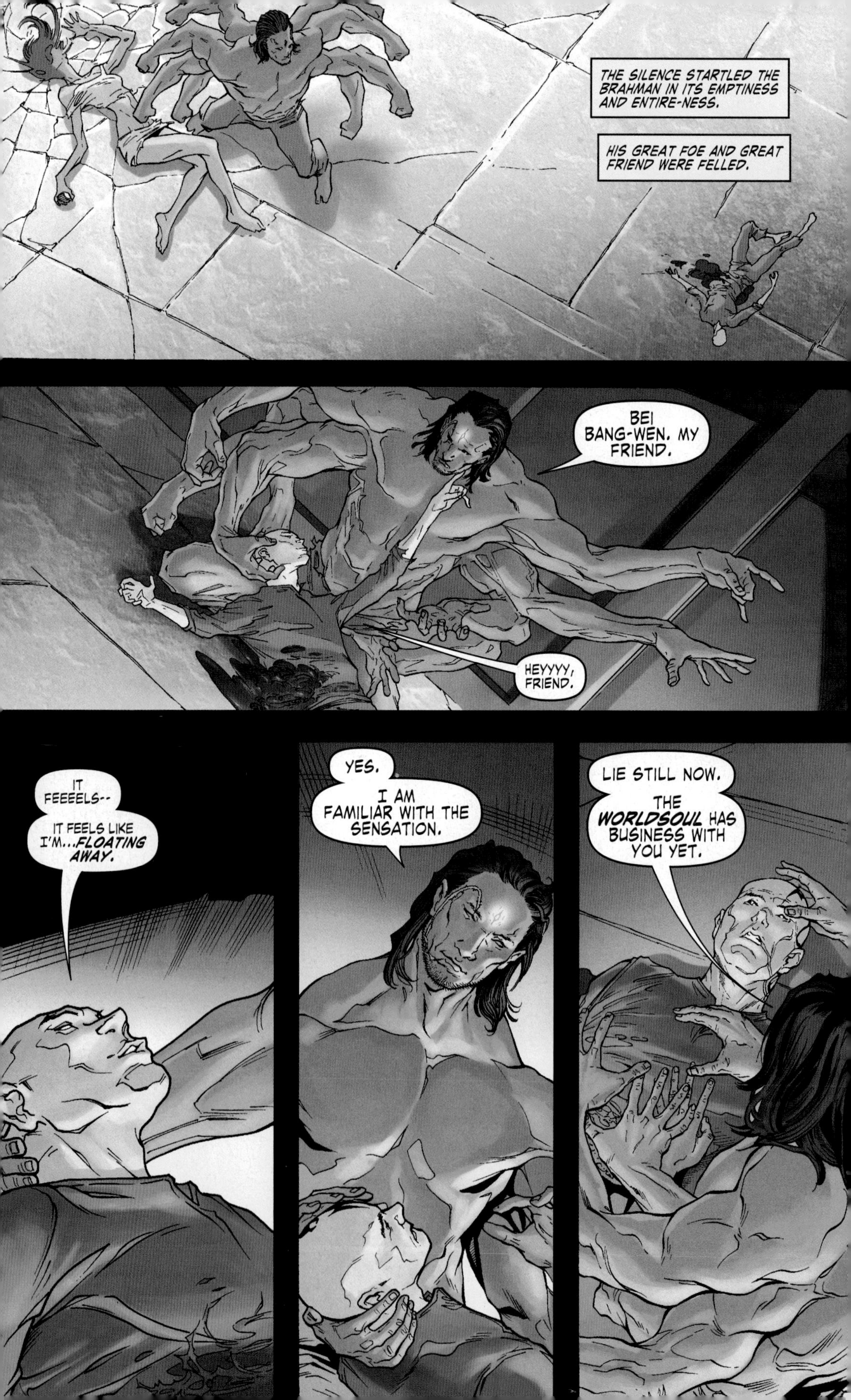
THE SILENCE STARTLED THE BRAHMAN IN ITS EMPTINESS AND ENTIRE-NESS.
HIS GREAT FOE AND GREAT FRIEND WERE FELLED.
BEI BANG-WEN. MY FRIEND.
HEYYYY, FRIEND.
IT FEEEELS--
IT FEELS LIKE I'M...FLOATING AWAY.
YES.
I AM FAMILIAR WITH THE SENSATION.
LIE STILL NOW.
THE WORLDSOUL HAS BUSINESS WITH YOU YET.

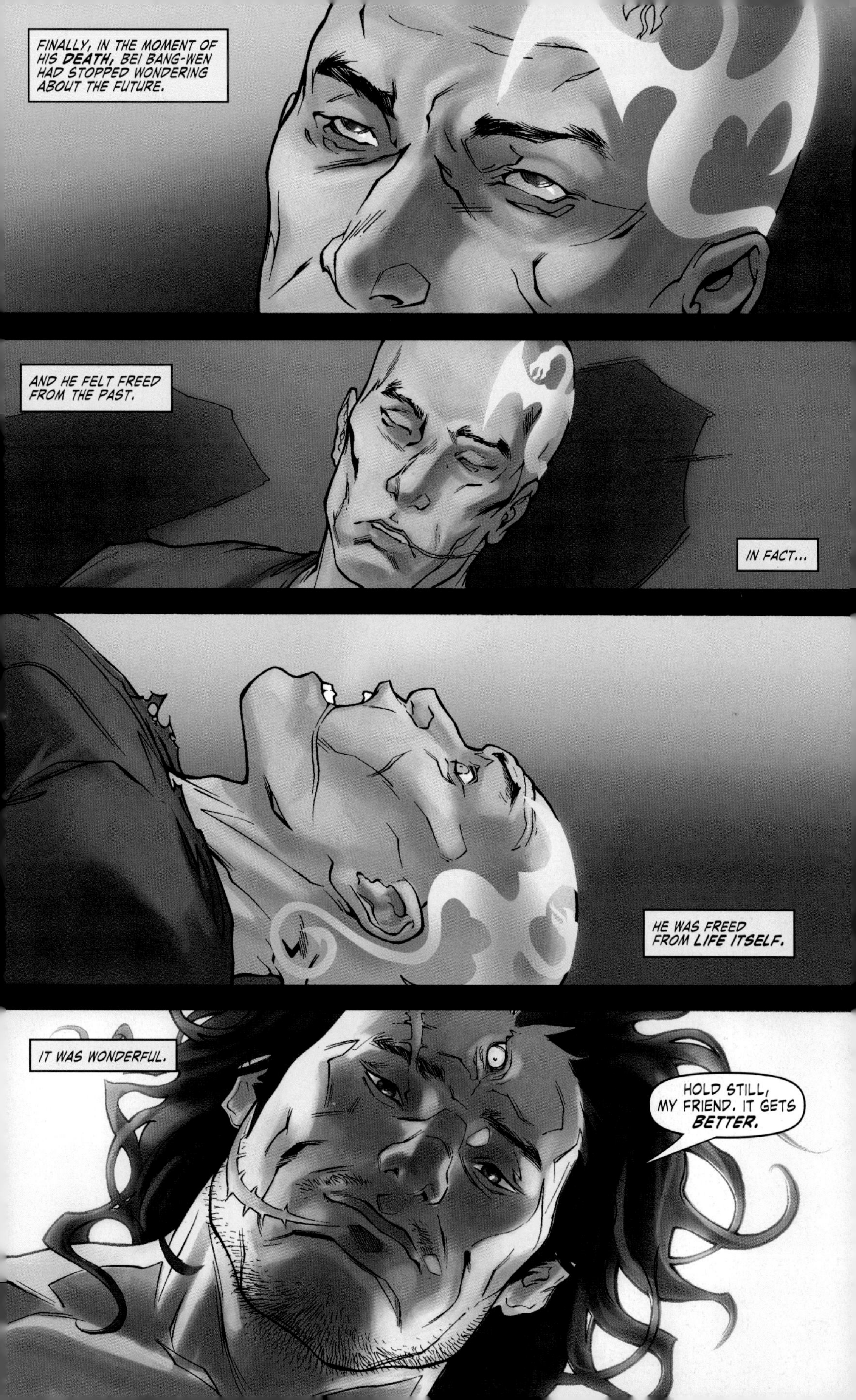
FINALLY, IN THE MOMENT OF HIS DEATH, BEI BANG-WEN HAD STOPPED WONDERING ABOUT THE FUTURE.
AND HE FELT FREED FROM THE PAST.
IN FACT...
HE WAS FREED FROM LIFE ITSELF.
IT WAS WONDERFUL.
HOLD STILL, MY FRIEND. IT GETS BETTER.

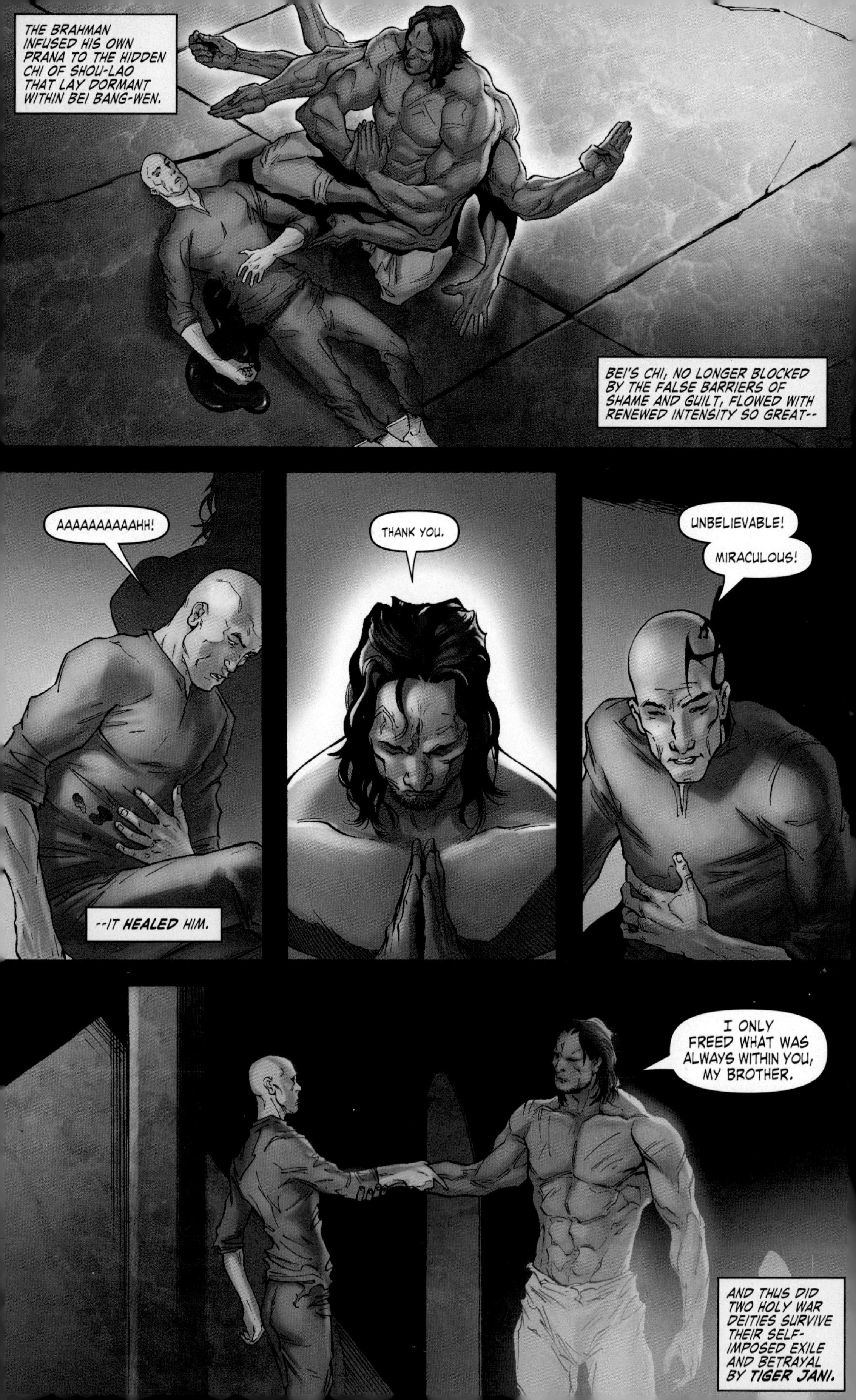
THE BRAHMAN INFUSED HIS OWN PRANA TO THE HIDDEN CHI OF SHOU-LAO THAT LAY DORMANT WITHIN BEI BANG-WEN.
BEI'S CHI, NO LONGER BLOCKED BY THE FALSE BARRIERS OF SHAME AND GUILT, FLOWED WITH RENEWED INTENSITY SO GREAT--
AAAAAAAAAAHH!
--IT **HEALED** HIM.
THANK YOU.
UNBELIEVABLE!
MIRACULOUS!
I ONLY FREED WHAT WAS ALWAYS WITHIN YOU, MY BROTHER.
AND THUS DID TWO HOLY WAR DEITIES SURVIVE THEIR SELF-IMPOSED EXILE AND BETRAYAL BY **TIGER JANI**.

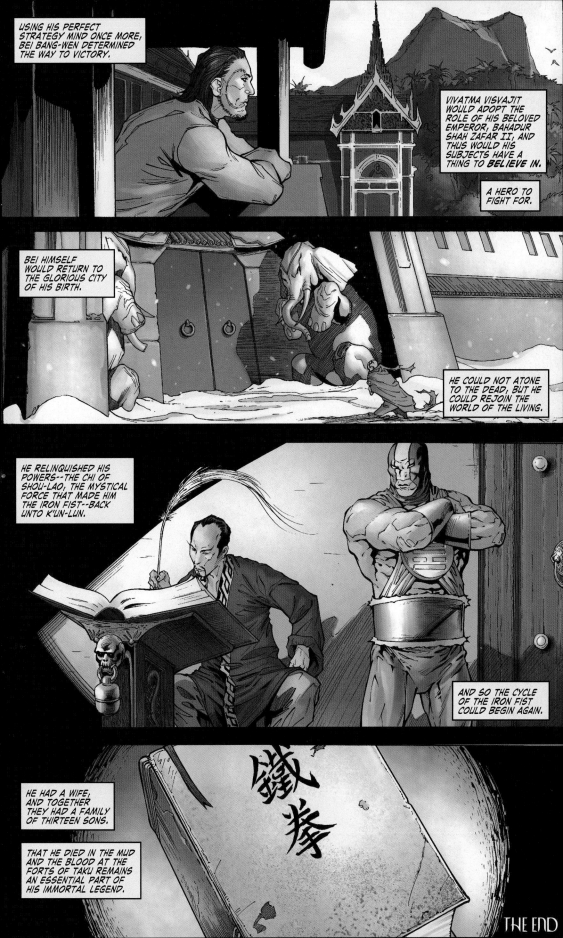

USING HIS PERFECT STRATEGY MIND ONCE MORE, BEI BANG-WEN DETERMINED THE WAY TO VICTORY.

VIVATMA VISVAJIT WOULD ADOPT THE ROLE OF HIS BELOVED EMPEROR, BAHADUR SHAH ZAFAR II, AND THUS WOULD HIS SUBJECTS HAVE A THING TO **BELIEVE IN.**

A HERO TO FIGHT FOR.

BEI HIMSELF WOULD RETURN TO THE GLORIOUS CITY OF HIS BIRTH.

HE COULD NOT ATONE TO THE DEAD, BUT HE COULD REJOIN THE WORLD OF THE LIVING.

HE RELINQUISHED HIS POWERS--THE CHI OF SHOU-LAO, THE MYSTICAL FORCE THAT MADE HIM THE IRON FIST--BACK UNTO K'UN-LUN.

AND SO THE CYCLE OF THE IRON FIST COULD BEGIN AGAIN.

HE HAD A WIFE, AND TOGETHER THEY HAD A FAMILY OF THIRTEEN SONS.

THAT HE DIED IN THE MUD AND THE BLOOD AT THE FORTS OF TAKU REMAINS AN ESSENTIAL PART OF HIS IMMORTAL LEGEND.

THE END

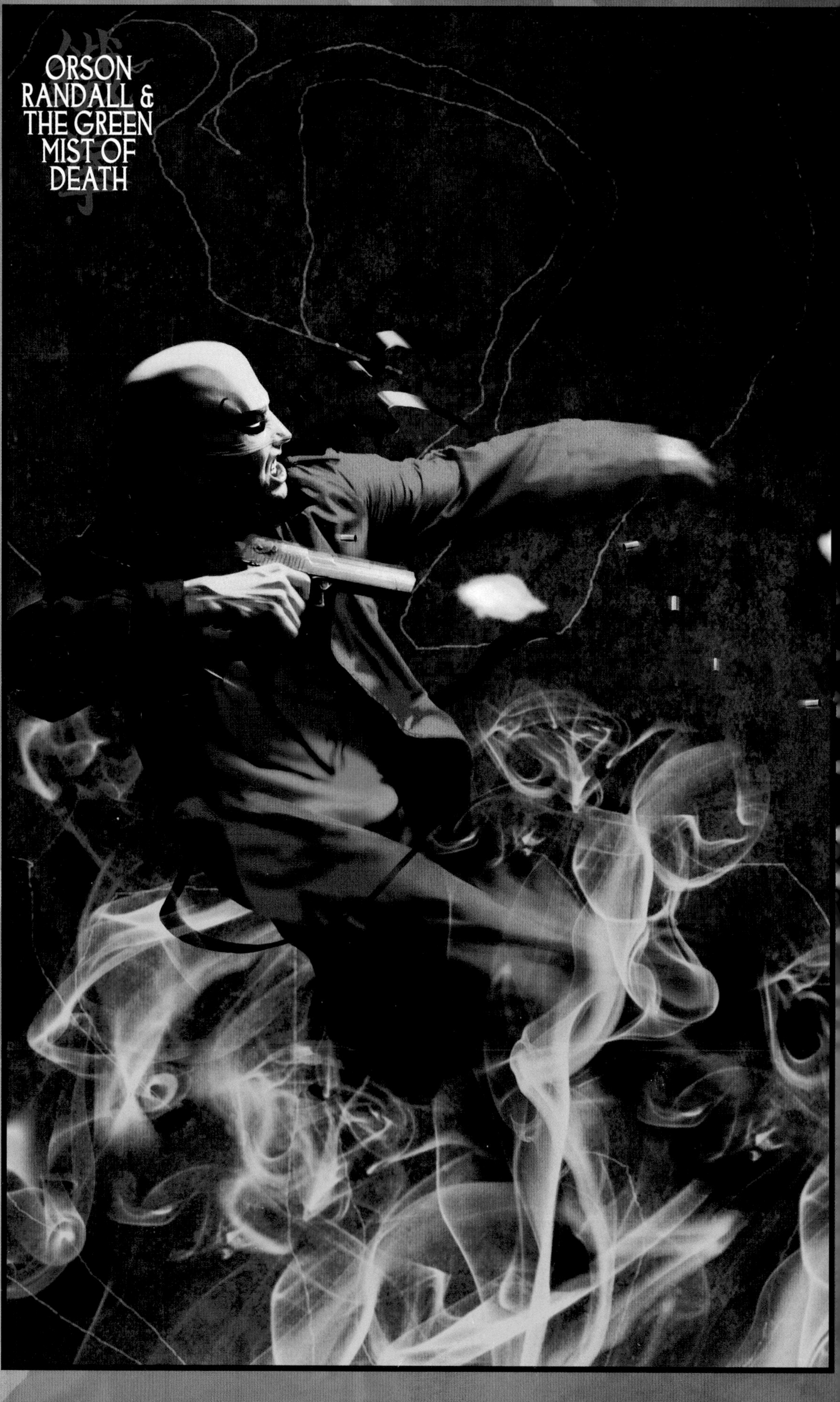
ORSON RANDALL & THE GREEN MIST OF DEATH

! Hero, adventurer, dashing rogue! Born and raised in the mystical city of K'un-Lun, Orson defeated the dragon Shou-Lao nd gained extraordinary powers. With superhuman strength, speed, and fighting prowess, he became the city's Immortal ut after traveling to Earth and enduring the horrors of World War I, Orson refused to take part in the deadly tournament 8 years between K'un-Lun and the six other mystical cities. Resisting his fellow Immortal Weapons' use of force, Orson accidentally killed the Crane Champion of K'un-Zi, and fled.

several decades — long before Danny Rand would travel to K'un-Lun and become successor to the title of the Immortal Orson roamed the Earth, a bounty on his head. In the company of his makeshift family, the Confederates of the Curious Danny's father, Wendell Rand — Orson has evaded the pursuits of the Immortal Weapons and quested around the globe for justice and adventure as…

THE GOLDEN AGE IRON FIST!

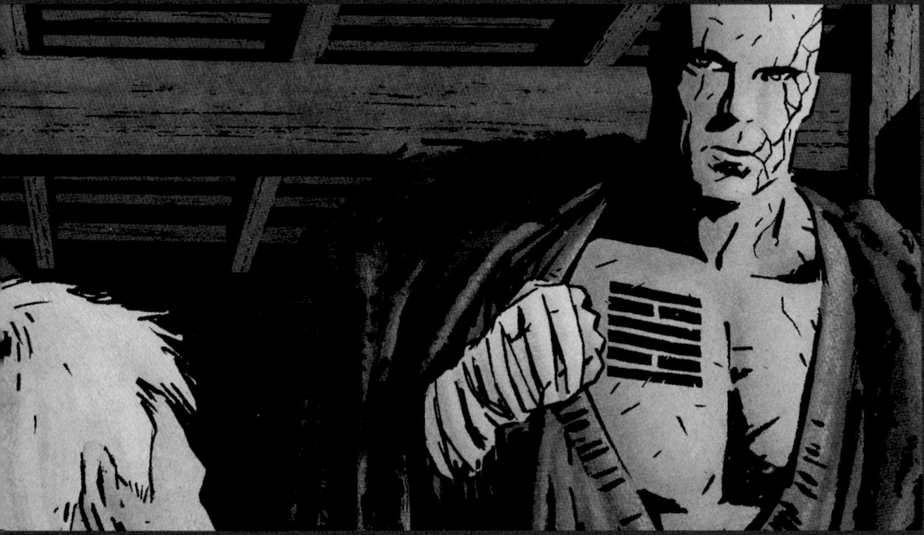

Previously:

— the Iron Fist and present-day Immortal Weapon of K'un-Lun — fights a war on many fronts. As the Tournament Cities unfolds, Danny must secure victory for K'un-Lun in order to return to Earth…and he's already lost his first hile the round robin elimination moves on, Danny's trainer and master, Lei Kung the Thunderer, has enlisted his aid n. Lei Kung is raising an army by training the women of K'un-Lun in the martial arts, and means to bring down the city's corrupt lord. They face overwhelming odds, and defeat is all but assured.

urnament, Danny attempted to befriend the Prince of Orphans — the oldest, most powerful and most venerated of nmortal Weapons — and the least known and most mysterious. But Danny was rebuffed by the enigmatic warrior.

yway. As Lei Kung and Danny steeled themselves to launch their rebellion at dawn and rewrite the destiny of the ities, Danny was paid a private visit in his quarters. It was the Prince of Orphans — a.k.a. John Aman. He came to g the mark of the Thunderer tattooed on his chest, announcing his allegiance to their cause…and asked how Danny him. Danny revealed that he'd learned of Aman by reading of the life and adventures of the Iron Fist Orson Randall, where Aman made several appearances…

MMORTAL IRON FIST: ORSON RANDALL AND THE GREEN MIST OF DEATH

ion

Nick Dragotta, Mike Allred and Laura Allred
Artists, Part One

Russ Heath
Artist, Part Two

Lewis LaRosa, Stefano Gaudiano and Matt Hollingsworth
Artists, Part Three

Mitch Breitweiser and Matt Hollingsworth
Artists, Part Four

Studios
rs

Paul Acerios
Production

Alejandro Arbona
Assistant Editor

Warren Simons
Editor

Joe Quesada
Editor in Chief

Dan Buckley
Publisher

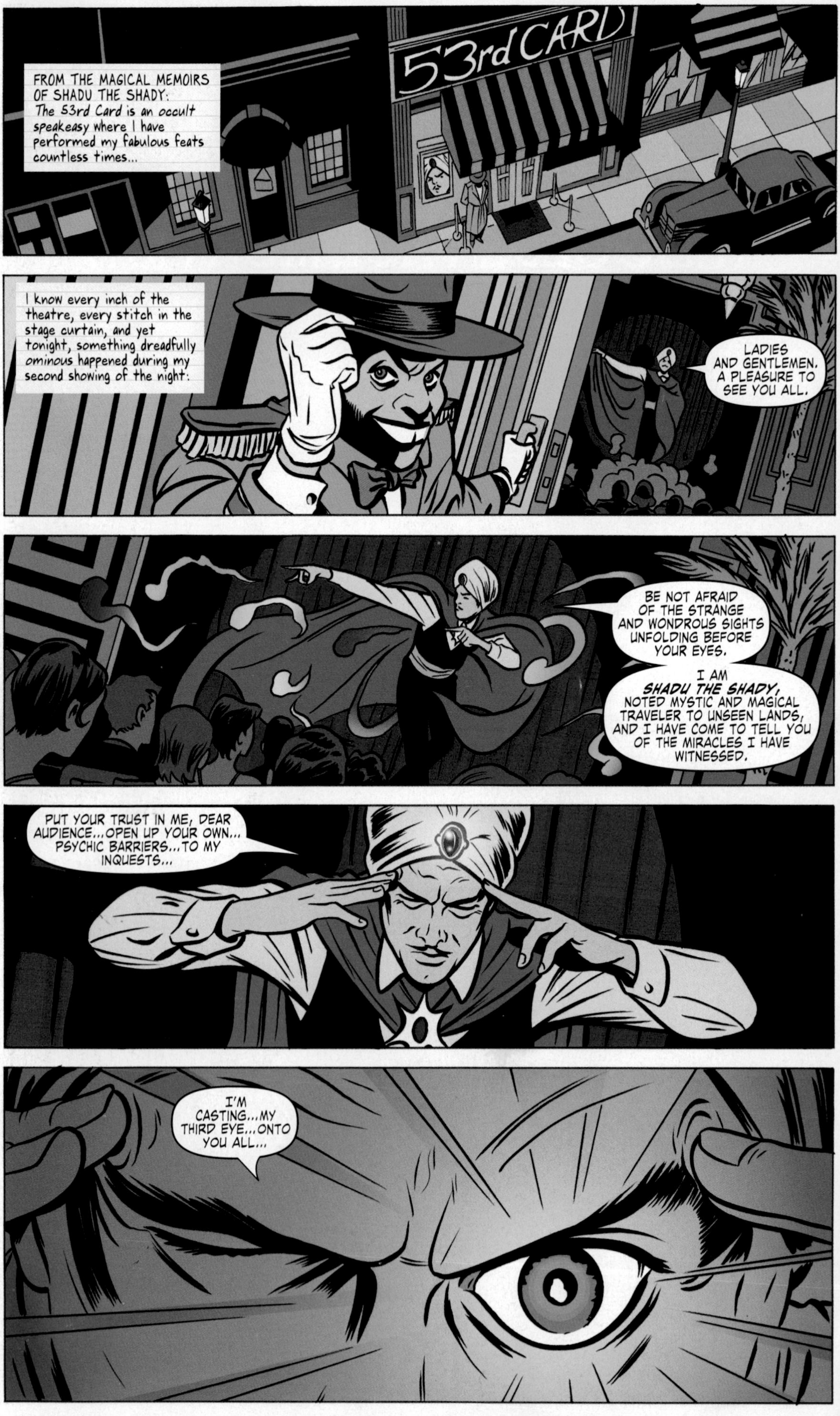
53rd CARD
FROM THE MAGICAL MEMOIRS OF SHADU THE SHADY: The 53rd Card is an occult speakeasy where I have performed my fabulous feats countless times...
I know every inch of the theatre, every stitch in the stage curtain, and yet tonight, something dreadfully ominous happened during my second showing of the night:
LADIES AND GENTLEMEN. A PLEASURE TO SEE YOU ALL.
BE NOT AFRAID OF THE STRANGE AND WONDROUS SIGHTS UNFOLDING BEFORE YOUR EYES.
I AM ***SHADU THE SHADY,*** NOTED MYSTIC AND MAGICAL TRAVELER TO UNSEEN LANDS, AND I HAVE COME TO TELL YOU OF THE MIRACLES I HAVE WITNESSED.
PUT YOUR TRUST IN ME, DEAR AUDIENCE...OPEN UP YOUR OWN... PSYCHIC BARRIERS...TO MY INQUESTS...
I'M CASTING...MY THIRD EYE...ONTO YOU ALL...

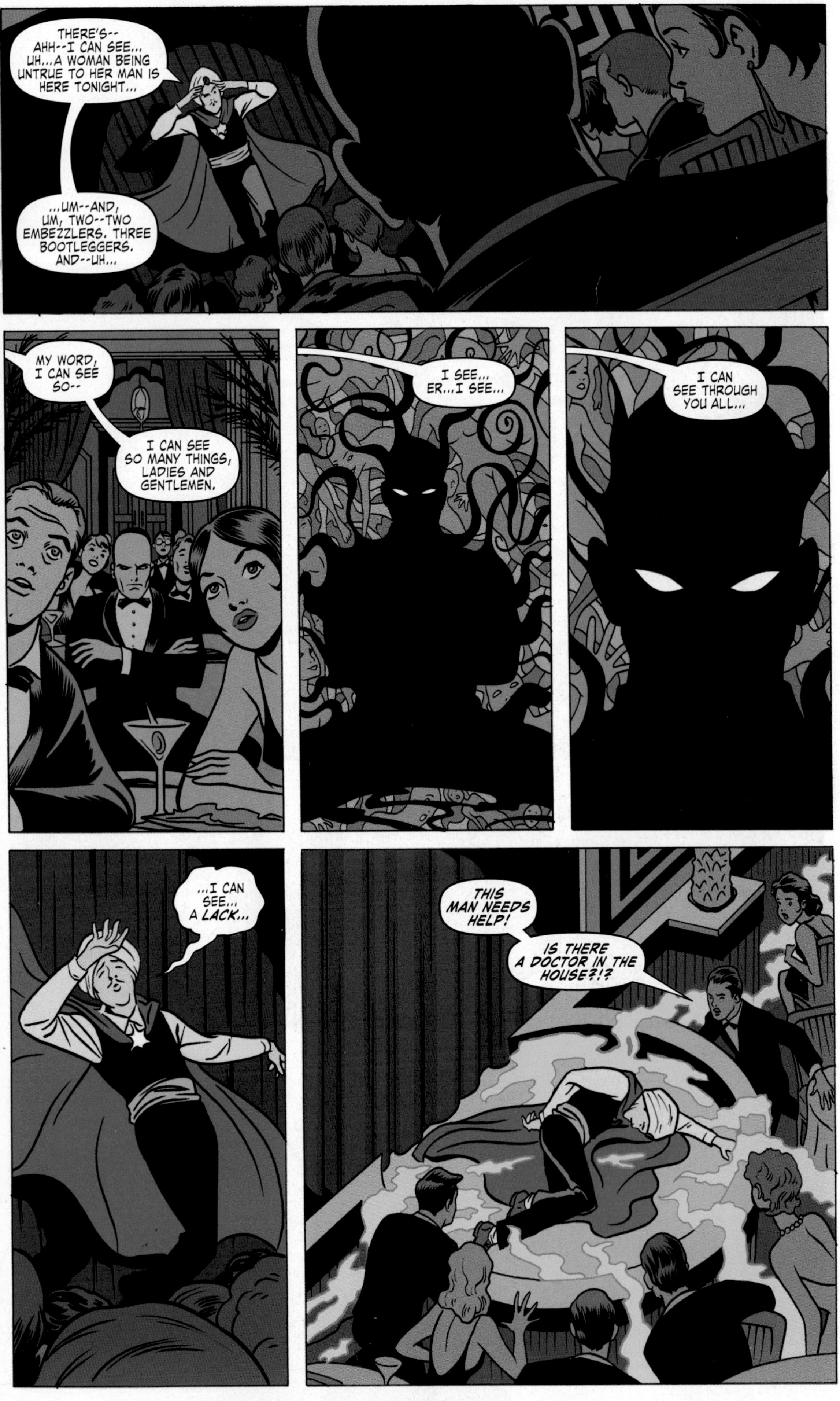
THERE'S-- AHH--I CAN SEE... UH...A WOMAN BEING UNTRUE TO HER MAN IS HERE TONIGHT...
...UM--AND, UM, TWO--TWO EMBEZZLERS. THREE BOOTLEGGERS. AND--UH...
MY WORD, I CAN SEE SO--
I CAN SEE SO MANY THINGS, LADIES AND GENTLEMEN.
I SEE... ER...I SEE...
I CAN SEE THROUGH YOU ALL...
...I CAN SEE... A *LACK*...
THIS MAN NEEDS HELP!
IS THERE A DOCTOR IN THE HOUSE?!?

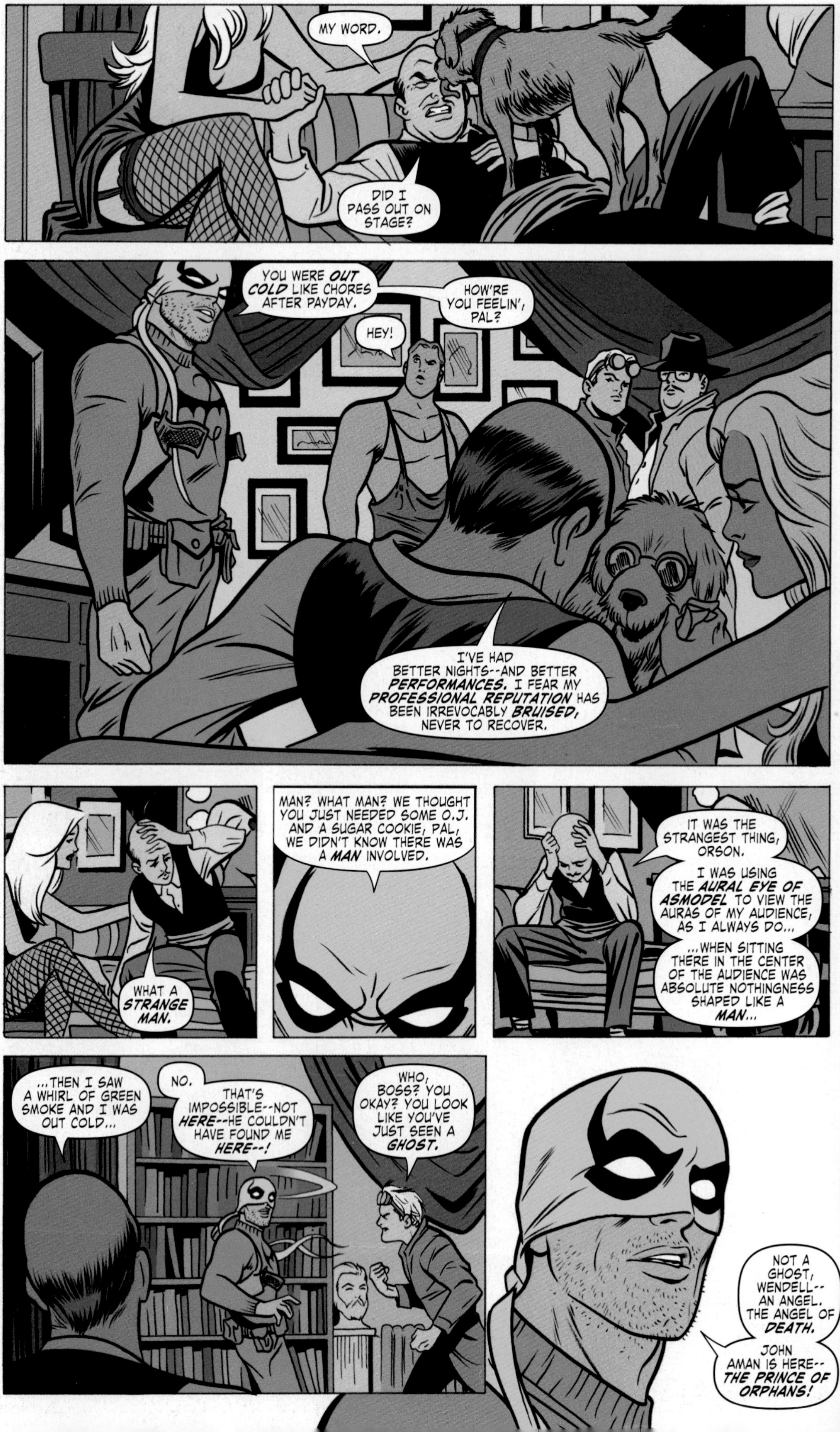
MY WORD.
DID I PASS OUT ON STAGE?
YOU WERE OUT COLD LIKE CHORES AFTER PAYDAY.
HOW'RE YOU FEELIN', PAL?
HEY!
I'VE HAD BETTER NIGHTS--AND BETTER PERFORMANCES. I FEAR MY PROFESSIONAL REPUTATION HAS BEEN IRREVOCABLY BRUISED, NEVER TO RECOVER.
WHAT A STRANGE MAN.
MAN? WHAT MAN? WE THOUGHT YOU JUST NEEDED SOME O.J. AND A SUGAR COOKIE, PAL, WE DIDN'T KNOW THERE WAS A MAN INVOLVED.
IT WAS THE STRANGEST THING, ORSON.
I WAS USING THE AURAL EYE OF ASMODEL TO VIEW THE AURAS OF MY AUDIENCE, AS I ALWAYS DO...
...WHEN SITTING THERE IN THE CENTER OF THE AUDIENCE WAS ABSOLUTE NOTHINGNESS SHAPED LIKE A MAN...
...THEN I SAW A WHIRL OF GREEN SMOKE AND I WAS OUT COLD...
NO.
THAT'S IMPOSSIBLE--NOT HERE--HE COULDN'T HAVE FOUND ME HERE--!
WHO, BOSS? YOU OKAY? YOU LOOK LIKE YOU'VE JUST SEEN A GHOST.
NOT A GHOST, WENDELL--AN ANGEL. THE ANGEL OF DEATH.
JOHN AMAN IS HERE--THE PRINCE OF ORPHANS!

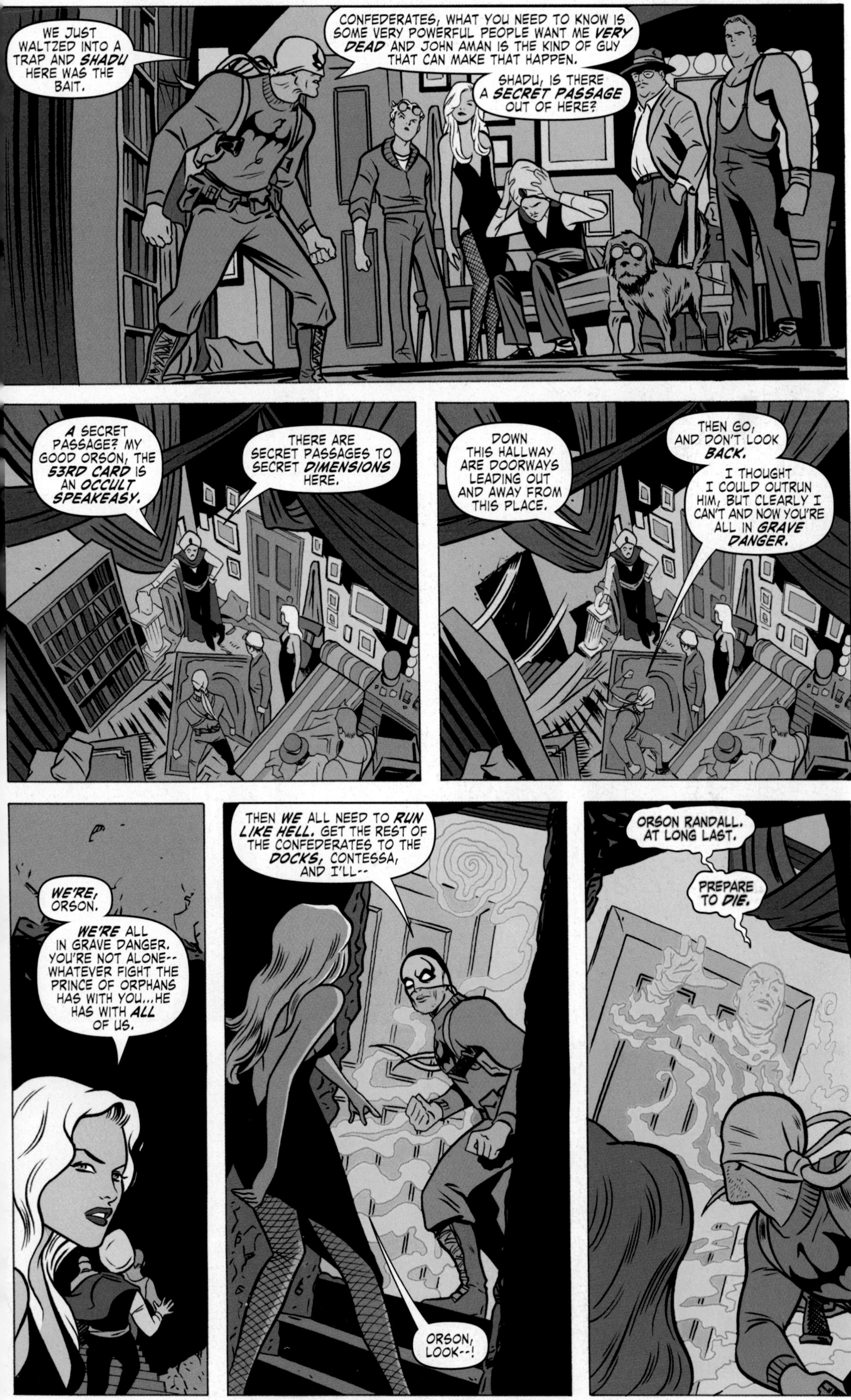
WE JUST WALTZED INTO A TRAP AND SHADU HERE WAS THE BAIT.
CONFEDERATES, WHAT YOU NEED TO KNOW IS SOME VERY POWERFUL PEOPLE WANT ME VERY DEAD AND JOHN AMAN IS THE KIND OF GUY THAT CAN MAKE THAT HAPPEN.
SHADU, IS THERE A SECRET PASSAGE OUT OF HERE?
A SECRET PASSAGE? MY GOOD ORSON, THE 53RD CARD IS AN OCCULT SPEAKEASY.
THERE ARE SECRET PASSAGES TO SECRET DIMENSIONS HERE.
DOWN THIS HALLWAY ARE DOORWAYS LEADING OUT AND AWAY FROM THIS PLACE.
THEN GO, AND DON'T LOOK BACK.
I THOUGHT I COULD OUTRUN HIM, BUT CLEARLY I CAN'T AND NOW YOU'RE ALL IN GRAVE DANGER.
WE'RE, ORSON.
WE'RE ALL IN GRAVE DANGER. YOU'RE NOT ALONE-- WHATEVER FIGHT THE PRINCE OF ORPHANS HAS WITH YOU...HE HAS WITH ALL OF US.
THEN WE ALL NEED TO RUN LIKE HELL. GET THE REST OF THE CONFEDERATES TO THE DOCKS, CONTESSA, AND I'LL--
ORSON, LOOK--!
ORSON RANDALL. AT LONG LAST.
PREPARE TO DIE.

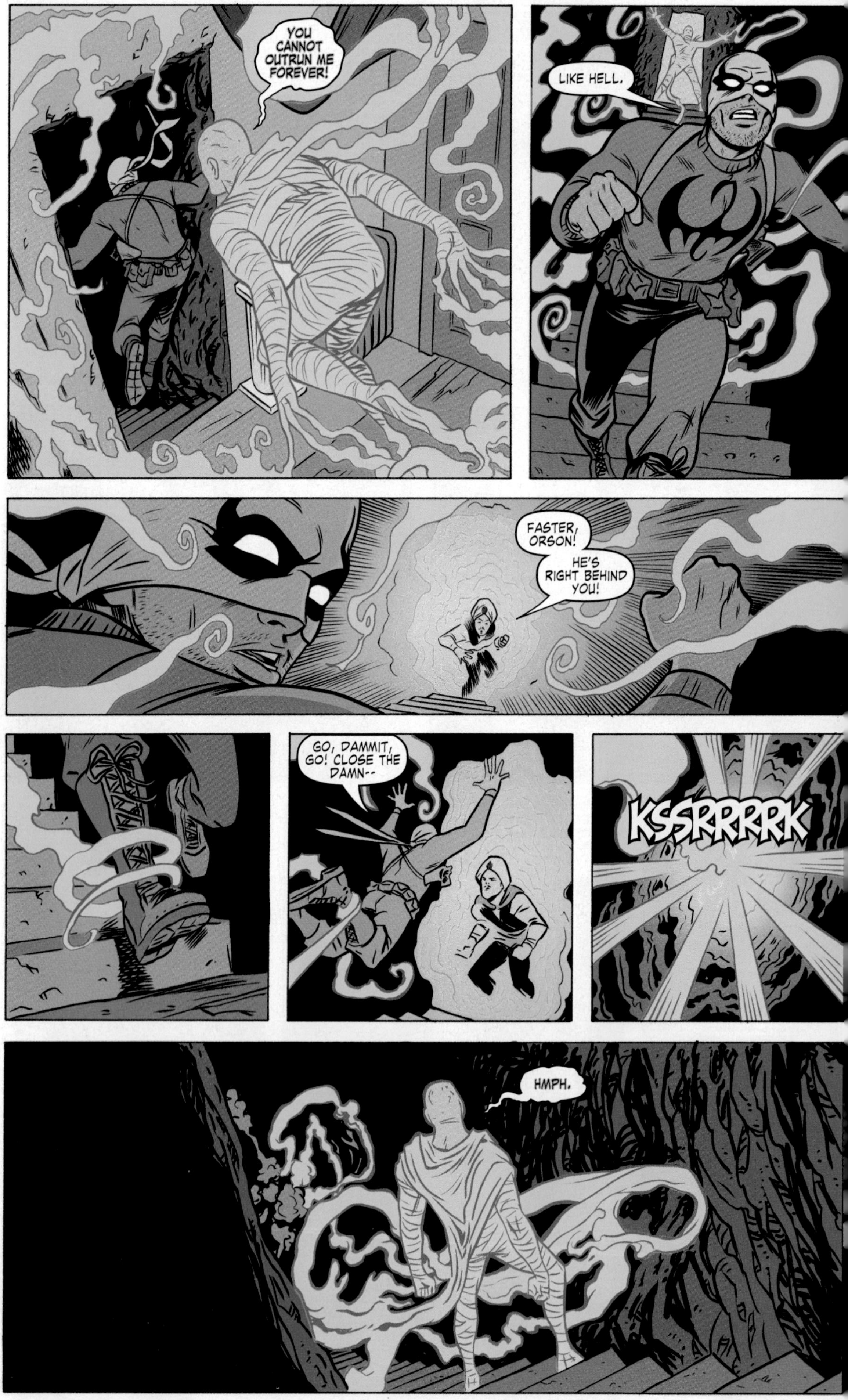
YOU CANNOT OUTRUN ME FOREVER!
LIKE HELL.
FASTER, ORSON!
HE'S RIGHT BEHIND YOU!
GO, DAMMIT, GO! CLOSE THE DAMN--
KSSRRRRK
HMPH.

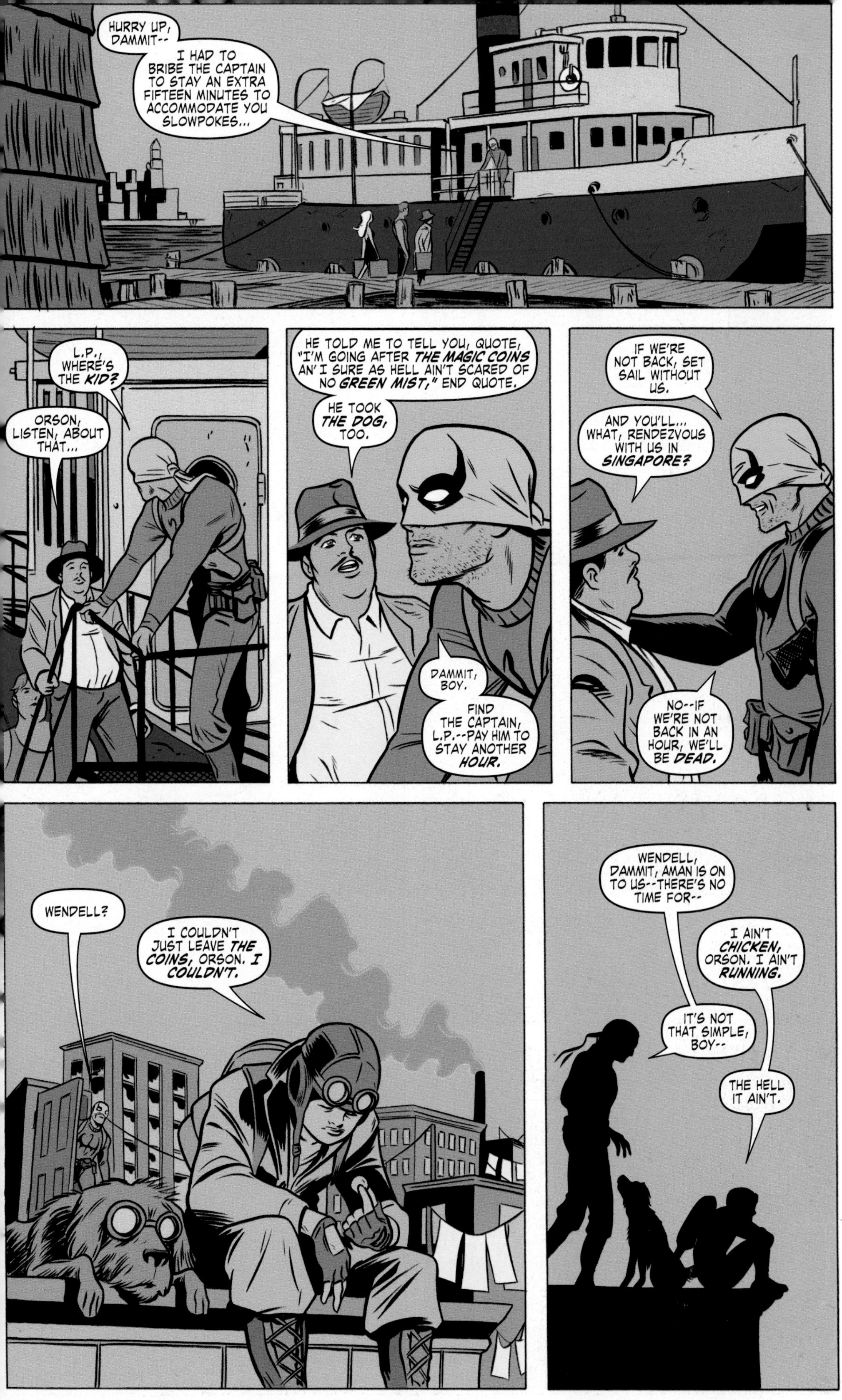
HURRY UP, DAMMIT--
I HAD TO BRIBE THE CAPTAIN TO STAY AN EXTRA FIFTEEN MINUTES TO ACCOMMODATE YOU SLOWPOKES...
L.P., WHERE'S THE KID?
ORSON, LISTEN, ABOUT THAT...
HE TOLD ME TO TELL YOU, QUOTE, "I'M GOING AFTER THE MAGIC COINS AN' I SURE AS HELL AIN'T SCARED OF NO GREEN MIST," END QUOTE.
HE TOOK THE DOG, TOO.
DAMMIT, BOY.
FIND THE CAPTAIN, L.P.--PAY HIM TO STAY ANOTHER HOUR.
IF WE'RE NOT BACK, SET SAIL WITHOUT US.
AND YOU'LL... WHAT, RENDEZVOUS WITH US IN SINGAPORE?
NO--IF WE'RE NOT BACK IN AN HOUR, WE'LL BE DEAD.
WENDELL?
I COULDN'T JUST LEAVE THE COINS, ORSON. I COULDN'T.
WENDELL, DAMMIT, AMAN IS ON TO US--THERE'S NO TIME FOR--
I AIN'T CHICKEN, ORSON. I AIN'T RUNNING.
IT'S NOT THAT SIMPLE, BOY--
THE HELL IT AIN'T.

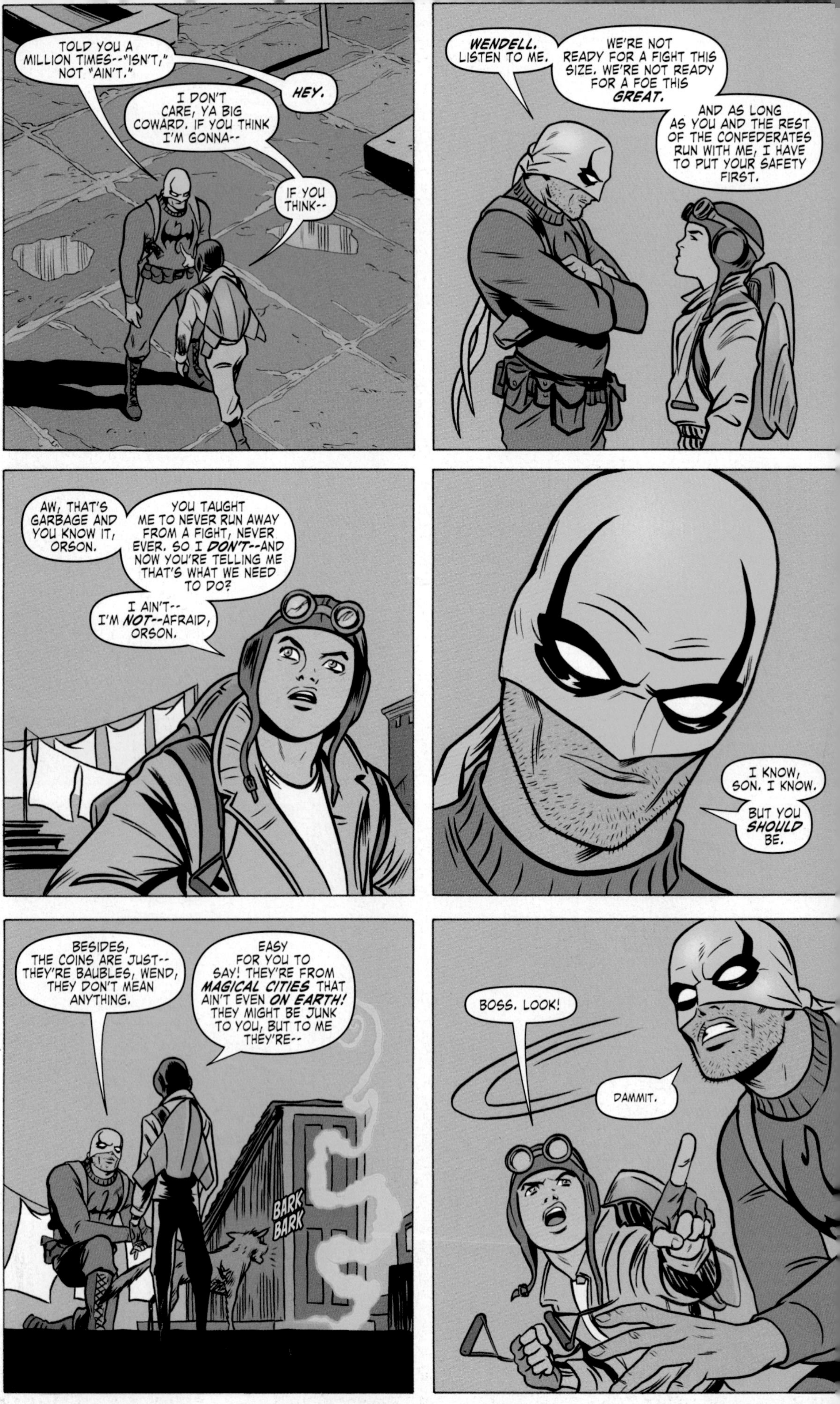
TOLD YOU A MILLION TIMES--"ISN'T," NOT "AIN'T."
HEY.
I DON'T CARE, YA BIG COWARD. IF YOU THINK I'M GONNA--
IF YOU THINK--
WENDELL. LISTEN TO ME.
WE'RE NOT READY FOR A FIGHT THIS SIZE. WE'RE NOT READY FOR A FOE THIS GREAT.
AND AS LONG AS YOU AND THE REST OF THE CONFEDERATES RUN WITH ME, I HAVE TO PUT YOUR SAFETY FIRST.
AW, THAT'S GARBAGE AND YOU KNOW IT, ORSON.
YOU TAUGHT ME TO NEVER RUN AWAY FROM A FIGHT, NEVER EVER. SO I DON'T--AND NOW YOU'RE TELLING ME THAT'S WHAT WE NEED TO DO?
I AIN'T-- I'M NOT--AFRAID, ORSON.
I KNOW, SON. I KNOW.
BUT YOU SHOULD BE.
BESIDES, THE COINS ARE JUST-- THEY'RE BAUBLES, WEND, THEY DON'T MEAN ANYTHING.
EASY FOR YOU TO SAY! THEY'RE FROM MAGICAL CITIES THAT AIN'T EVEN ON EARTH! THEY MIGHT BE JUNK TO YOU, BUT TO ME THEY'RE--
BARK BARK
BOSS. LOOK!
DAMMIT.

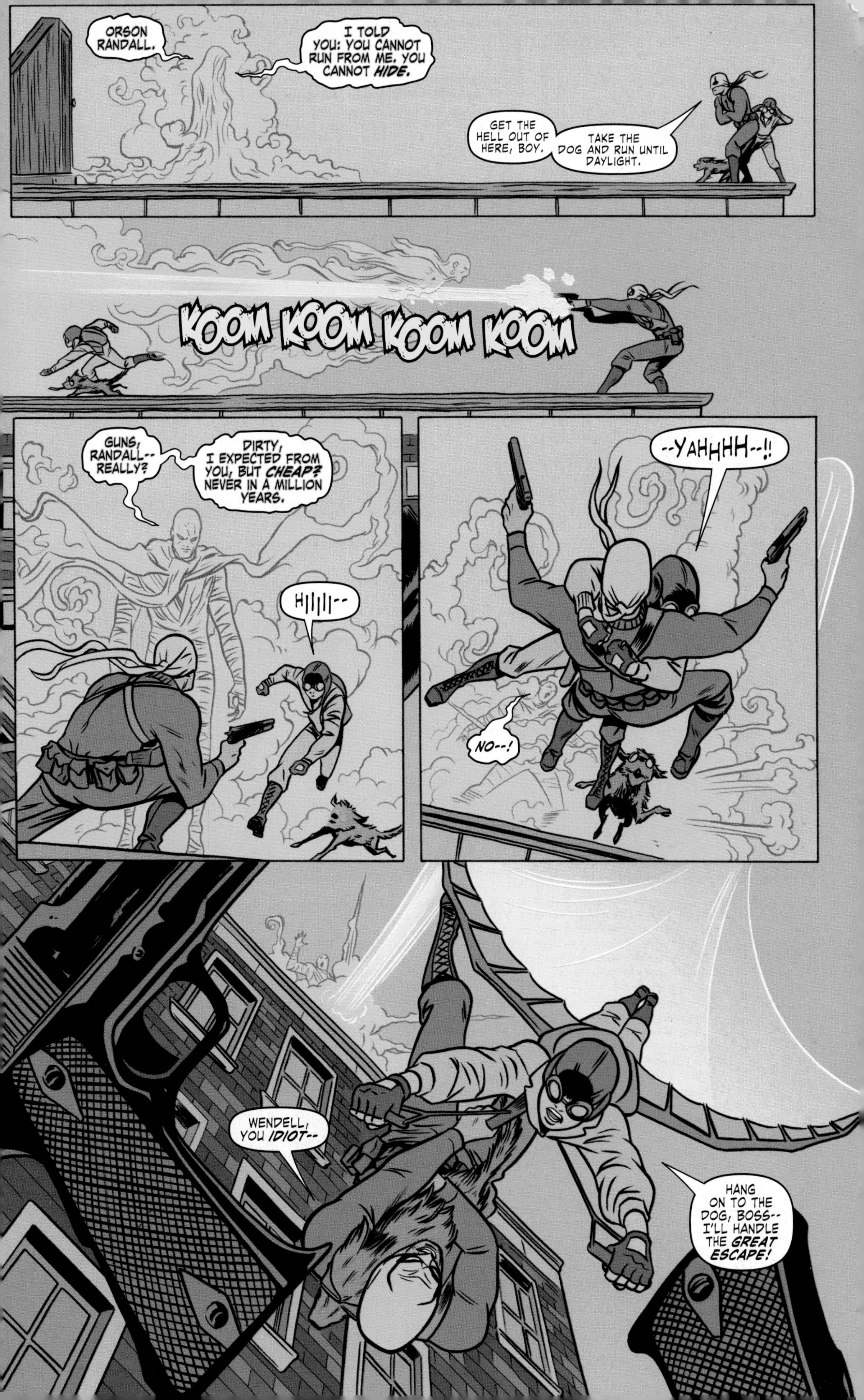
ORSON RANDALL.
I TOLD YOU: YOU CANNOT RUN FROM ME. YOU CANNOT *HIDE.*
GET THE HELL OUT OF HERE, BOY.
TAKE THE DOG AND RUN UNTIL DAYLIGHT.
KOOM KOOM KOOM KOOM
GUNS, RANDALL-- REALLY?
DIRTY, I EXPECTED FROM YOU, BUT *CHEAP?* NEVER IN A MILLION YEARS.
HIIIII--
--YAHHHH--!!
NO--!
WENDELL, YOU *IDIOT--*
HANG ON TO THE DOG, BOSS-- I'LL HANDLE THE *GREAT ESCAPE!*

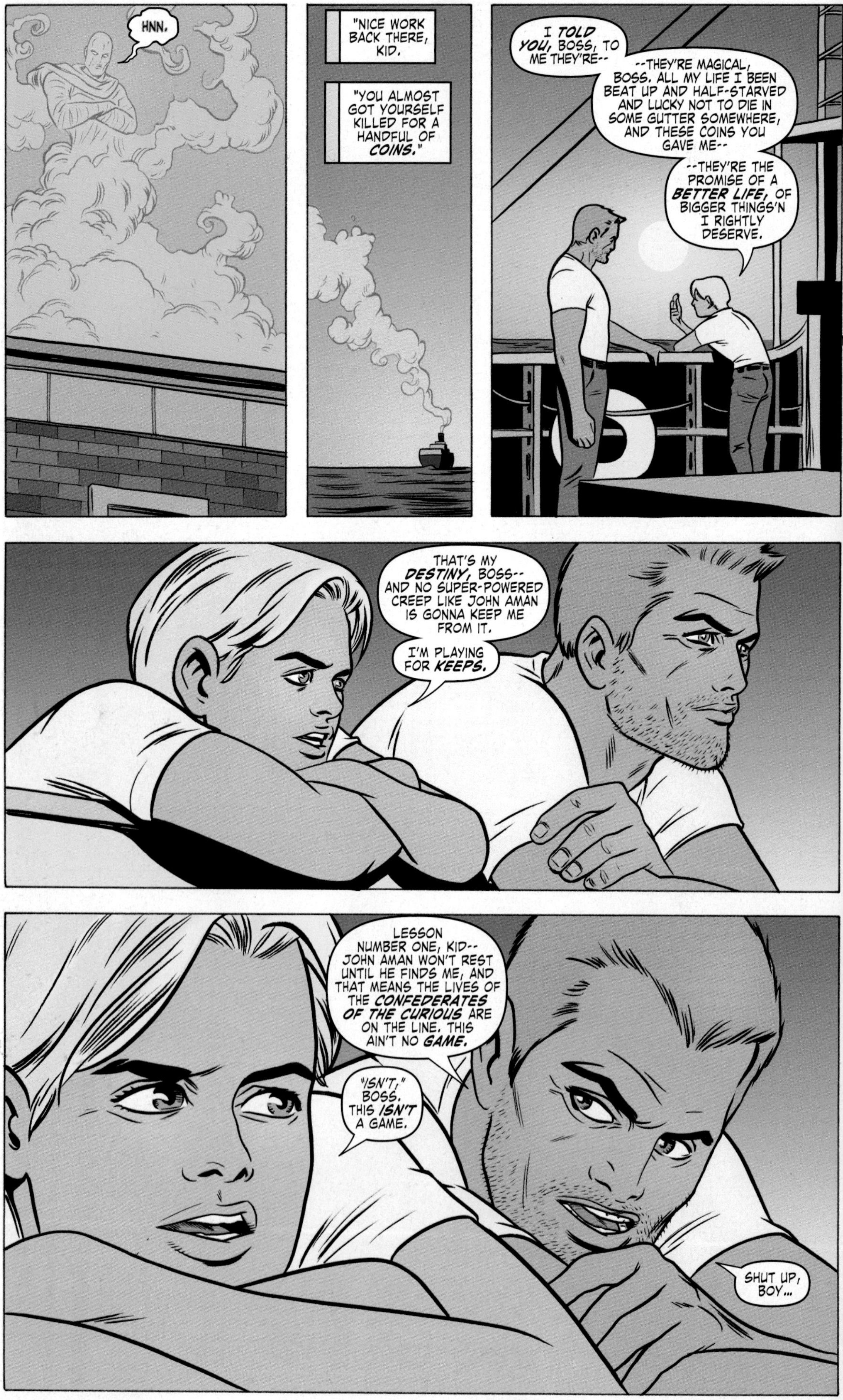

HNN.
"NICE WORK BACK THERE, KID.
"YOU ALMOST GOT YOURSELF KILLED FOR A HANDFUL OF COINS."
I TOLD YOU, BOSS, TO ME THEY'RE--
--THEY'RE MAGICAL, BOSS. ALL MY LIFE I BEEN BEAT UP AND HALF-STARVED AND LUCKY NOT TO DIE IN SOME GUTTER SOMEWHERE, AND THESE COINS YOU GAVE ME--
--THEY'RE THE PROMISE OF A BETTER LIFE, OF BIGGER THINGS'N I RIGHTLY DESERVE.
THAT'S MY DESTINY, BOSS-- AND NO SUPER-POWERED CREEP LIKE JOHN AMAN IS GONNA KEEP ME FROM IT.
I'M PLAYING FOR KEEPS.
LESSON NUMBER ONE, KID-- JOHN AMAN WON'T REST UNTIL HE FINDS ME, AND THAT MEANS THE LIVES OF THE CONFEDERATES OF THE CURIOUS ARE ON THE LINE. THIS AIN'T NO GAME.
"ISN'T," BOSS. THIS ISN'T A GAME.
SHUT UP, BOY...

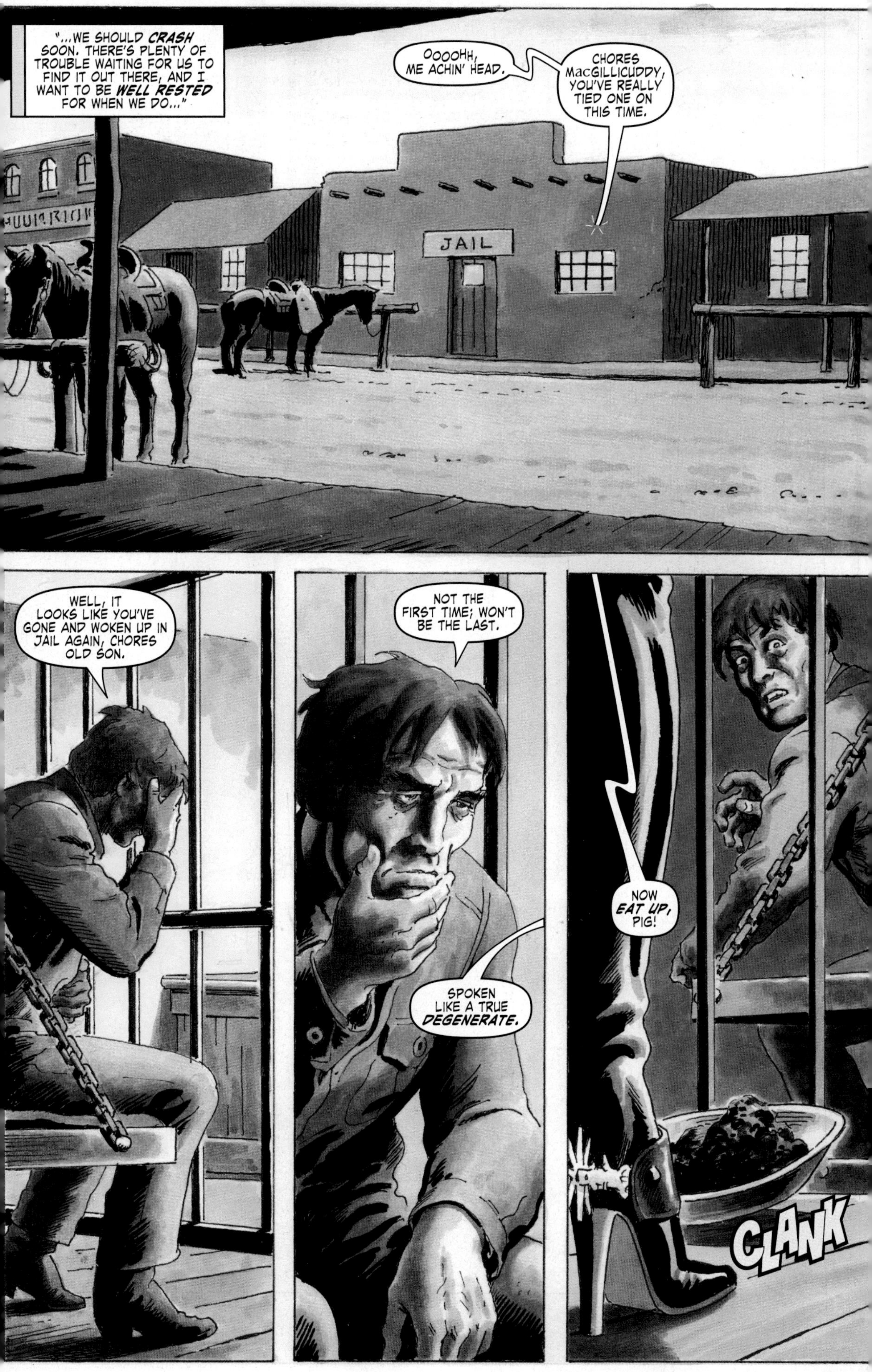
"...WE SHOULD *CRASH* SOON. THERE'S PLENTY OF TROUBLE WAITING FOR US TO FIND IT OUT THERE, AND I WANT TO BE *WELL RESTED* FOR WHEN WE DO..."
OOOOHH, ME ACHIN' HEAD.
CHORES MacGILLICUDDY, YOU'VE REALLY TIED ONE ON THIS TIME.
JAIL
WELL, IT LOOKS LIKE YOU'VE GONE AND WOKEN UP IN JAIL AGAIN, CHORES OLD SON.
NOT THE FIRST TIME; WON'T BE THE LAST.
SPOKEN LIKE A TRUE *DEGENERATE.*
NOW *EAT UP,* PIG!
CLANK

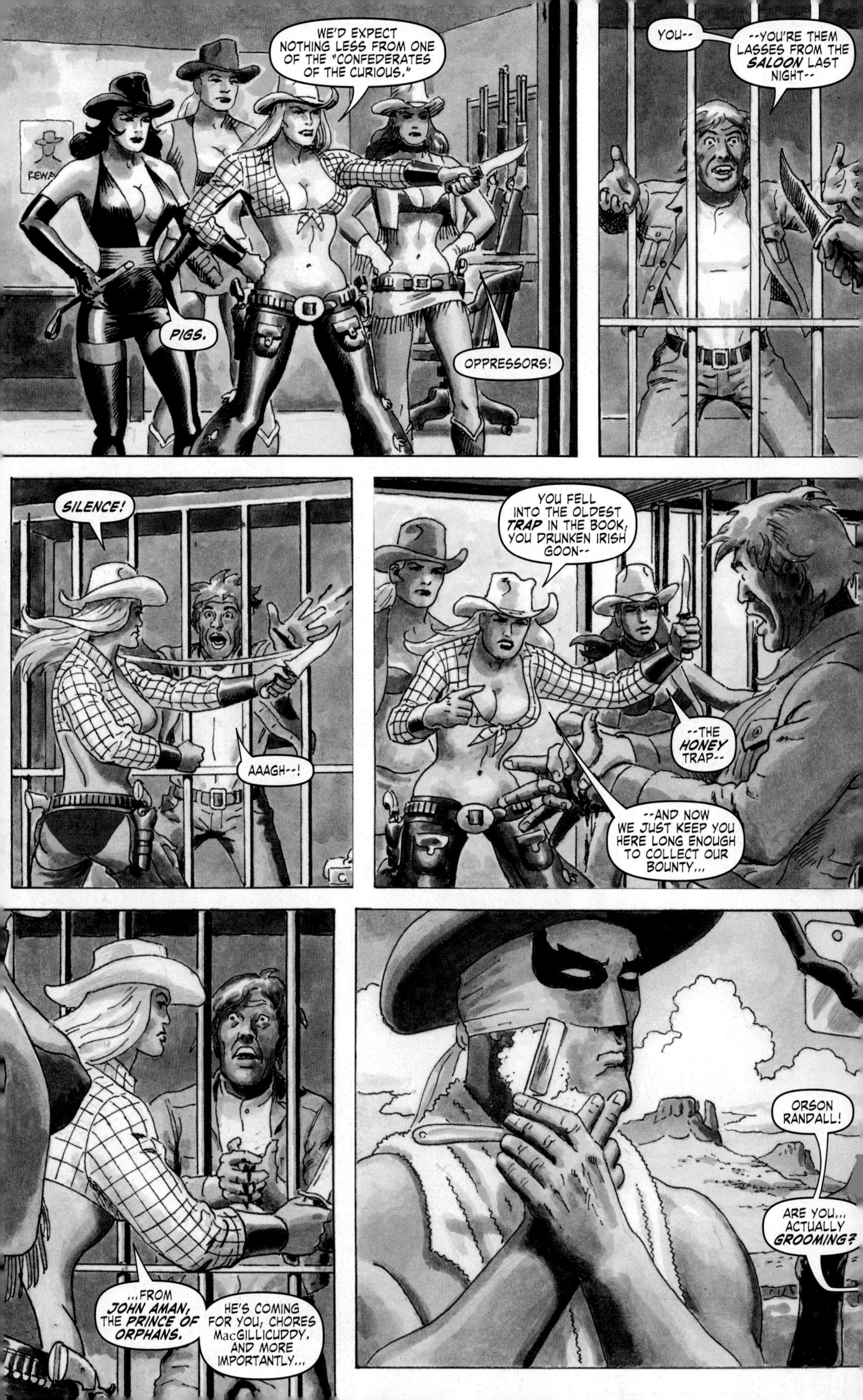

WE'D EXPECT NOTHING LESS FROM ONE OF THE "CONFEDERATES OF THE CURIOUS."
PIGS.
OPPRESSORS!
YOU--
--YOU'RE THEM LASSES FROM THE SALOON LAST NIGHT--
SILENCE!
AAAGH--!
YOU FELL INTO THE OLDEST TRAP IN THE BOOK, YOU DRUNKEN IRISH GOON--
--THE HONEY TRAP--
--AND NOW WE JUST KEEP YOU HERE LONG ENOUGH TO COLLECT OUR BOUNTY...
...FROM JOHN AMAN, THE PRINCE OF ORPHANS.
HE'S COMING FOR YOU, CHORES MacGILLICUDDY. AND MORE IMPORTANTLY...
ORSON RANDALL!
ARE YOU... ACTUALLY GROOMING?

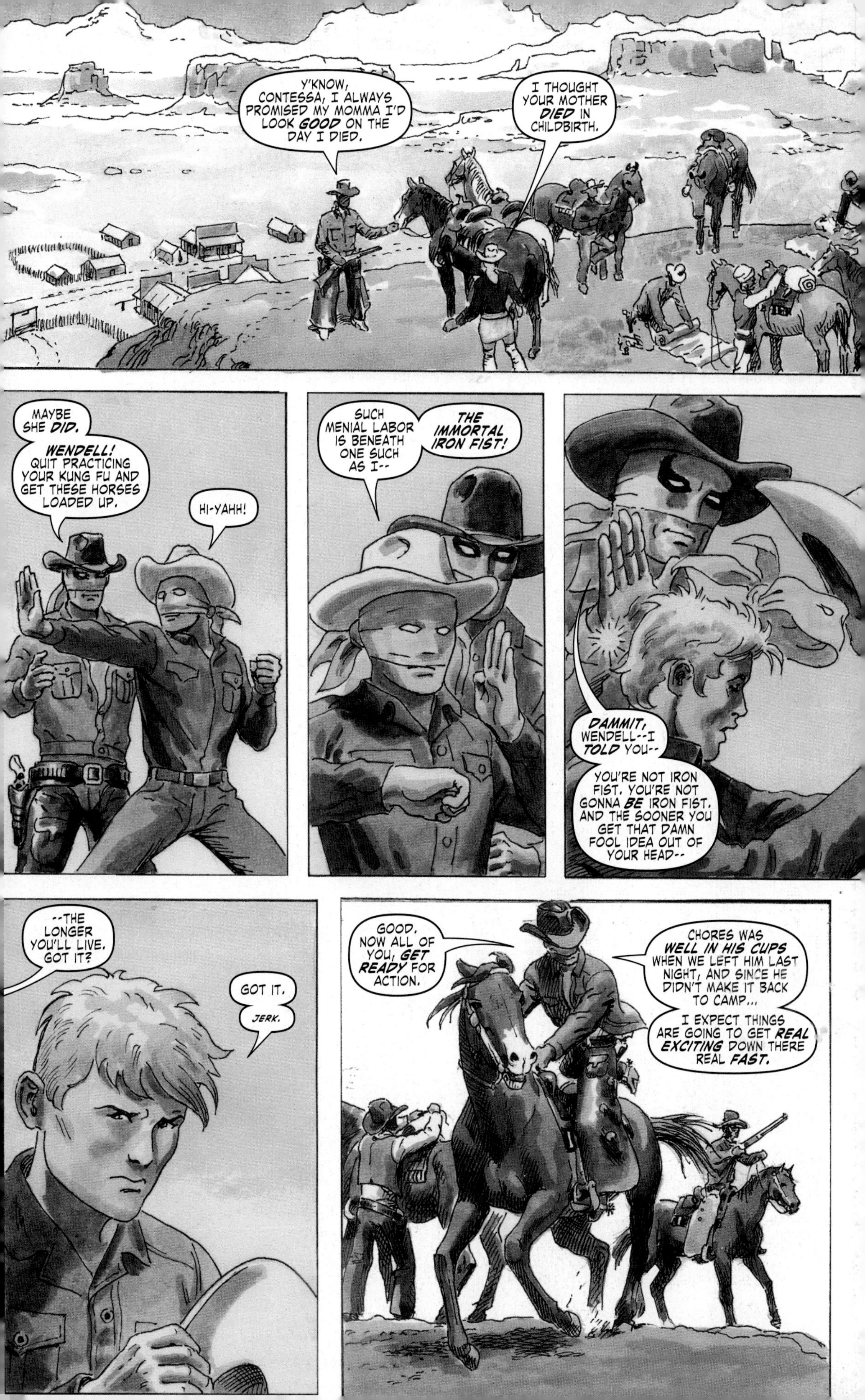
Y'KNOW, CONTESSA, I ALWAYS PROMISED MY MOMMA I'D LOOK GOOD ON THE DAY I DIED.
I THOUGHT YOUR MOTHER DIED IN CHILDBIRTH.
MAYBE SHE DID.
WENDELL! QUIT PRACTICING YOUR KUNG FU AND GET THESE HORSES LOADED UP.
HI-YAHH!
SUCH MENIAL LABOR IS BENEATH ONE SUCH AS I--
THE IMMORTAL IRON FIST!
DAMMIT, WENDELL--I TOLD YOU--
YOU'RE NOT IRON FIST. YOU'RE NOT GONNA BE IRON FIST. AND THE SOONER YOU GET THAT DAMN FOOL IDEA OUT OF YOUR HEAD--
--THE LONGER YOU'LL LIVE. GOT IT?
GOT IT.
JERK.
GOOD. NOW ALL OF YOU, GET READY FOR ACTION.
CHORES WAS WELL IN HIS CUPS WHEN WE LEFT HIM LAST NIGHT, AND SINCE HE DIDN'T MAKE IT BACK TO CAMP...
I EXPECT THINGS ARE GOING TO GET REAL EXCITING DOWN THERE REAL FAST.

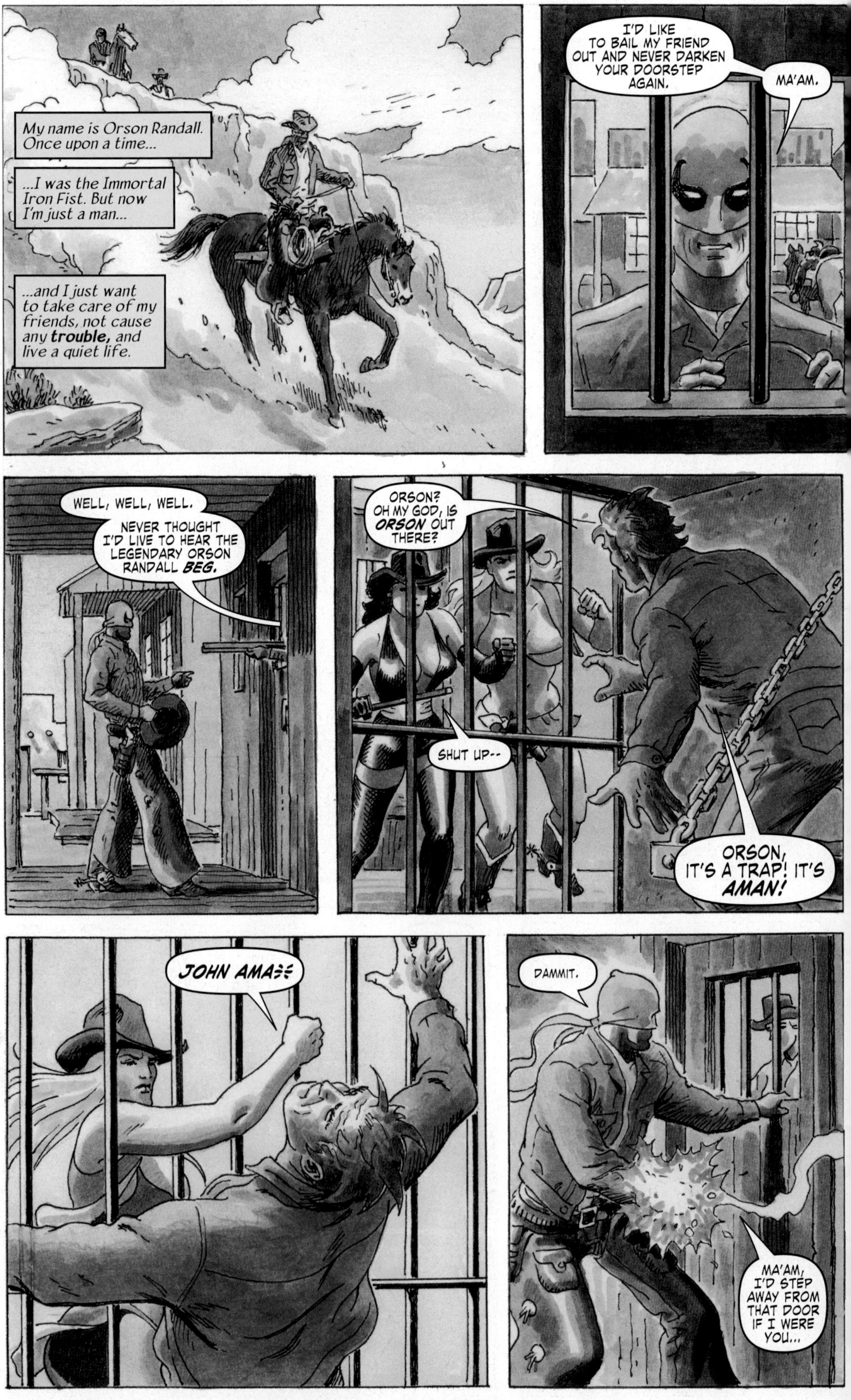

My name is Orson Randall. Once upon a time...
...I was the Immortal Iron Fist. But now I'm just a man...
...and I just want to take care of my friends, not cause any **trouble,** and live a quiet life.
I'D LIKE TO BAIL MY FRIEND OUT AND NEVER DARKEN YOUR DOORSTEP AGAIN.
MA'AM.
WELL, WELL, WELL.
NEVER THOUGHT I'D LIVE TO HEAR THE LEGENDARY ORSON RANDALL BEG.
ORSON? OH MY GOD, IS ORSON OUT THERE?
SHUT UP--
ORSON, IT'S A TRAP! IT'S AMAN!
JOHN AMA
DAMMIT.
MA'AM, I'D STEP AWAY FROM THAT DOOR IF I WERE YOU...

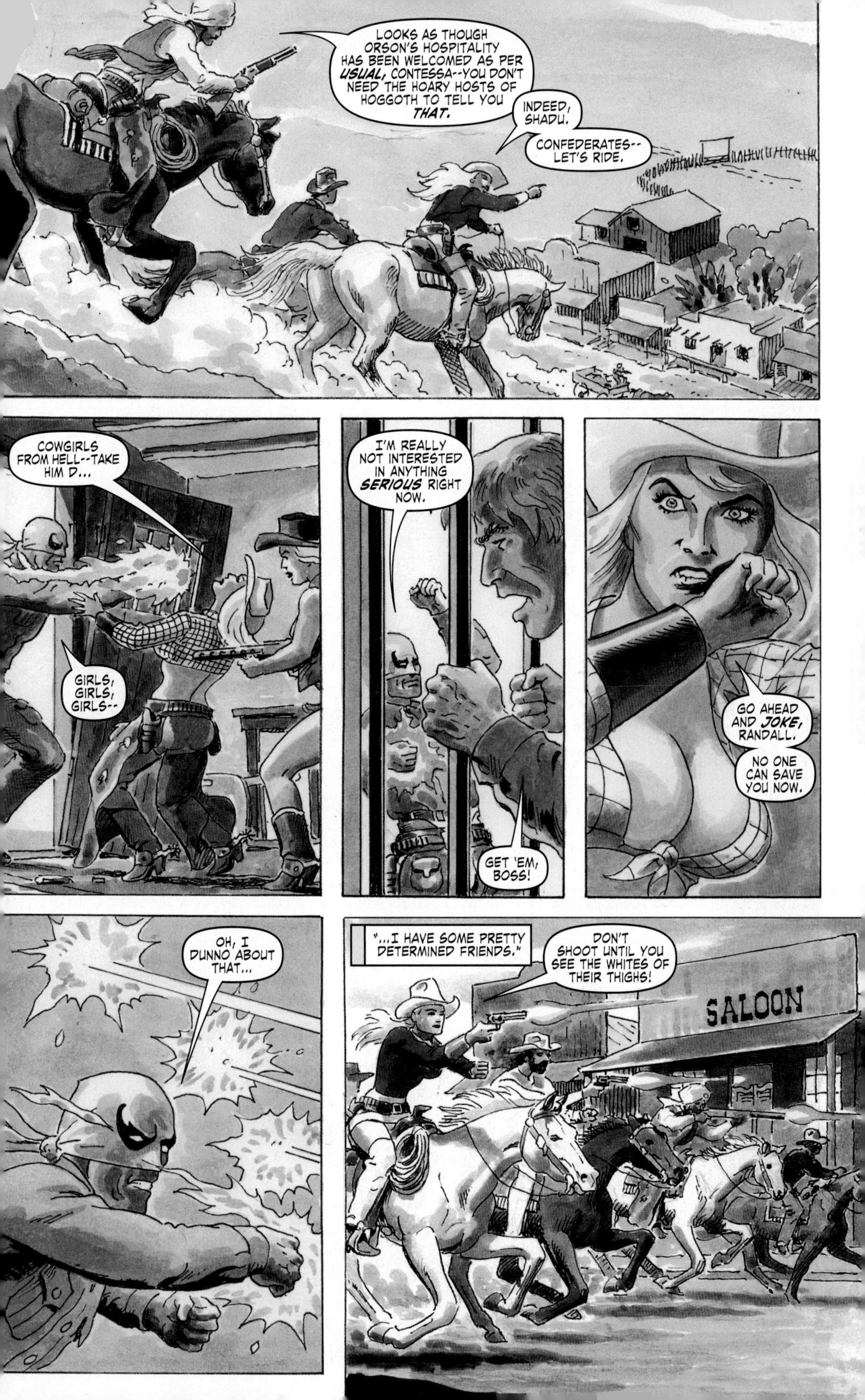
LOOKS AS THOUGH ORSON'S HOSPITALITY HAS BEEN WELCOMED AS PER USUAL, CONTESSA--YOU DON'T NEED THE HOARY HOSTS OF HOGGOTH TO TELL YOU THAT.
INDEED, SHADU.
CONFEDERATES--LET'S RIDE.
COWGIRLS FROM HELL--TAKE HIM D...
GIRLS, GIRLS, GIRLS--
I'M REALLY NOT INTERESTED IN ANYTHING SERIOUS RIGHT NOW.
GET 'EM, BOSS!
GO AHEAD AND JOKE, RANDALL.
NO ONE CAN SAVE YOU NOW.
OH, I DUNNO ABOUT THAT...
"...I HAVE SOME PRETTY DETERMINED FRIENDS."
DON'T SHOOT UNTIL YOU SEE THE WHITES OF THEIR THIGHS!
SALOON

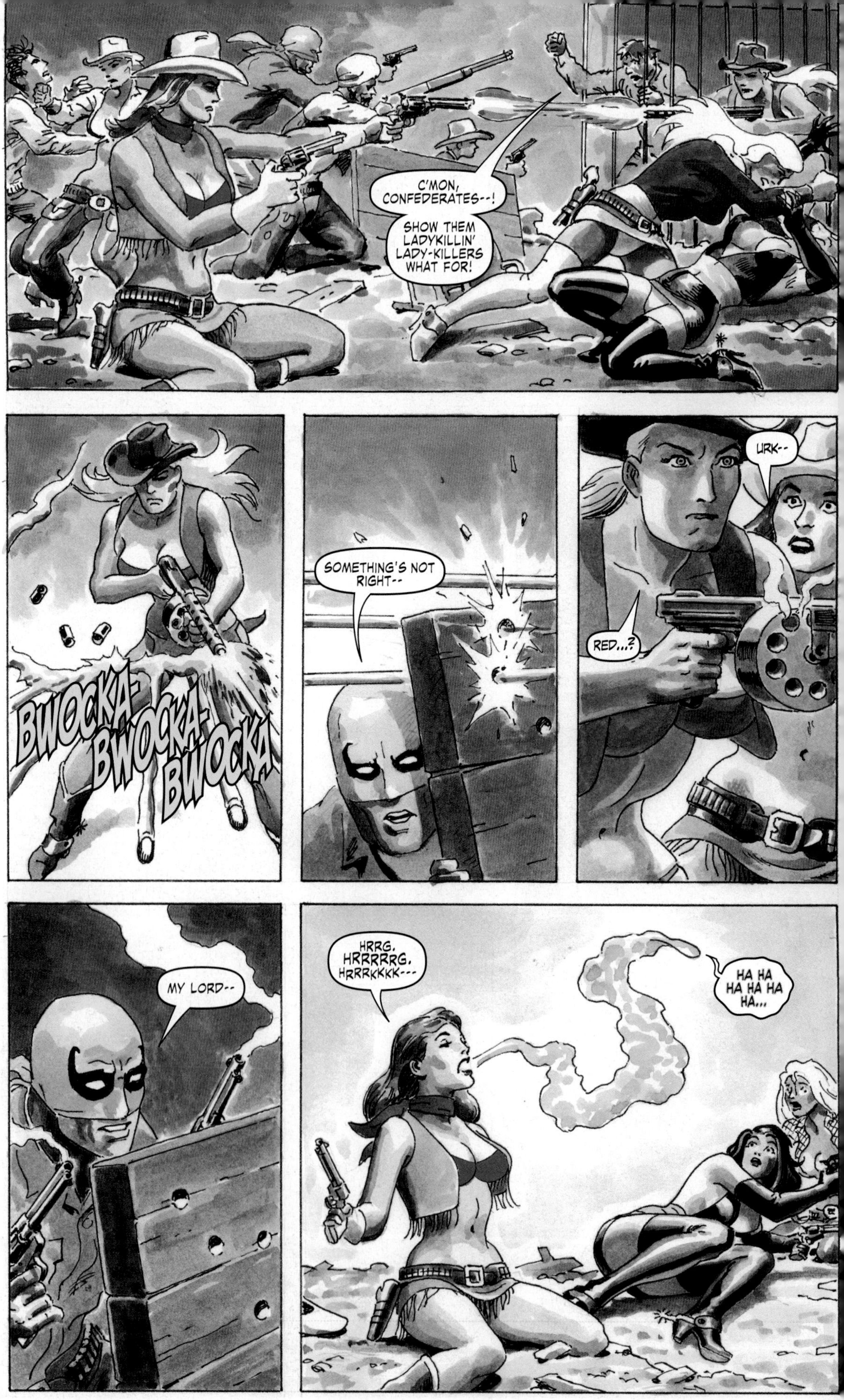
C'MON, CONFEDERATES--!
SHOW THEM LADYKILLIN' LADY-KILLERS WHAT FOR!
BWOCKA-BWOCKA-BWOCKA
SOMETHING'S NOT RIGHT--
URK--
RED...?
MY LORD--
HRRG, HRRRRRG, HRRRKKKK---
HA HA HA HA HA HA...

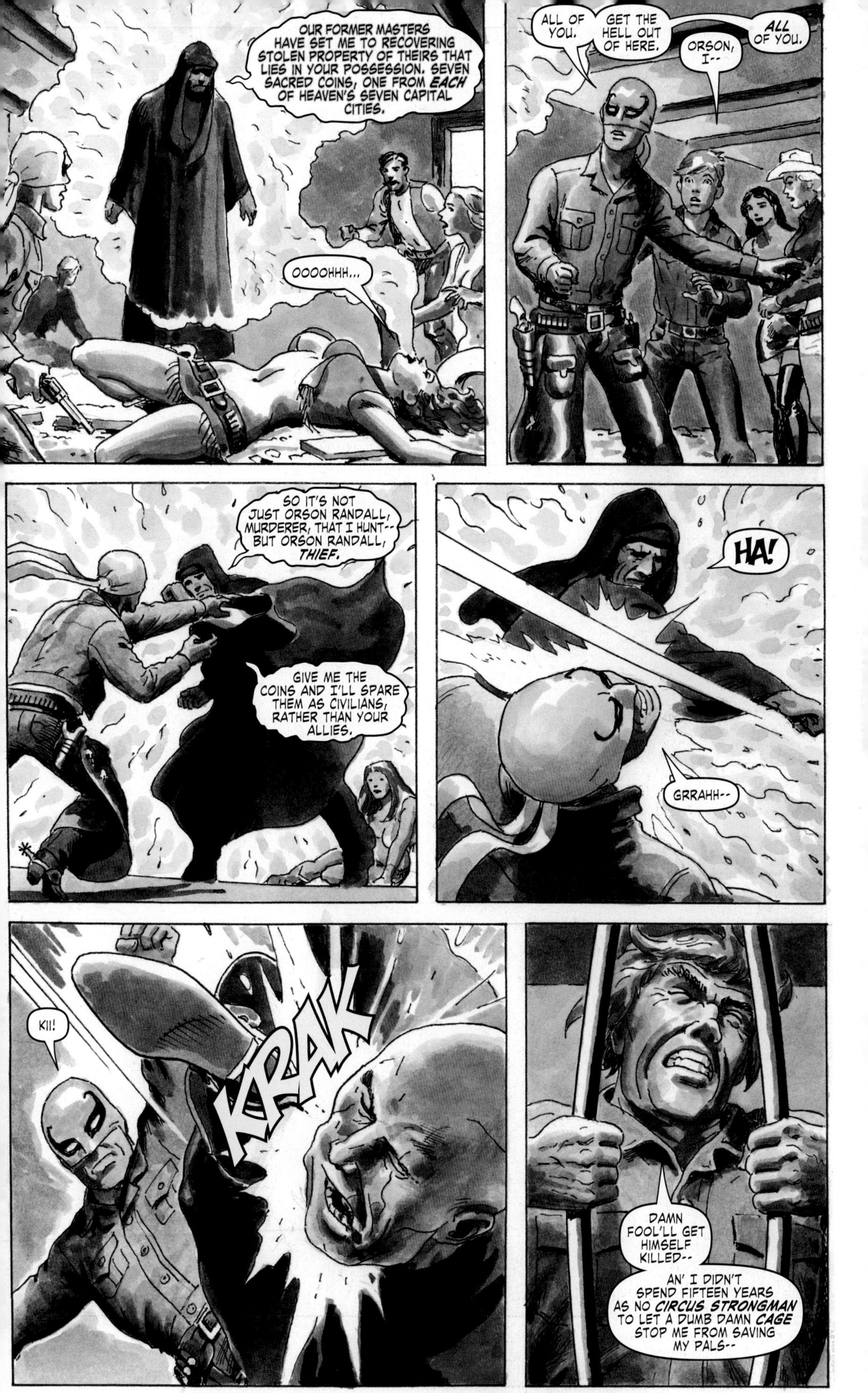
OUR FORMER MASTERS HAVE SET ME TO RECOVERING STOLEN PROPERTY OF THEIRS THAT LIES IN YOUR POSSESSION. SEVEN SACRED COINS, ONE FROM EACH OF HEAVEN'S SEVEN CAPITAL CITIES.
OOOOHHH...
ALL OF YOU.
GET THE HELL OUT OF HERE.
ALL OF YOU.
ORSON, I--
SO IT'S NOT JUST ORSON RANDALL, MURDERER, THAT I HUNT-- BUT ORSON RANDALL, THIEF.
GIVE ME THE COINS AND I'LL SPARE THEM AS CIVILIANS, RATHER THAN YOUR ALLIES.
HA!
GRRAHH--
KII!
KRAK
DAMN FOOL'LL GET HIMSELF KILLED--
AN' I DIDN'T SPEND FIFTEEN YEARS AS NO CIRCUS STRONGMAN TO LET A DUMB DAMN CAGE STOP ME FROM SAVING MY PALS--

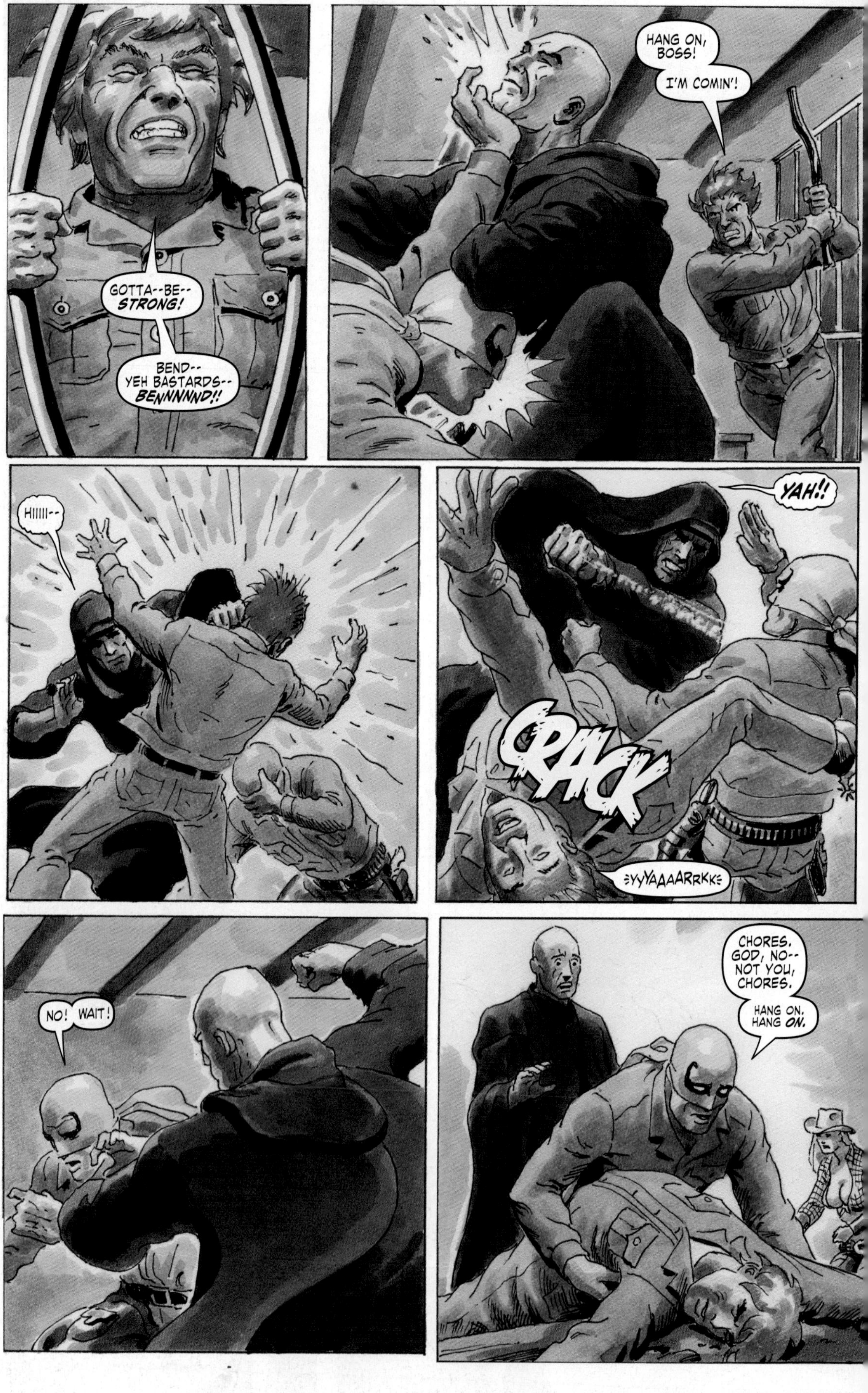
GOTTA--BE--
STRONG!
BEND--
YEH BASTARDS--
BENNNNND!!
HANG ON, BOSS!
I'M COMIN'!
HIIIII--
YAH!!
CRACK
YYYAAAARRKK
NO! WAIT!
CHORES. GOD, NO-- NOT YOU, CHORES.
HANG ON. HANG ON.

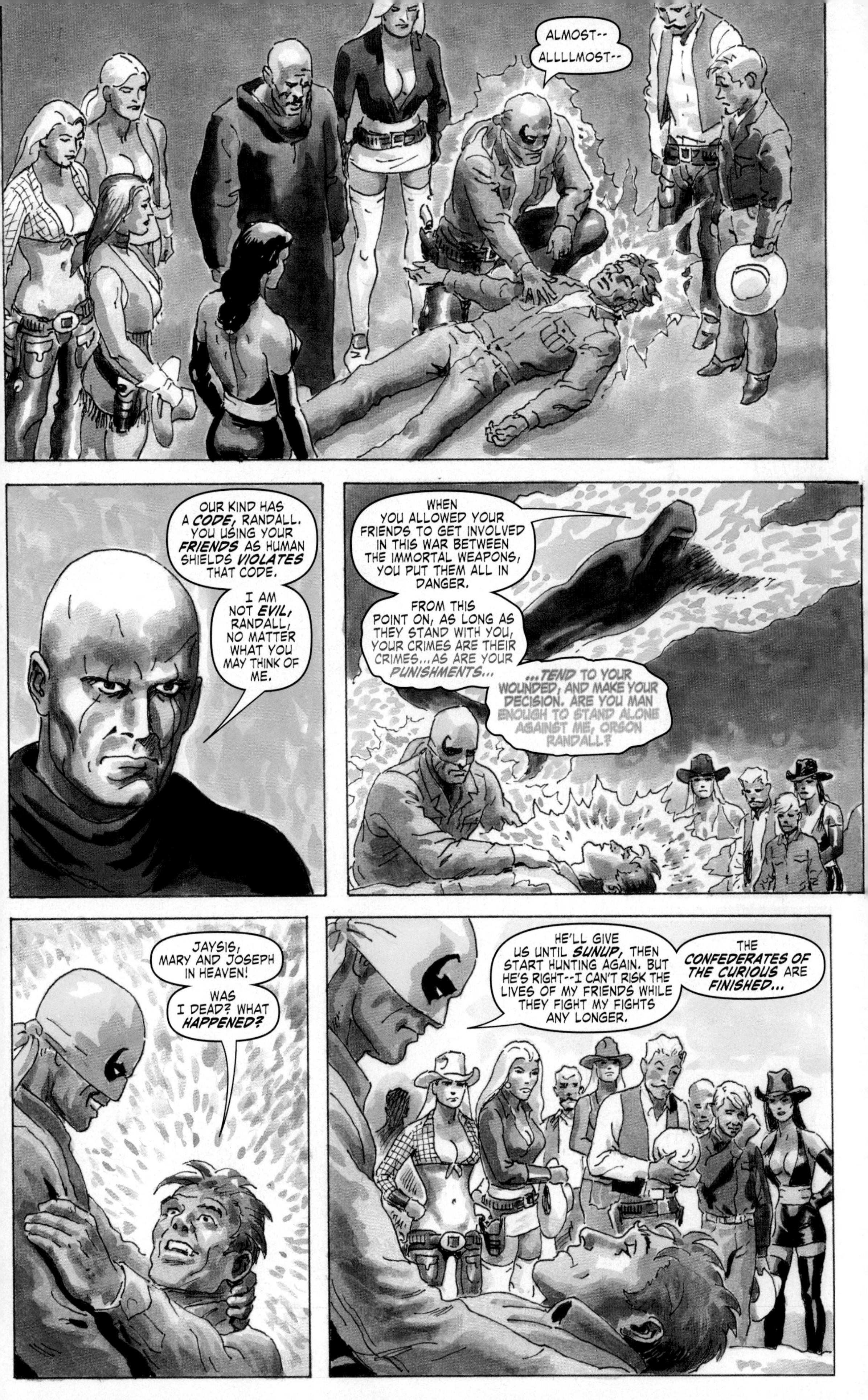
ALMOST--
ALLLLMOST--
OUR KIND HAS A CODE, RANDALL. YOU USING YOUR FRIENDS AS HUMAN SHIELDS VIOLATES THAT CODE.
I AM NOT EVIL, RANDALL, NO MATTER WHAT YOU MAY THINK OF ME.
WHEN YOU ALLOWED YOUR FRIENDS TO GET INVOLVED IN THIS WAR BETWEEN THE IMMORTAL WEAPONS, YOU PUT THEM ALL IN DANGER.
FROM THIS POINT ON, AS LONG AS THEY STAND WITH YOU, YOUR CRIMES ARE THEIR CRIMES...AS ARE YOUR PUNISHMENTS...
...TEND TO YOUR WOUNDED, AND MAKE YOUR DECISION. ARE YOU MAN ENOUGH TO STAND ALONE AGAINST ME, ORSON RANDALL?
JAYSIS, MARY AND JOSEPH IN HEAVEN!
WAS I DEAD? WHAT HAPPENED?
HE'LL GIVE US UNTIL SUNUP, THEN START HUNTING AGAIN. BUT HE'S RIGHT--I CAN'T RISK THE LIVES OF MY FRIENDS WHILE THEY FIGHT MY FIGHTS ANY LONGER.
THE CONFEDERATES OF THE CURIOUS ARE FINISHED...

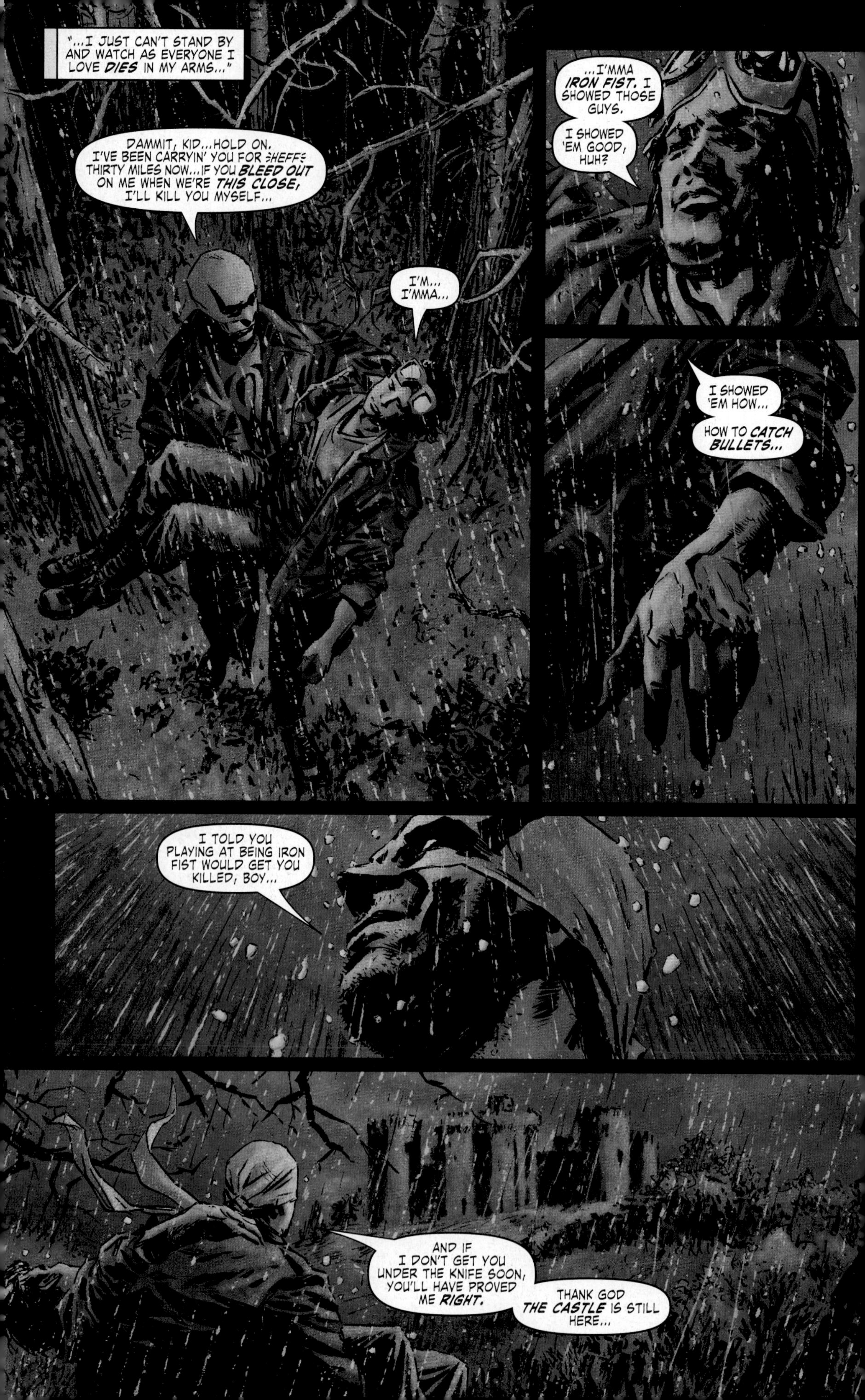
"...I JUST CAN'T STAND BY AND WATCH AS EVERYONE I LOVE *DIES* IN MY ARMS..."
DAMMIT, KID...HOLD ON. I'VE BEEN CARRYIN' YOU FOR THIRTY MILES NOW...IF YOU *BLEED OUT* ON ME WHEN WE'RE *THIS CLOSE,* I'LL KILL YOU MYSELF...
I'M... I'MMA...
...I'MMA *IRON FIST.* I SHOWED THOSE GUYS.
I SHOWED 'EM GOOD, HUH?
I SHOWED 'EM HOW...
HOW TO *CATCH BULLETS...*
I TOLD YOU PLAYING AT BEING IRON FIST WOULD GET YOU KILLED, BOY...
AND IF I DON'T GET YOU UNDER THE KNIFE SOON, YOU'LL HAVE PROVED ME *RIGHT.*
THANK GOD *THE CASTLE* IS STILL HERE...

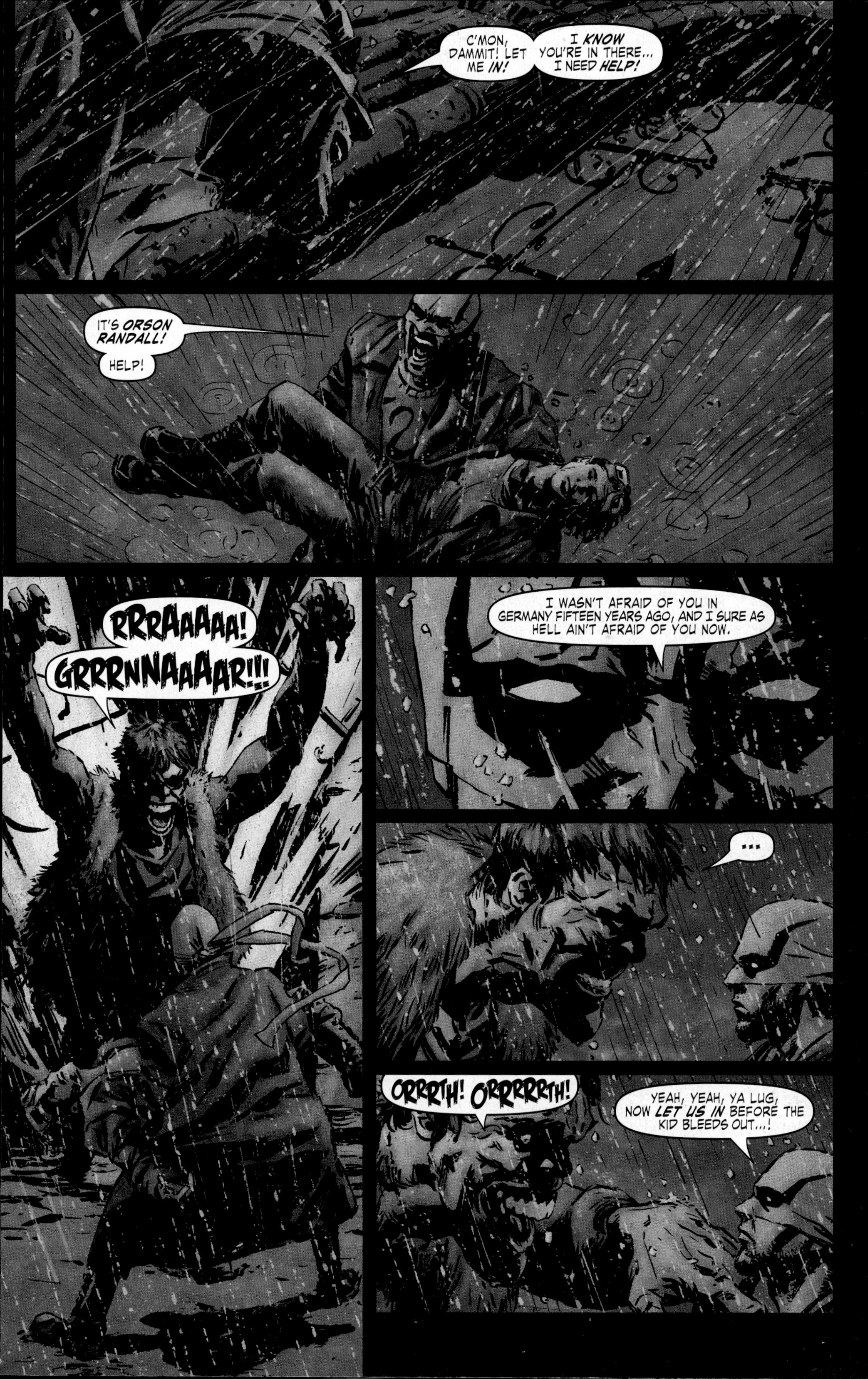
C'MON, DAMMIT! LET ME *IN!*
I *KNOW* YOU'RE IN THERE... I NEED *HELP!*
IT'S *ORSON RANDALL!*
HELP!
RRRAAAAA!
GRRRNNAAAAR!!!
I WASN'T AFRAID OF YOU IN GERMANY FIFTEEN YEARS AGO, AND I SURE AS HELL AIN'T AFRAID OF YOU NOW.
...
ORRRTH! ORRRRRTH!
YEAH, YEAH, YA LUG, NOW *LET US IN* BEFORE THE KID BLEEDS OUT...!

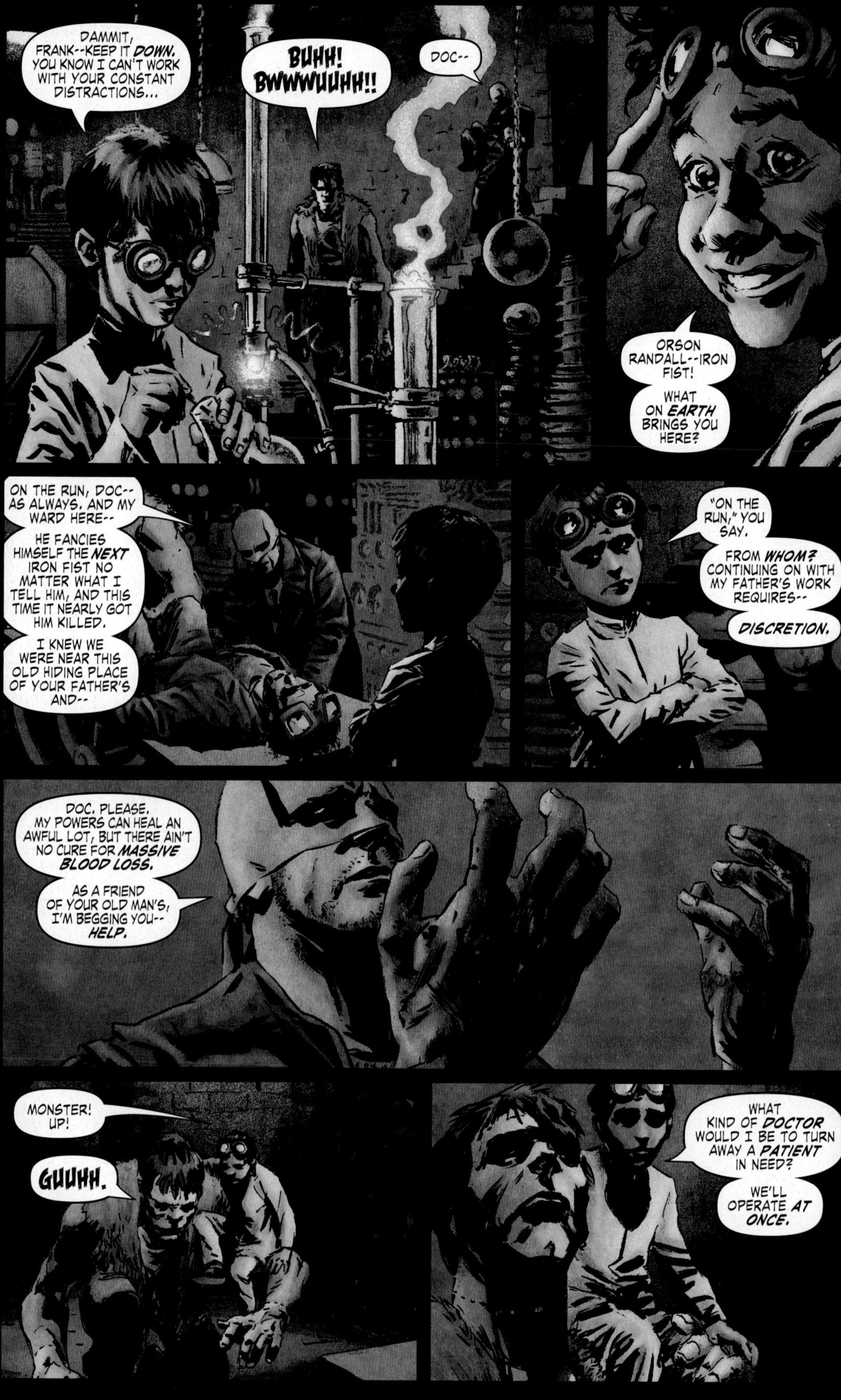
DAMMIT, FRANK--KEEP IT DOWN. YOU KNOW I CAN'T WORK WITH YOUR CONSTANT DISTRACTIONS...
BUHH! BWWWUUHH!!
DOC--
ORSON RANDALL--IRON FIST!
WHAT ON EARTH BRINGS YOU HERE?
ON THE RUN, DOC--AS ALWAYS. AND MY WARD HERE--
HE FANCIES HIMSELF THE NEXT IRON FIST NO MATTER WHAT I TELL HIM, AND THIS TIME IT NEARLY GOT HIM KILLED.
I KNEW WE WERE NEAR THIS OLD HIDING PLACE OF YOUR FATHER'S AND--
"ON THE RUN," YOU SAY.
FROM WHOM? CONTINUING ON WITH MY FATHER'S WORK REQUIRES--
DISCRETION.
DOC. PLEASE. MY POWERS CAN HEAL AN AWFUL LOT, BUT THERE AIN'T NO CURE FOR MASSIVE BLOOD LOSS.
AS A FRIEND OF YOUR OLD MAN'S, I'M BEGGING YOU--HELP.
MONSTER! UP!
GUUHH.
WHAT KIND OF DOCTOR WOULD I BE TO TURN AWAY A PATIENT IN NEED?
WE'LL OPERATE AT ONCE.

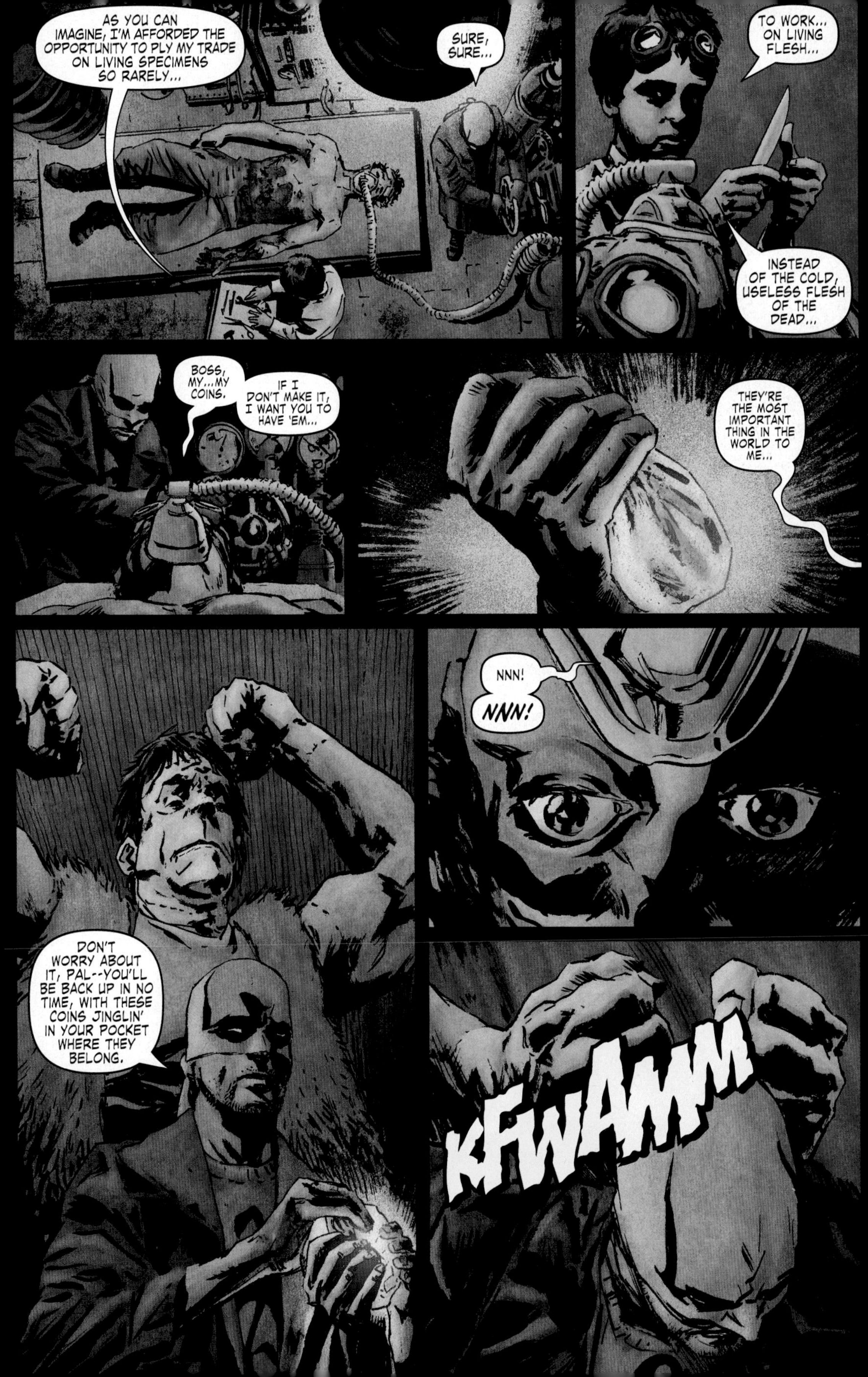
AS YOU CAN IMAGINE, I'M AFFORDED THE OPPORTUNITY TO PLY MY TRADE ON LIVING SPECIMENS SO RARELY...
SURE, SURE...
TO WORK... ON LIVING FLESH...
INSTEAD OF THE COLD, USELESS FLESH OF THE DEAD...
BOSS, MY...MY COINS.
IF I DON'T MAKE IT, I WANT YOU TO HAVE 'EM...
THEY'RE THE MOST IMPORTANT THING IN THE WORLD TO ME...
NNN!
NNN!
DON'T WORRY ABOUT IT, PAL--YOU'LL BE BACK UP IN NO TIME, WITH THESE COINS JINGLIN' IN YOUR POCKET WHERE THEY BELONG.
KFWAMM

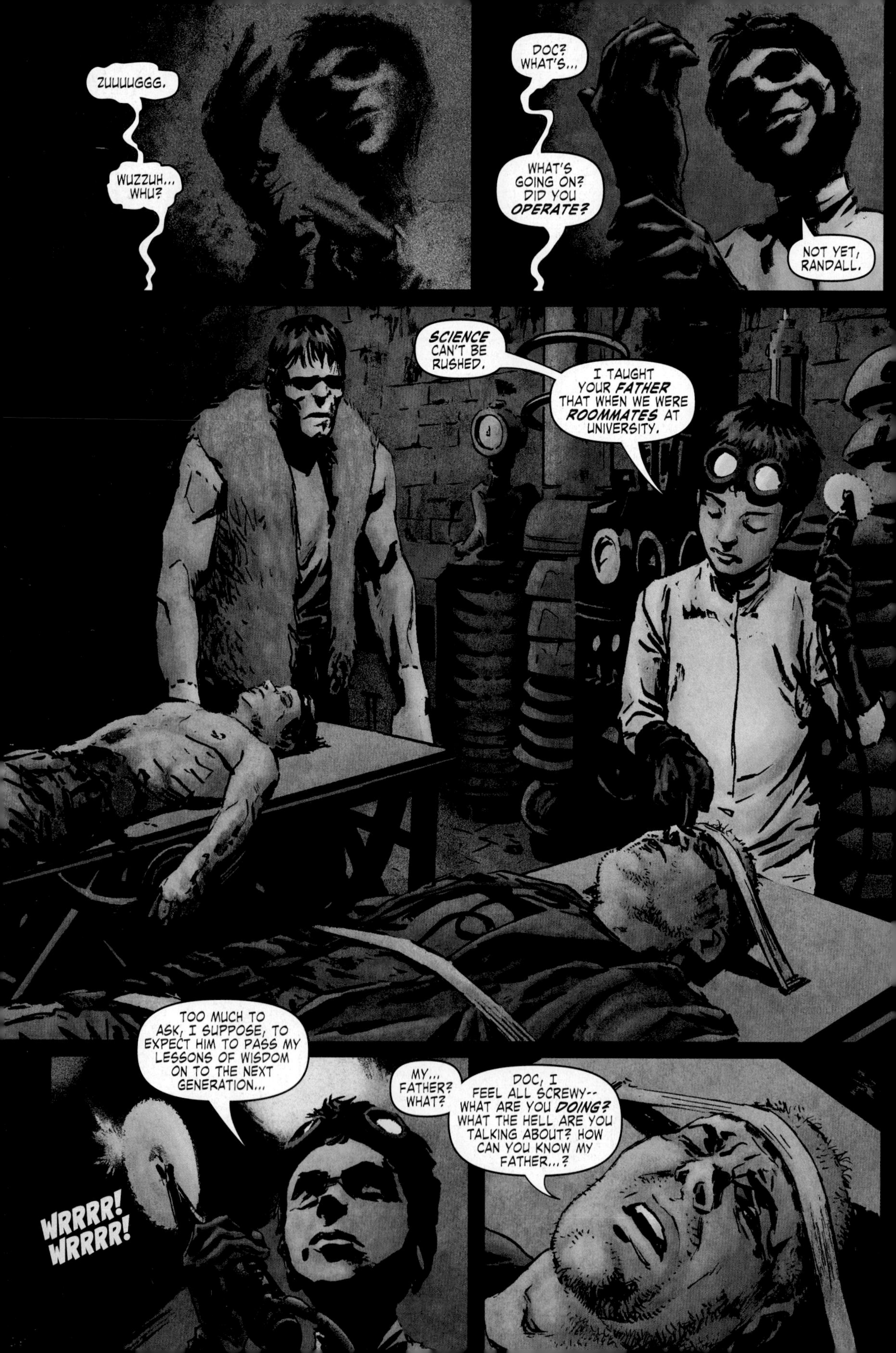
ZUUUUGGG.
WUZZUH... WHU?
DOC? WHAT'S...
WHAT'S GOING ON? DID YOU OPERATE?
NOT YET, RANDALL.
SCIENCE CAN'T BE RUSHED.
I TAUGHT YOUR FATHER THAT WHEN WE WERE ROOMMATES AT UNIVERSITY.
TOO MUCH TO ASK, I SUPPOSE, TO EXPECT HIM TO PASS MY LESSONS OF WISDOM ON TO THE NEXT GENERATION...
WRRRR! WRRRR!
MY... FATHER? WHAT?
DOC, I FEEL ALL SCREWY-- WHAT ARE YOU DOING? WHAT THE HELL ARE YOU TALKING ABOUT? HOW CAN YOU KNOW MY FATHER...?

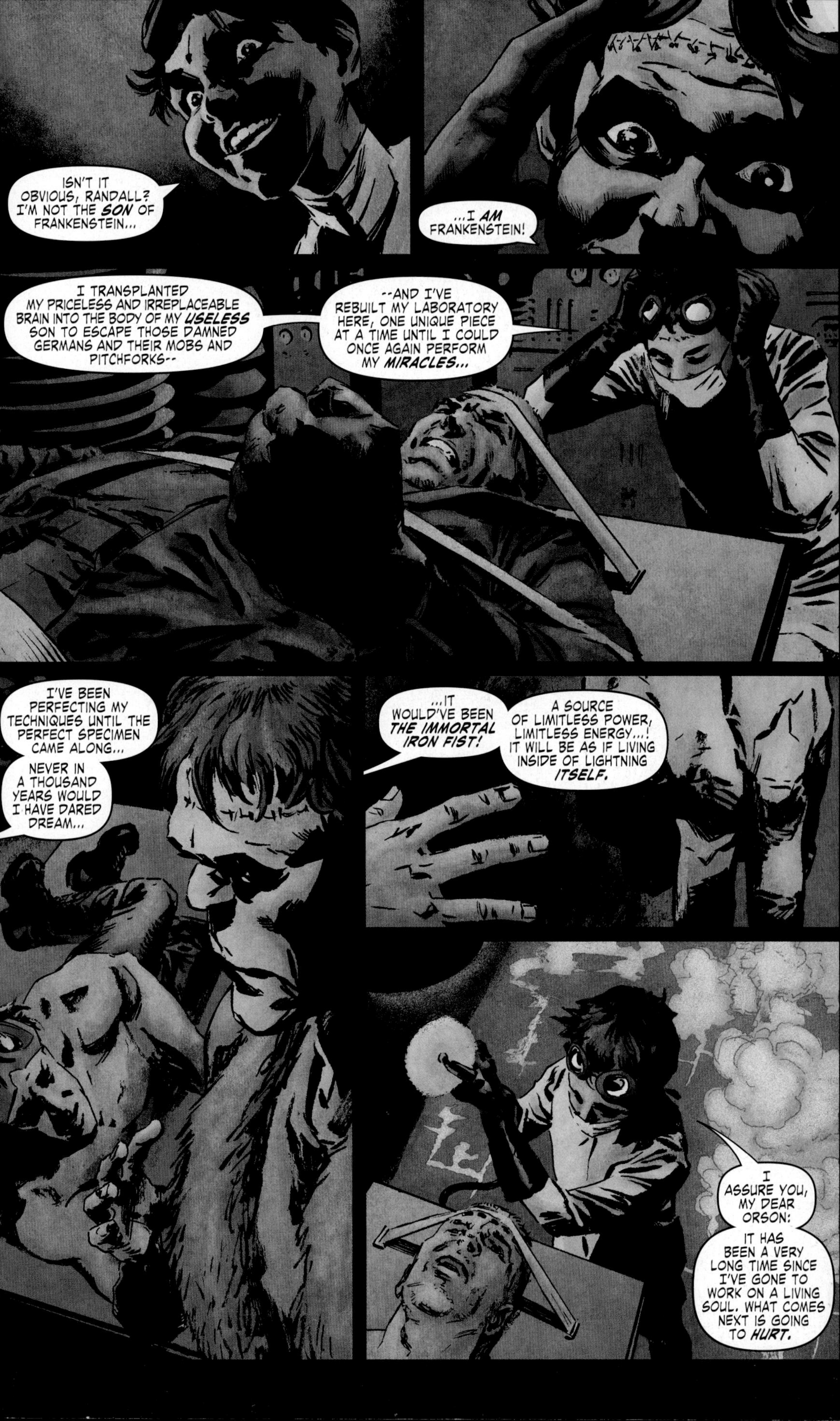
ISN'T IT OBVIOUS, RANDALL? I'M NOT THE SON OF FRANKENSTEIN...
...I AM FRANKENSTEIN!
I TRANSPLANTED MY PRICELESS AND IRREPLACEABLE BRAIN INTO THE BODY OF MY USELESS SON TO ESCAPE THOSE DAMNED GERMANS AND THEIR MOBS AND PITCHFORKS--
--AND I'VE REBUILT MY LABORATORY HERE, ONE UNIQUE PIECE AT A TIME UNTIL I COULD ONCE AGAIN PERFORM MY MIRACLES...
I'VE BEEN PERFECTING MY TECHNIQUES UNTIL THE PERFECT SPECIMEN CAME ALONG...
NEVER IN A THOUSAND YEARS WOULD I HAVE DARED DREAM...
...IT WOULD'VE BEEN THE IMMORTAL IRON FIST!
A SOURCE OF LIMITLESS POWER, LIMITLESS ENERGY...! IT WILL BE AS IF LIVING INSIDE OF LIGHTNING ITSELF.
I ASSURE YOU, MY DEAR ORSON:
IT HAS BEEN A VERY LONG TIME SINCE I'VE GONE TO WORK ON A LIVING SOUL. WHAT COMES NEXT IS GOING TO HURT.

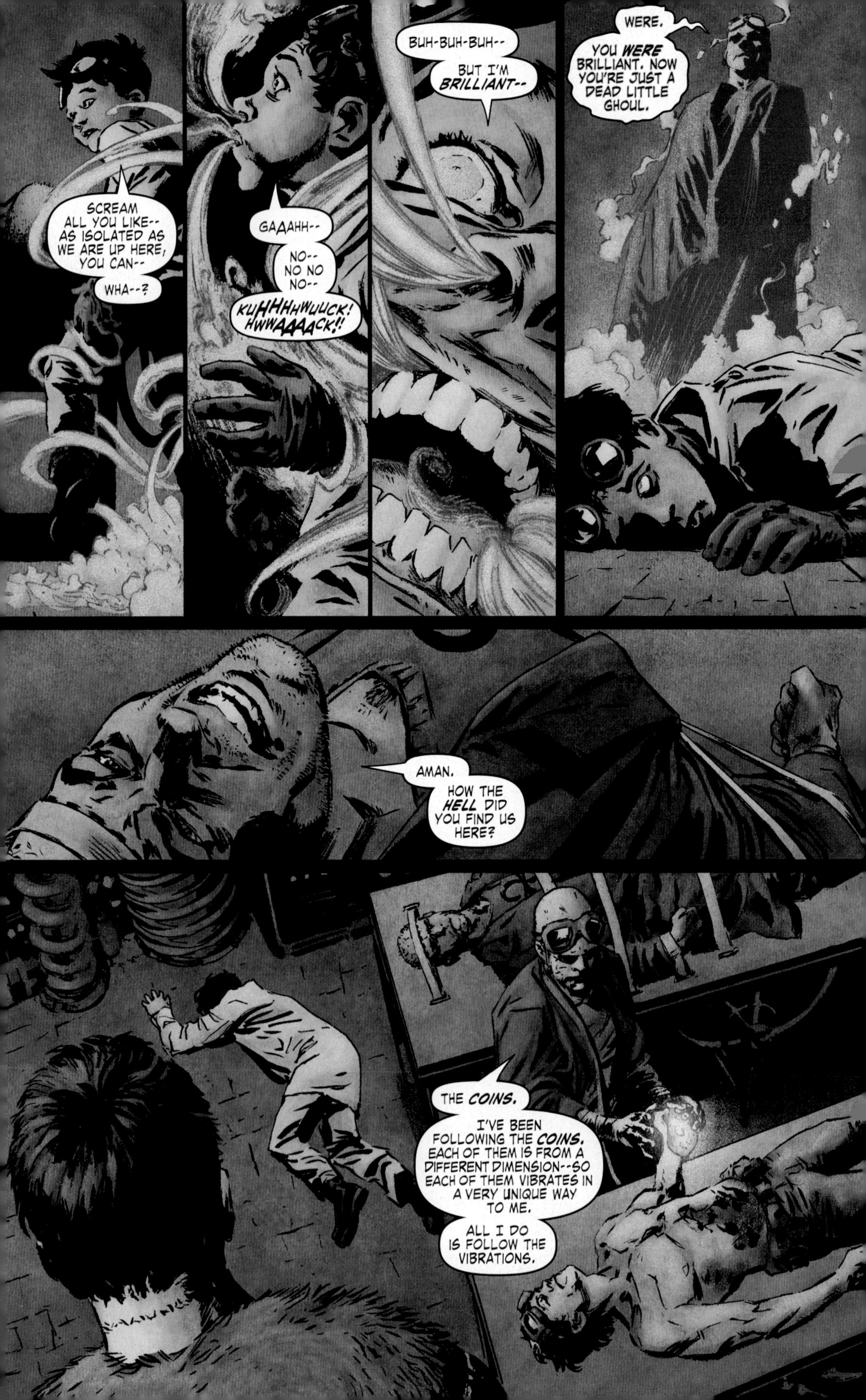
SCREAM ALL YOU LIKE-- AS ISOLATED AS WE ARE UP HERE, YOU CAN--
WHA--?
GAAAHH--
NO-- NO NO NO--
KUHHHHWUUCK! HWWAAAACK!!
BUH-BUH-BUH--
BUT I'M BRILLIANT--
WERE.
YOU WERE BRILLIANT. NOW YOU'RE JUST A DEAD LITTLE GHOUL.
AMAN.
HOW THE HELL DID YOU FIND US HERE?
THE COINS.
I'VE BEEN FOLLOWING THE COINS. EACH OF THEM IS FROM A DIFFERENT DIMENSION--SO EACH OF THEM VIBRATES IN A VERY UNIQUE WAY TO ME.
ALL I DO IS FOLLOW THE VIBRATIONS.

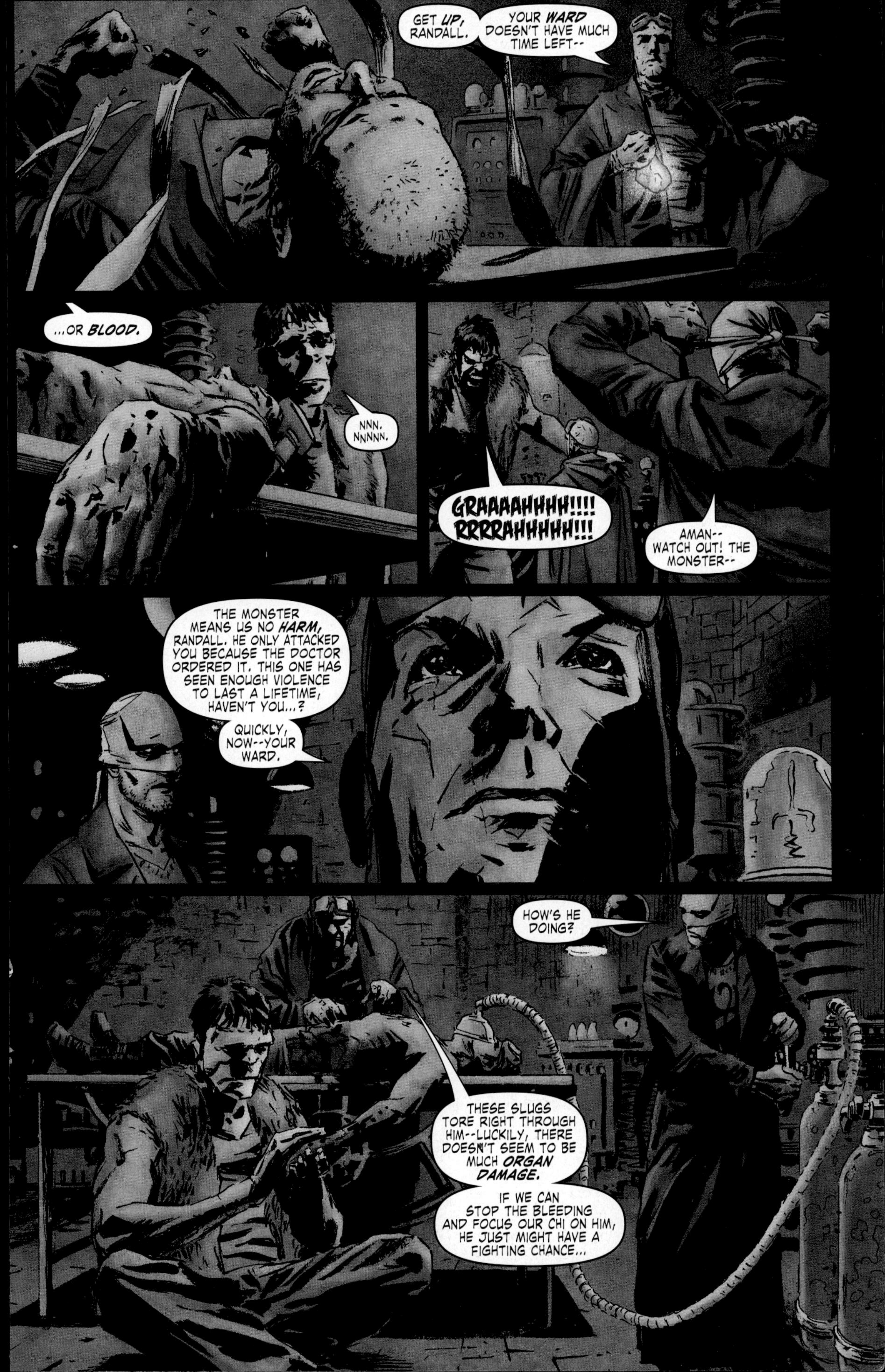
GET UP, RANDALL.
YOUR WARD DOESN'T HAVE MUCH TIME LEFT--
...OR BLOOD.
NNN. NNNNN.
GRAAAAHHHH!!!! RRRRAHHHHH!!!
AMAN-- WATCH OUT! THE MONSTER--
THE MONSTER MEANS US NO HARM, RANDALL. HE ONLY ATTACKED YOU BECAUSE THE DOCTOR ORDERED IT. THIS ONE HAS SEEN ENOUGH VIOLENCE TO LAST A LIFETIME, HAVEN'T YOU...?
QUICKLY, NOW--YOUR WARD.
HOW'S HE DOING?
THESE SLUGS TORE RIGHT THROUGH HIM--LUCKILY, THERE DOESN'T SEEM TO BE MUCH ORGAN DAMAGE.
IF WE CAN STOP THE BLEEDING AND FOCUS OUR CHI ON HIM, HE JUST MIGHT HAVE A FIGHTING CHANCE...

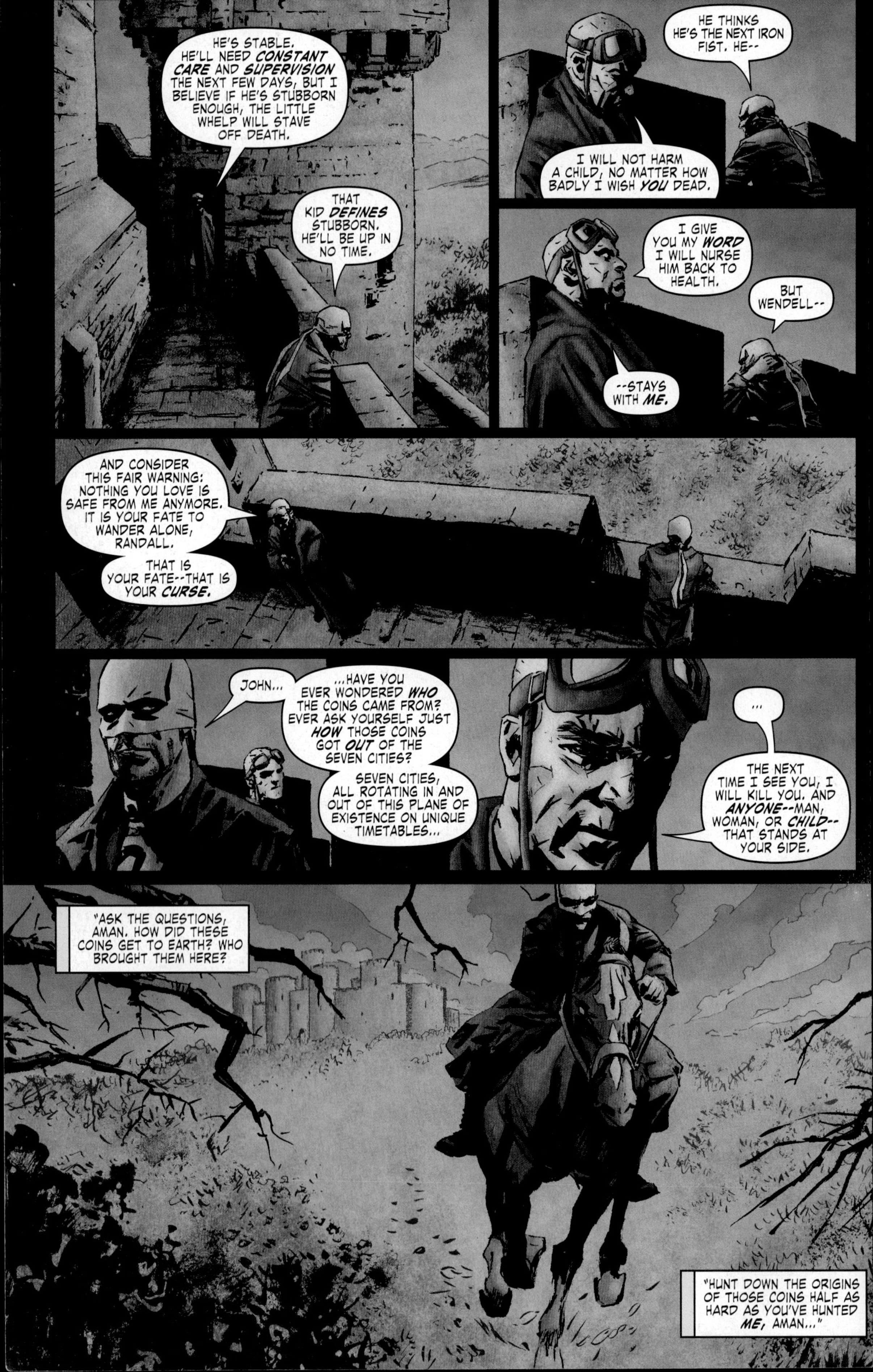

HE'S STABLE. HE'LL NEED CONSTANT CARE AND SUPERVISION THE NEXT FEW DAYS, BUT I BELIEVE IF HE'S STUBBORN ENOUGH, THE LITTLE WHELP WILL STAVE OFF DEATH.
THAT KID DEFINES STUBBORN. HE'LL BE UP IN NO TIME.
HE THINKS HE'S THE NEXT IRON FIST. HE--
I WILL NOT HARM A CHILD, NO MATTER HOW BADLY I WISH YOU DEAD.
I GIVE YOU MY WORD I WILL NURSE HIM BACK TO HEALTH.
BUT WENDELL--
--STAYS WITH ME.
AND CONSIDER THIS FAIR WARNING: NOTHING YOU LOVE IS SAFE FROM ME ANYMORE. IT IS YOUR FATE TO WANDER ALONE, RANDALL.
THAT IS YOUR FATE--THAT IS YOUR CURSE.
JOHN...
...HAVE YOU EVER WONDERED WHO THE COINS CAME FROM? EVER ASK YOURSELF JUST HOW THOSE COINS GOT OUT OF THE SEVEN CITIES?
SEVEN CITIES, ALL ROTATING IN AND OUT OF THIS PLANE OF EXISTENCE ON UNIQUE TIMETABLES...
...
THE NEXT TIME I SEE YOU, I WILL KILL YOU. AND ANYONE--MAN, WOMAN, OR CHILD--THAT STANDS AT YOUR SIDE.
"ASK THE QUESTIONS, AMAN. HOW DID THESE COINS GET TO EARTH? WHO BROUGHT THEM HERE?
"HUNT DOWN THE ORIGINS OF THOSE COINS HALF AS HARD AS YOU'VE HUNTED ME, AMAN..."

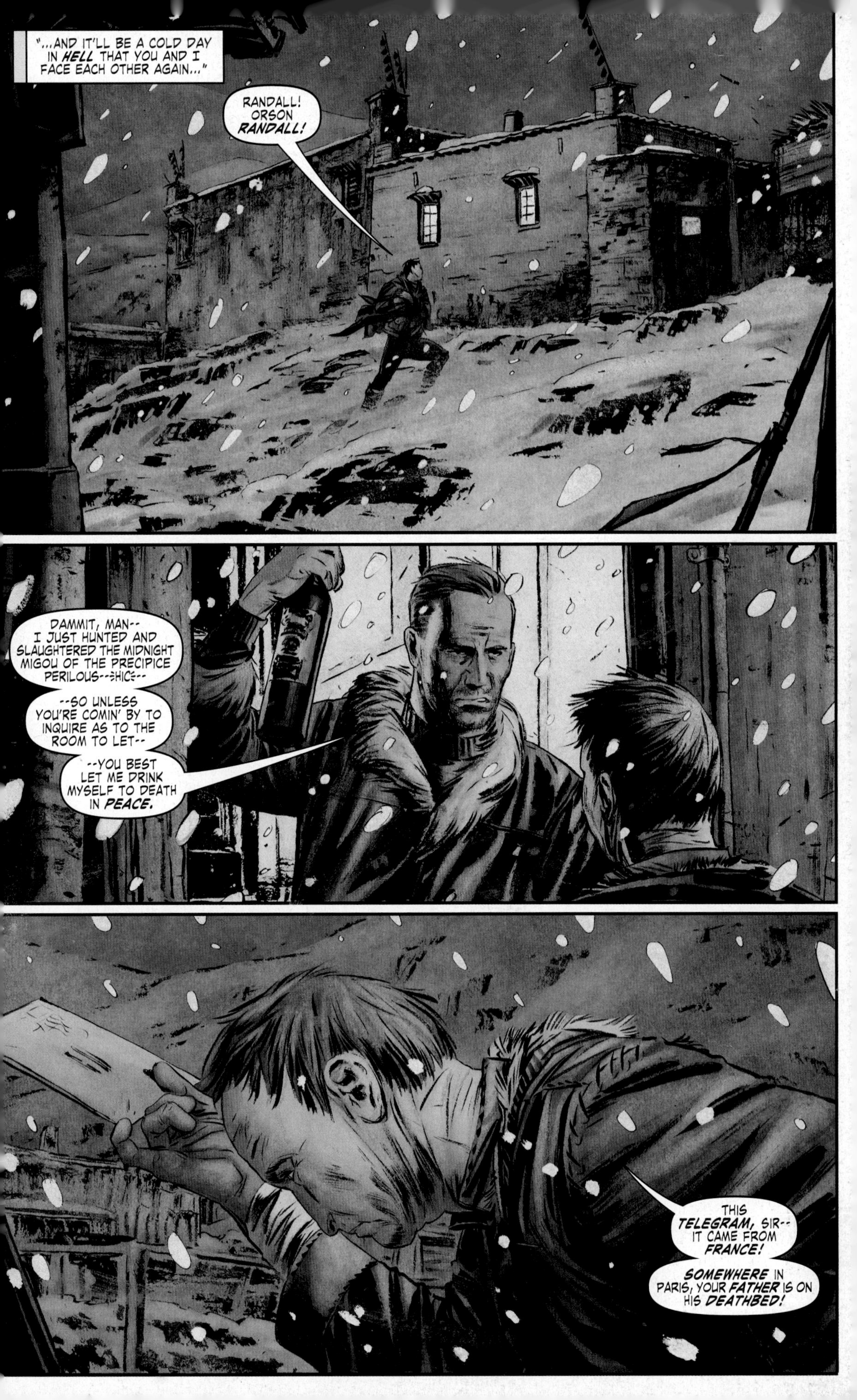
"...AND IT'LL BE A COLD DAY IN HELL THAT YOU AND I FACE EACH OTHER AGAIN..."
RANDALL! ORSON RANDALL!
DAMMIT, MAN-- I JUST HUNTED AND SLAUGHTERED THE MIDNIGHT MIGOU OF THE PRECIPICE PERILOUS--HIC--
--SO UNLESS YOU'RE COMIN' BY TO INQUIRE AS TO THE ROOM TO LET--
--YOU BEST LET ME DRINK MYSELF TO DEATH IN PEACE.
THIS TELEGRAM, SIR-- IT CAME FROM FRANCE!
SOMEWHERE IN PARIS, YOUR FATHER IS ON HIS DEATHBED!

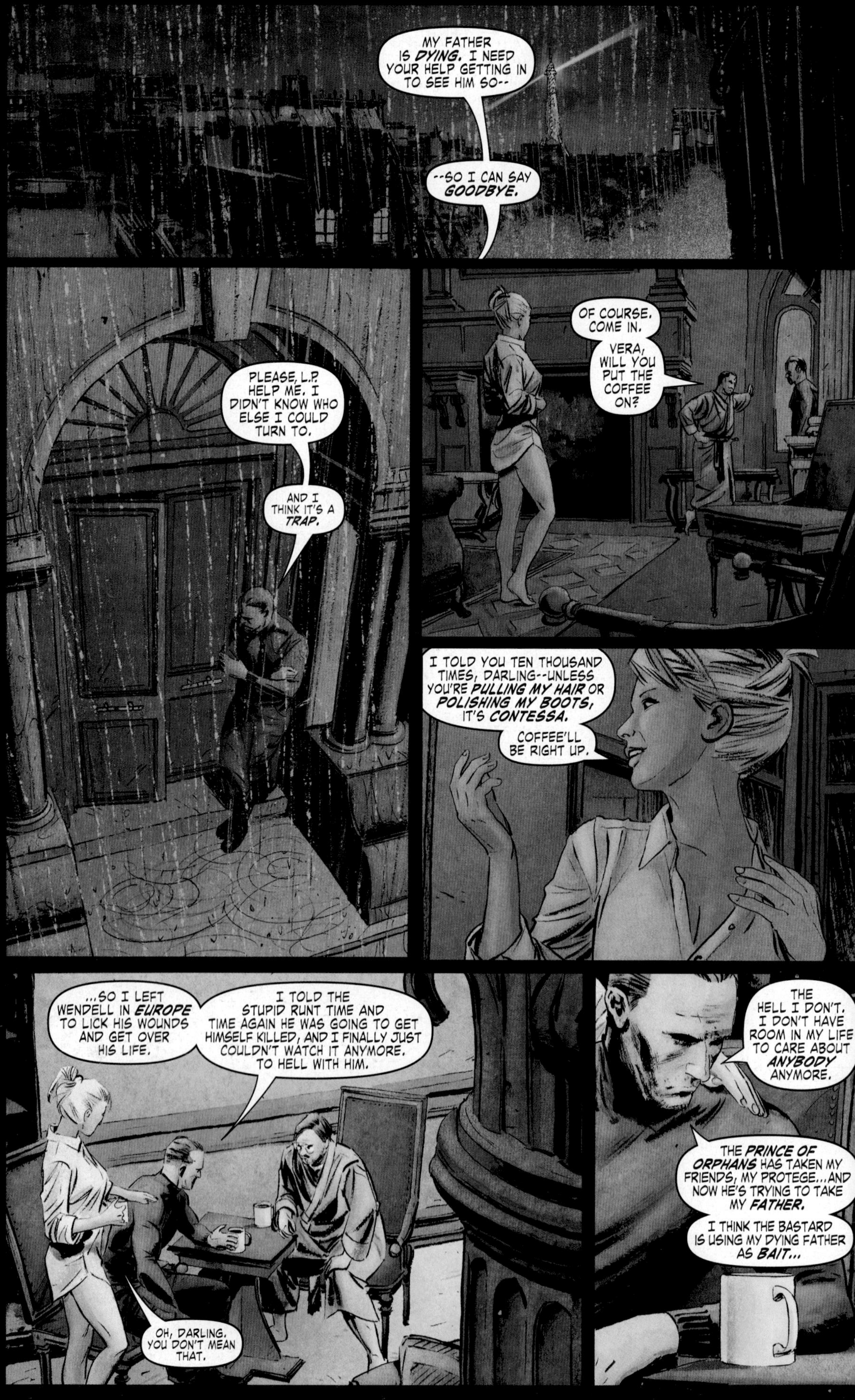
MY FATHER IS DYING. I NEED YOUR HELP GETTING IN TO SEE HIM SO--
--SO I CAN SAY GOODBYE.
PLEASE, L.P. HELP ME. I DIDN'T KNOW WHO ELSE I COULD TURN TO.
AND I THINK IT'S A TRAP.
OF COURSE. COME IN.
VERA, WILL YOU PUT THE COFFEE ON?
I TOLD YOU TEN THOUSAND TIMES, DARLING--UNLESS YOU'RE PULLING MY HAIR OR POLISHING MY BOOTS, IT'S CONTESSA.
COFFEE'LL BE RIGHT UP.
...SO I LEFT WENDELL IN EUROPE TO LICK HIS WOUNDS AND GET OVER HIS LIFE.
I TOLD THE STUPID RUNT TIME AND TIME AGAIN HE WAS GOING TO GET HIMSELF KILLED, AND I FINALLY JUST COULDN'T WATCH IT ANYMORE. TO HELL WITH HIM.
OH, DARLING. YOU DON'T MEAN THAT.
THE HELL I DON'T. I DON'T HAVE ROOM IN MY LIFE TO CARE ABOUT ANYBODY ANYMORE.
THE PRINCE OF ORPHANS HAS TAKEN MY FRIENDS, MY PROTEGE...AND NOW HE'S TRYING TO TAKE MY FATHER.
I THINK THE BASTARD IS USING MY DYING FATHER AS BAIT...

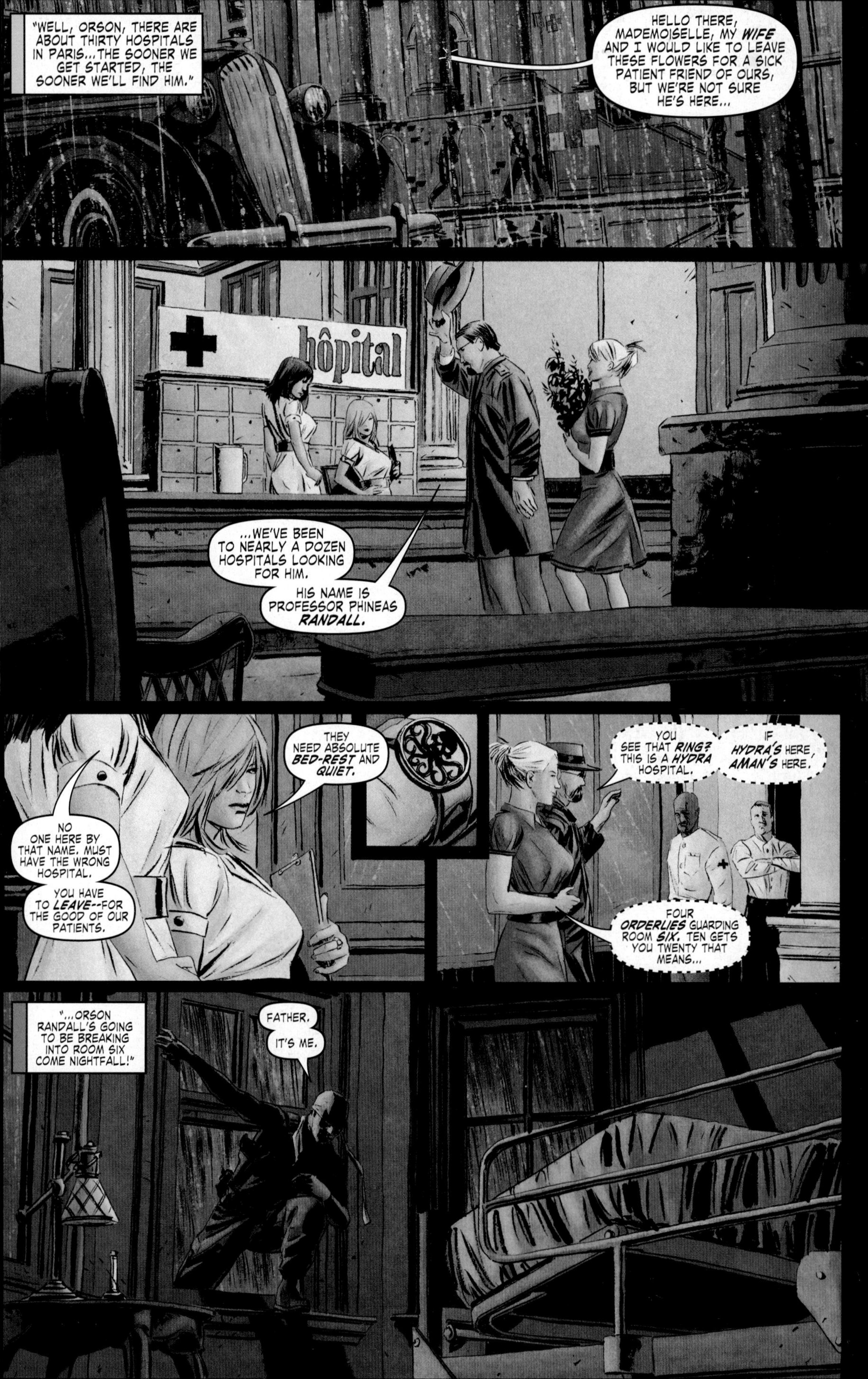
"WELL, ORSON, THERE ARE ABOUT THIRTY HOSPITALS IN PARIS...THE SOONER WE GET STARTED, THE SOONER WE'LL FIND HIM."
HELLO THERE, MADEMOISELLE, MY WIFE AND I WOULD LIKE TO LEAVE THESE FLOWERS FOR A SICK PATIENT FRIEND OF OURS, BUT WE'RE NOT SURE HE'S HERE...
hôpital
...WE'VE BEEN TO NEARLY A DOZEN HOSPITALS LOOKING FOR HIM.
HIS NAME IS PROFESSOR PHINEAS RANDALL.
NO ONE HERE BY THAT NAME. MUST HAVE THE WRONG HOSPITAL.
YOU HAVE TO LEAVE--FOR THE GOOD OF OUR PATIENTS.
THEY NEED ABSOLUTE BED-REST AND QUIET.
YOU SEE THAT RING? THIS IS A HYDRA HOSPITAL.
IF HYDRA'S HERE, AMAN'S HERE.
FOUR ORDERLIES GUARDING ROOM SIX. TEN GETS YOU TWENTY THAT MEANS...
"...ORSON RANDALL'S GOING TO BE BREAKING INTO ROOM SIX COME NIGHTFALL!"
FATHER.
IT'S ME.

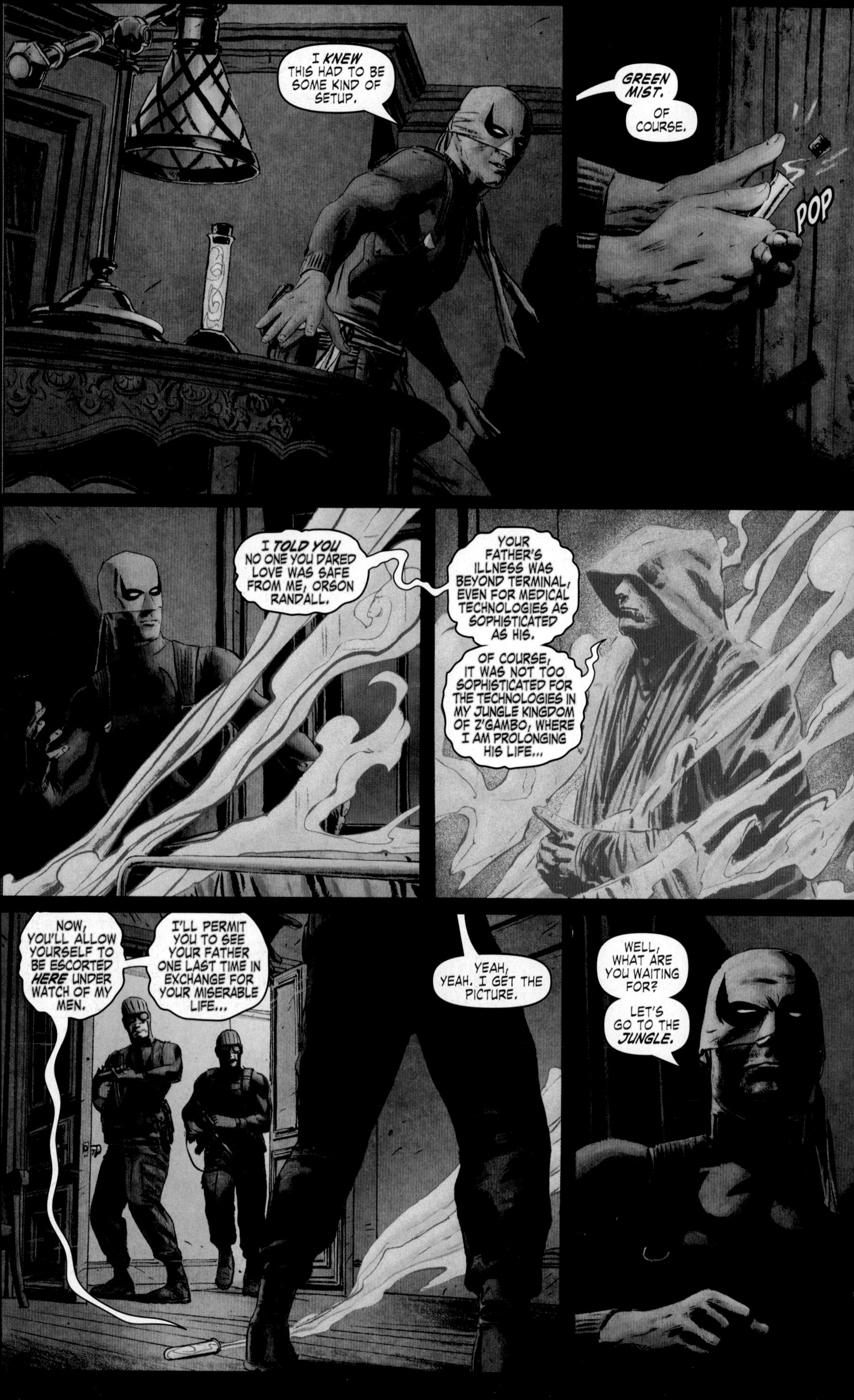
I KNEW THIS HAD TO BE SOME KIND OF SETUP.
GREEN MIST.
OF COURSE.
POP
I TOLD YOU NO ONE YOU DARED LOVE WAS SAFE FROM ME, ORSON RANDALL.
YOUR FATHER'S ILLNESS WAS BEYOND TERMINAL, EVEN FOR MEDICAL TECHNOLOGIES AS SOPHISTICATED AS HIS.
OF COURSE, IT WAS NOT TOO SOPHISTICATED FOR THE TECHNOLOGIES IN MY JUNGLE KINGDOM OF Z'GAMBO, WHERE I AM PROLONGING HIS LIFE...
NOW, YOU'LL ALLOW YOURSELF TO BE ESCORTED HERE UNDER WATCH OF MY MEN.
I'LL PERMIT YOU TO SEE YOUR FATHER ONE LAST TIME IN EXCHANGE FOR YOUR MISERABLE LIFE...
YEAH, YEAH. I GET THE PICTURE.
WELL, WHAT ARE YOU WAITING FOR?
LET'S GO TO THE JUNGLE.

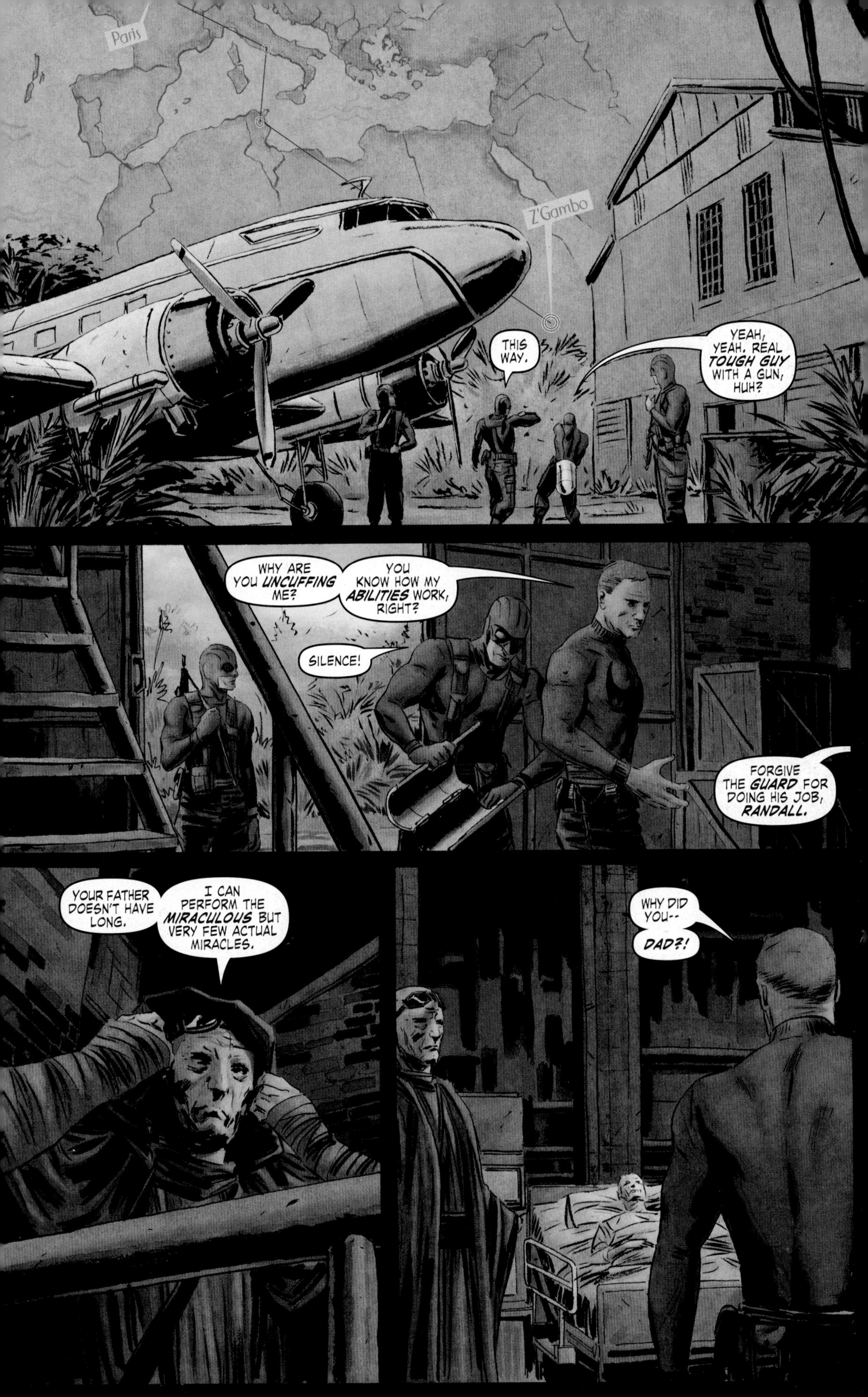
Paris
Z'Gambo
THIS WAY.
YEAH, YEAH. REAL TOUGH GUY WITH A GUN, HUH?
WHY ARE YOU UNCUFFING ME?
YOU KNOW HOW MY ABILITIES WORK, RIGHT?
SILENCE!
FORGIVE THE GUARD FOR DOING HIS JOB, RANDALL.
YOUR FATHER DOESN'T HAVE LONG.
I CAN PERFORM THE MIRACULOUS BUT VERY FEW ACTUAL MIRACLES.
WHY DID YOU--
DAD?!

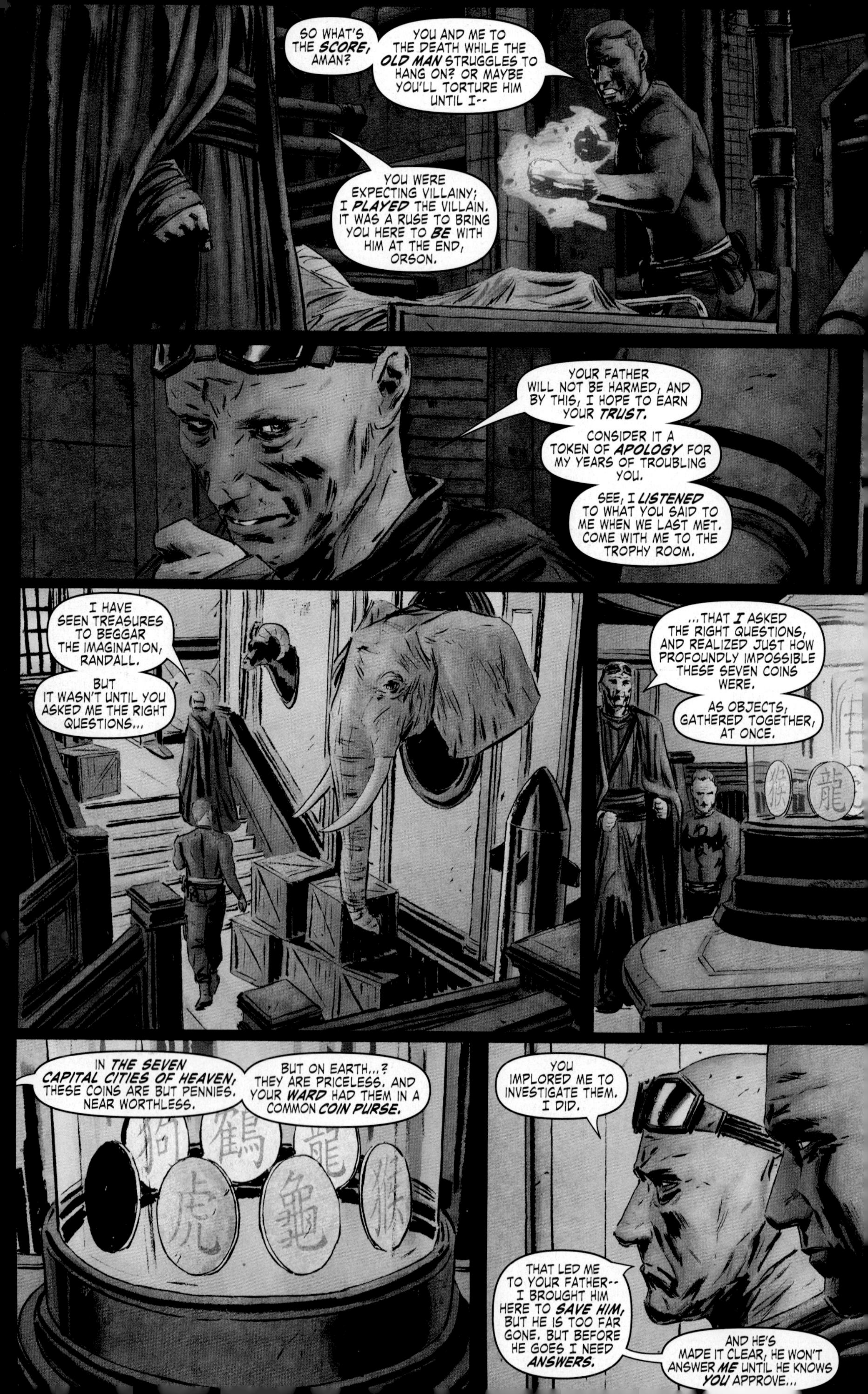
SO WHAT'S THE SCORE, AMAN?
YOU AND ME TO THE DEATH WHILE THE OLD MAN STRUGGLES TO HANG ON? OR MAYBE YOU'LL TORTURE HIM UNTIL I--
YOU WERE EXPECTING VILLAINY; I PLAYED THE VILLAIN. IT WAS A RUSE TO BRING YOU HERE TO BE WITH HIM AT THE END, ORSON.
YOUR FATHER WILL NOT BE HARMED, AND BY THIS, I HOPE TO EARN YOUR TRUST.
CONSIDER IT A TOKEN OF APOLOGY FOR MY YEARS OF TROUBLING YOU.
SEE, I LISTENED TO WHAT YOU SAID TO ME WHEN WE LAST MET. COME WITH ME TO THE TROPHY ROOM.
I HAVE SEEN TREASURES TO BEGGAR THE IMAGINATION, RANDALL.
BUT IT WASN'T UNTIL YOU ASKED ME THE RIGHT QUESTIONS...
...THAT I ASKED THE RIGHT QUESTIONS, AND REALIZED JUST HOW PROFOUNDLY IMPOSSIBLE THESE SEVEN COINS WERE.
AS OBJECTS, GATHERED TOGETHER, AT ONCE.
IN THE SEVEN CAPITAL CITIES OF HEAVEN, THESE COINS ARE BUT PENNIES. NEAR WORTHLESS.
BUT ON EARTH...? THEY ARE PRICELESS. AND YOUR WARD HAD THEM IN A COMMON COIN PURSE.
YOU IMPLORED ME TO INVESTIGATE THEM. I DID.
THAT LED ME TO YOUR FATHER-- I BROUGHT HIM HERE TO SAVE HIM, BUT HE IS TOO FAR GONE. BUT BEFORE HE GOES I NEED ANSWERS.
AND HE'S MADE IT CLEAR, HE WON'T ANSWER ME UNTIL HE KNOWS YOU APPROVE...

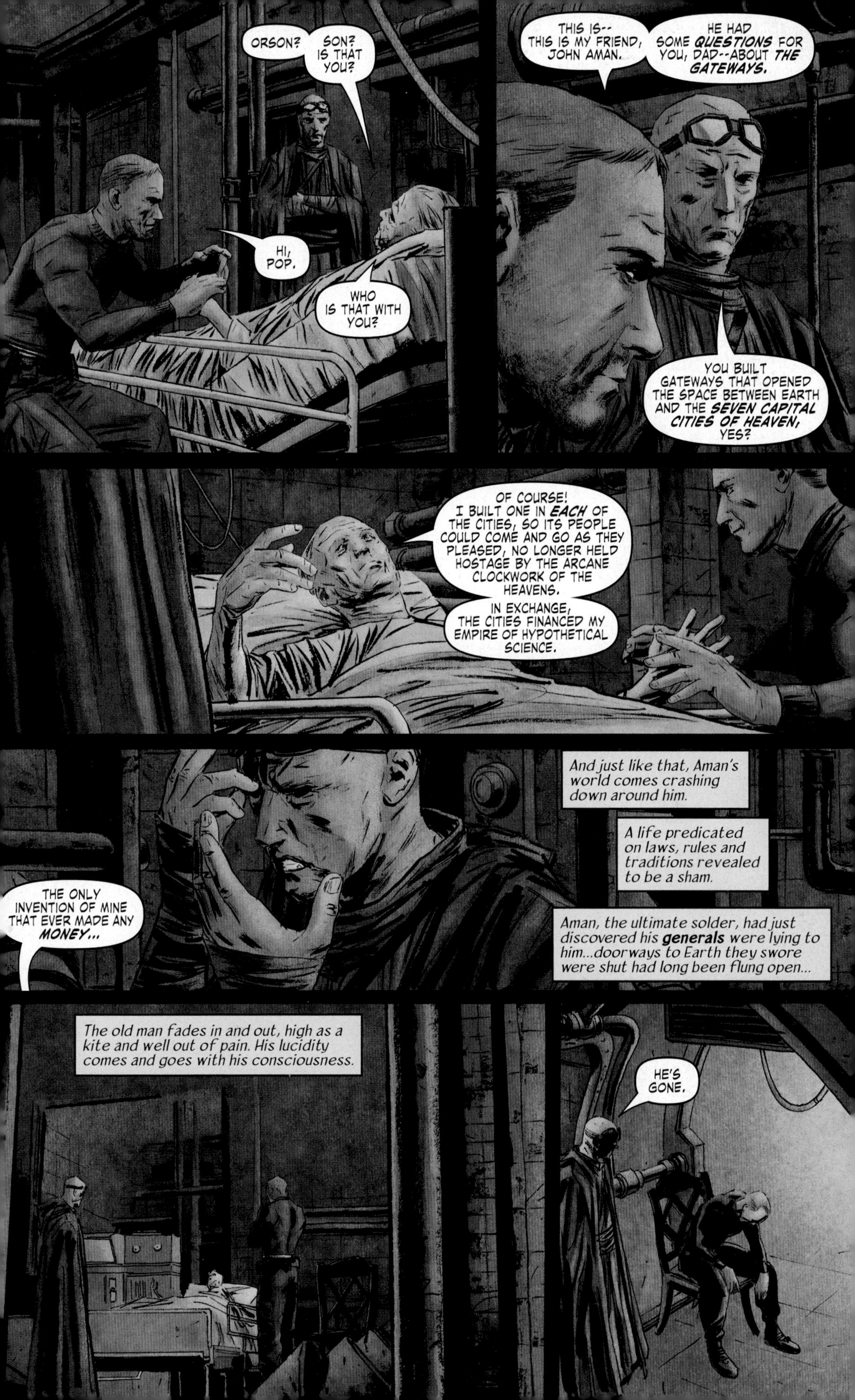
ORSON?
SON? IS THAT YOU?
HI, POP.
WHO IS THAT WITH YOU?
THIS IS-- THIS IS MY FRIEND, JOHN AMAN.
HE HAD SOME **QUESTIONS** FOR YOU, DAD--ABOUT ***THE GATEWAYS.***
YOU BUILT GATEWAYS THAT OPENED THE SPACE BETWEEN EARTH AND THE ***SEVEN CAPITAL CITIES OF HEAVEN,*** YES?
OF COURSE! I BUILT ONE IN ***EACH*** OF THE CITIES, SO ITS PEOPLE COULD COME AND GO AS THEY PLEASED, NO LONGER HELD HOSTAGE BY THE ARCANE CLOCKWORK OF THE HEAVENS.
IN EXCHANGE, THE CITIES FINANCED MY EMPIRE OF HYPOTHETICAL SCIENCE.
And just like that, Aman's world comes crashing down around him.
A life predicated on laws, rules and traditions revealed to be a sham.
THE ONLY INVENTION OF MINE THAT EVER MADE ANY ***MONEY...***
*Aman, the ultimate solder, had just discovered his **generals** were lying to him...doorways to Earth they swore were shut had long been flung open...*
The old man fades in and out, high as a kite and well out of pain. His lucidity comes and goes with his consciousness.
HE'S GONE.

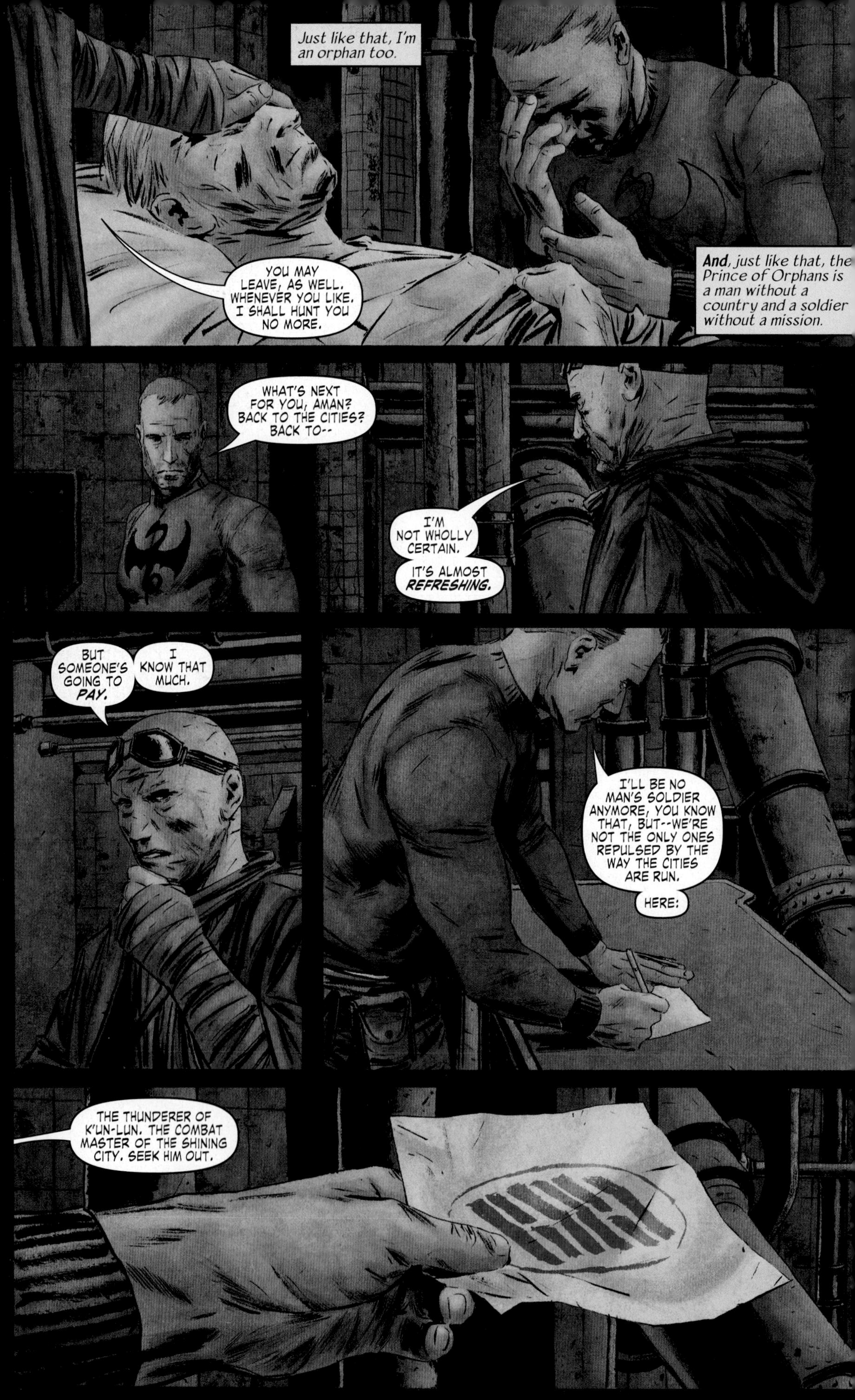
Just like that, I'm an orphan too.
YOU MAY LEAVE, AS WELL. WHENEVER YOU LIKE. I SHALL HUNT YOU NO MORE.
And, just like that, the Prince of Orphans is a man without a country and a soldier without a mission.
WHAT'S NEXT FOR YOU, AMAN? BACK TO THE CITIES? BACK TO--
I'M NOT WHOLLY CERTAIN.
IT'S ALMOST REFRESHING.
I KNOW THAT MUCH.
BUT SOMEONE'S GOING TO PAY.
I'LL BE NO MAN'S SOLDIER ANYMORE, YOU KNOW THAT, BUT--WE'RE NOT THE ONLY ONES REPULSED BY THE WAY THE CITIES ARE RUN.
HERE:
THE THUNDERER OF K'UN-LUN. THE COMBAT MASTER OF THE SHINING CITY. SEEK HIM OUT.

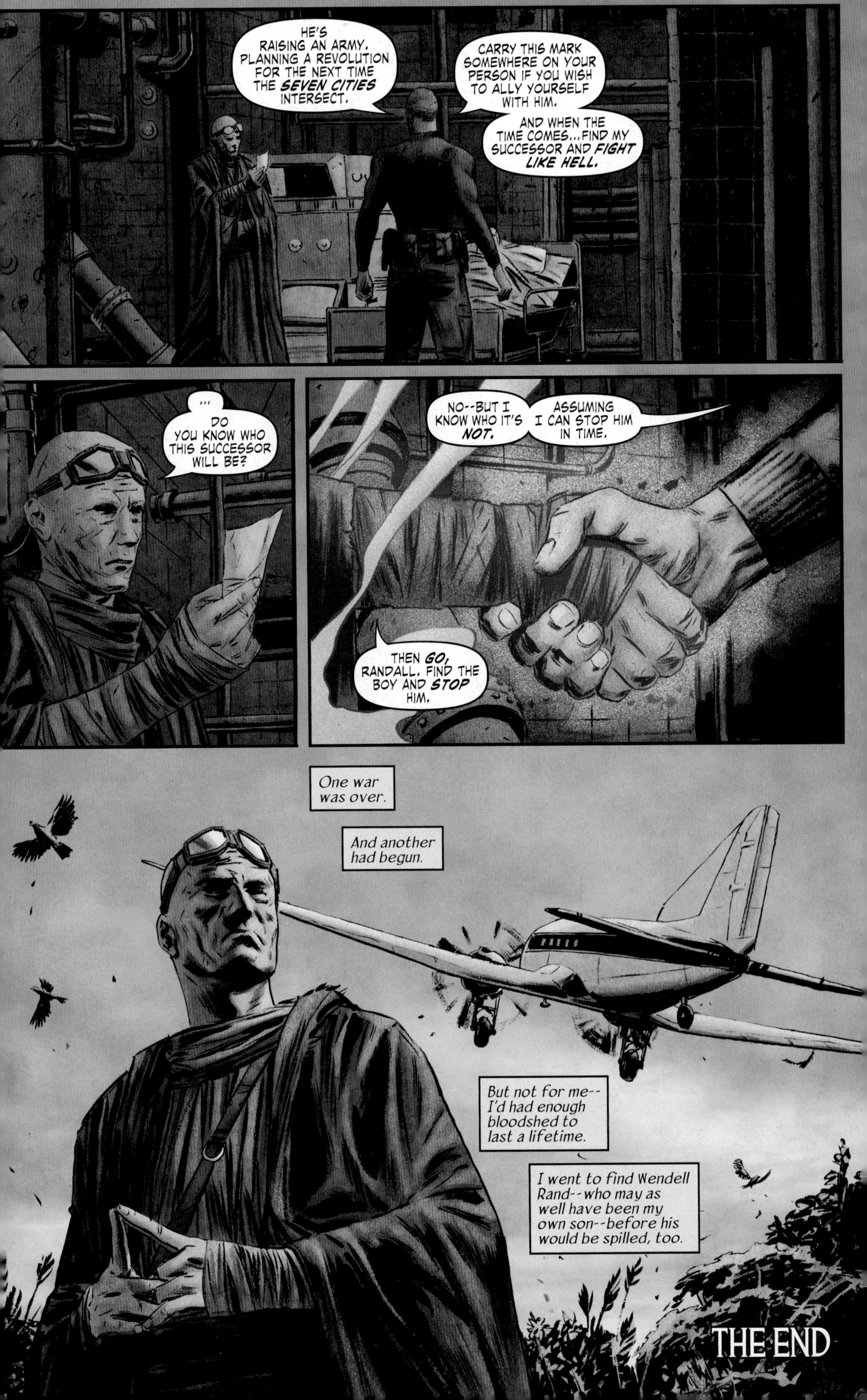

HE'S RAISING AN ARMY. PLANNING A REVOLUTION FOR THE NEXT TIME THE SEVEN CITIES INTERSECT.
CARRY THIS MARK SOMEWHERE ON YOUR PERSON IF YOU WISH TO ALLY YOURSELF WITH HIM.
AND WHEN THE TIME COMES...FIND MY SUCCESSOR AND FIGHT LIKE HELL.
... DO YOU KNOW WHO THIS SUCCESSOR WILL BE?
NO--BUT I KNOW WHO IT'S NOT.
ASSUMING I CAN STOP HIM IN TIME.
THEN GO, RANDALL. FIND THE BOY AND STOP HIM.
One war was over.
And another had begun.
But not for me--I'd had enough bloodshed to last a lifetime.
I went to find Wendell Rand--who may as well have been my own son--before his would be spilled, too.
THE END

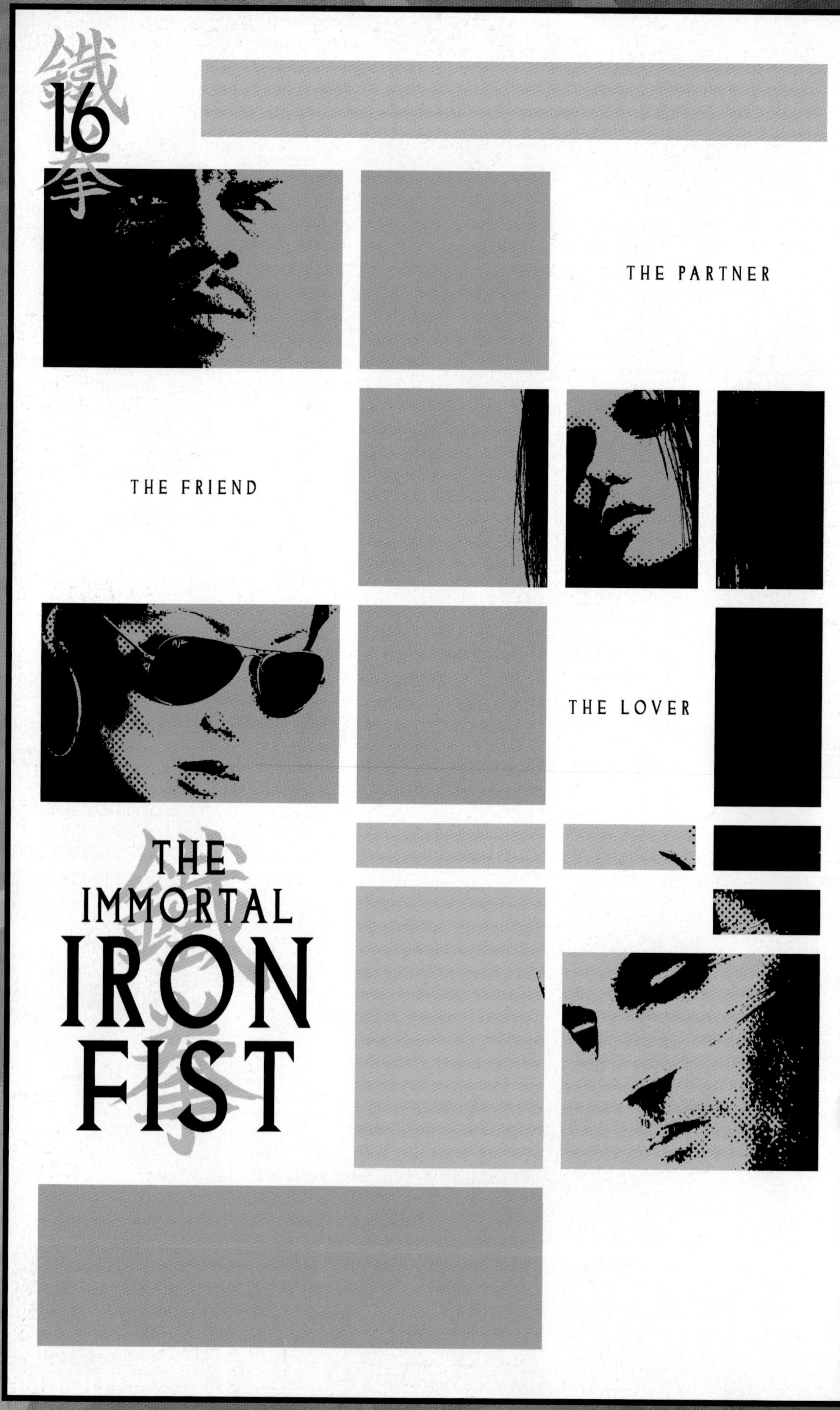

16

THE PARTNER

THE FRIEND

THE LOVER

THE
IMMORTAL
IRON
FIST

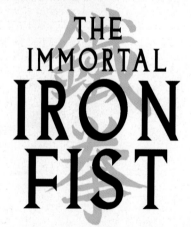

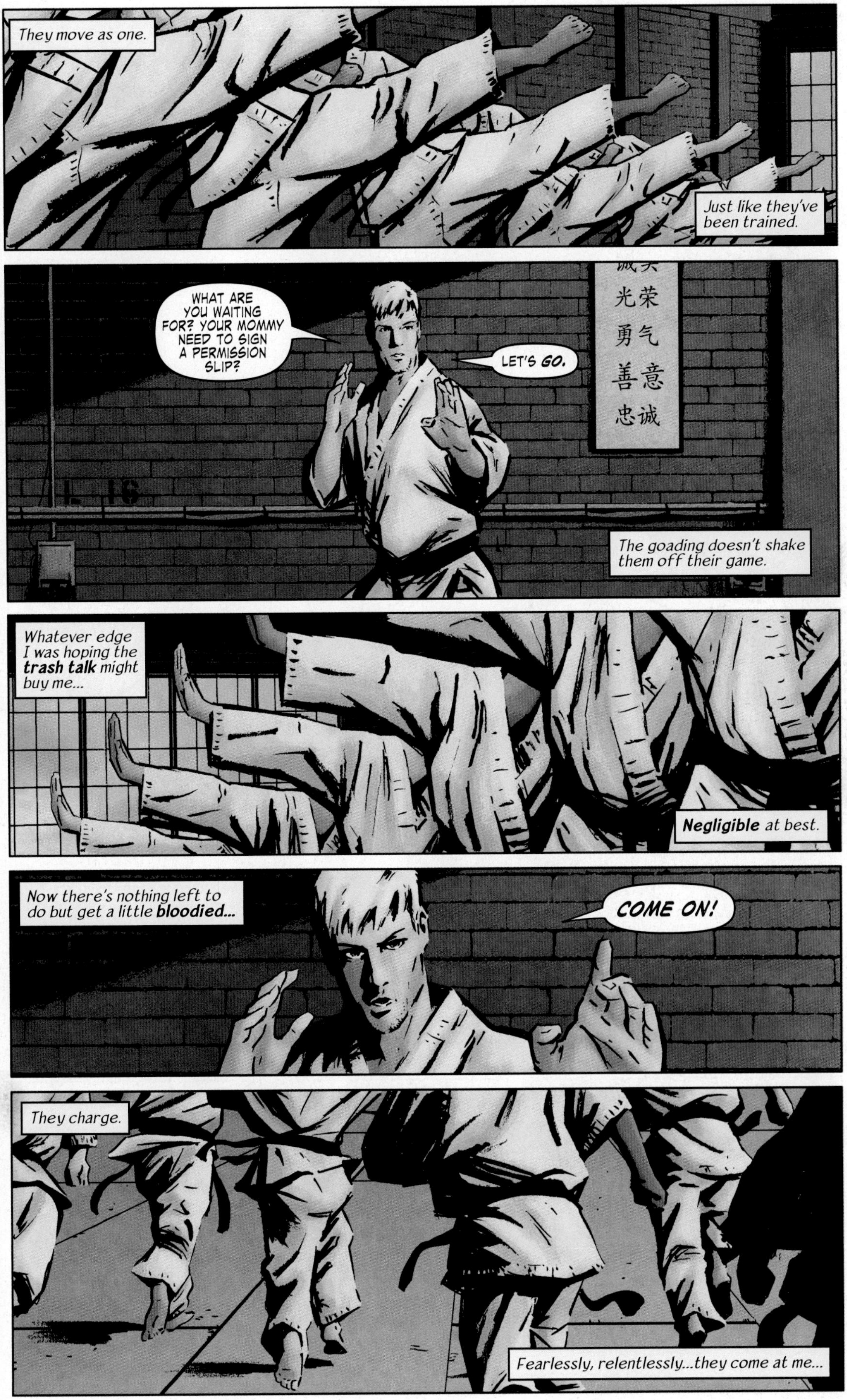
They move as one.
Just like they've been trained.
WHAT ARE YOU WAITING FOR? YOUR MOMMY NEED TO SIGN A PERMISSION SLIP?
LET'S GO.
荣气意诚
光勇善忠
The goading doesn't shake them off their game.
Whatever edge I was hoping the trash talk might buy me...
Negligible at best.
Now there's nothing left to do but get a little bloodied...
COME ON!
They charge.
Fearlessly, relentlessly...they come at me...

The Thunder Dojo teaches its students no less.

I couldn't be prouder of them.

"Happy Birthday Danny"

Matt Fraction Writer   **David Aja** Art   **Matt Hollingsworth** Color Art   **Dave Lanphear** Letterer

Alejandro Arbona Assistant Editor   **Warren Simons** Editor   **Joe Quesada** Editor in Chief   **Dan Buckley** Publisher

The space was apparently an old furniture warehouse that **Rand International** had acquired somewhere along the line, up in **Harlem.**

It's in the heart of a neighborhood that's seen better days.

And it's a neighborhood full of kids...

  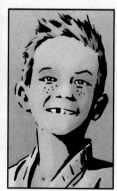  

...almost all of 'em needing a place like the **Dojo** to come after school.

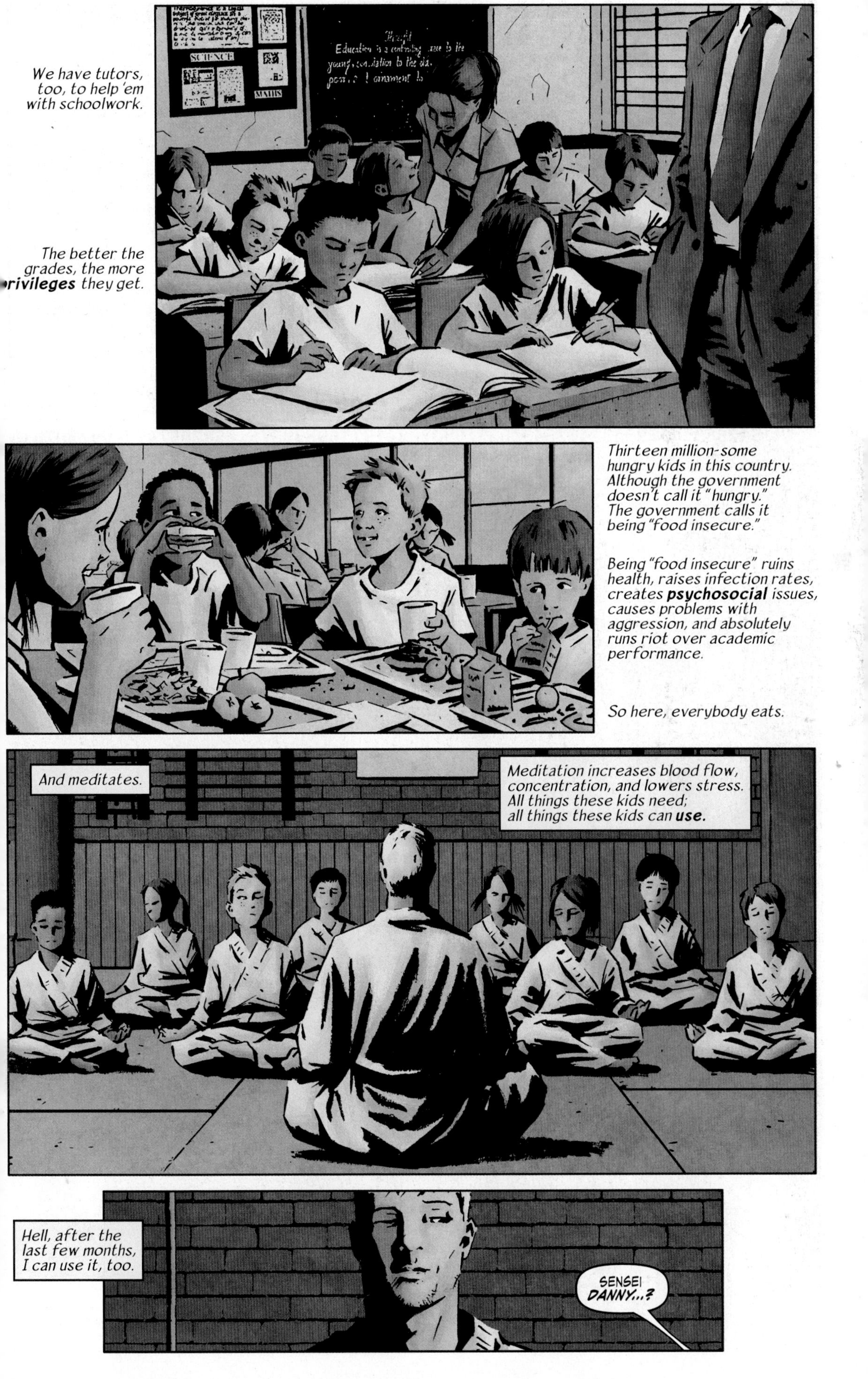
We have tutors, too, to help 'em with schoolwork.
SCIENCE
MATHS
The better the grades, the more **privileges** they get.
Thirteen million-some hungry kids in this country. Although the government doesn't call it "hungry." The government calls it being "food insecure."
Being "food insecure" ruins health, raises infection rates, creates **psychosocial** issues, causes problems with aggression, and absolutely runs riot over academic performance.
So here, everybody eats.
And meditates.
Meditation increases blood flow, concentration, and lowers stress. All things these kids need; all things these kids can **use.**
Hell, after the last few months, I can use it, too.
SENSEI DANNY...?

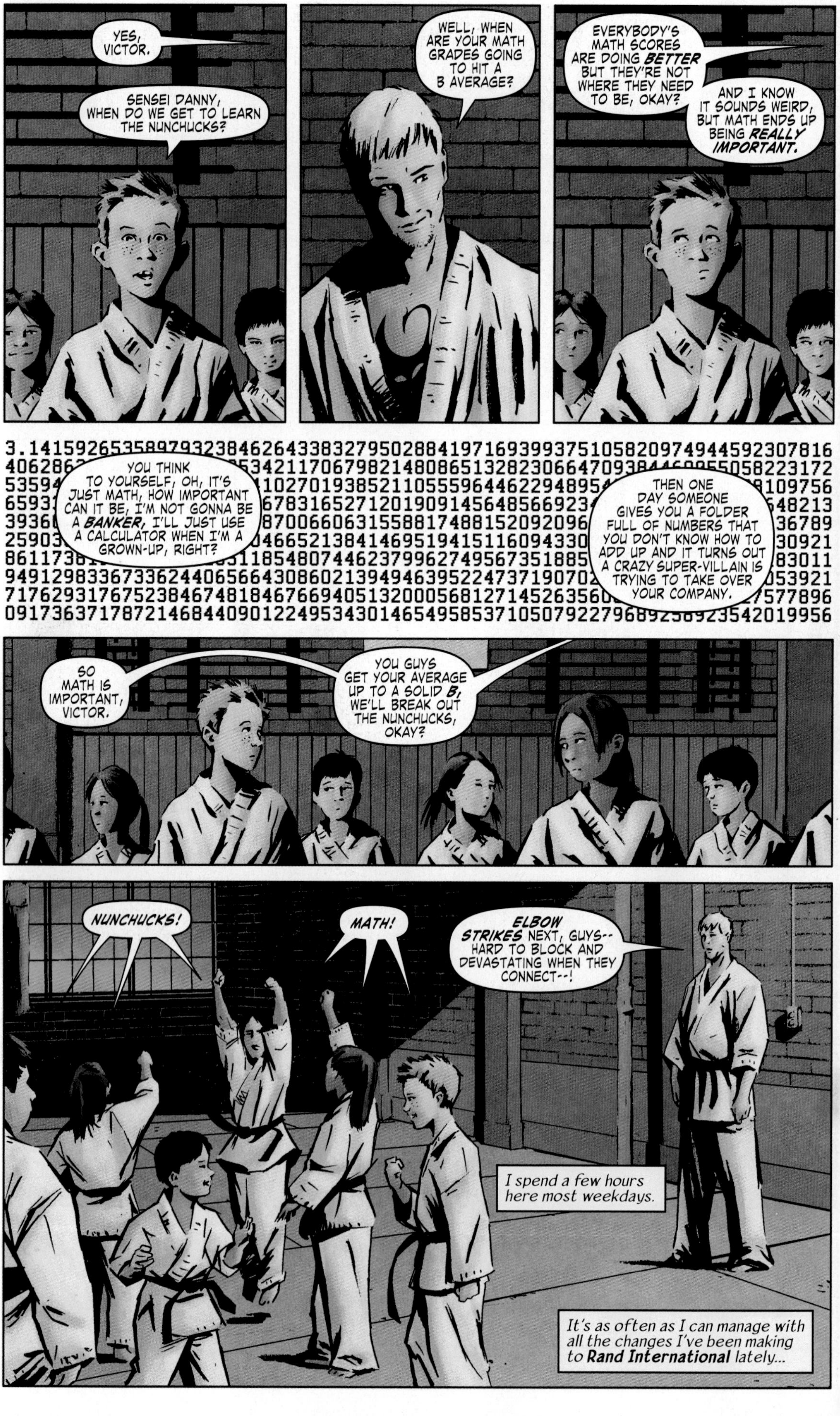
YES, VICTOR.
SENSEI DANNY, WHEN DO WE GET TO LEARN THE NUNCHUCKS?
WELL, WHEN ARE YOUR MATH GRADES GOING TO HIT A B AVERAGE?
EVERYBODY'S MATH SCORES ARE DOING **BETTER** BUT THEY'RE NOT WHERE THEY NEED TO BE, OKAY?
AND I KNOW IT SOUNDS WEIRD, BUT MATH ENDS UP BEING ***REALLY IMPORTANT.***
3.141592653589793238462643383279502884197169399375105820974944592307816
YOU THINK TO YOURSELF, OH, IT'S JUST MATH, HOW IMPORTANT CAN IT BE, I'M NOT GONNA BE A ***BANKER,*** I'LL JUST USE A CALCULATOR WHEN I'M A GROWN-UP, RIGHT?
THEN ONE DAY SOMEONE GIVES YOU A FOLDER FULL OF NUMBERS THAT YOU DON'T KNOW HOW TO ADD UP AND IT TURNS OUT A CRAZY SUPER-VILLAIN IS TRYING TO TAKE OVER YOUR COMPANY.
SO MATH IS IMPORTANT, VICTOR.
YOU GUYS GET YOUR AVERAGE UP TO A SOLID ***B,*** WE'LL BREAK OUT THE NUNCHUCKS, OKAY?
NUNCHUCKS!
MATH!
ELBOW STRIKES NEXT, GUYS-- HARD TO BLOCK AND DEVASTATING WHEN THEY CONNECT--!
I spend a few hours here most weekdays.
It's as often as I can manage with all the changes I've been making to ***Rand International*** *lately...*

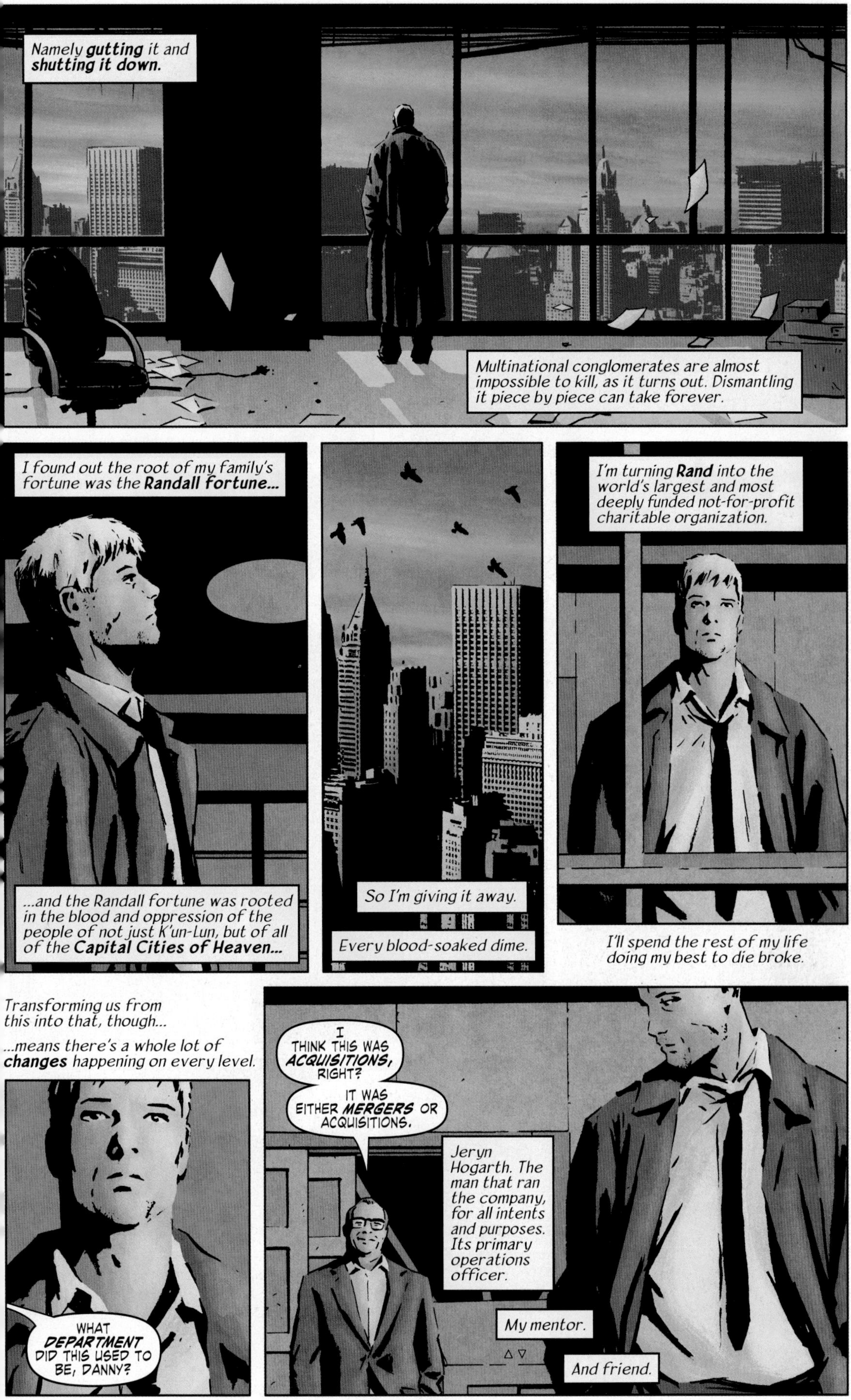
Namely **gutting** it and **shutting it down.**
Multinational conglomerates are almost impossible to kill, as it turns out. Dismantling it piece by piece can take forever.
I found out the root of my family's fortune was the **Randall fortune...**
...and the Randall fortune was rooted in the blood and oppression of the people of not just K'un-Lun, but of all of the **Capital Cities of Heaven...**
So I'm giving it away.
Every blood-soaked dime.
I'm turning **Rand** into the world's largest and most deeply funded not-for-profit charitable organization.
I'll spend the rest of my life doing my best to die broke.
Transforming us from this into that, though...
...means there's a whole lot of **changes** happening on every level.
WHAT *DEPARTMENT* DID THIS USED TO BE, DANNY?
I THINK THIS WAS *ACQUISITIONS,* RIGHT?
IT WAS EITHER *MERGERS* OR ACQUISITIONS.
Jeryn Hogarth. The man that ran the company, for all intents and purposes. Its primary operations officer.
My mentor.
And friend.

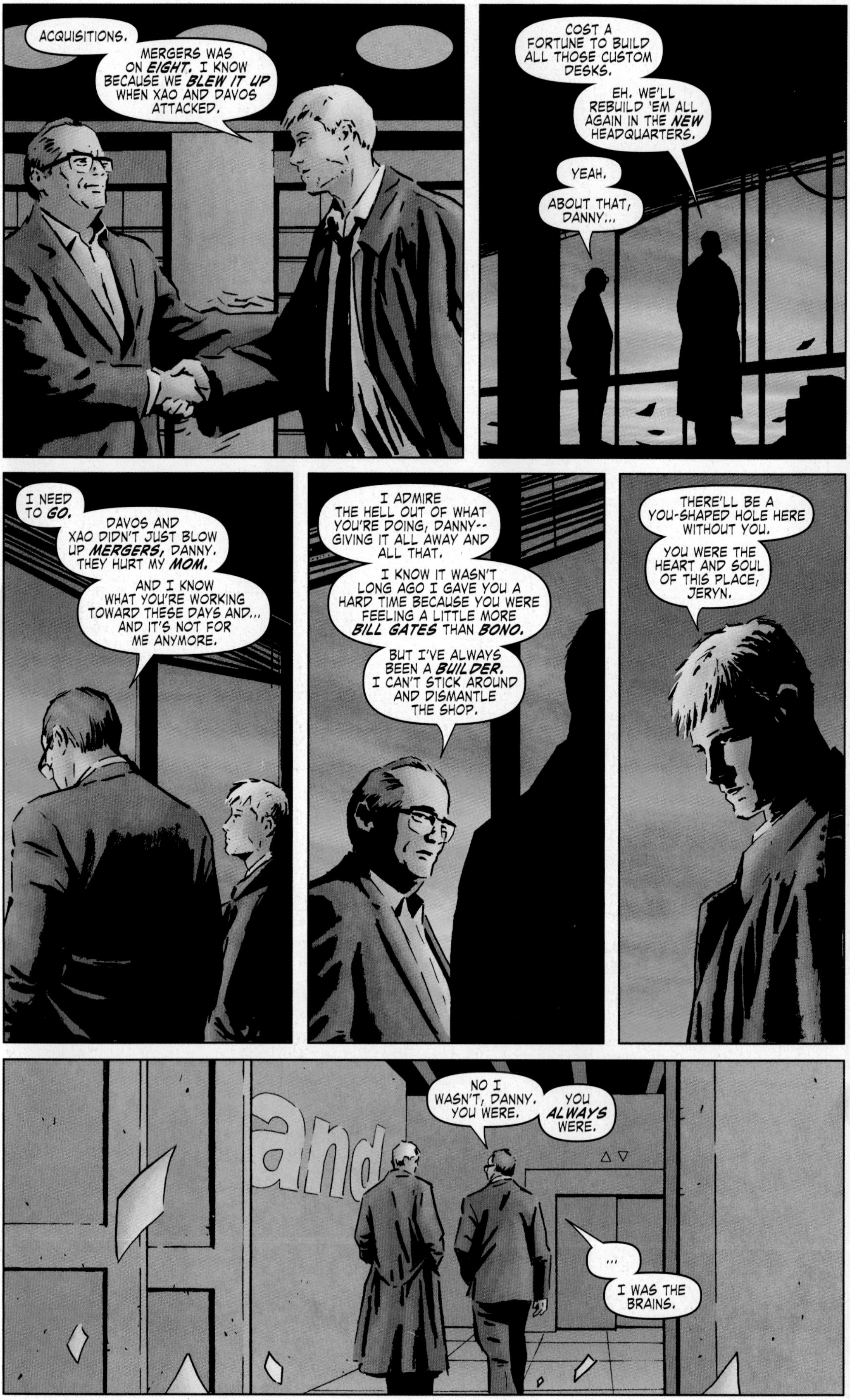
ACQUISITIONS.
MERGERS WAS ON *EIGHT*. I KNOW BECAUSE WE *BLEW IT UP* WHEN XAO AND DAVOS ATTACKED.
COST A FORTUNE TO BUILD ALL THOSE CUSTOM DESKS.
EH. WE'LL REBUILD 'EM ALL AGAIN IN THE *NEW* HEADQUARTERS.
YEAH.
ABOUT THAT, DANNY...
I NEED TO *GO.*
DAVOS AND XAO DIDN'T JUST BLOW UP *MERGERS,* DANNY. THEY HURT MY *MOM.*
AND I KNOW WHAT YOU'RE WORKING TOWARD THESE DAYS AND... AND IT'S NOT FOR ME ANYMORE.
I ADMIRE THE HELL OUT OF WHAT YOU'RE DOING, DANNY-- GIVING IT ALL AWAY AND ALL THAT.
I KNOW IT WASN'T LONG AGO I GAVE YOU A HARD TIME BECAUSE YOU WERE FEELING A LITTLE MORE *BILL GATES* THAN *BONO.*
BUT I'VE ALWAYS BEEN A *BUILDER.* I CAN'T STICK AROUND AND DISMANTLE THE SHOP.
THERE'LL BE A YOU-SHAPED HOLE HERE WITHOUT YOU.
YOU WERE THE HEART AND SOUL OF THIS PLACE, JERYN.
NO I WASN'T, DANNY. YOU WERE.
YOU *ALWAYS* WERE.
and
...
I WAS THE BRAINS.

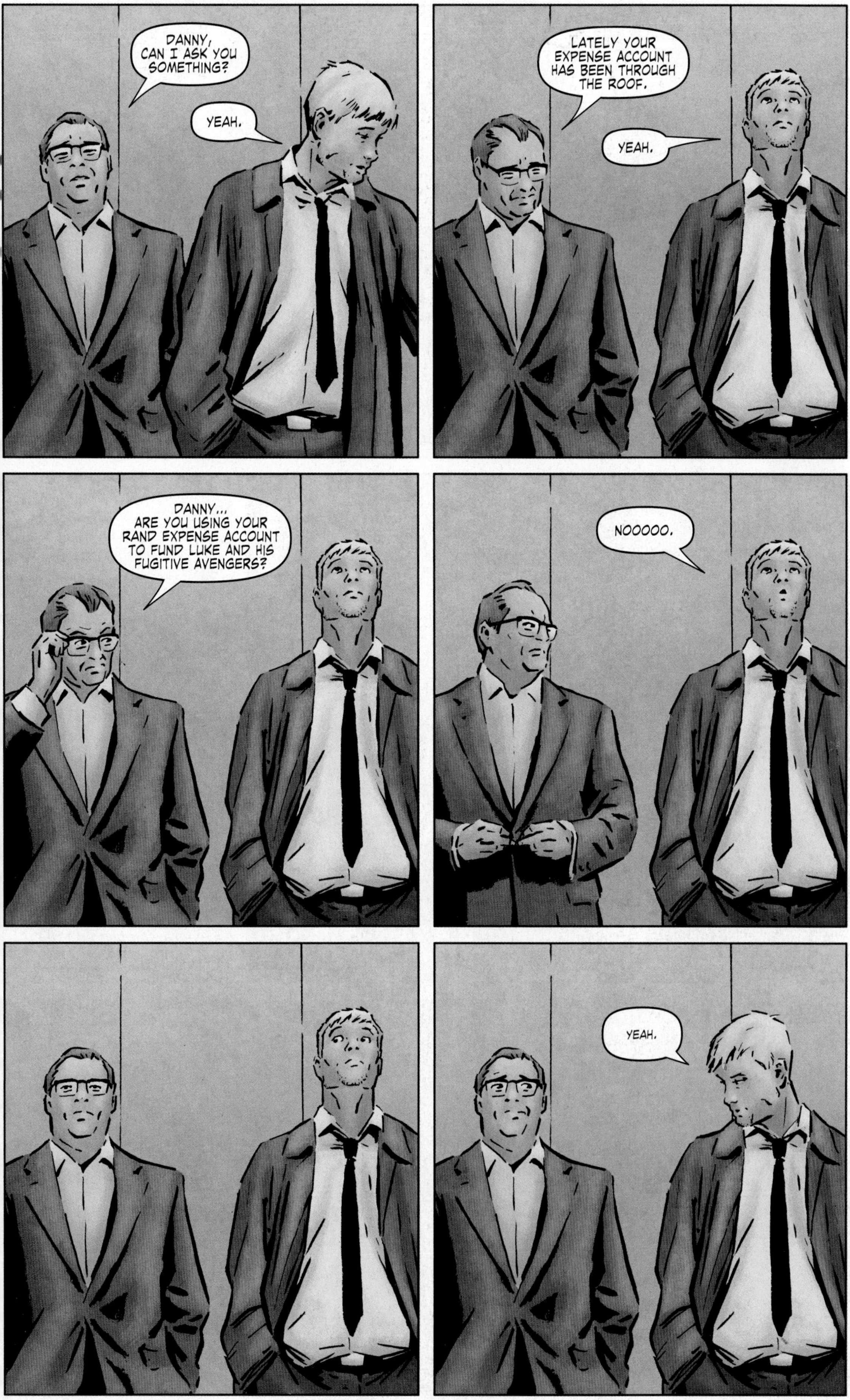
DANNY, CAN I ASK YOU SOMETHING?
YEAH.
LATELY YOUR EXPENSE ACCOUNT HAS BEEN THROUGH THE ROOF.
YEAH.
DANNY... ARE YOU USING YOUR RAND EXPENSE ACCOUNT TO FUND LUKE AND HIS FUGITIVE AVENGERS?
NOOOOO.
YEAH.

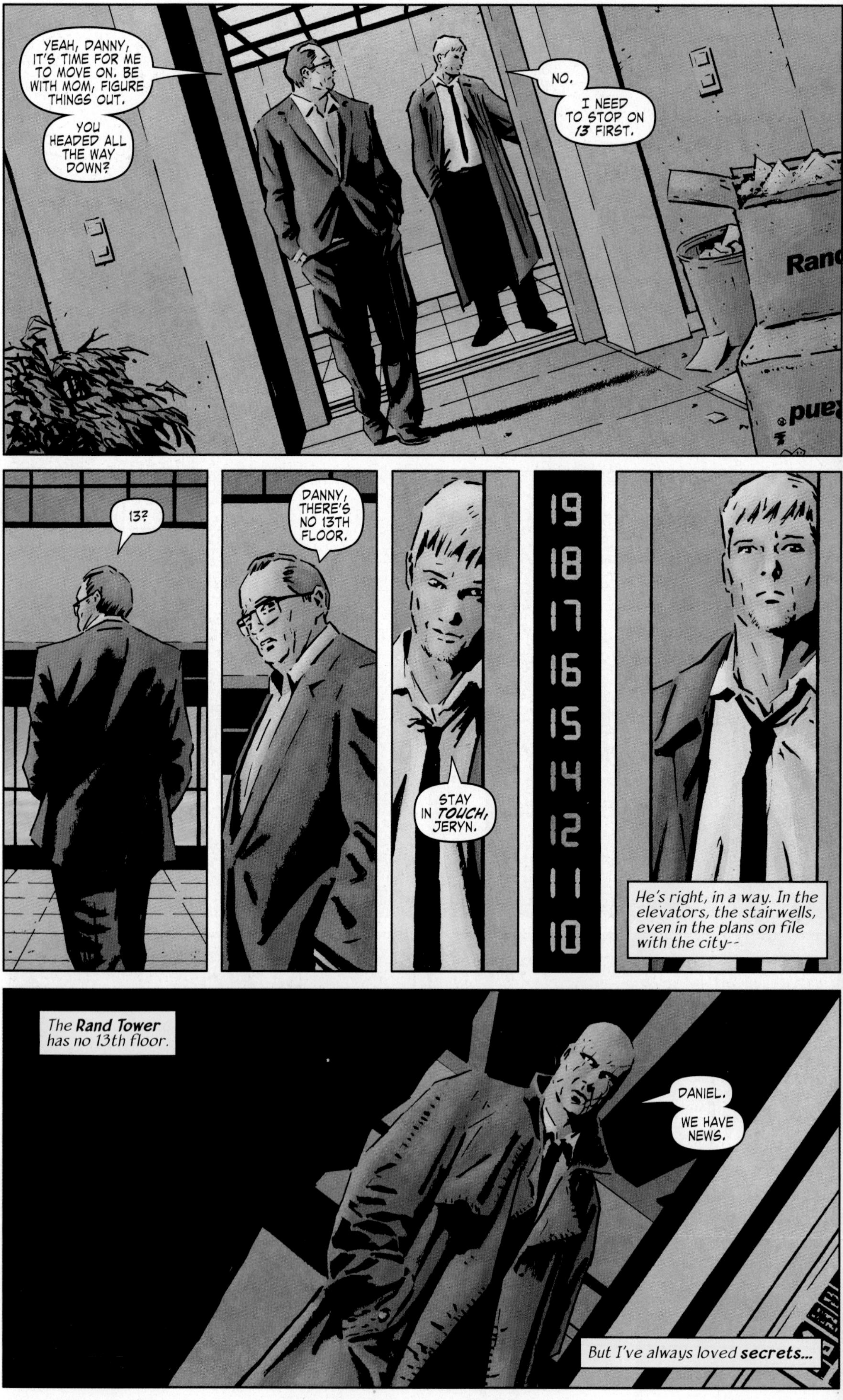
YEAH, DANNY, IT'S TIME FOR ME TO MOVE ON. BE WITH MOM, FIGURE THINGS OUT.
YOU HEADED ALL THE WAY DOWN?
NO.
I NEED TO STOP ON 13 FIRST.
13?
DANNY, THERE'S NO 13TH FLOOR.
STAY IN TOUCH, JERYN.
19
18
17
16
15
14
12
11
10
He's right, in a way. In the elevators, the stairwells, even in the plans on file with the city--
The Rand Tower has no 13th floor.
DANIEL.
WE HAVE NEWS.
But I've always loved secrets...

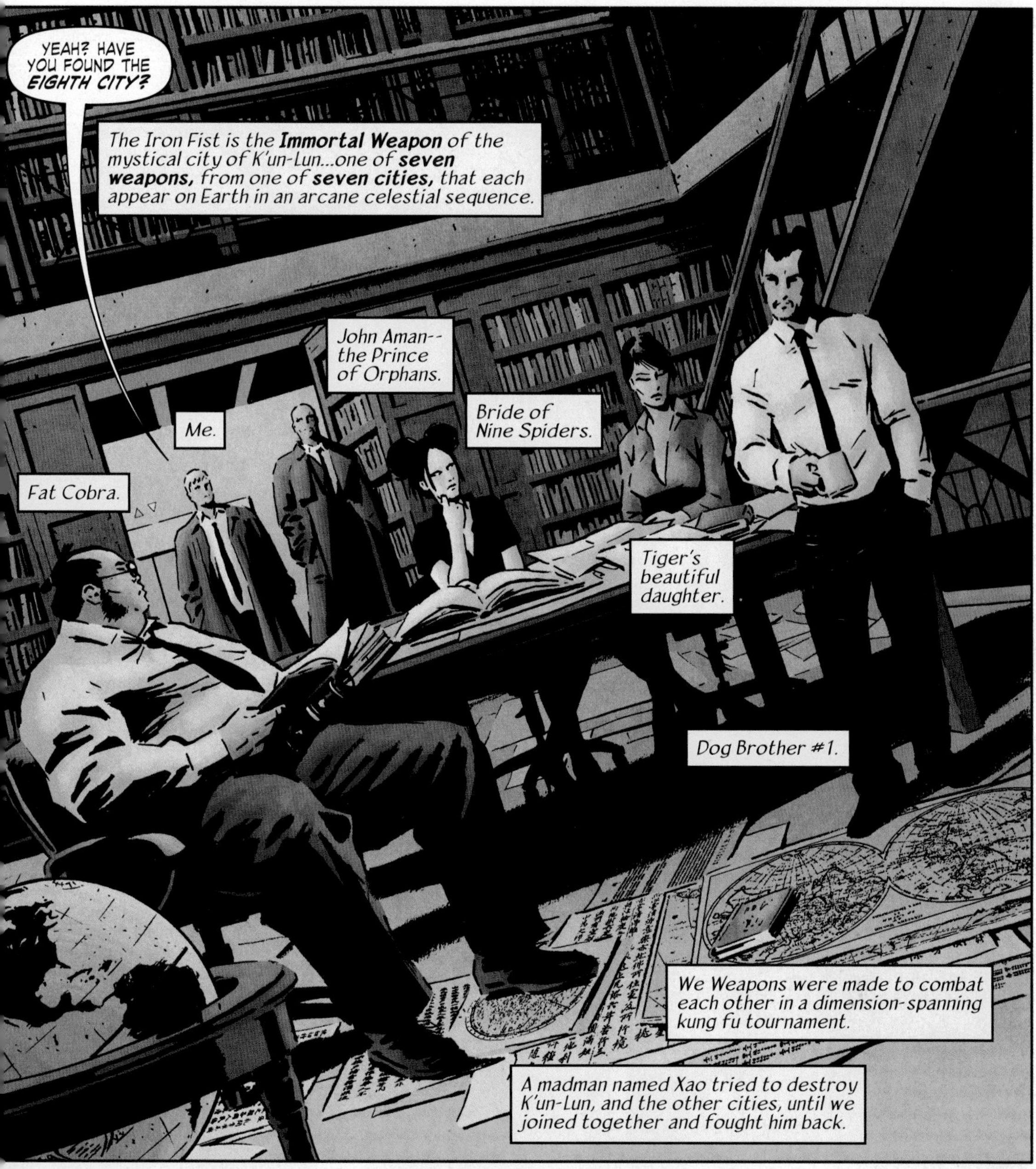
YEAH? HAVE YOU FOUND THE EIGHTH CITY?
The Iron Fist is the Immortal Weapon of the mystical city of K'un-Lun...one of seven weapons, from one of seven cities, that each appear on Earth in an arcane celestial sequence.
John Aman-- the Prince of Orphans.
Bride of Nine Spiders.
Me.
Fat Cobra.
Tiger's beautiful daughter.
Dog Brother #1.
We Weapons were made to combat each other in a dimension-spanning kung fu tournament.
A madman named Xao tried to destroy K'un-Lun, and the other cities, until we joined together and fought him back.

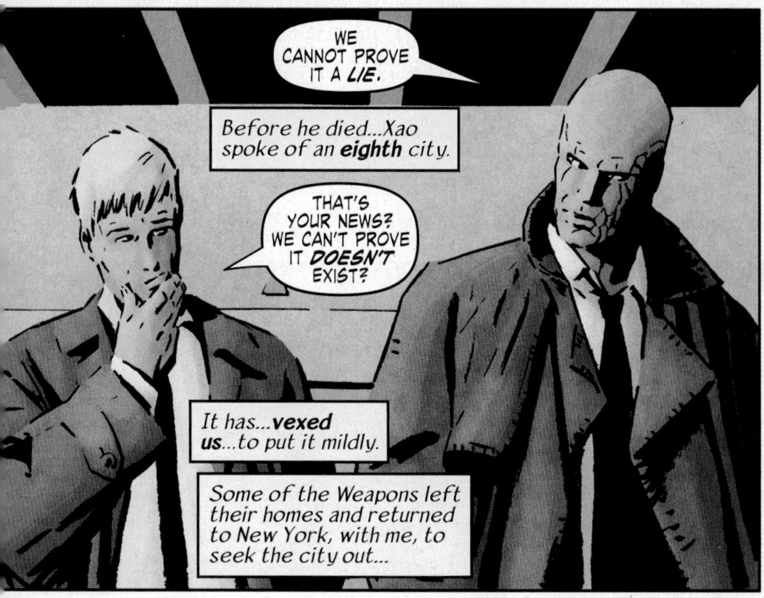
WE CANNOT PROVE IT A LIE.
Before he died...Xao spoke of an eighth city.
THAT'S YOUR NEWS? WE CAN'T PROVE IT DOESN'T EXIST?
It has...vexed us...to put it mildly.
Some of the Weapons left their homes and returned to New York, with me, to seek the city out...

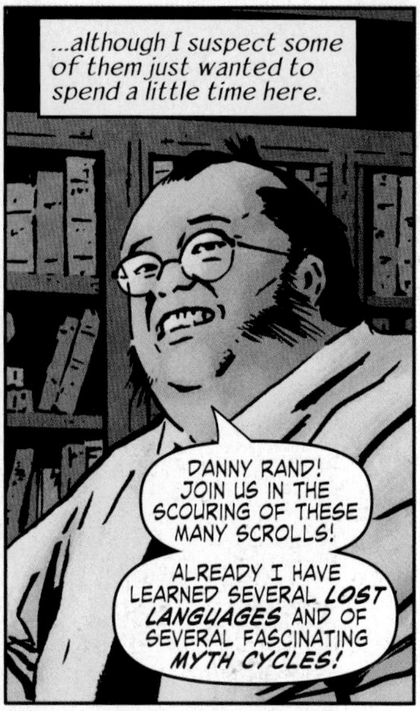
...although I suspect some of them just wanted to spend a little time here.
DANNY RAND! JOIN US IN THE SCOURING OF THESE MANY SCROLLS!
ALREADY I HAVE LEARNED SEVERAL LOST LANGUAGES AND OF SEVERAL FASCINATING MYTH CYCLES!

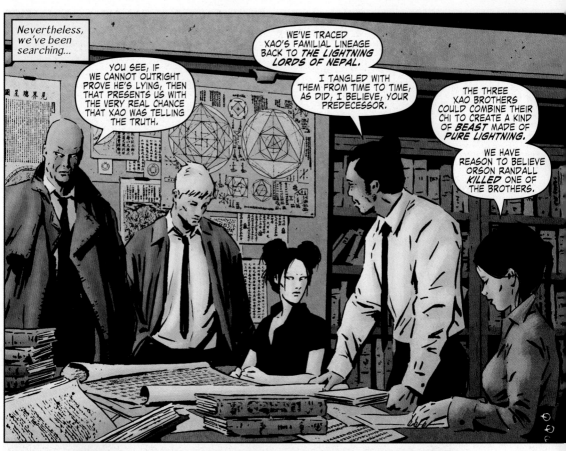

Nevertheless, we've been searching...

YOU SEE, IF WE CANNOT OUTRIGHT PROVE HE'S LYING, THEN THAT PRESENTS US WITH THE VERY REAL CHANCE THAT XAO WAS TELLING THE TRUTH.

WE'VE TRACED XAO'S FAMILIAL LINEAGE BACK TO *THE LIGHTNING LORDS OF NEPAL.*

I TANGLED WITH THEM FROM TIME TO TIME, AS DID, I BELIEVE, YOUR PREDECESSOR.

THE THREE XAO BROTHERS COULD COMBINE THEIR CHI TO CREATE A KIND OF *BEAST* MADE OF *PURE LIGHTNING.*

WE HAVE REASON TO BELIEVE ORSON RANDALL *KILLED* ONE OF THE BROTHERS.

IT LOOKS LIKE *YOUR PREDECESSOR* EMPLOYED XAO, IF I'M READING THIS RIGHT. USED HIM AS A BOUNTY HUNTER TO HUNT *DOWN* ORSON.

DID THE PREVIOUS *BRIDE* EVER MENTION--

AAH--

III KNOW WHAAAT DAY ITTT ISSS, DANNNIEL RANNND.

OHHHHH-KAY. THAT WAS CREEPY.

KEEP DIGGING. I'LL BE BACK *SOON.*

I HAVE A MEETING ACROSS TOWN I HAVE TO GET TO. BIG MEETING. *CRAZY* IMPORTANT.

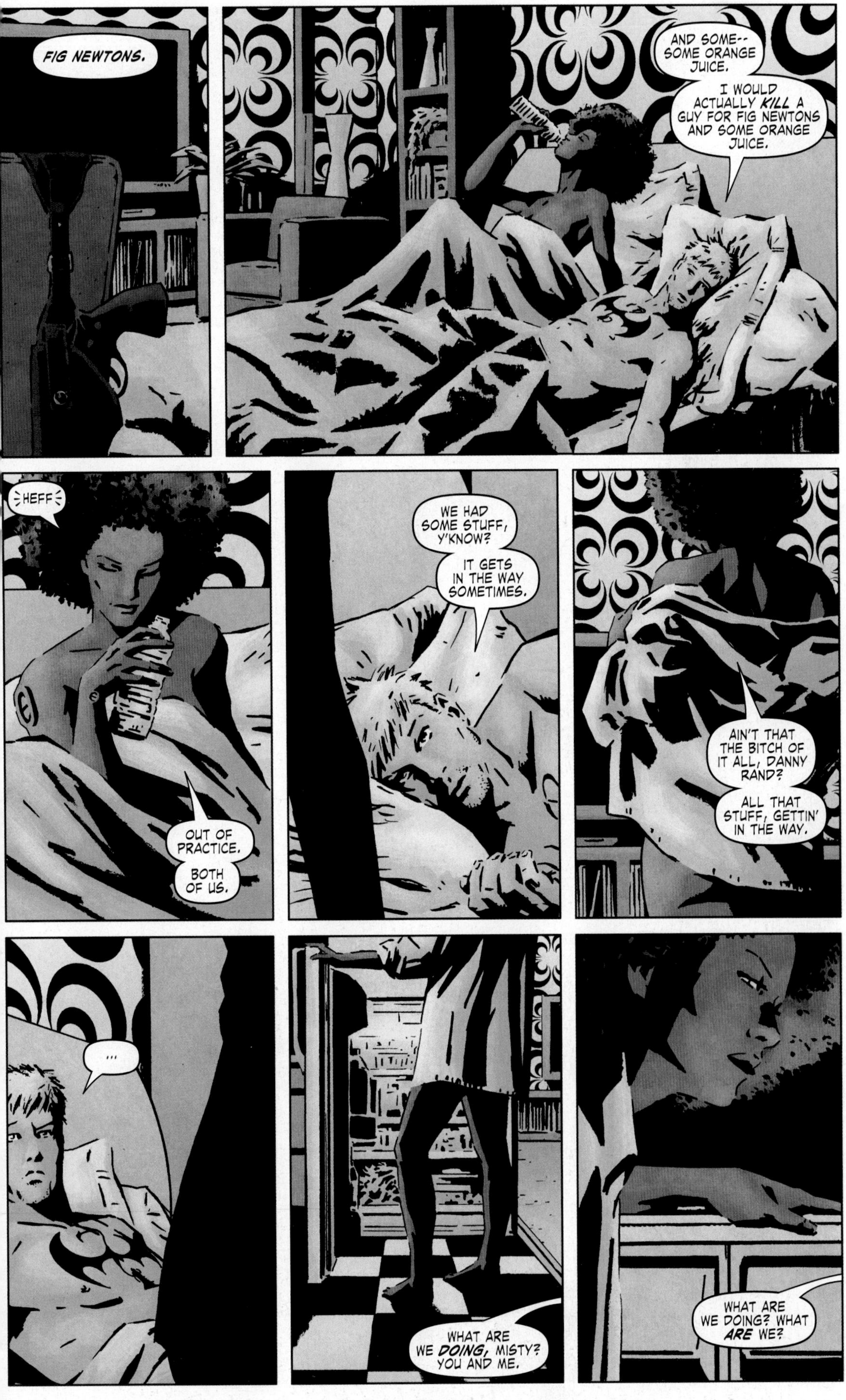
FIG NEWTONS.
AND SOME-- SOME ORANGE JUICE.
I WOULD ACTUALLY KILL A GUY FOR FIG NEWTONS AND SOME ORANGE JUICE.
HEFF
OUT OF PRACTICE.
BOTH OF US.
WE HAD SOME STUFF, Y'KNOW?
IT GETS IN THE WAY SOMETIMES.
AIN'T THAT THE BITCH OF IT ALL, DANNY RAND?
ALL THAT STUFF, GETTIN' IN THE WAY.
...
WHAT ARE WE DOING, MISTY? YOU AND ME.
WHAT ARE WE DOING? WHAT ARE WE?

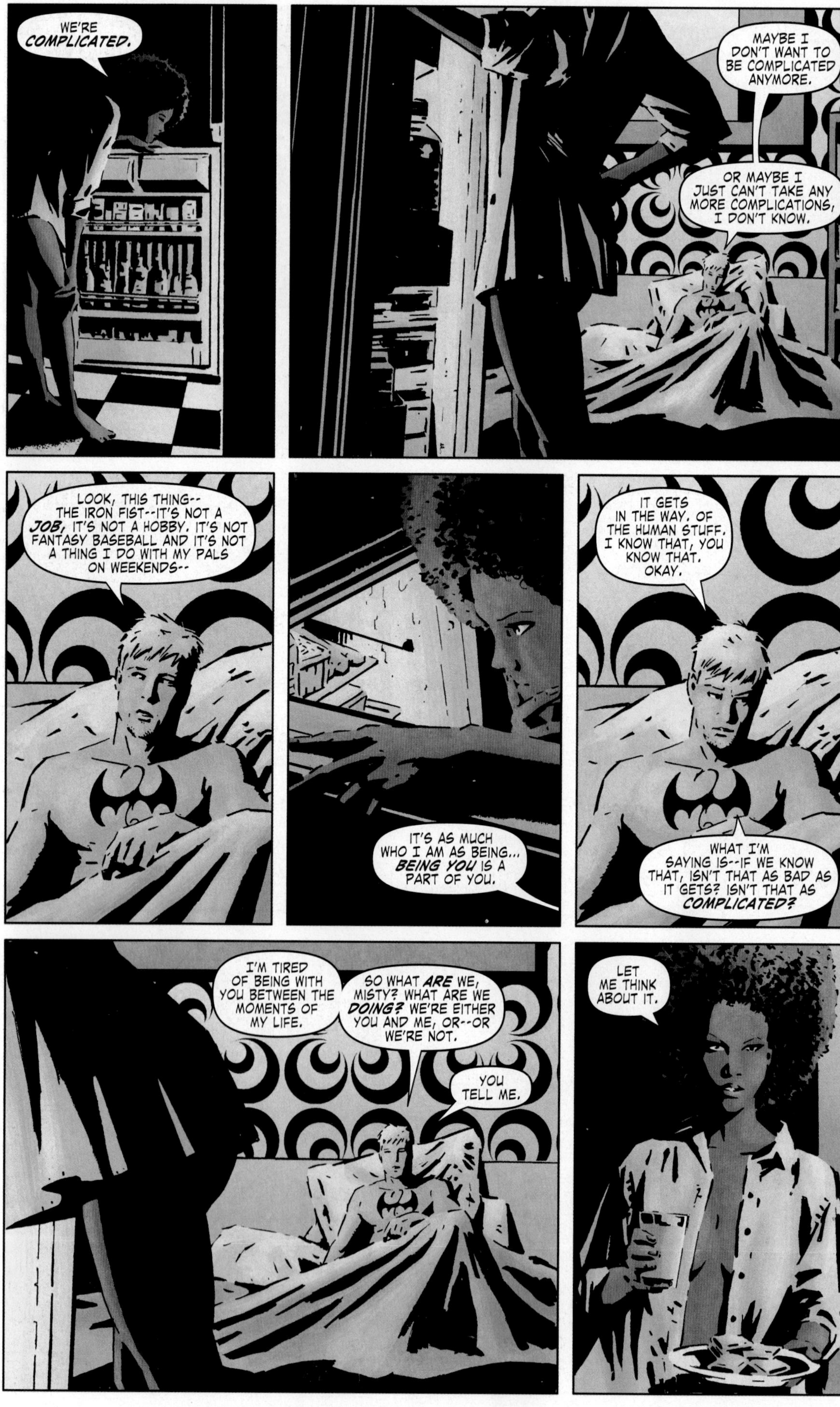
WE'RE COMPLICATED.
MAYBE I DON'T WANT TO BE COMPLICATED ANYMORE.
OR MAYBE I JUST CAN'T TAKE ANY MORE COMPLICATIONS, I DON'T KNOW.
LOOK, THIS THING-- THE IRON FIST--IT'S NOT A JOB, IT'S NOT A HOBBY. IT'S NOT FANTASY BASEBALL AND IT'S NOT A THING I DO WITH MY PALS ON WEEKENDS--
IT'S AS MUCH WHO I AM AS BEING... BEING YOU IS A PART OF YOU.
IT GETS IN THE WAY. OF THE HUMAN STUFF. I KNOW THAT, YOU KNOW THAT. OKAY.
WHAT I'M SAYING IS--IF WE KNOW THAT, ISN'T THAT AS BAD AS IT GETS? ISN'T THAT AS COMPLICATED?
I'M TIRED OF BEING WITH YOU BETWEEN THE MOMENTS OF MY LIFE.
SO WHAT ARE WE, MISTY? WHAT ARE WE DOING? WE'RE EITHER YOU AND ME, OR--OR WE'RE NOT.
YOU TELL ME.
LET ME THINK ABOUT IT.

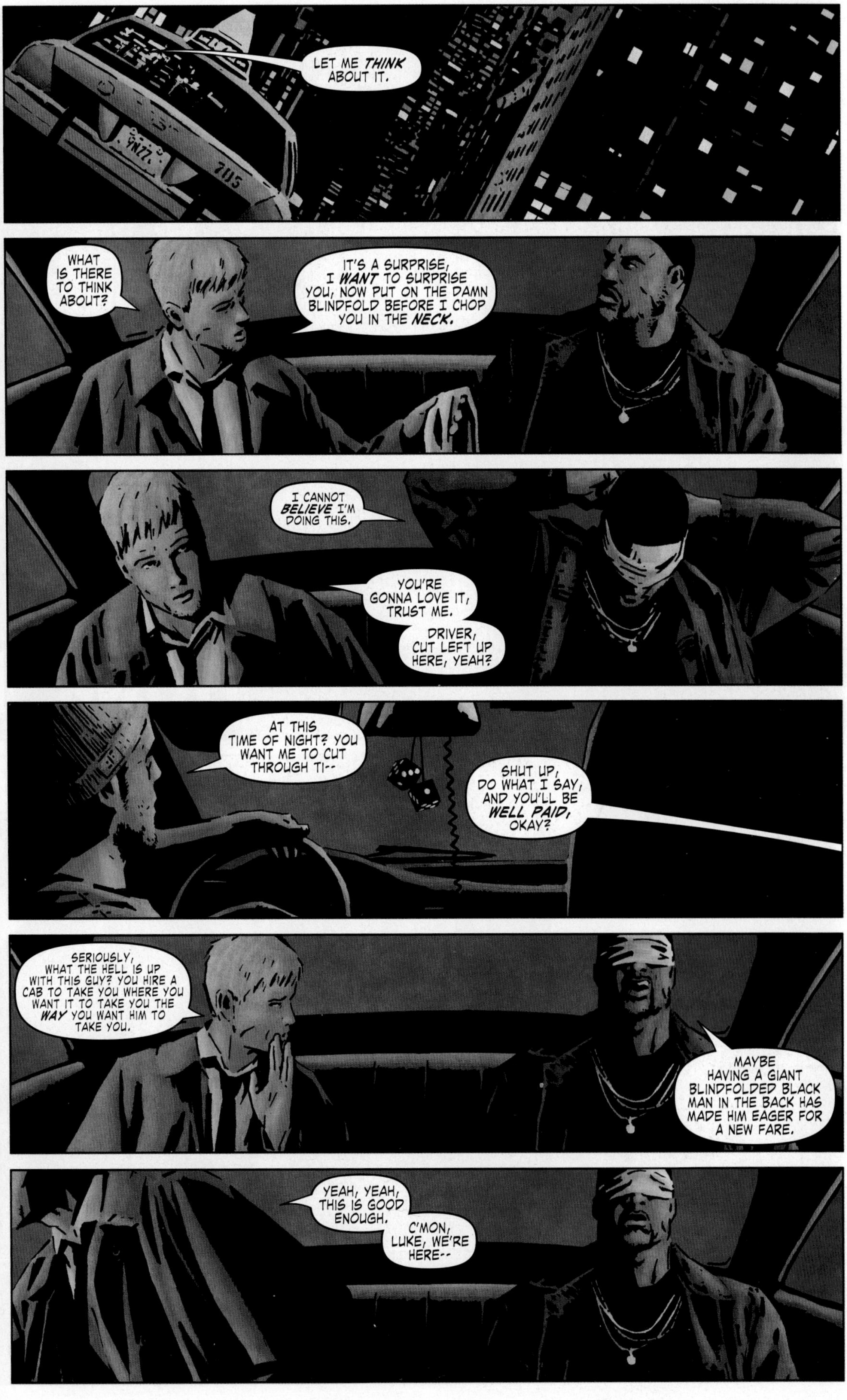
LET ME THINK ABOUT IT.
WHAT IS THERE TO THINK ABOUT?
IT'S A SURPRISE, I WANT TO SURPRISE YOU, NOW PUT ON THE DAMN BLINDFOLD BEFORE I CHOP YOU IN THE NECK.
I CANNOT BELIEVE I'M DOING THIS.
YOU'RE GONNA LOVE IT, TRUST ME.
DRIVER, CUT LEFT UP HERE, YEAH?
AT THIS TIME OF NIGHT? YOU WANT ME TO CUT THROUGH TI--
SHUT UP, DO WHAT I SAY, AND YOU'LL BE WELL PAID, OKAY?
SERIOUSLY, WHAT THE HELL IS UP WITH THIS GUY? YOU HIRE A CAB TO TAKE YOU WHERE YOU WANT IT TO TAKE YOU THE WAY YOU WANT HIM TO TAKE YOU.
MAYBE HAVING A GIANT BLINDFOLDED BLACK MAN IN THE BACK HAS MADE HIM EAGER FOR A NEW FARE.
YEAH, YEAH, THIS IS GOOD ENOUGH.
C'MON, LUKE, WE'RE HERE--

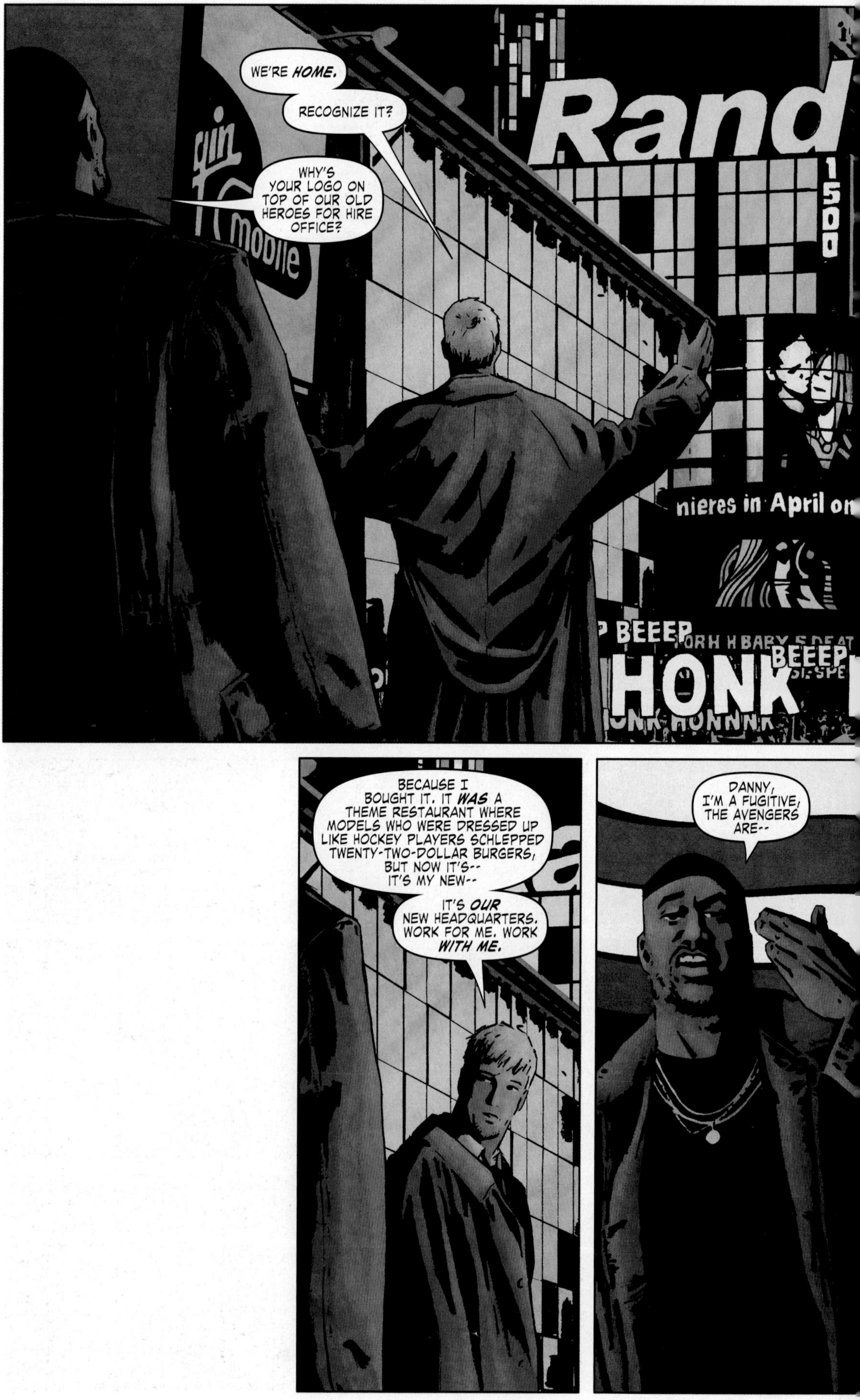
WE'RE *HOME.*
RECOGNIZE IT?
WHY'S YOUR LOGO ON TOP OF OUR OLD HEROES FOR HIRE OFFICE?
Rand
1500
nieres in April on
BEEEP
HONK
BEEEP
BECAUSE I BOUGHT IT. IT *WAS* A THEME RESTAURANT WHERE MODELS WHO WERE DRESSED UP LIKE HOCKEY PLAYERS SCHLEPPED TWENTY-TWO-DOLLAR BURGERS, BUT NOW IT'S-- IT'S MY NEW--
IT'S *OUR* NEW HEADQUARTERS. WORK FOR ME. WORK *WITH ME.*
DANNY, I'M A FUGITIVE, THE AVENGERS ARE--

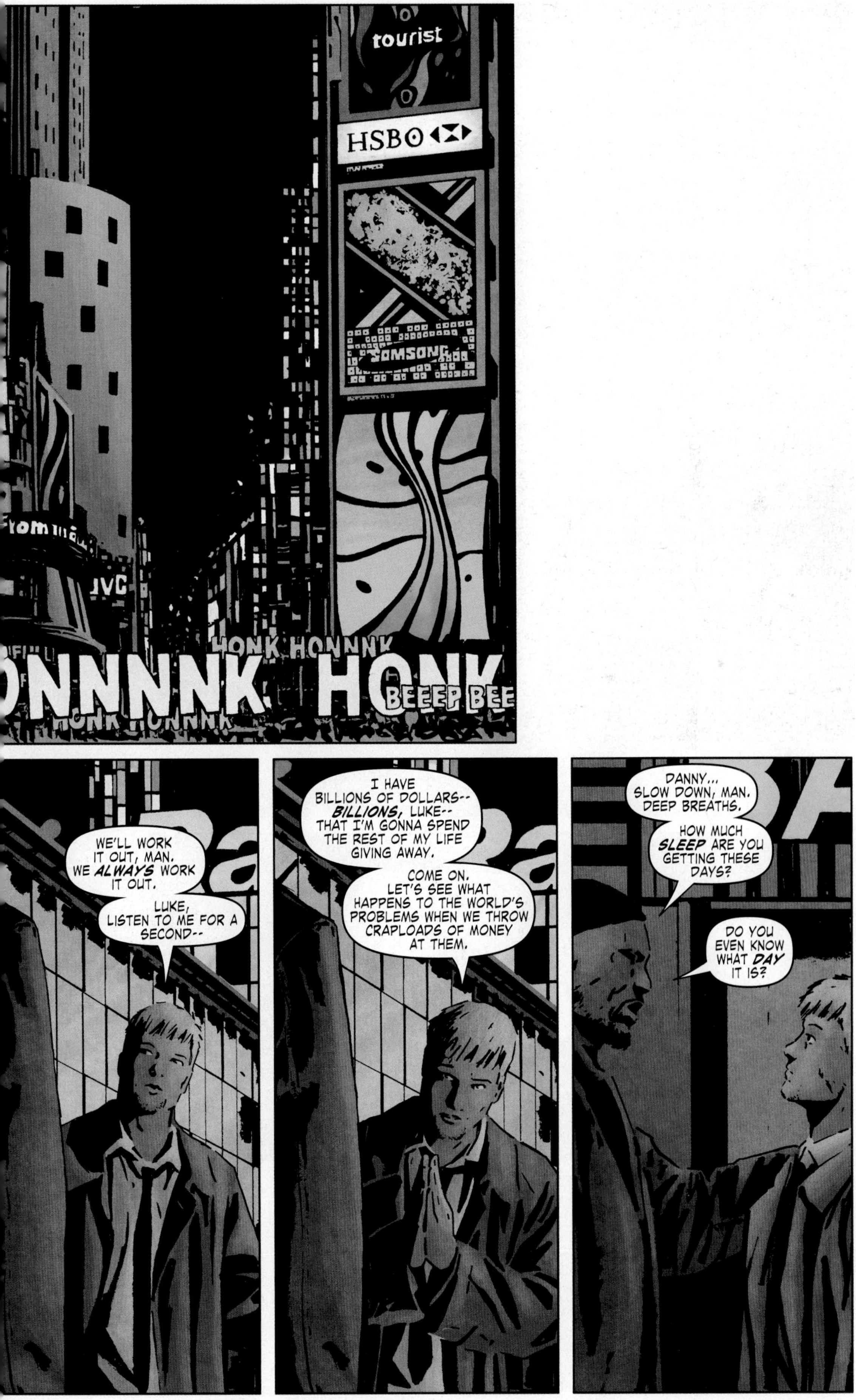
tourist
HSBO
SOMSONG
JVC
HONK HONNNK
ONNNNK. HONK
BEEEP BEE
WE'LL WORK IT OUT, MAN. WE *ALWAYS* WORK IT OUT.
LUKE, LISTEN TO ME FOR A SECOND--
I HAVE BILLIONS OF DOLLARS-- *BILLIONS,* LUKE-- THAT I'M GONNA SPEND THE REST OF MY LIFE GIVING AWAY.
COME ON. LET'S SEE WHAT HAPPENS TO THE WORLD'S PROBLEMS WHEN WE THROW CRAPLOADS OF MONEY AT THEM.
DANNY... SLOW DOWN, MAN. DEEP BREATHS.
HOW MUCH *SLEEP* ARE YOU GETTING THESE DAYS?
DO YOU EVEN KNOW WHAT *DAY* IT IS?

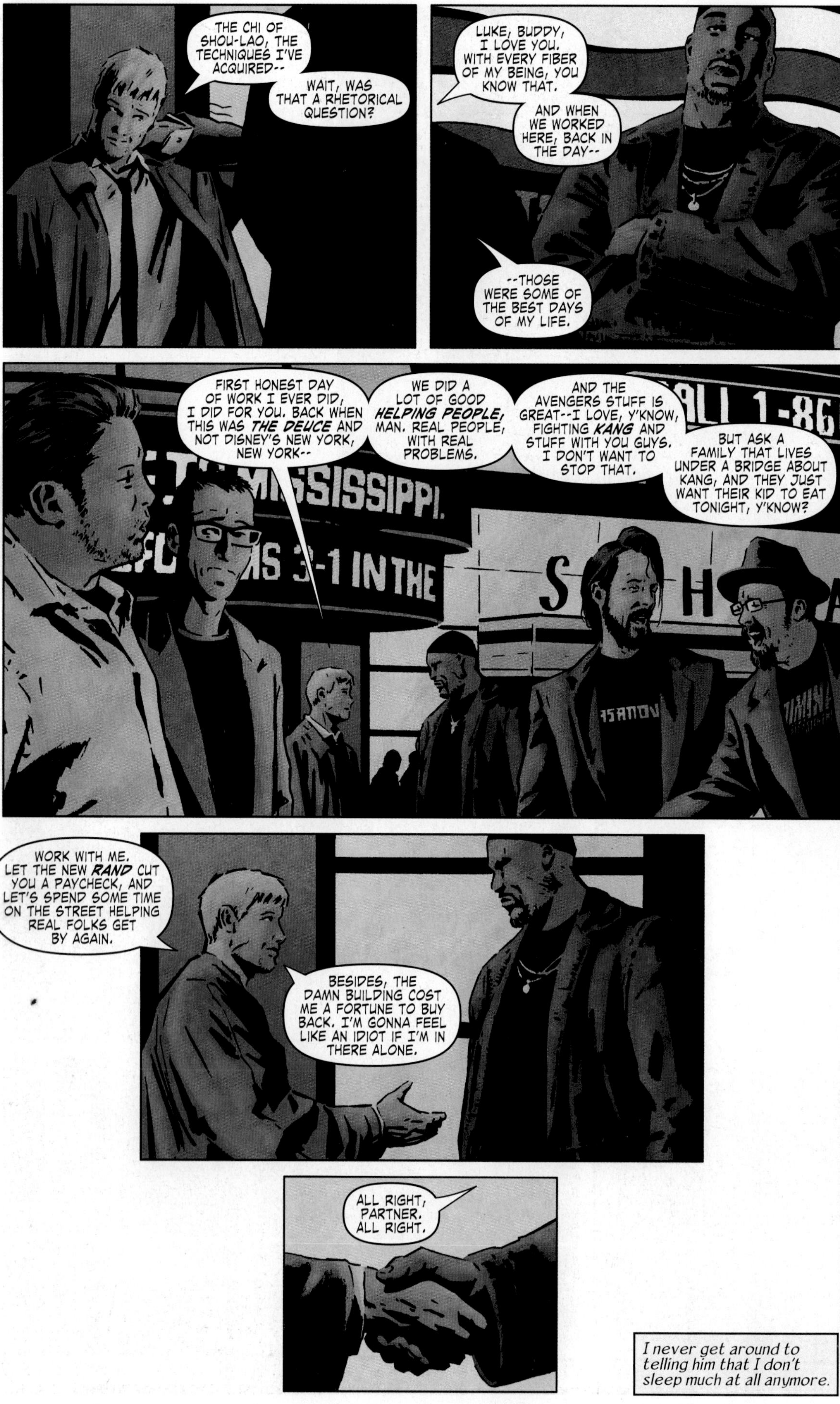
THE CHI OF SHOU-LAO, THE TECHNIQUES I'VE ACQUIRED--
WAIT, WAS THAT A RHETORICAL QUESTION?
LUKE, BUDDY, I LOVE YOU. WITH EVERY FIBER OF MY BEING, YOU KNOW THAT.
AND WHEN WE WORKED HERE, BACK IN THE DAY--
--THOSE WERE SOME OF THE BEST DAYS OF MY LIFE.
FIRST HONEST DAY OF WORK I EVER DID, I DID FOR YOU. BACK WHEN THIS WAS THE DEUCE AND NOT DISNEY'S NEW YORK, NEW YORK--
WE DID A LOT OF GOOD HELPING PEOPLE, MAN. REAL PEOPLE, WITH REAL PROBLEMS.
AND THE AVENGERS STUFF IS GREAT--I LOVE, Y'KNOW, FIGHTING KANG AND STUFF WITH YOU GUYS. I DON'T WANT TO STOP THAT.
BUT ASK A FAMILY THAT LIVES UNDER A BRIDGE ABOUT KANG, AND THEY JUST WANT THEIR KID TO EAT TONIGHT, Y'KNOW?
WORK WITH ME. LET THE NEW RAND CUT YOU A PAYCHECK, AND LET'S SPEND SOME TIME ON THE STREET HELPING REAL FOLKS GET BY AGAIN.
BESIDES, THE DAMN BUILDING COST ME A FORTUNE TO BUY BACK. I'M GONNA FEEL LIKE AN IDIOT IF I'M IN THERE ALONE.
ALL RIGHT, PARTNER. ALL RIGHT.
I never get around to telling him that I don't sleep much at all anymore.

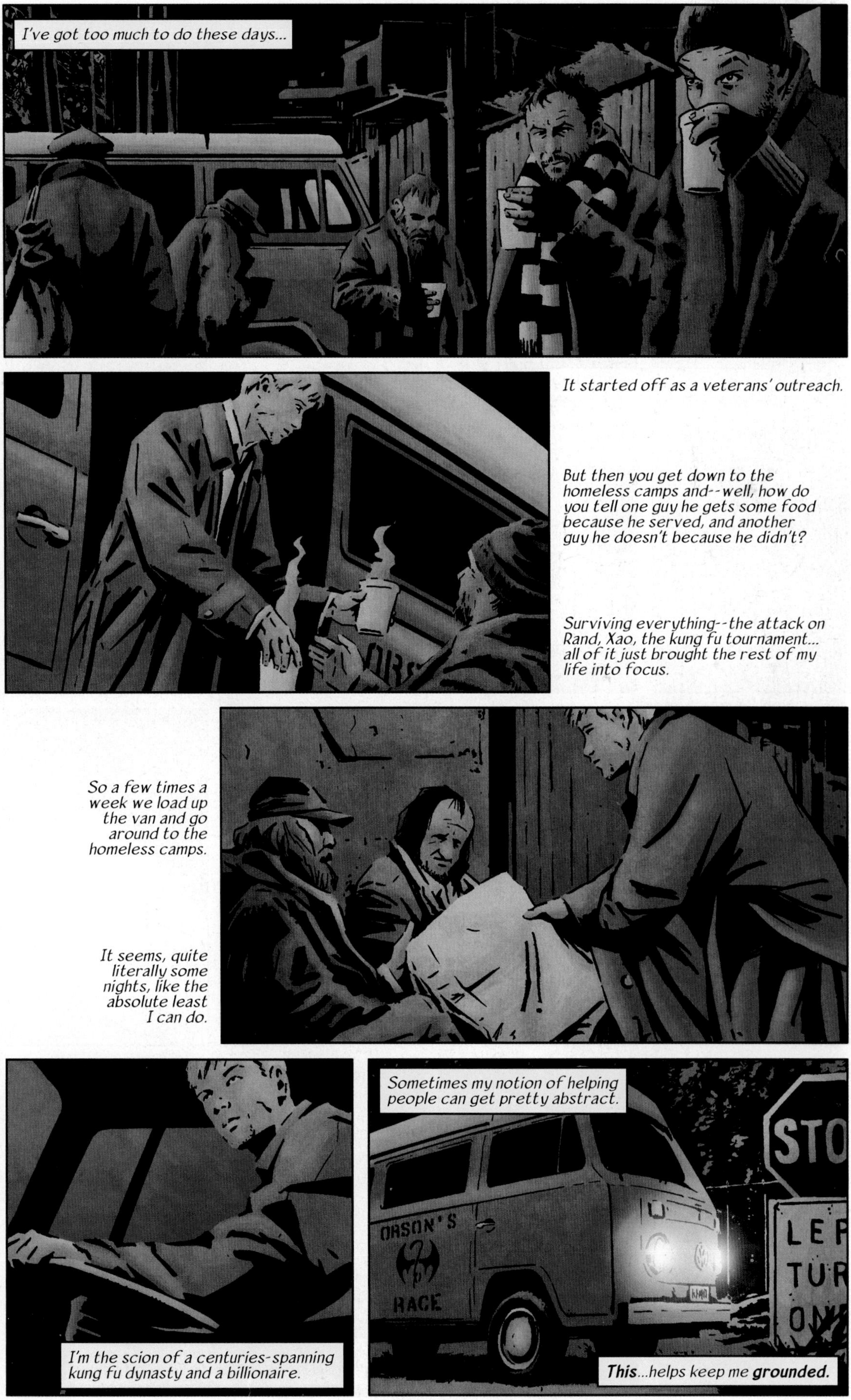

I've got too much to do these days...
It started off as a veterans' outreach.
But then you get down to the homeless camps and--well, how do you tell one guy he gets some food because he served, and another guy he doesn't because he didn't?
Surviving everything--the attack on Rand, Xao, the kung fu tournament... all of it just brought the rest of my life into focus.
So a few times a week we load up the van and go around to the homeless camps.
It seems, quite literally some nights, like the absolute least I can do.
I'm the scion of a centuries-spanning kung fu dynasty and a billionaire.
Sometimes my notion of helping people can get pretty abstract.
ORSON'S
RACE
This...helps keep me grounded.

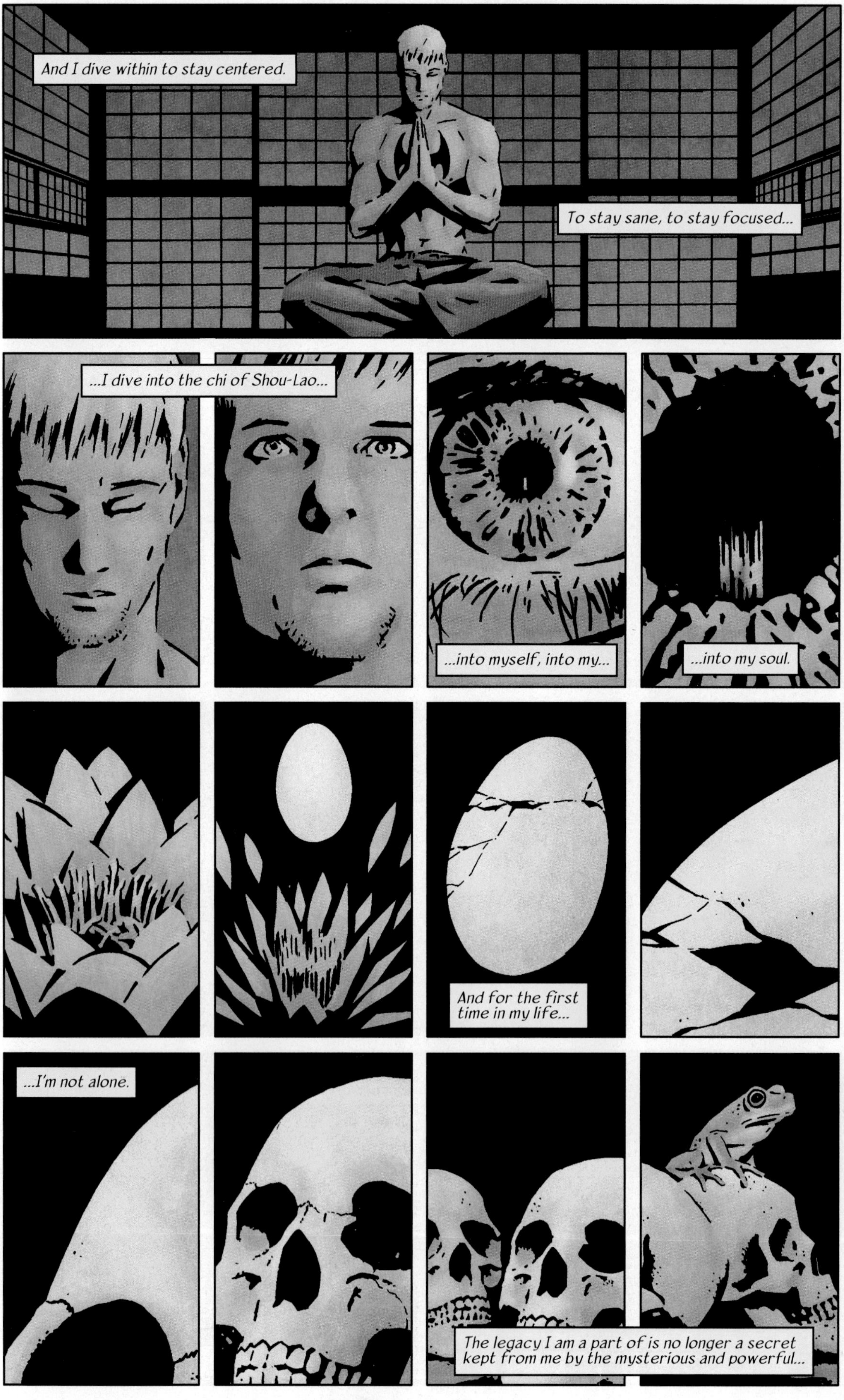
And I dive within to stay centered.
To stay sane, to stay focused...
...I dive into the chi of Shou-Lao...
...into myself, into my...
...into my soul.
And for the first time in my life...
...I'm not alone.
The legacy I am a part of is no longer a secret kept from me by the mysterious and powerful...

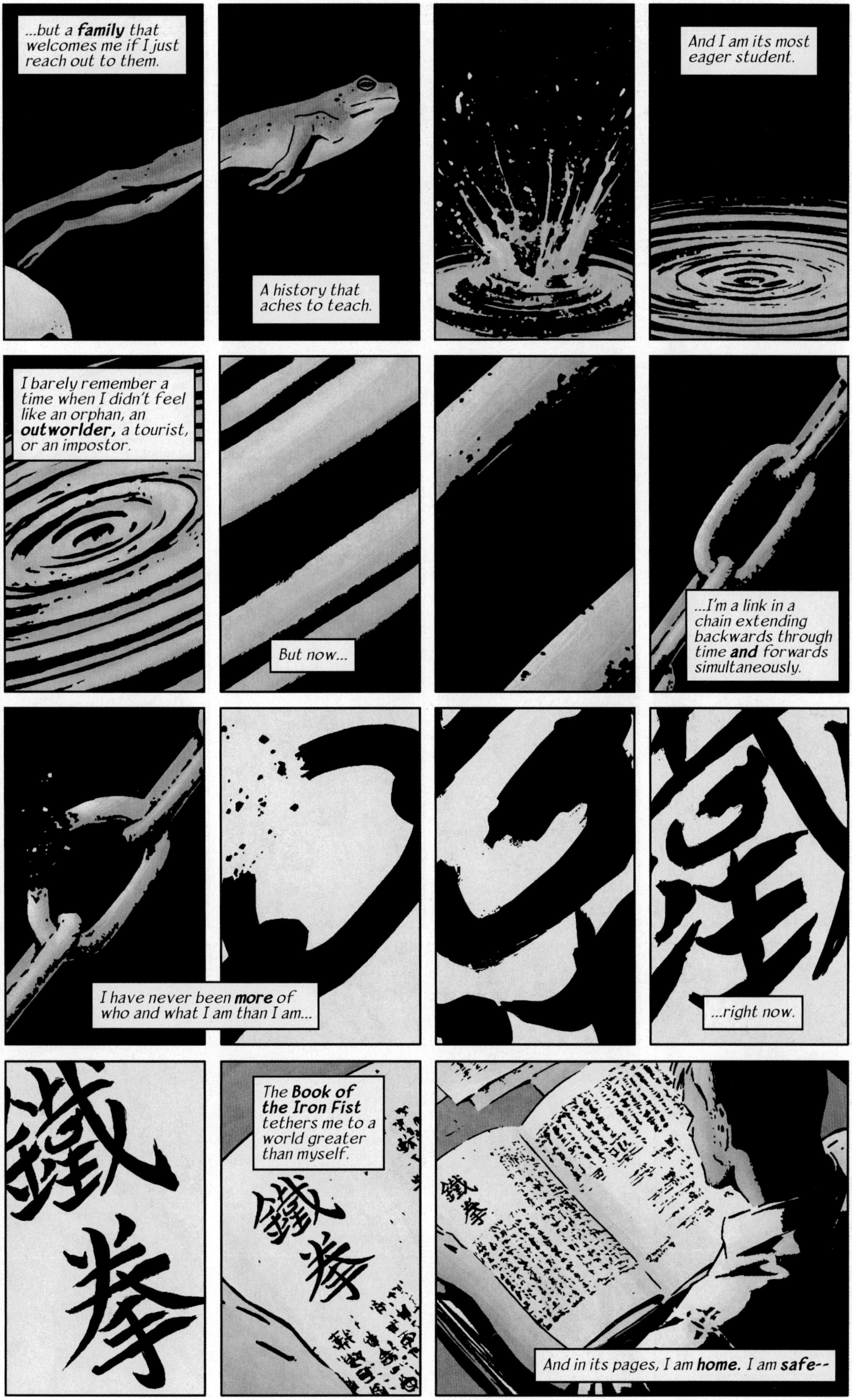
...but a **family** that welcomes me if I just reach out to them.
A history that aches to teach.
And I am its most eager student.
I barely remember a time when I didn't feel like an orphan, an **outworlder,** a tourist, or an impostor.
But now...
...I'm a link in a chain extending backwards through time **and** forwards simultaneously.
I have never been **more** of who and what I am than I am...
...right now.
鐵拳
The **Book of the Iron Fist** tethers me to a world greater than myself.
鐵拳
And in its pages, I am **home.** I am **safe--**

WHOA.

WAIT.

C'MON C'MON C'MON--

--DAMMIT. NO.

NO NO NO NO--

Stupid--

Stupid, stupid--

How could I have missed this before? How could I not have caught this--?

Every Iron Fist--

BANG-WEN 1827-1860

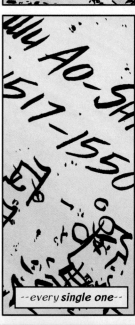

AO-SH 1517-1550

--every single one--

MING-TIAN 1194-1227

--even back to the very first--

They've all died at thirty-three.

The same age Orson was when he went missing.

DANNY...?

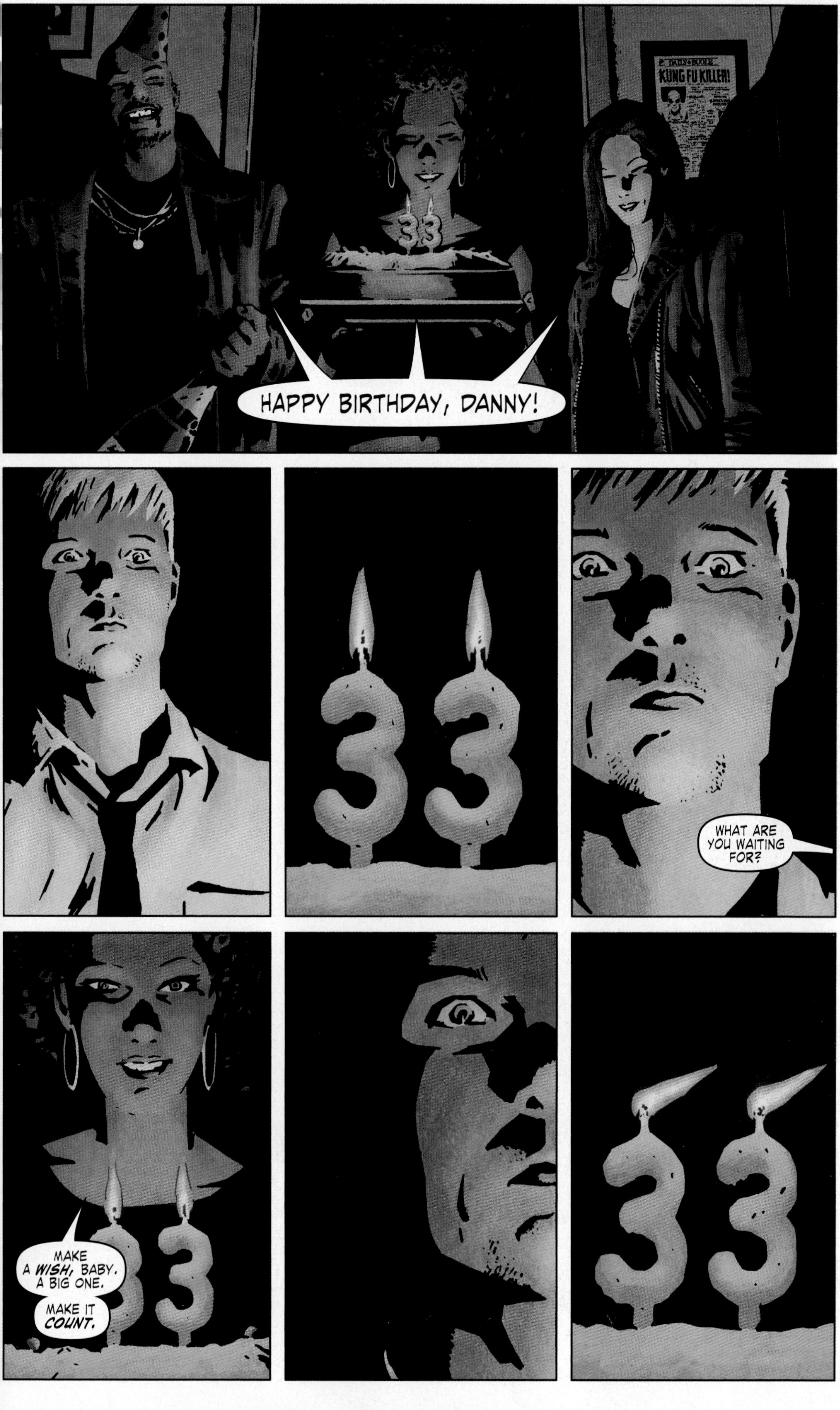
DAILY BUGLE
KUNG FU KILLER!
HAPPY BIRTHDAY, DANNY!
WHAT ARE YOU WAITING FOR?
MAKE A WISH, BABY. A BIG ONE.
MAKE IT COUNT.

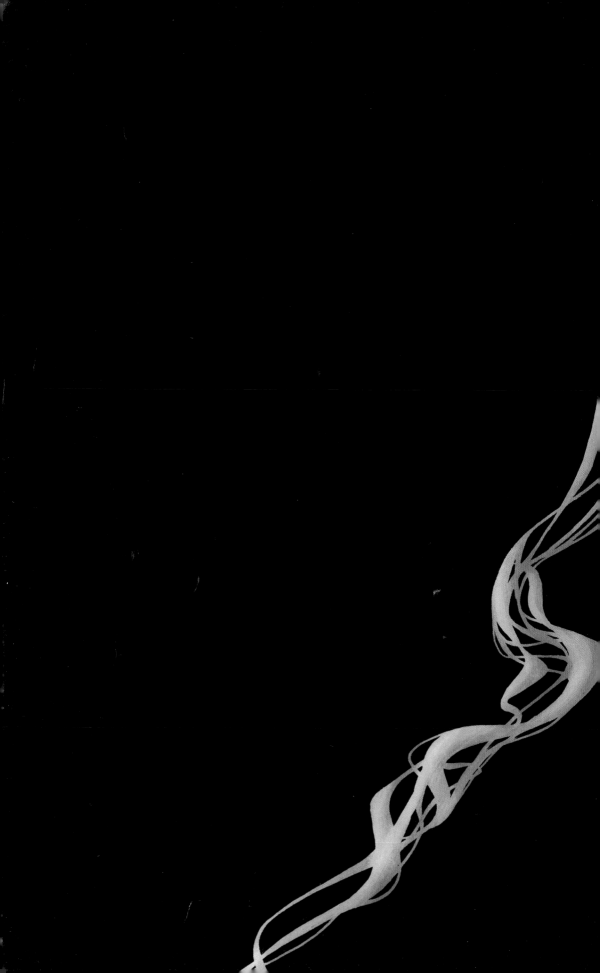

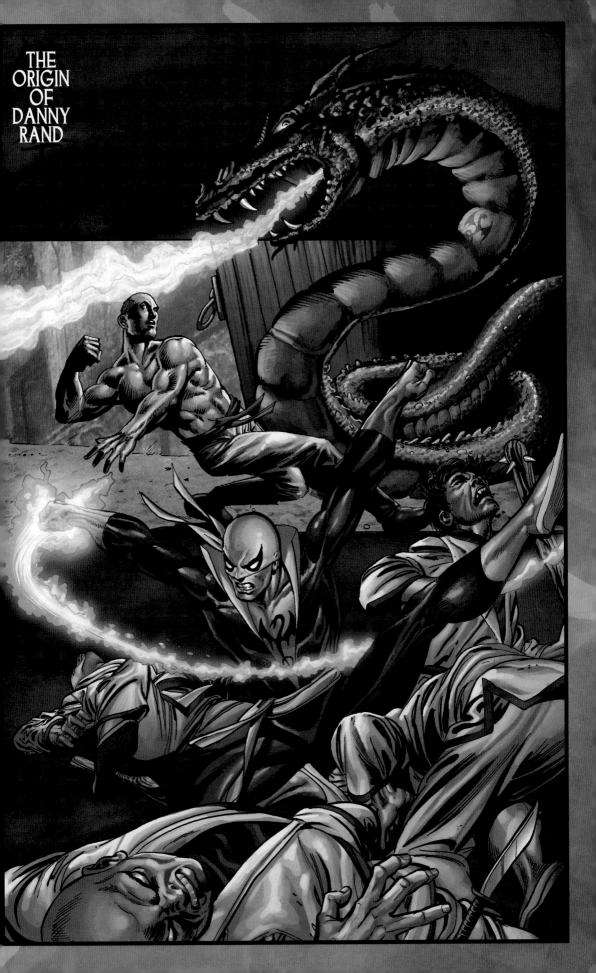

THE
ORIGIN
OF
DANNY
RAND

THE IMMORTAL IRON FIST

THE ORIGIN OF DANNY RAND

Framing Sequence
Writer: Matt Fraction
Artist: Kano
Letterer: Dave Lanphear

Chapter 1: "The Fury of Iron Fist"
Writer: Roy Thomas
Penciler: Gil Kane

Chapter 2: "Heart of the Dragon"
Writer: Len Wein
Penciler: Larry Hama

Inker: Dick Giordano
Colorist: Sotocolor's A. Crossley
Letterer: L.P. Gregory

Cover Artists: Gil Kane, Larry Hama & Rain Beredo

Special Thanks to Warren Simons & Alejandro Arbona

Editor: Jeff Youngquist
Assistant Editor: Cory Levine
Production: Spring Hoteling & Nelson Ribeiro
Select Art Reconstruction: Tom Smith
Senior Vice President of Sales: David Gabriel

Editor in Chief: Joe Quesada
Publisher: Dan Buckley

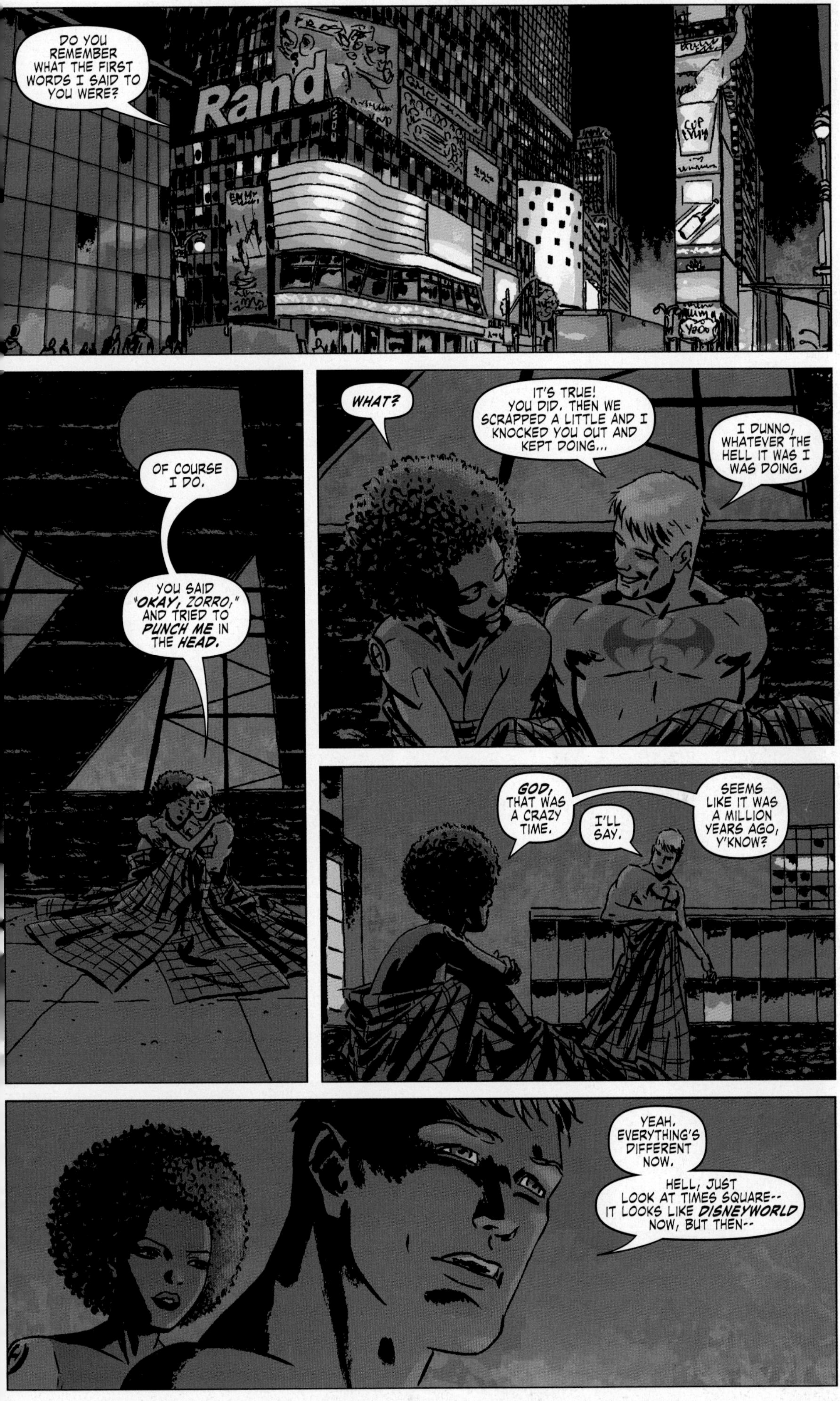
DO YOU REMEMBER WHAT THE FIRST WORDS I SAID TO YOU WERE?
Rand
OF COURSE I DO.
YOU SAID "OKAY, ZORRO," AND TRIED TO PUNCH ME IN THE HEAD.
WHAT?
IT'S TRUE! YOU DID. THEN WE SCRAPPED A LITTLE AND I KNOCKED YOU OUT AND KEPT DOING...
I DUNNO, WHATEVER THE HELL IT WAS I WAS DOING.
GOD, THAT WAS A CRAZY TIME.
I'LL SAY.
SEEMS LIKE IT WAS A MILLION YEARS AGO, Y'KNOW?
YEAH. EVERYTHING'S DIFFERENT NOW.
HELL, JUST LOOK AT TIMES SQUARE-- IT LOOKS LIKE DISNEYWORLD NOW, BUT THEN--

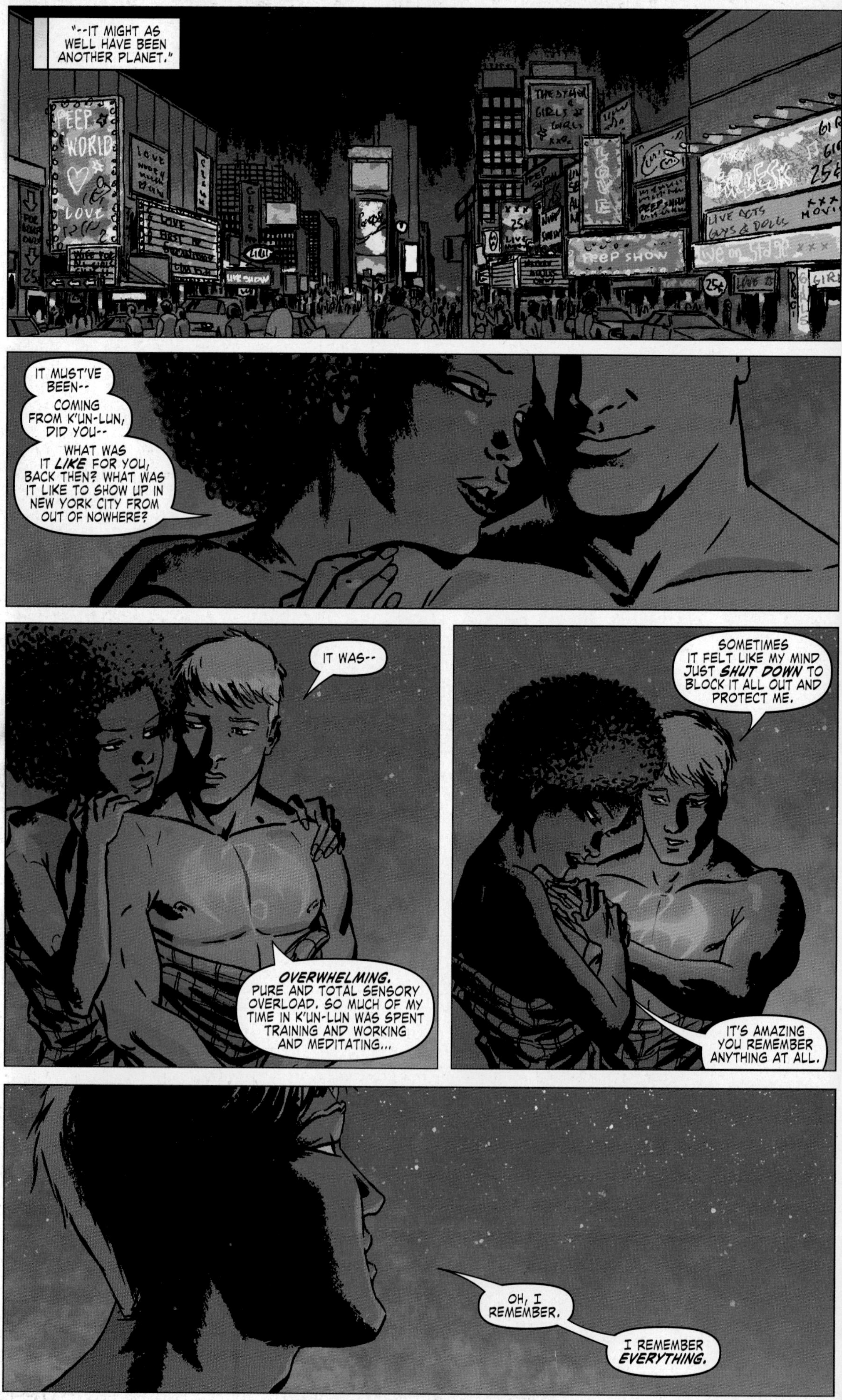
"--IT MIGHT AS WELL HAVE BEEN ANOTHER PLANET."
PEEP WORLD
PEEP SHOW
LIVE SHOW
IT MUST'VE BEEN--
COMING FROM K'UN-LUN, DID YOU--
WHAT WAS IT *LIKE* FOR YOU, BACK THEN? WHAT WAS IT LIKE TO SHOW UP IN NEW YORK CITY FROM OUT OF NOWHERE?
IT WAS--
OVERWHELMING. PURE AND TOTAL SENSORY OVERLOAD. SO MUCH OF MY TIME IN K'UN-LUN WAS SPENT TRAINING AND WORKING AND MEDITATING...
SOMETIMES IT FELT LIKE MY MIND JUST *SHUT DOWN* TO BLOCK IT ALL OUT AND PROTECT ME.
IT'S AMAZING YOU REMEMBER ANYTHING AT ALL.
OH, I REMEMBER.
I REMEMBER *EVERYTHING.*

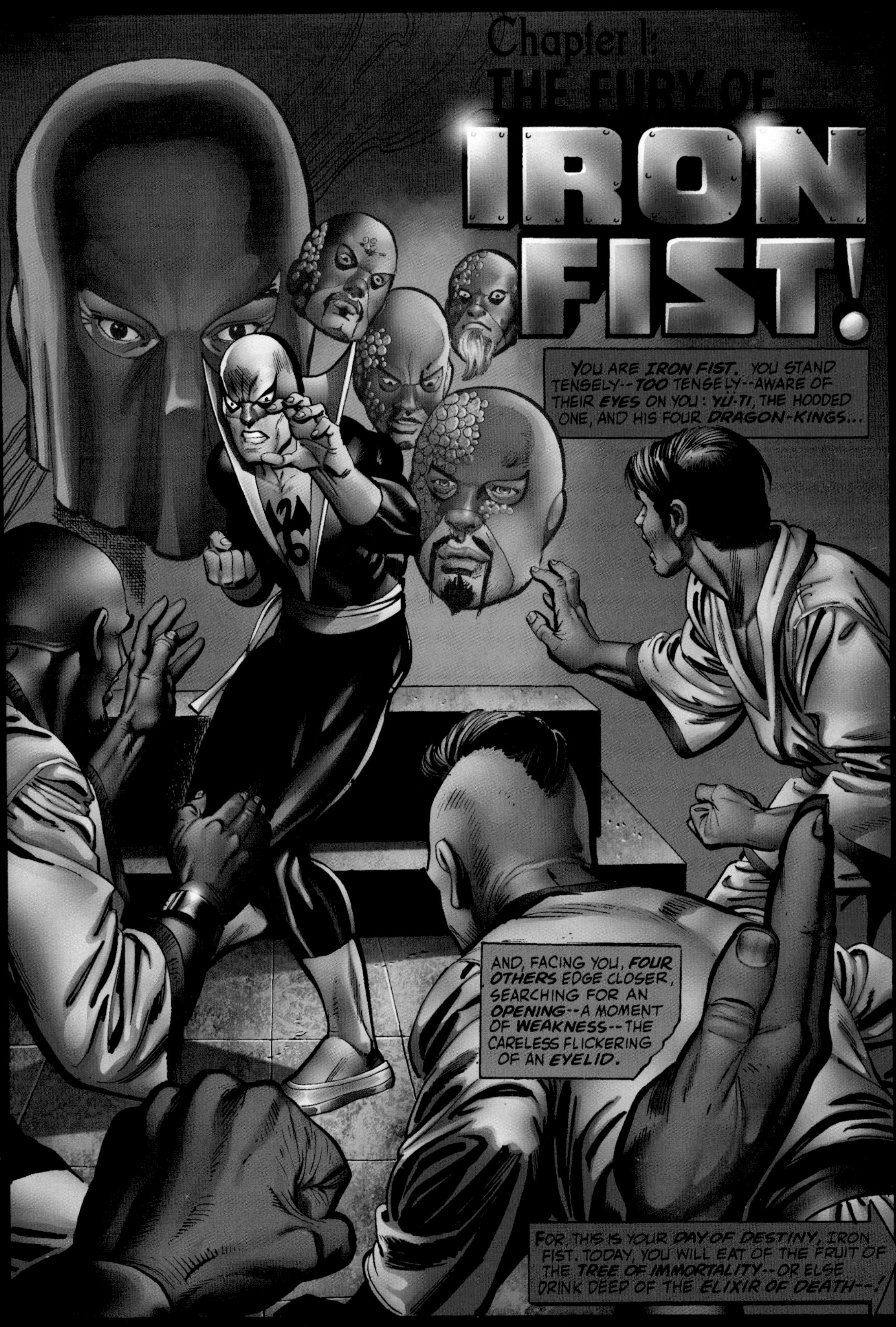
Chapter 1:
THE FURY OF
IRON FIST!
YOU ARE IRON FIST. YOU STAND TENSELY--TOO TENSELY--AWARE OF THEIR EYES ON YOU: YÜ-TI, THE HOODED ONE, AND HIS FOUR DRAGON-KINGS...
AND, FACING YOU, FOUR OTHERS EDGE CLOSER, SEARCHING FOR AN OPENING--A MOMENT OF WEAKNESS--THE CARELESS FLICKERING OF AN EYELID.
FOR, THIS IS YOUR DAY OF DESTINY, IRON FIST. TODAY, YOU WILL EAT OF THE FRUIT OF THE TREE OF IMMORTALITY--OR ELSE DRINK DEEP OF THE ELIXIR OF DEATH--!

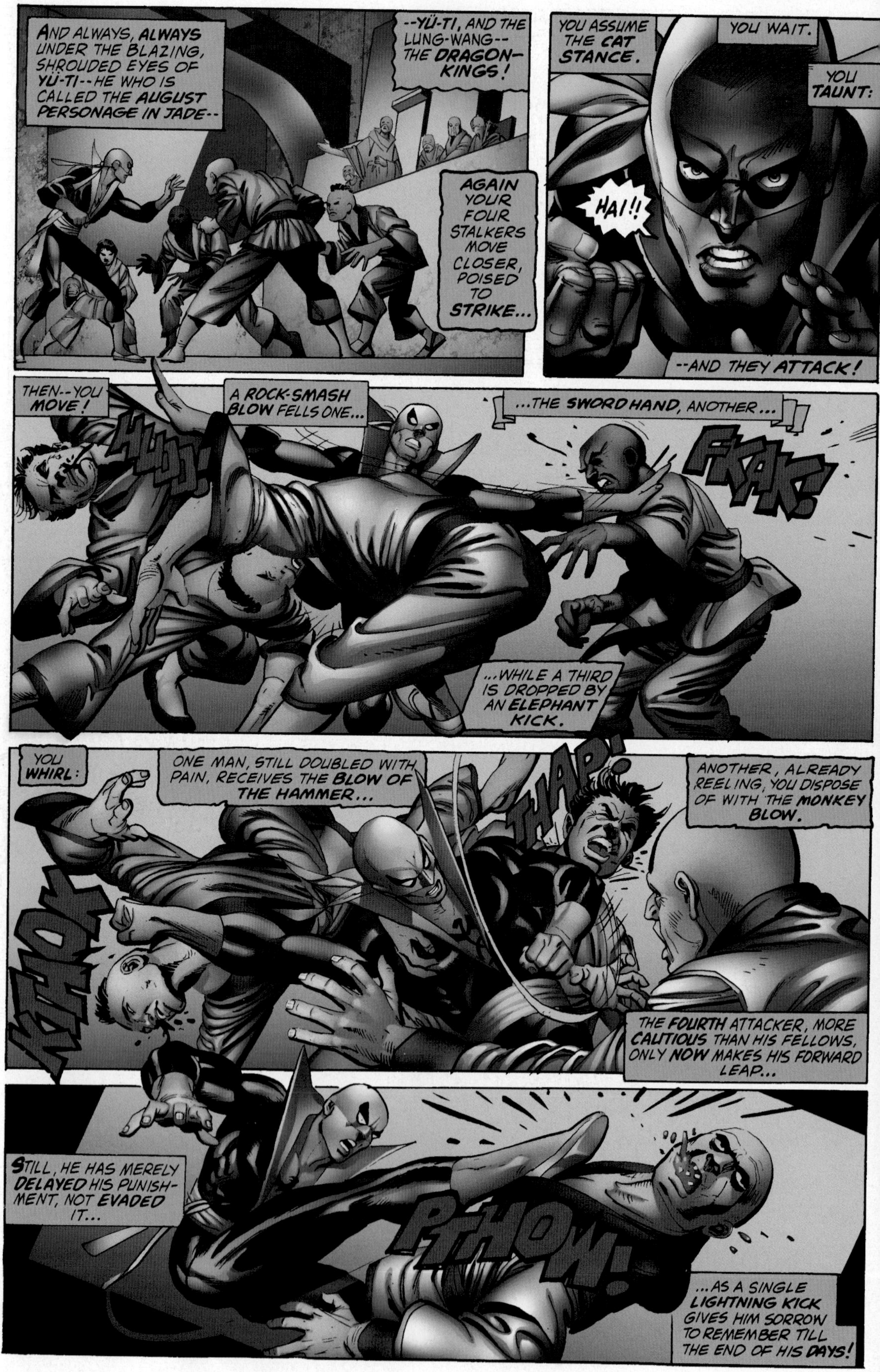

AND ALWAYS, ALWAYS UNDER THE BLAZING, SHROUDED EYES OF YÜ-TI--HE WHO IS CALLED THE AUGUST PERSONAGE IN JADE--
--YÜ-TI, AND THE LUNG-WANG--THE DRAGON-KINGS!
AGAIN YOUR FOUR STALKERS MOVE CLOSER, POISED TO STRIKE...
YOU ASSUME THE CAT STANCE.
YOU WAIT.
YOU TAUNT:
HAI!!
--AND THEY ATTACK!
THEN--YOU MOVE!
A ROCK-SMASH BLOW FELLS ONE...
...THE SWORD HAND, ANOTHER...
FKAK!
...WHILE A THIRD IS DROPPED BY AN ELEPHANT KICK.
YOU WHIRL:
ONE MAN, STILL DOUBLED WITH PAIN, RECEIVES THE BLOW OF THE HAMMER...
THAP!
ANOTHER, ALREADY REELING, YOU DISPOSE OF WITH THE MONKEY BLOW.
KTHOK!
THE FOURTH ATTACKER, MORE CAUTIOUS THAN HIS FELLOWS, ONLY NOW MAKES HIS FORWARD LEAP...
STILL, HE HAS MERELY DELAYED HIS PUNISHMENT, NOT EVADED IT...
PTHOW!
...AS A SINGLE LIGHTNING KICK GIVES HIM SORROW TO REMEMBER TILL THE END OF HIS DAYS!

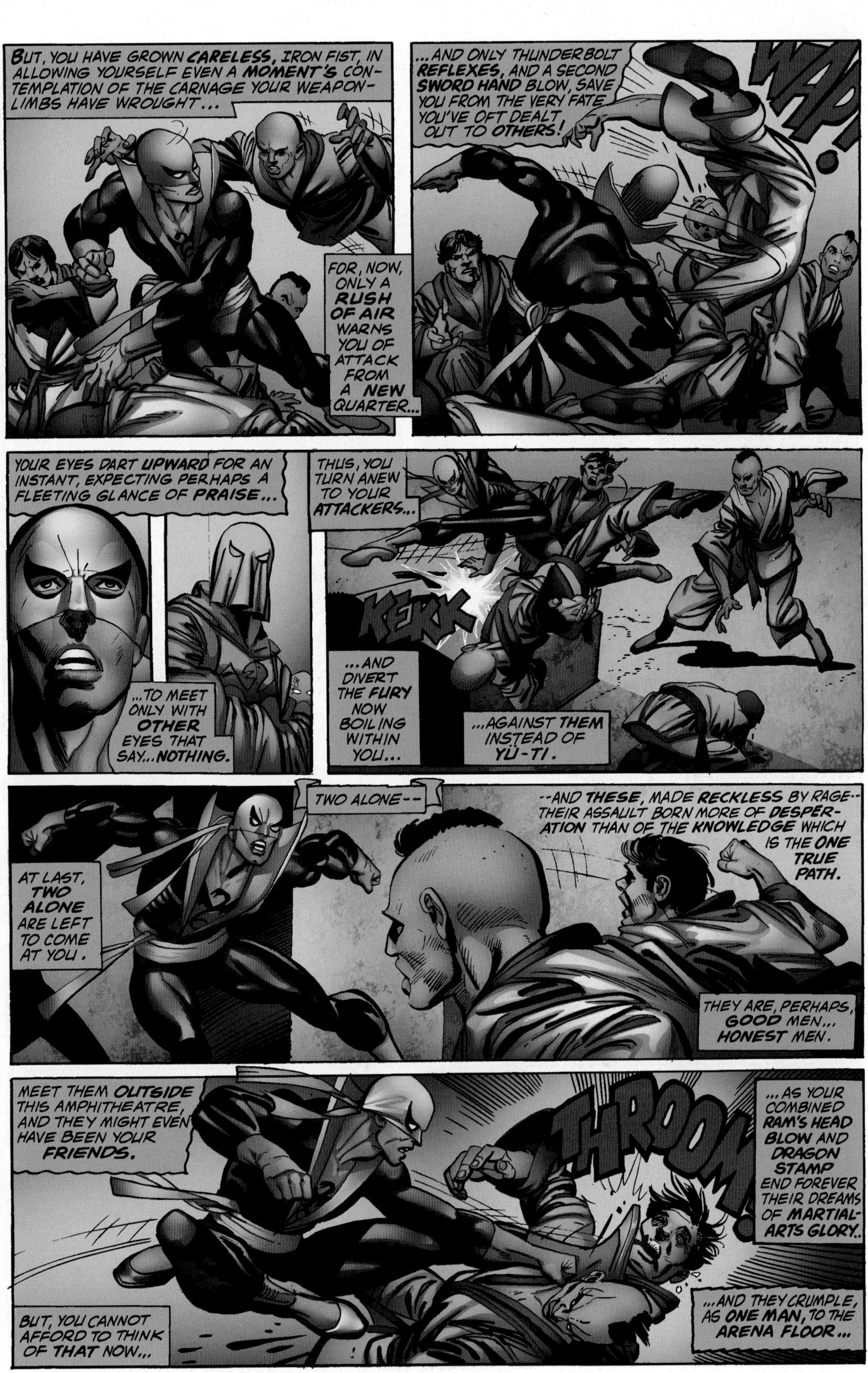
BUT, YOU HAVE GROWN CARELESS, IRON FIST, IN ALLOWING YOURSELF EVEN A MOMENT'S CONTEMPLATION OF THE CARNAGE YOUR WEAPON-LIMBS HAVE WROUGHT...
FOR, NOW, ONLY A RUSH OF AIR WARNS YOU OF ATTACK FROM A NEW QUARTER...
...AND ONLY THUNDERBOLT REFLEXES, AND A SECOND SWORD HAND BLOW, SAVE YOU FROM THE VERY FATE YOU'VE OFT DEALT OUT TO OTHERS!
WAP!
YOUR EYES DART UPWARD FOR AN INSTANT, EXPECTING PERHAPS A FLEETING GLANCE OF PRAISE...
...TO MEET ONLY WITH OTHER EYES THAT SAY...NOTHING.
THUS, YOU TURN ANEW TO YOUR ATTACKERS...
KEKK
...AND DIVERT THE FURY NOW BOILING WITHIN YOU...
...AGAINST THEM INSTEAD OF YÜ-TI.
TWO ALONE--
AT LAST, TWO ALONE ARE LEFT TO COME AT YOU.
--AND THESE, MADE RECKLESS BY RAGE--THEIR ASSAULT BORN MORE OF DESPERATION THAN OF THE KNOWLEDGE WHICH IS THE ONE TRUE PATH.
THEY ARE, PERHAPS, GOOD MEN... HONEST MEN.
MEET THEM OUTSIDE THIS AMPHITHEATRE, AND THEY MIGHT EVEN HAVE BEEN YOUR FRIENDS.
THROOM!
...AS YOUR COMBINED RAM'S HEAD BLOW AND DRAGON STAMP END FOREVER THEIR DREAMS OF MARTIAL-ARTS GLORY...
BUT, YOU CANNOT AFFORD TO THINK OF THAT NOW...
...AND THEY CRUMPLE, AS ONE MAN, TO THE ARENA FLOOR...

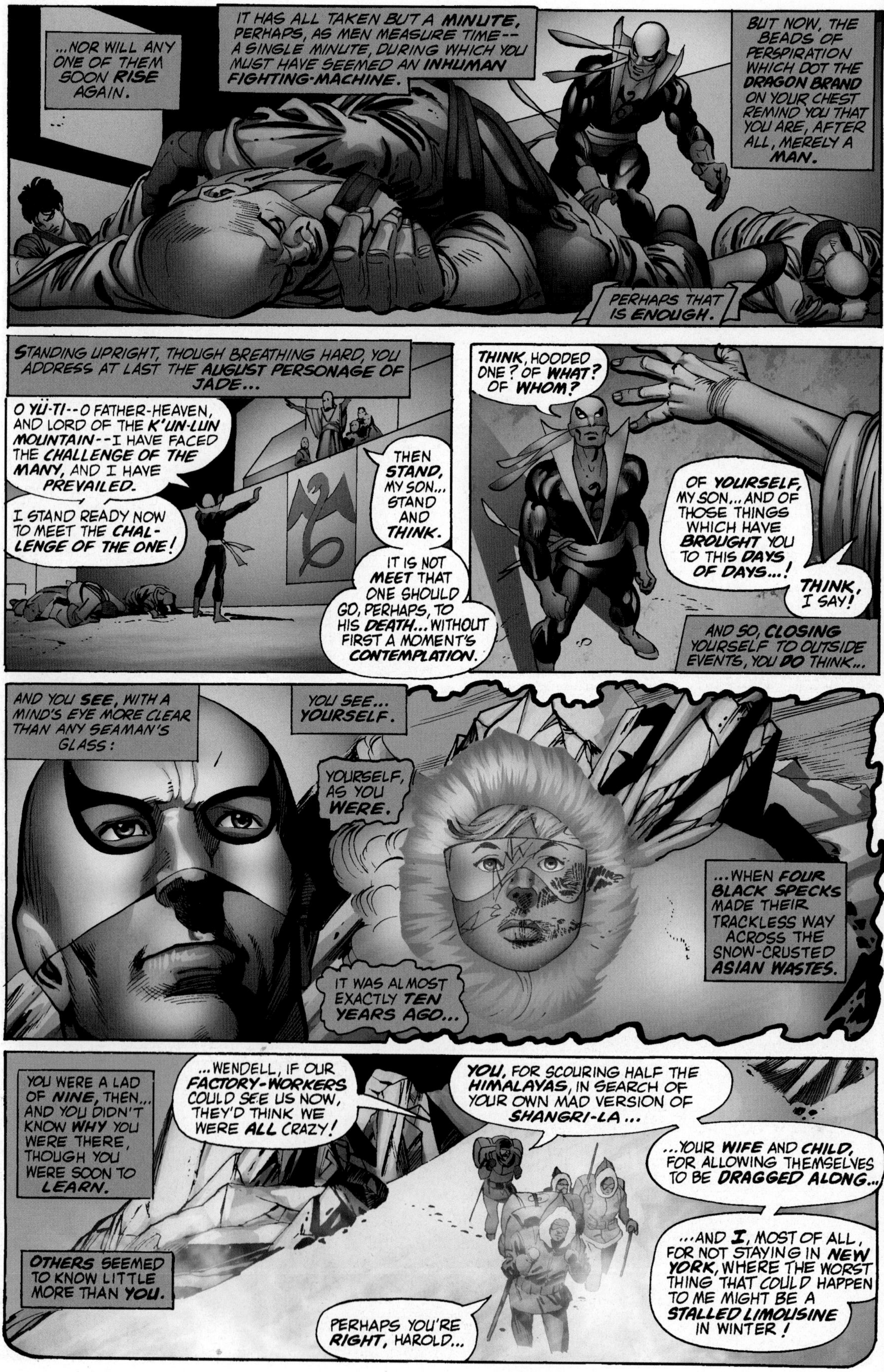
...NOR WILL ANY ONE OF THEM SOON RISE AGAIN.
IT HAS ALL TAKEN BUT A MINUTE, PERHAPS, AS MEN MEASURE TIME-- A SINGLE MINUTE, DURING WHICH YOU MUST HAVE SEEMED AN INHUMAN FIGHTING-MACHINE.
BUT NOW, THE BEADS OF PERSPIRATION WHICH DOT THE DRAGON BRAND ON YOUR CHEST REMIND YOU THAT YOU ARE, AFTER ALL, MERELY A MAN.
PERHAPS THAT IS ENOUGH.
STANDING UPRIGHT, THOUGH BREATHING HARD, YOU ADDRESS AT LAST THE AUGUST PERSONAGE OF JADE...
O YÜ-TI--O FATHER-HEAVEN, AND LORD OF THE K'UN-LUN MOUNTAIN--I HAVE FACED THE CHALLENGE OF THE MANY, AND I HAVE PREVAILED.
I STAND READY NOW TO MEET THE CHALLENGE OF THE ONE!
THEN STAND, MY SON... STAND AND THINK.
IT IS NOT MEET THAT ONE SHOULD GO, PERHAPS, TO HIS DEATH... WITHOUT FIRST A MOMENT'S CONTEMPLATION.
THINK, HOODED ONE? OF WHAT? OF WHOM?
OF YOURSELF, MY SON... AND OF THOSE THINGS WHICH HAVE BROUGHT YOU TO THIS DAYS OF DAYS...!
THINK, I SAY!
AND SO, CLOSING YOURSELF TO OUTSIDE EVENTS, YOU DO THINK...
AND YOU SEE, WITH A MIND'S EYE MORE CLEAR THAN ANY SEAMAN'S GLASS:
YOU SEE... YOURSELF.
YOURSELF, AS YOU WERE.
IT WAS ALMOST EXACTLY TEN YEARS AGO...
...WHEN FOUR BLACK SPECKS MADE THEIR TRACKLESS WAY ACROSS THE SNOW-CRUSTED ASIAN WASTES.
YOU WERE A LAD OF NINE, THEN... AND YOU DIDN'T KNOW WHY YOU WERE THERE, THOUGH YOU WERE SOON TO LEARN.
...WENDELL, IF OUR FACTORY-WORKERS COULD SEE US NOW, THEY'D THINK WE WERE ALL CRAZY!
YOU, FOR SCOURING HALF THE HIMALAYAS, IN SEARCH OF YOUR OWN MAD VERSION OF SHANGRI-LA...
...YOUR WIFE AND CHILD, FOR ALLOWING THEMSELVES TO BE DRAGGED ALONG...
...AND I, MOST OF ALL, FOR NOT STAYING IN NEW YORK, WHERE THE WORST THING THAT COULD HAPPEN TO ME MIGHT BE A STALLED LIMOUSINE IN WINTER!
OTHERS SEEMED TO KNOW LITTLE MORE THAN YOU.
PERHAPS YOU'RE RIGHT, HAROLD...

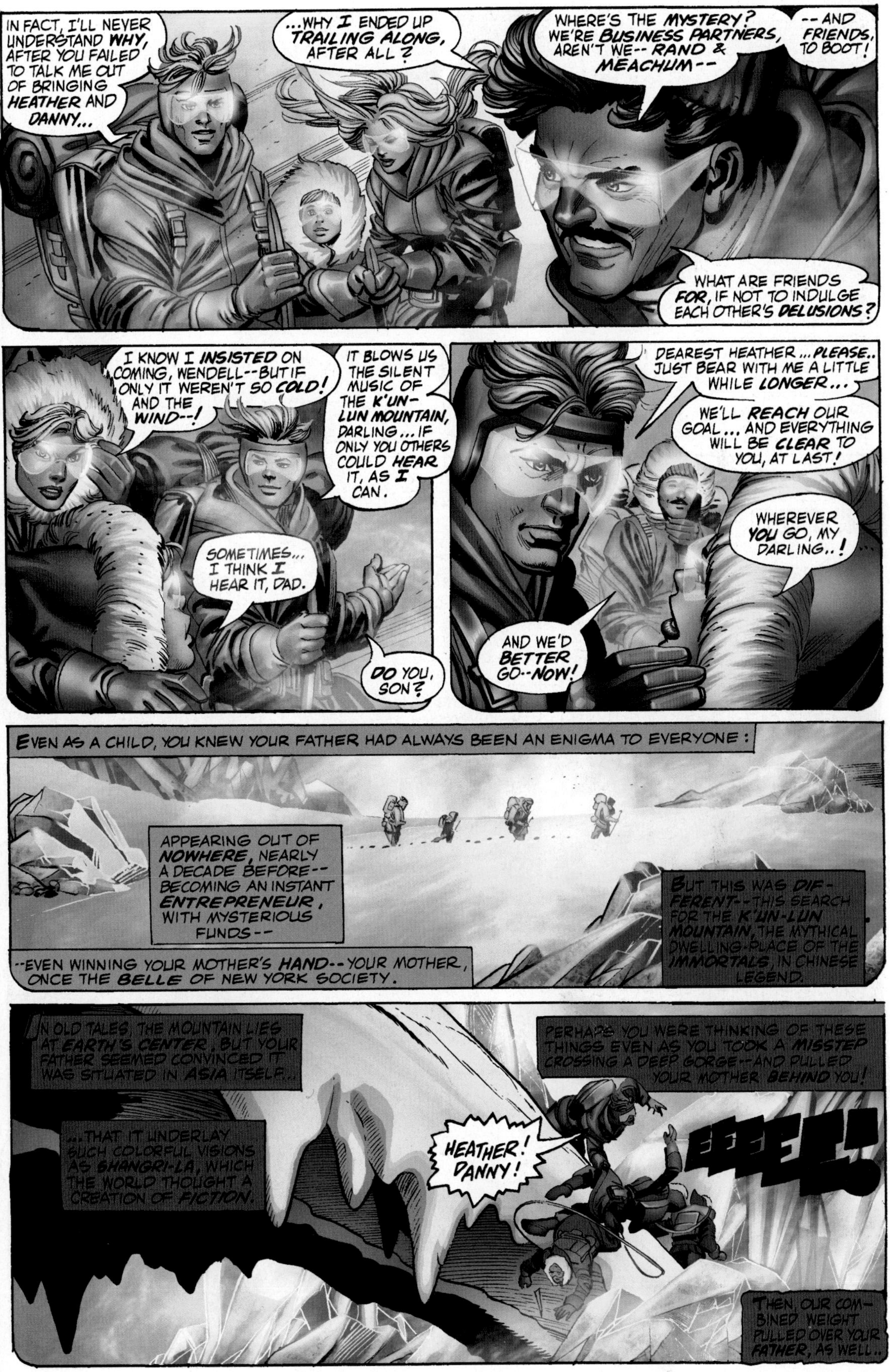

IN FACT, I'LL NEVER UNDERSTAND WHY, AFTER YOU FAILED TO TALK ME OUT OF BRINGING HEATHER AND DANNY...
...WHY I ENDED UP TRAILING ALONG, AFTER ALL?
WHERE'S THE MYSTERY? WE'RE BUSINESS PARTNERS, AREN'T WE-- RAND & MEACHUM--
--AND FRIENDS, TO BOOT!
WHAT ARE FRIENDS FOR, IF NOT TO INDULGE EACH OTHER'S DELUSIONS?
I KNOW I INSISTED ON COMING, WENDELL--BUT IF ONLY IT WEREN'T SO COLD! AND THE WIND--!
IT BLOWS US THE SILENT MUSIC OF THE K'UN-LUN MOUNTAIN, DARLING... IF ONLY YOU OTHERS COULD HEAR IT, AS I CAN.
SOMETIMES... I THINK I HEAR IT, DAD.
DO YOU, SON?
DEAREST HEATHER... PLEASE.. JUST BEAR WITH ME A LITTLE WHILE LONGER...
WE'LL REACH OUR GOAL... AND EVERYTHING WILL BE CLEAR TO YOU, AT LAST!
WHEREVER YOU GO, MY DARLING..!
AND WE'D BETTER GO--NOW!
EVEN AS A CHILD, YOU KNEW YOUR FATHER HAD ALWAYS BEEN AN ENIGMA TO EVERYONE:
APPEARING OUT OF NOWHERE, NEARLY A DECADE BEFORE-- BECOMING AN INSTANT ENTREPRENEUR, WITH MYSTERIOUS FUNDS--
--EVEN WINNING YOUR MOTHER'S HAND--YOUR MOTHER, ONCE THE BELLE OF NEW YORK SOCIETY.
BUT THIS WAS DIFFERENT--THIS SEARCH FOR THE K'UN-LUN MOUNTAIN, THE MYTHICAL DWELLING-PLACE OF THE IMMORTALS, IN CHINESE LEGEND.
IN OLD TALES, THE MOUNTAIN LIES AT EARTH'S CENTER, BUT YOUR FATHER SEEMED CONVINCED IT WAS SITUATED IN ASIA ITSELF...
...THAT IT UNDERLAY SUCH COLORFUL VISIONS AS SHANGRI-LA, WHICH THE WORLD THOUGHT A CREATION OF FICTION.
PERHAPS YOU WERE THINKING OF THESE THINGS EVEN AS YOU TOOK A MISSTEP CROSSING A DEEP GORGE--AND PULLED YOUR MOTHER BEHIND YOU!
HEATHER! DANNY!
EEEEE!
THEN, OUR COMBINED WEIGHT PULLED OVER YOUR FATHER, AS WELL..

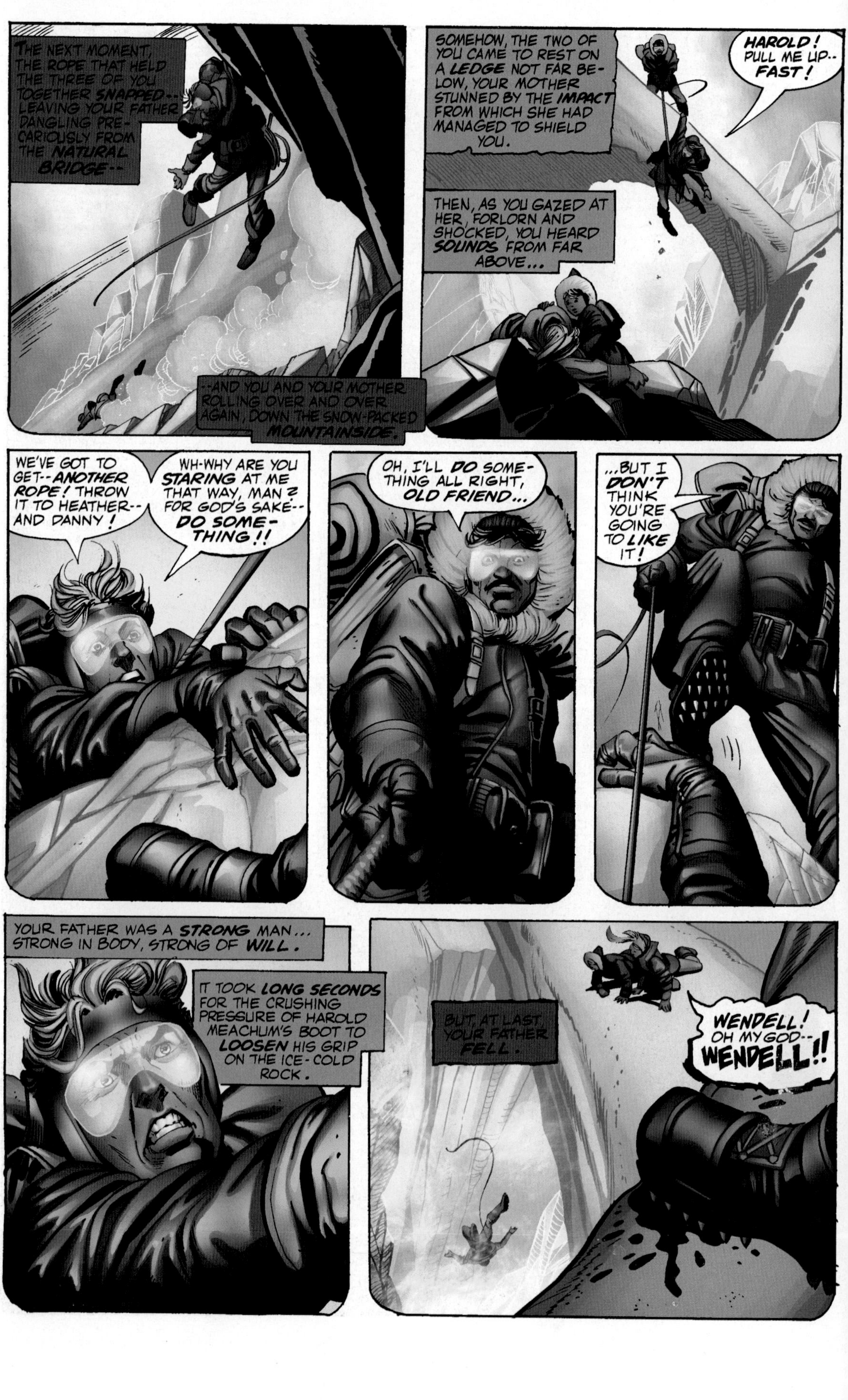
THE NEXT MOMENT, THE ROPE THAT HELD THE THREE OF YOU TOGETHER SNAPPED-- LEAVING YOUR FATHER DANGLING PRECARIOUSLY FROM THE NATURAL BRIDGE--
--AND YOU AND YOUR MOTHER ROLLING OVER AND OVER AGAIN, DOWN THE SNOW-PACKED MOUNTAINSIDE.
SOMEHOW, THE TWO OF YOU CAME TO REST ON A LEDGE NOT FAR BELOW, YOUR MOTHER STUNNED BY THE IMPACT FROM WHICH SHE HAD MANAGED TO SHIELD YOU.
HAROLD! PULL ME UP-- FAST!
THEN, AS YOU GAZED AT HER, FORLORN AND SHOCKED, YOU HEARD SOUNDS FROM FAR ABOVE...
WE'VE GOT TO GET--ANOTHER ROPE! THROW IT TO HEATHER-- AND DANNY!
WH-WHY ARE YOU STARING AT ME THAT WAY, MAN? FOR GOD'S SAKE-- DO SOMETHING!!
OH, I'LL DO SOMETHING ALL RIGHT, OLD FRIEND...
...BUT I DON'T THINK YOU'RE GOING TO LIKE IT!
YOUR FATHER WAS A STRONG MAN... STRONG IN BODY, STRONG OF WILL.
IT TOOK LONG SECONDS FOR THE CRUSHING PRESSURE OF HAROLD MEACHUM'S BOOT TO LOOSEN HIS GRIP ON THE ICE-COLD ROCK.
BUT, AT LAST, YOUR FATHER FELL.
WENDELL! OH MY GOD-- WENDELL!!

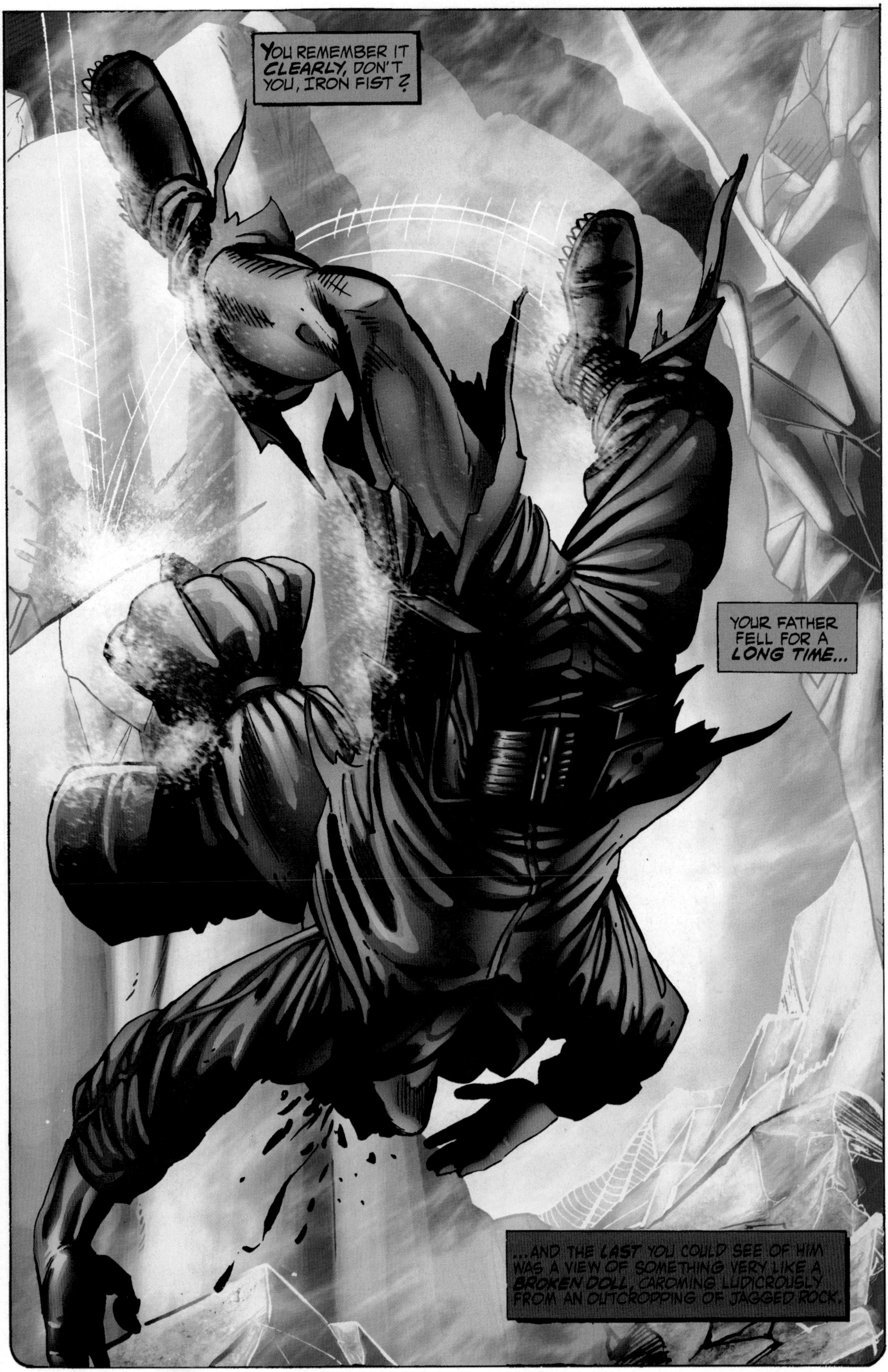
YOU REMEMBER IT CLEARLY, DON'T YOU, IRON FIST?
YOUR FATHER FELL FOR A LONG TIME...
...AND THE LAST YOU COULD SEE OF HIM WAS A VIEW OF SOMETHING VERY LIKE A BROKEN DOLL, CAROMING LUDICROUSLY FROM AN OUTCROPPING OF JAGGED ROCK.

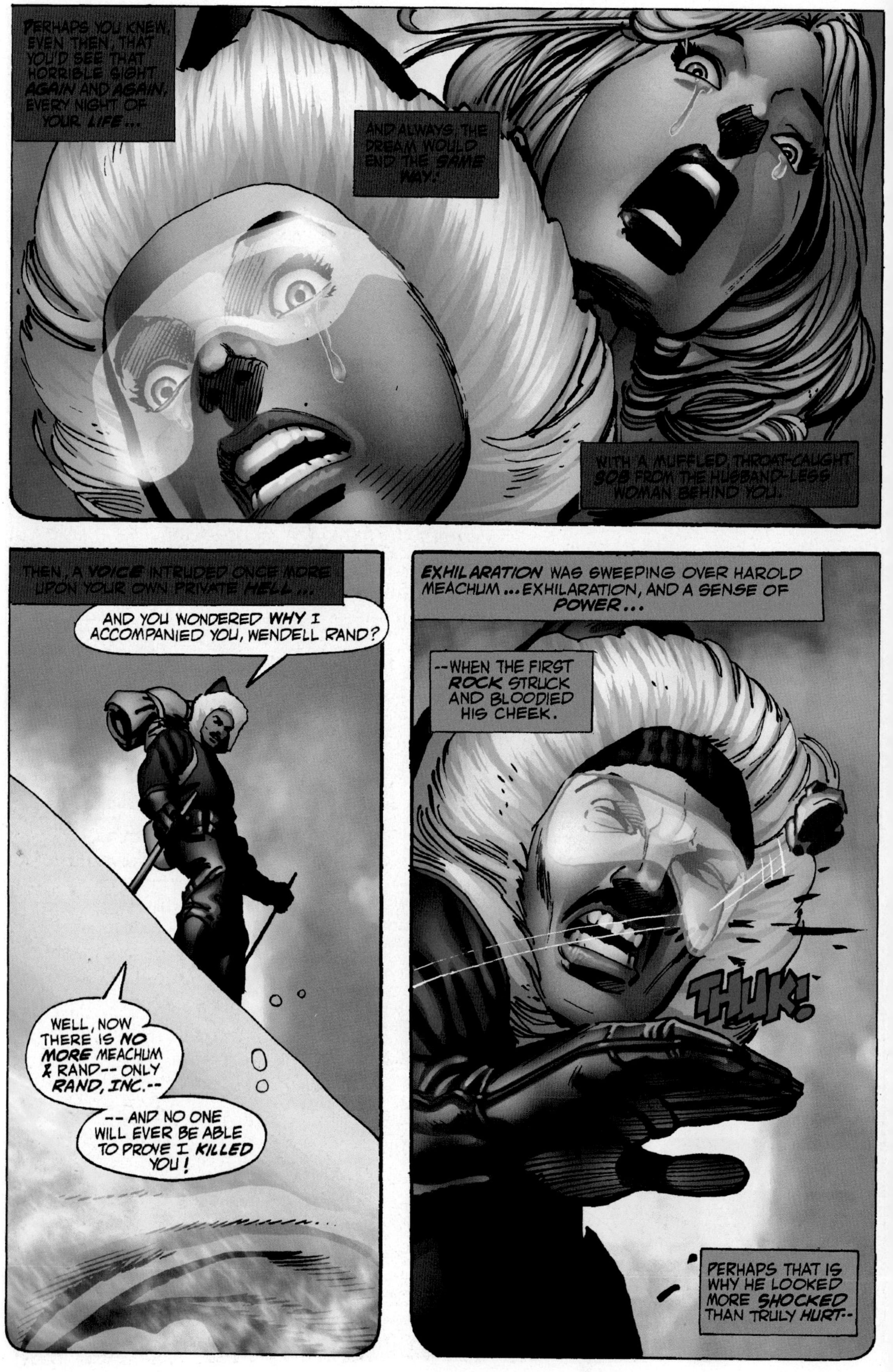
PERHAPS YOU KNEW, EVEN THEN, THAT YOU'D SEE THAT HORRIBLE SIGHT AGAIN AND AGAIN, EVERY NIGHT OF YOUR LIFE...
AND ALWAYS THE DREAM WOULD END THE SAME WAY:
WITH A MUFFLED, THROAT-CAUGHT SOB FROM THE HUSBAND-LESS WOMAN BEHIND YOU.
THEN, A VOICE INTRUDED ONCE MORE UPON YOUR OWN PRIVATE HELL...
AND YOU WONDERED WHY I ACCOMPANIED YOU, WENDELL RAND?
WELL, NOW THERE IS NO MORE MEACHUM & RAND-- ONLY RAND, INC.--
-- AND NO ONE WILL EVER BE ABLE TO PROVE I KILLED YOU!
EXHILARATION WAS SWEEPING OVER HAROLD MEACHUM ... EXHILARATION, AND A SENSE OF POWER...
--WHEN THE FIRST ROCK STRUCK AND BLOODIED HIS CHEEK.
THUK!
PERHAPS THAT IS WHY HE LOOKED MORE SHOCKED THAN TRULY HURT--

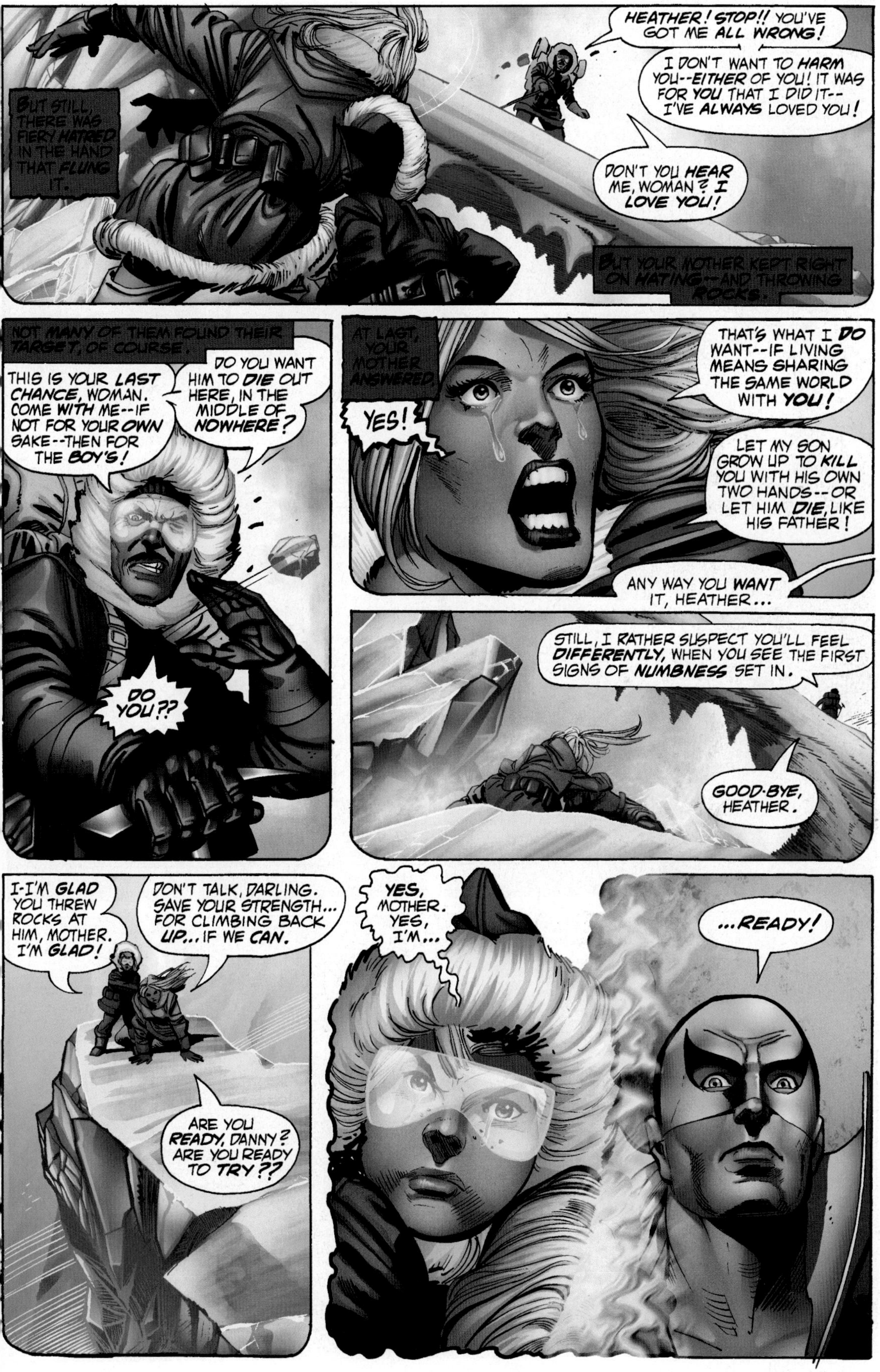
BUT STILL, THERE WAS FIERY HATRED IN THE HAND THAT FLUNG IT.
HEATHER! STOP!! YOU'VE GOT ME ALL WRONG!
I DON'T WANT TO HARM YOU--EITHER OF YOU! IT WAS FOR YOU THAT I DID IT-- I'VE ALWAYS LOVED YOU!
DON'T YOU HEAR ME, WOMAN? I LOVE YOU!
BUT YOUR MOTHER KEPT RIGHT ON HATING--AND THROWING ROCKS.
NOT MANY OF THEM FOUND THEIR TARGET, OF COURSE.
THIS IS YOUR LAST CHANCE, WOMAN. COME WITH ME--IF NOT FOR YOUR OWN SAKE--THEN FOR THE BOY'S!
DO YOU WANT HIM TO DIE OUT HERE, IN THE MIDDLE OF NOWHERE?
DO YOU??
AT LAST, YOUR MOTHER ANSWERED.
YES!
THAT'S WHAT I DO WANT--IF LIVING MEANS SHARING THE SAME WORLD WITH YOU!
LET MY SON GROW UP TO KILL YOU WITH HIS OWN TWO HANDS--OR LET HIM DIE, LIKE HIS FATHER!
ANY WAY YOU WANT IT, HEATHER...
STILL, I RATHER SUSPECT YOU'LL FEEL DIFFERENTLY, WHEN YOU SEE THE FIRST SIGNS OF NUMBNESS SET IN.
GOOD-BYE, HEATHER.
I-I'M GLAD YOU THREW ROCKS AT HIM, MOTHER. I'M GLAD!
DON'T TALK, DARLING. SAVE YOUR STRENGTH... FOR CLIMBING BACK UP... IF WE CAN.
ARE YOU READY, DANNY? ARE YOU READY TO TRY??
YES, MOTHER. YES, I'M...
...READY!

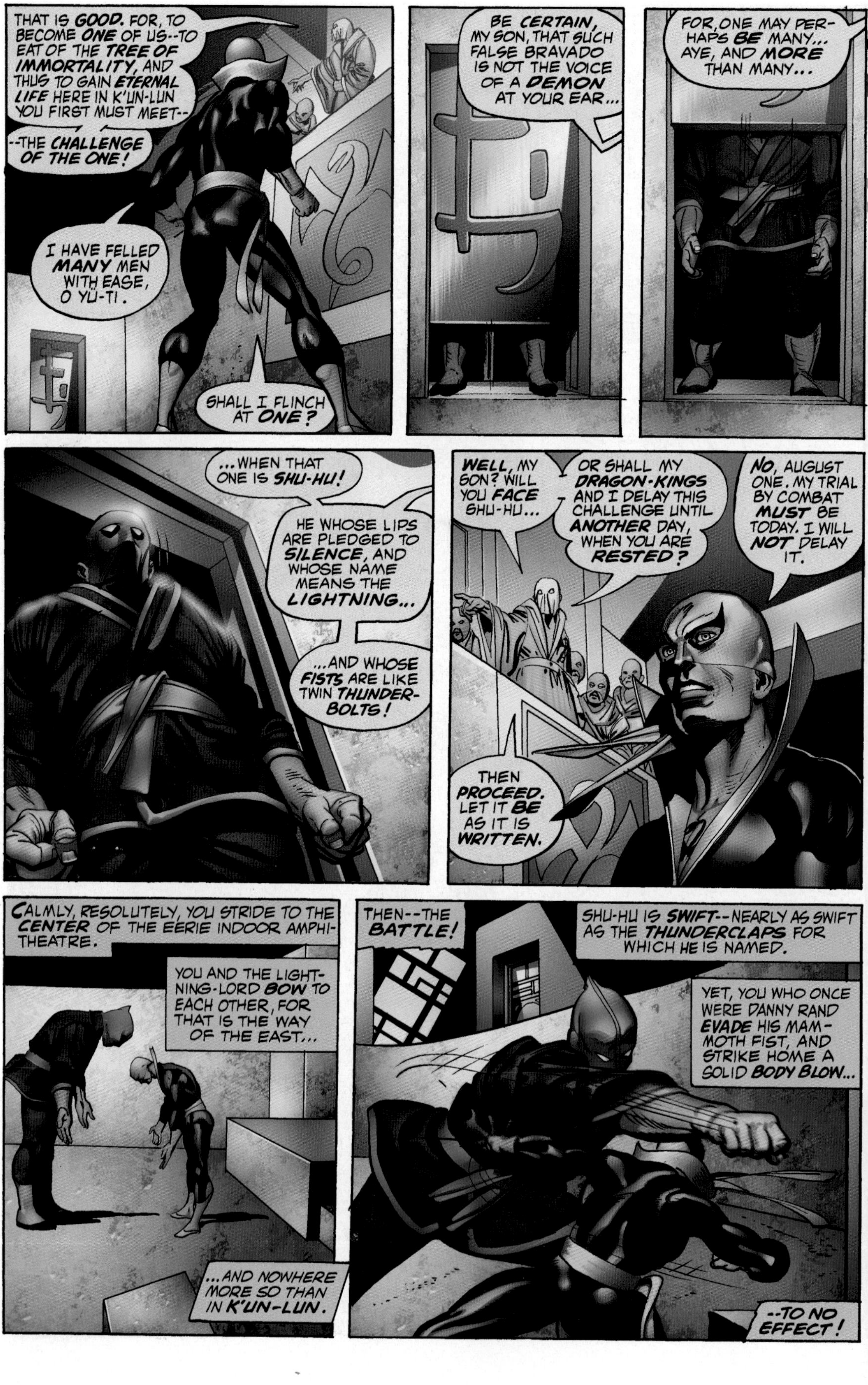

THAT IS GOOD. FOR, TO BECOME ONE OF US--TO EAT OF THE TREE OF IMMORTALITY, AND THUS TO GAIN ETERNAL LIFE HERE IN K'UN-LUN YOU FIRST MUST MEET--
--THE CHALLENGE OF THE ONE!
I HAVE FELLED MANY MEN WITH EASE, O YÜ-TI.
SHALL I FLINCH AT ONE?
BE CERTAIN, MY SON, THAT SUCH FALSE BRAVADO IS NOT THE VOICE OF A DEMON AT YOUR EAR...
FOR, ONE MAY PERHAPS BE MANY... AYE, AND MORE THAN MANY...
...WHEN THAT ONE IS SHU-HU!
HE WHOSE LIPS ARE PLEDGED TO SILENCE, AND WHOSE NAME MEANS THE LIGHTNING...
...AND WHOSE FISTS ARE LIKE TWIN THUNDER-BOLTS!
WELL, MY SON? WILL YOU FACE SHU-HU...
OR SHALL MY DRAGON-KINGS AND I DELAY THIS CHALLENGE UNTIL ANOTHER DAY, WHEN YOU ARE RESTED?
NO, AUGUST ONE. MY TRIAL BY COMBAT MUST BE TODAY. I WILL NOT DELAY IT.
THEN PROCEED. LET IT BE AS IT IS WRITTEN.
CALMLY, RESOLUTELY, YOU STRIDE TO THE CENTER OF THE EERIE INDOOR AMPHI-THEATRE.
YOU AND THE LIGHTNING-LORD BOW TO EACH OTHER, FOR THAT IS THE WAY OF THE EAST...
...AND NOWHERE MORE SO THAN IN K'UN-LUN.
THEN--THE BATTLE!
SHU-HU IS SWIFT--NEARLY AS SWIFT AS THE THUNDERCLAPS FOR WHICH HE IS NAMED.
YET, YOU WHO ONCE WERE DANNY RAND EVADE HIS MAMMOTH FIST, AND STRIKE HOME A SOLID BODY BLOW...
--TO NO EFFECT!

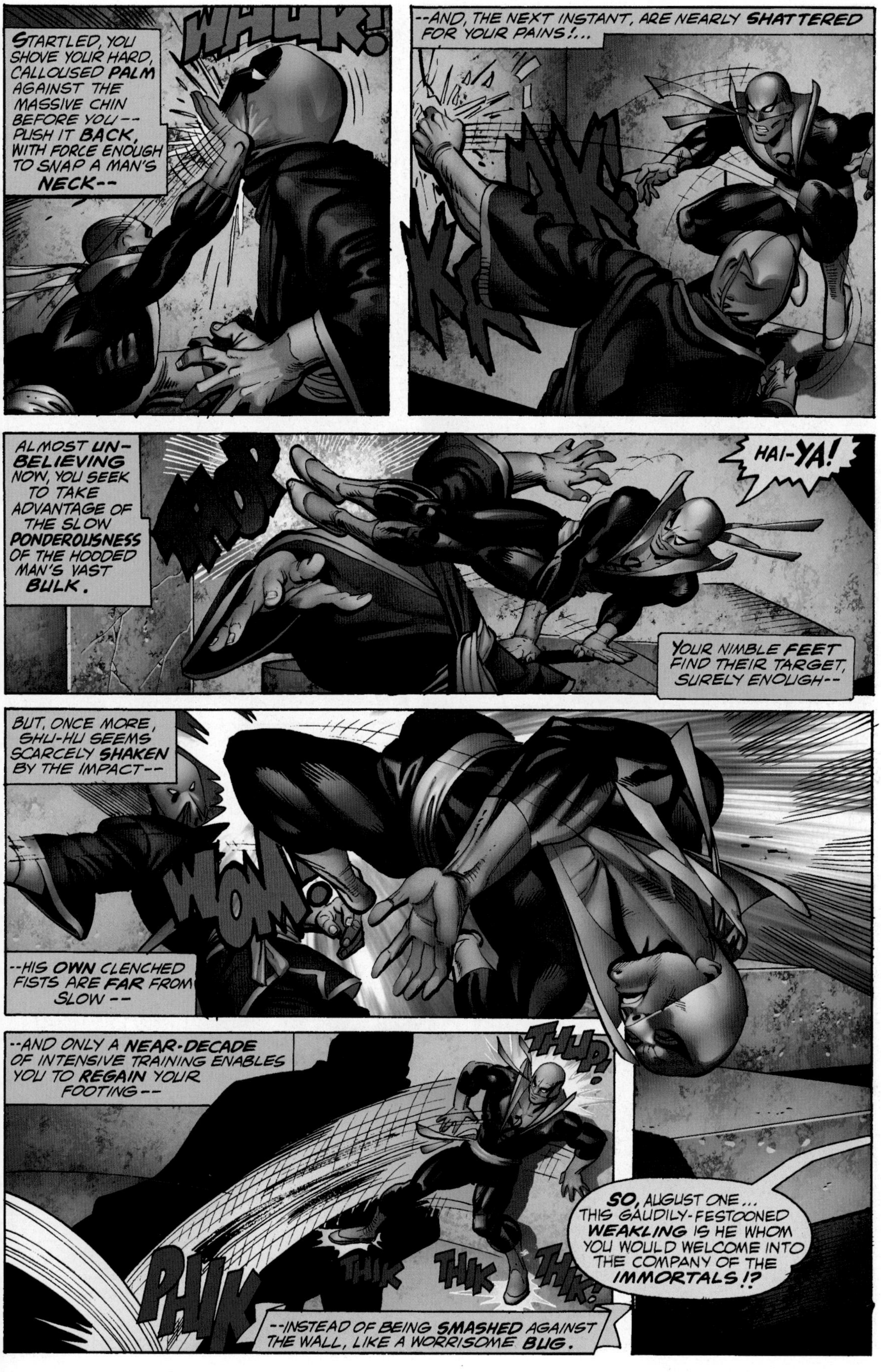
STARTLED, YOU SHOVE YOUR HARD, CALLOUSED PALM AGAINST THE MASSIVE CHIN BEFORE YOU -- PUSH IT BACK, WITH FORCE ENOUGH TO SNAP A MAN'S NECK--
WHUK!
--AND, THE NEXT INSTANT, ARE NEARLY SHATTERED FOR YOUR PAINS!...
ALMOST UN-BELIEVING NOW, YOU SEEK TO TAKE ADVANTAGE OF THE SLOW PONDEROUSNESS OF THE HOODED MAN'S VAST BULK.
HAI-YA!
YOUR NIMBLE FEET FIND THEIR TARGET, SURELY ENOUGH--
BUT, ONCE MORE, SHU-HU SEEMS SCARCELY SHAKEN BY THE IMPACT--
WOM
--HIS OWN CLENCHED FISTS ARE FAR FROM SLOW --
--AND ONLY A NEAR-DECADE OF INTENSIVE TRAINING ENABLES YOU TO REGAIN YOUR FOOTING--
THUP!
SO, AUGUST ONE... THIS GAUDILY-FESTOONED WEAKLING IS HE WHOM YOU WOULD WELCOME INTO THE COMPANY OF THE IMMORTALS!?
PHUK
THIK THIK THIK!
--INSTEAD OF BEING SMASHED AGAINST THE WALL, LIKE A WORRISOME BUG.

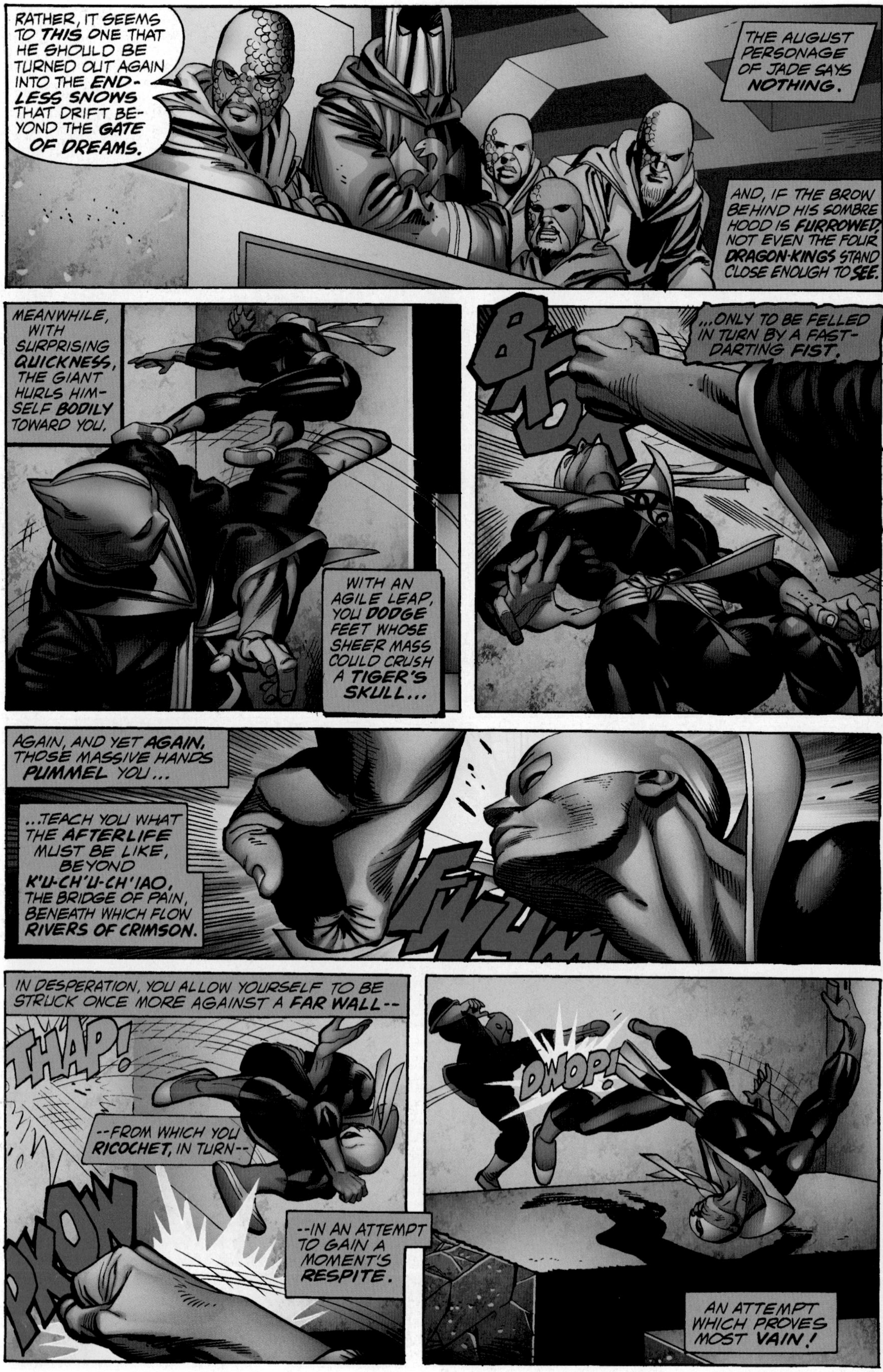
RATHER, IT SEEMS TO THIS ONE THAT HE SHOULD BE TURNED OUT AGAIN INTO THE ENDLESS SNOWS THAT DRIFT BEYOND THE GATE OF DREAMS.
THE AUGUST PERSONAGE OF JADE SAYS NOTHING.
AND, IF THE BROW BEHIND HIS SOMBRE HOOD IS FURROWED, NOT EVEN THE FOUR DRAGON-KINGS STAND CLOSE ENOUGH TO SEE.
MEANWHILE, WITH SURPRISING QUICKNESS, THE GIANT HURLS HIMSELF BODILY TOWARD YOU.
WITH AN AGILE LEAP, YOU DODGE FEET WHOSE SHEER MASS COULD CRUSH A TIGER'S SKULL...
...ONLY TO BE FELLED IN TURN BY A FAST-DARTING FIST.
AGAIN, AND YET AGAIN, THOSE MASSIVE HANDS PUMMEL YOU...
...TEACH YOU WHAT THE AFTERLIFE MUST BE LIKE, BEYOND K'U-CH'U-CH'IAO, THE BRIDGE OF PAIN, BENEATH WHICH FLOW RIVERS OF CRIMSON.
FWUM
IN DESPERATION, YOU ALLOW YOURSELF TO BE STRUCK ONCE MORE AGAINST A FAR WALL--
THAP!
--FROM WHICH YOU RICOCHET, IN TURN--
PKOW
--IN AN ATTEMPT TO GAIN A MOMENT'S RESPITE.
DWOP!
AN ATTEMPT WHICH PROVES MOST VAIN!

IT SEEMS TO BE SLIPPING AWAY NOW--YOUR GRIP ON CONSCIOUSNESS.

WOULD IT NOT BE SIMPLER FAR TO LET IT GO-- TO COLLAPSE INTO SWEET OBLIVION?

BUT WHY, THEN, DOES YOUR MIND RACE BACK ONCE MORE TO THAT WINDBLOWN LEDGE?

WHY DO YOU HEAR AGAIN YOUR MOTHER'S VOICE FROM OUT OF THE DEAD PAST?

COME ON, DANNY! WE'RE GOING TO CLIMB NOW...!

YOUR HEART BEATS FASTER WITHIN YOUR BREAST...

BUT, IS IT HERE THAT IT BEATS... HERE, WITHIN THE ARENA OF YOUR THROBBING PAIN...

...OR IS IT THERE, WHERE TWO PEOPLE MADE THAT MOST INHUMAN EFFORT, TEN YEARS GONE?

YOU MADE IT THEN, DIDN'T YOU?

SOMEHOW, IT WAS EASIER THEN, IN SPITE OF THE NUMBING COLD...IN SPITE OF THE VIVID MEMORY OF MURDER MOST FOUL!

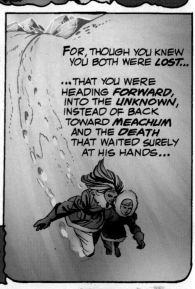

FOR, THOUGH YOU KNEW YOU BOTH WERE LOST...

...THAT YOU WERE HEADING FORWARD, INTO THE UNKNOWN, INSTEAD OF BACK TOWARD MEACHUM AND THE DEATH THAT WAITED SURELY AT HIS HANDS...

...STILL, YOU HAD EACH OTHER.

DANNY, I... I WANT YOU TO PROMISE ME SOME-THING.

PROMISE ME YOU DON'T HATE YOUR FATHER FOR BRINGING YOU HERE!

FOR, HE HAD A VISION OF A BETTER WORLD, WAITING SOME-WHERE FOR THE THREE OF US...

...SOMEWHERE ALWAYS JUST BEYOND THE NEXT RIDGE.

PROMISE ME, DANNY!

I...PROMISE, MOTHER.

AND SO YOU WANDERED ALONE, FOR DAYS. THEN, EVEN AS YOUR STRENGTH GREW EVER WEAKER...

...YOUR STEPS EVER MORE FALTERING...

...SUDDENLY, YOU BOTH WEREN'T ALONE ANY LONGER.

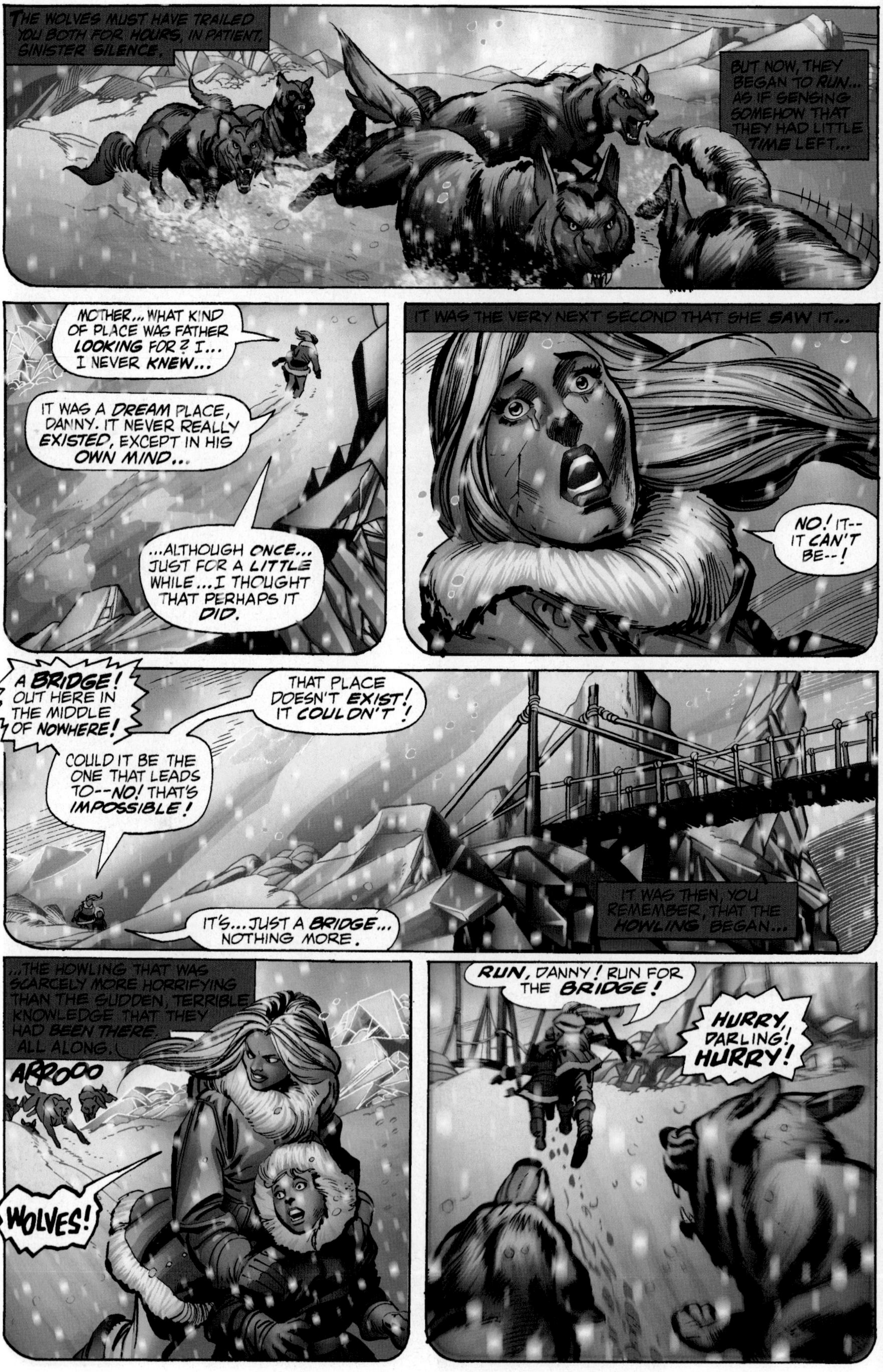
THE WOLVES MUST HAVE TRAILED YOU BOTH FOR HOURS, IN PATIENT, SINISTER SILENCE.
BUT NOW, THEY BEGAN TO RUN... AS IF SENSING SOMEHOW THAT THEY HAD LITTLE TIME LEFT...
MOTHER... WHAT KIND OF PLACE WAS FATHER LOOKING FOR? I... I NEVER KNEW...
IT WAS A DREAM PLACE, DANNY. IT NEVER REALLY EXISTED, EXCEPT IN HIS OWN MIND...
...ALTHOUGH ONCE... JUST FOR A LITTLE WHILE... I THOUGHT THAT PERHAPS IT DID.
IT WAS THE VERY NEXT SECOND THAT SHE SAW IT...
NO! IT-- IT CAN'T BE--!
A BRIDGE! OUT HERE IN THE MIDDLE OF NOWHERE!
THAT PLACE DOESN'T EXIST! IT COULDN'T!
COULD IT BE THE ONE THAT LEADS TO--NO! THAT'S IMPOSSIBLE!
IT'S... JUST A BRIDGE... NOTHING MORE.
IT WAS THEN, YOU REMEMBER, THAT THE HOWLING BEGAN...
...THE HOWLING THAT WAS SCARCELY MORE HORRIFYING THAN THE SUDDEN, TERRIBLE KNOWLEDGE THAT THEY HAD BEEN THERE ALL ALONG.
ARROOO
WOLVES!
RUN, DANNY! RUN FOR THE BRIDGE!
HURRY, DARLING! HURRY!

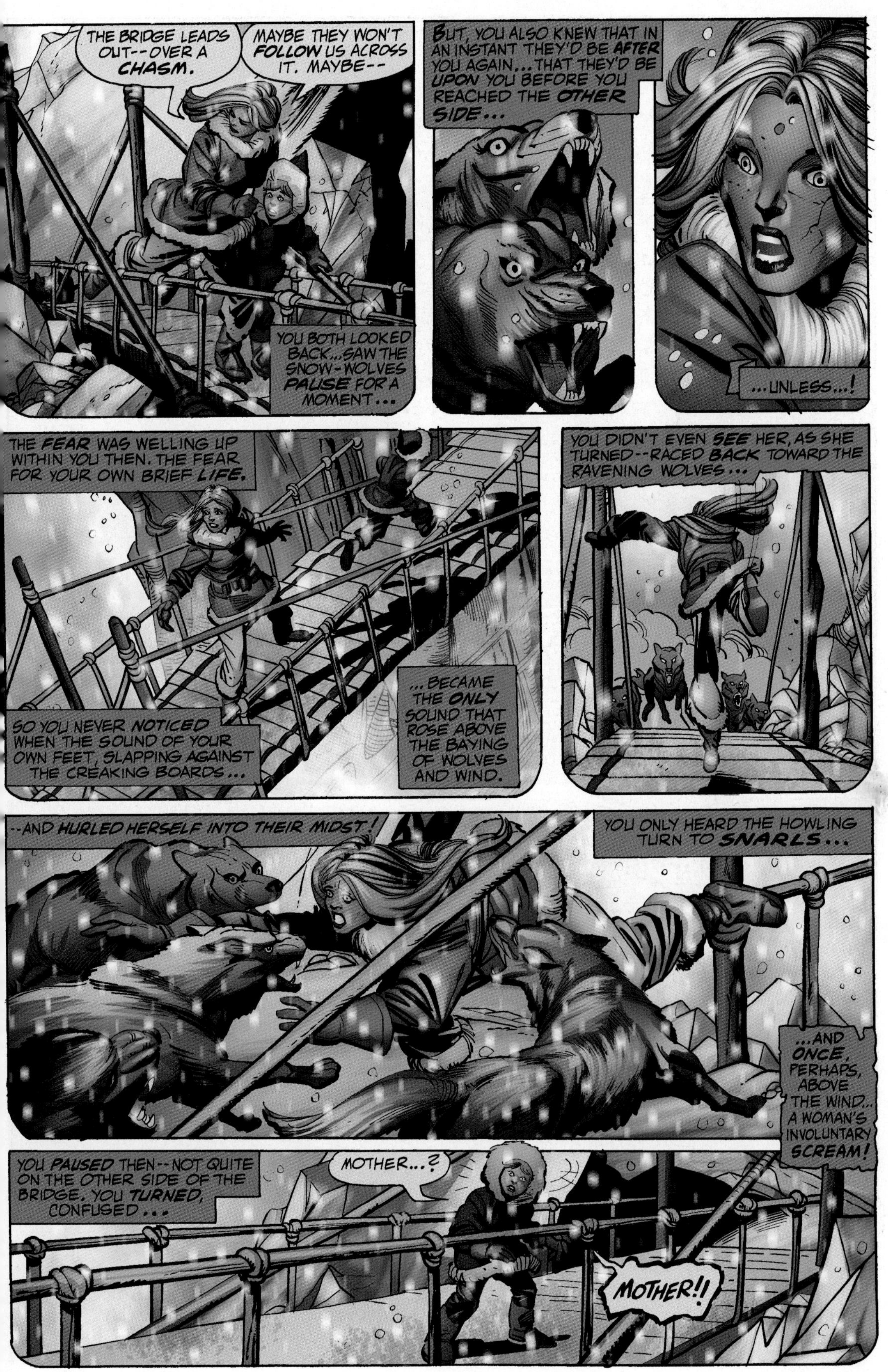
THE BRIDGE LEADS OUT--OVER A CHASM.
MAYBE THEY WON'T FOLLOW US ACROSS IT. MAYBE--
YOU BOTH LOOKED BACK...SAW THE SNOW-WOLVES PAUSE FOR A MOMENT...
BUT, YOU ALSO KNEW THAT IN AN INSTANT THEY'D BE AFTER YOU AGAIN...THAT THEY'D BE UPON YOU BEFORE YOU REACHED THE OTHER SIDE...
...UNLESS...!
THE FEAR WAS WELLING UP WITHIN YOU THEN. THE FEAR FOR YOUR OWN BRIEF LIFE.
SO YOU NEVER NOTICED WHEN THE SOUND OF YOUR OWN FEET, SLAPPING AGAINST THE CREAKING BOARDS...
...BECAME THE ONLY SOUND THAT ROSE ABOVE THE BAYING OF WOLVES AND WIND.
YOU DIDN'T EVEN SEE HER, AS SHE TURNED--RACED BACK TOWARD THE RAVENING WOLVES...
--AND HURLED HERSELF INTO THEIR MIDST!
YOU ONLY HEARD THE HOWLING TURN TO SNARLS...
...AND ONCE, PERHAPS, ABOVE THE WIND... A WOMAN'S INVOLUNTARY SCREAM!
YOU PAUSED THEN--NOT QUITE ON THE OTHER SIDE OF THE BRIDGE. YOU TURNED, CONFUSED...
MOTHER...?
MOTHER!!

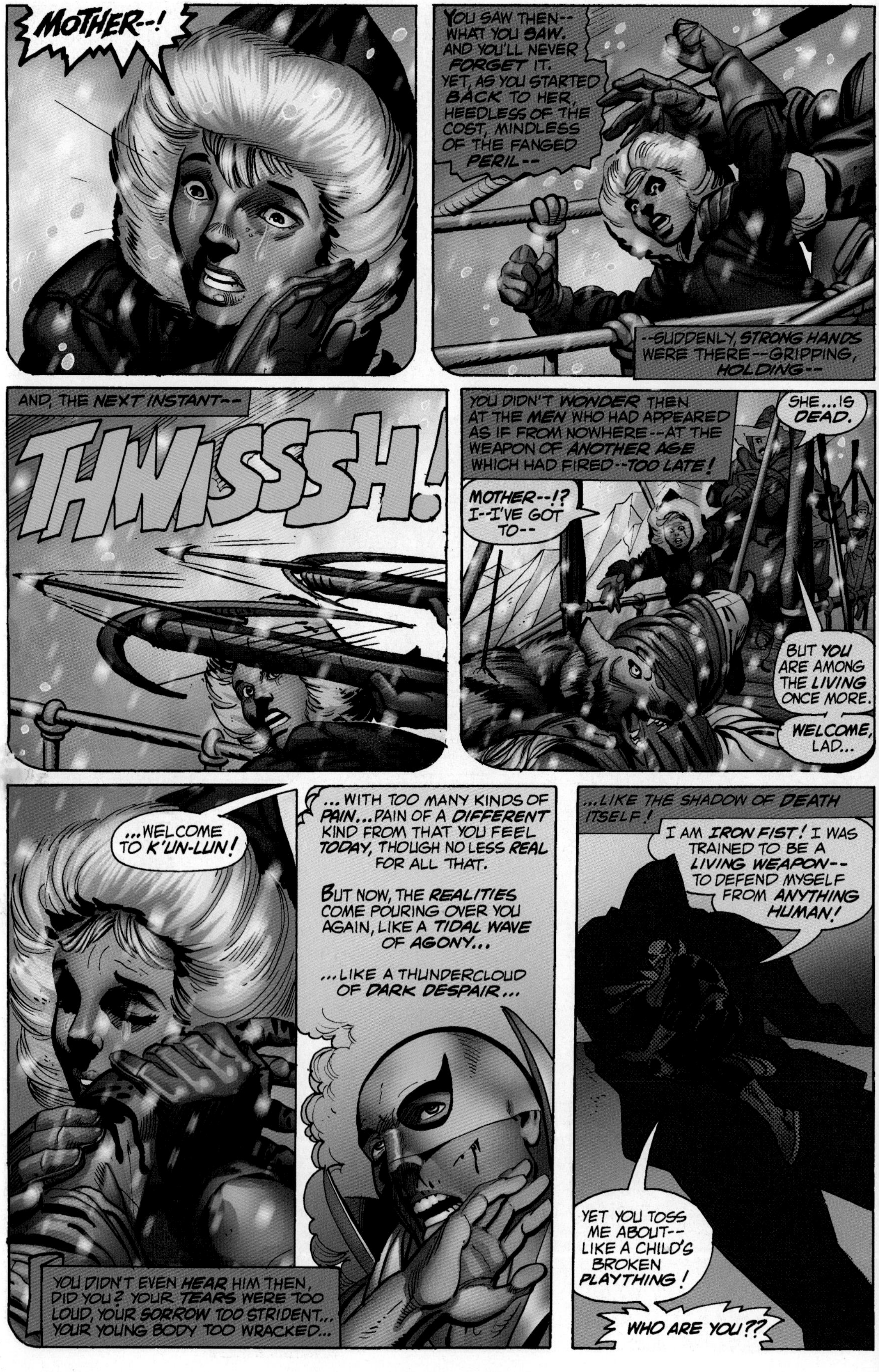
MOTHER--!
YOU SAW THEN-- WHAT YOU SAW. AND YOU'LL NEVER FORGET IT. YET, AS YOU STARTED BACK TO HER, HEEDLESS OF THE COST, MINDLESS OF THE FANGED PERIL--
--SUDDENLY, STRONG HANDS WERE THERE--GRIPPING, HOLDING--
AND, THE NEXT INSTANT--
THWISSSH!
YOU DIDN'T WONDER THEN AT THE MEN WHO HAD APPEARED AS IF FROM NOWHERE--AT THE WEAPON OF ANOTHER AGE WHICH HAD FIRED--TOO LATE!
SHE...IS DEAD.
MOTHER--!? I--I'VE GOT TO--
BUT YOU ARE AMONG THE LIVING ONCE MORE.
WELCOME, LAD...
...WELCOME TO K'UN-LUN!
YOU DIDN'T EVEN HEAR HIM THEN, DID YOU? YOUR TEARS WERE TOO LOUD, YOUR SORROW TOO STRIDENT... YOUR YOUNG BODY TOO WRACKED...
...WITH TOO MANY KINDS OF PAIN...PAIN OF A DIFFERENT KIND FROM THAT YOU FEEL TODAY, THOUGH NO LESS REAL FOR ALL THAT.
BUT NOW, THE REALITIES COME POURING OVER YOU AGAIN, LIKE A TIDAL WAVE OF AGONY...
...LIKE A THUNDERCLOUD OF DARK DESPAIR...
...LIKE THE SHADOW OF DEATH ITSELF!
I AM IRON FIST! I WAS TRAINED TO BE A LIVING WEAPON-- TO DEFEND MYSELF FROM ANYTHING HUMAN!
YET YOU TOSS ME ABOUT-- LIKE A CHILD'S BROKEN PLAYTHING!
WHO ARE YOU??

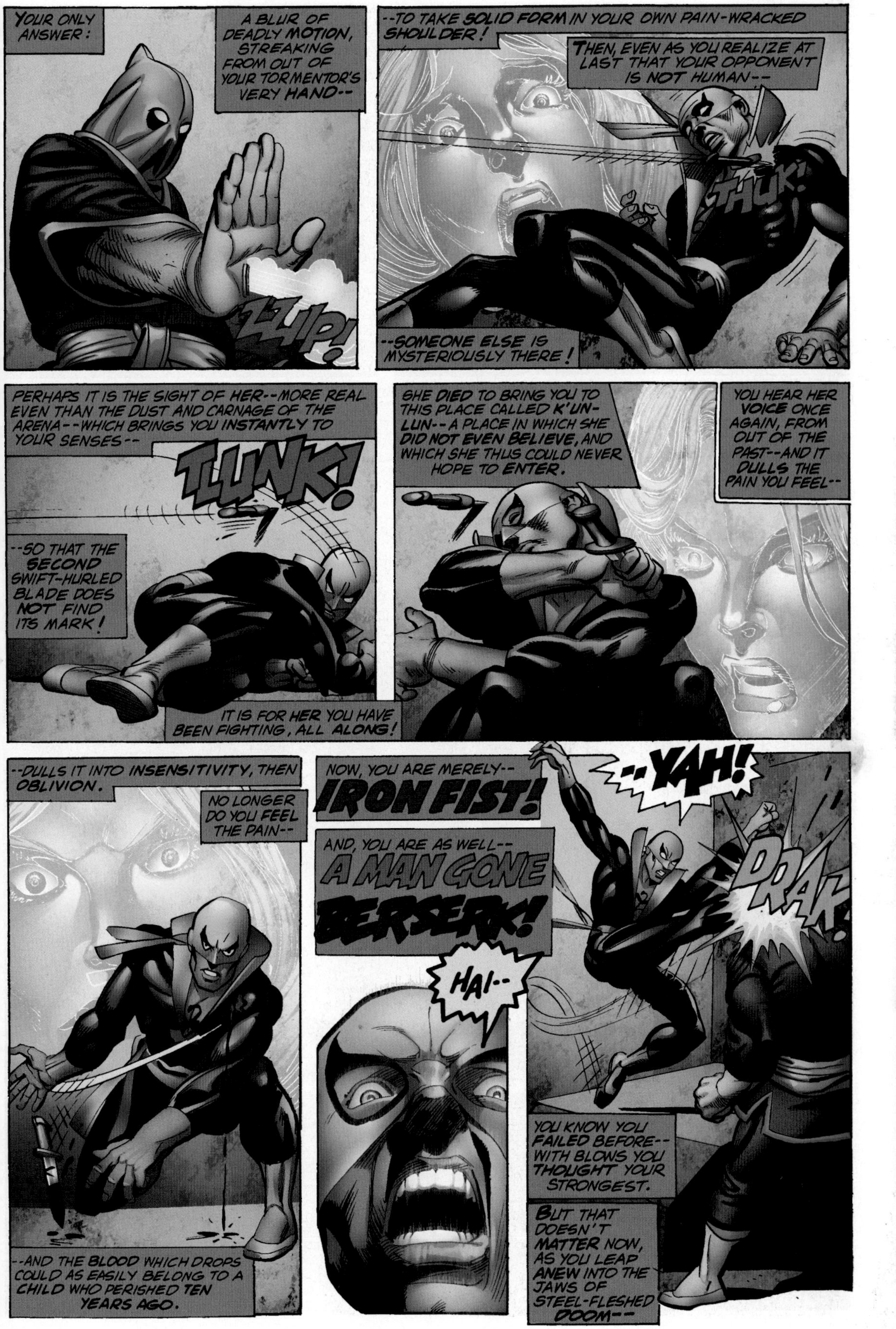
YOUR ONLY ANSWER:
A BLUR OF DEADLY MOTION, STREAKING FROM OUT OF YOUR TORMENTOR'S VERY HAND--
ZZUP!
--TO TAKE SOLID FORM IN YOUR OWN PAIN-WRACKED SHOULDER!
THEN, EVEN AS YOU REALIZE AT LAST THAT YOUR OPPONENT IS NOT HUMAN--
THUK!
--SOMEONE ELSE IS MYSTERIOUSLY THERE!
PERHAPS IT IS THE SIGHT OF HER--MORE REAL EVEN THAN THE DUST AND CARNAGE OF THE ARENA--WHICH BRINGS YOU INSTANTLY TO YOUR SENSES--
TUNK!
--SO THAT THE SECOND SWIFT-HURLED BLADE DOES NOT FIND ITS MARK!
IT IS FOR HER YOU HAVE BEEN FIGHTING, ALL ALONG!
SHE DIED TO BRING YOU TO THIS PLACE CALLED K'UN-LUN--A PLACE IN WHICH SHE DID NOT EVEN BELIEVE, AND WHICH SHE THUS COULD NEVER HOPE TO ENTER.
YOU HEAR HER VOICE ONCE AGAIN, FROM OUT OF THE PAST--AND IT DULLS THE PAIN YOU FEEL--
--DULLS IT INTO INSENSITIVITY, THEN OBLIVION.
NO LONGER DO YOU FEEL THE PAIN--
--AND THE BLOOD WHICH DROPS COULD AS EASILY BELONG TO A CHILD WHO PERISHED TEN YEARS AGO.
NOW, YOU ARE MERELY--
IRON FIST!
AND, YOU ARE AS WELL--
A MAN GONE BERSERK!
HAI--
--YAH!
DRAK!
YOU KNOW YOU FAILED BEFORE--WITH BLOWS YOU THOUGHT YOUR STRONGEST.
BUT THAT DOESN'T MATTER NOW, AS YOU LEAP ANEW INTO THE JAWS OF STEEL-FLESHED DOOM--

--AS YOU STRIKE AGAIN--

WHUMP!

--AND AGAIN--

BK K K K

--AND YET *AGAIN*--

Now, you can feel the hard, man-forged metal beneath the hood--feel it start to give and bend and twist.

The ponderous giant's moves become sluggish-- slow--mechanical--

AND, IF HE--IF IT COULD FEEL PAIN--

F W AKK!

--ITS PAIN WOULD DWARF ANY THAT YOU HAVE EVER KNOWN!

AT LAST IT TOTTERS-- REELS--YET, IT IS STILL *TOO STRONG* TO FALL.

AND NOW, AN ICY CALM SETTLES OVER YOU--

--A CALM WHICH IS, FINALLY, YOUR GREATEST STRENGTH.

YOU CALL SILENTLY, INWARDLY, UPON THE INVINCIBLE WILL WHICH FORMS THE VERY *CORE* OF YOUR BEING.

UNFATHOMED RESERVES OF CONCENTRATION AND RE- SOLVE FLOW FROM YOUR BRAIN, YOUR SHOULDERS, YOUR LEGS, FROM EVERY PART OF A BODY HONED FOR TEN *LONG YEARS--*

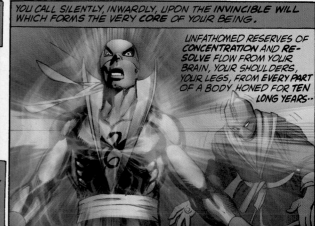

--INTO YOUR HAND--

--UNTIL IT BECOMES LIKE UNTO--

--A THING OF *IRON!*

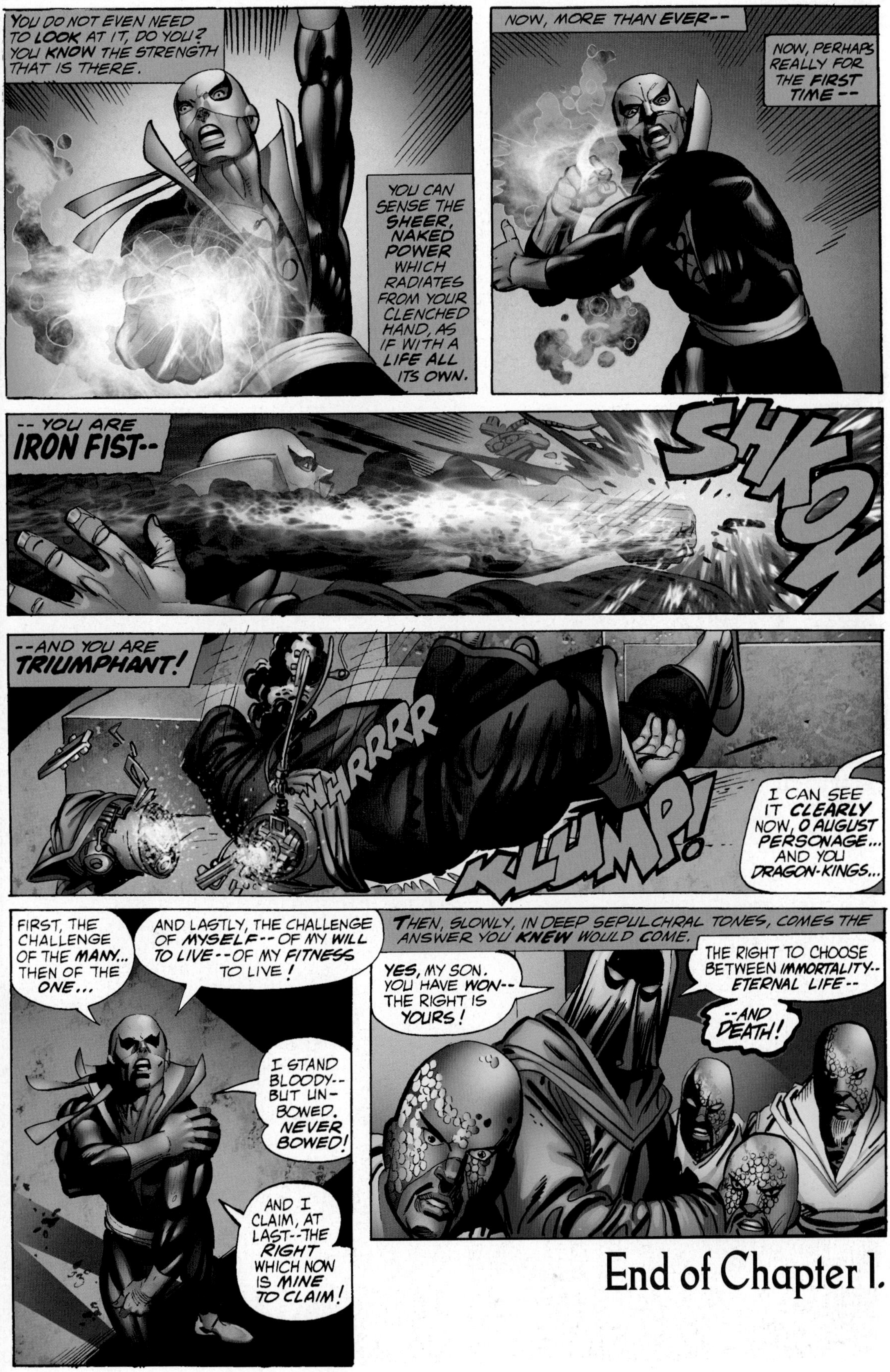
YOU DO NOT EVEN NEED TO LOOK AT IT, DO YOU? YOU KNOW THE STRENGTH THAT IS THERE.
YOU CAN SENSE THE SHEER, NAKED POWER WHICH RADIATES FROM YOUR CLENCHED HAND, AS IF WITH A LIFE ALL ITS OWN.
NOW, MORE THAN EVER--
NOW, PERHAPS REALLY FOR THE FIRST TIME --
-- YOU ARE IRON FIST--
SHKOW
--AND YOU ARE TRIUMPHANT!
WHRRRR
KLUMP!
I CAN SEE IT CLEARLY NOW, O AUGUST PERSONAGE... AND YOU DRAGON-KINGS...
FIRST, THE CHALLENGE OF THE MANY... THEN OF THE ONE...
AND LASTLY, THE CHALLENGE OF MYSELF--OF MY WILL TO LIVE--OF MY FITNESS TO LIVE!
I STAND BLOODY--BUT UNBOWED. NEVER BOWED!
AND I CLAIM, AT LAST--THE RIGHT WHICH NOW IS MINE TO CLAIM!
THEN, SLOWLY, IN DEEP SEPULCHRAL TONES, COMES THE ANSWER YOU KNEW WOULD COME.
YES, MY SON. YOU HAVE WON-- THE RIGHT IS YOURS!
THE RIGHT TO CHOOSE BETWEEN IMMORTALITY-- ETERNAL LIFE --
--AND DEATH!

End of Chapter I.

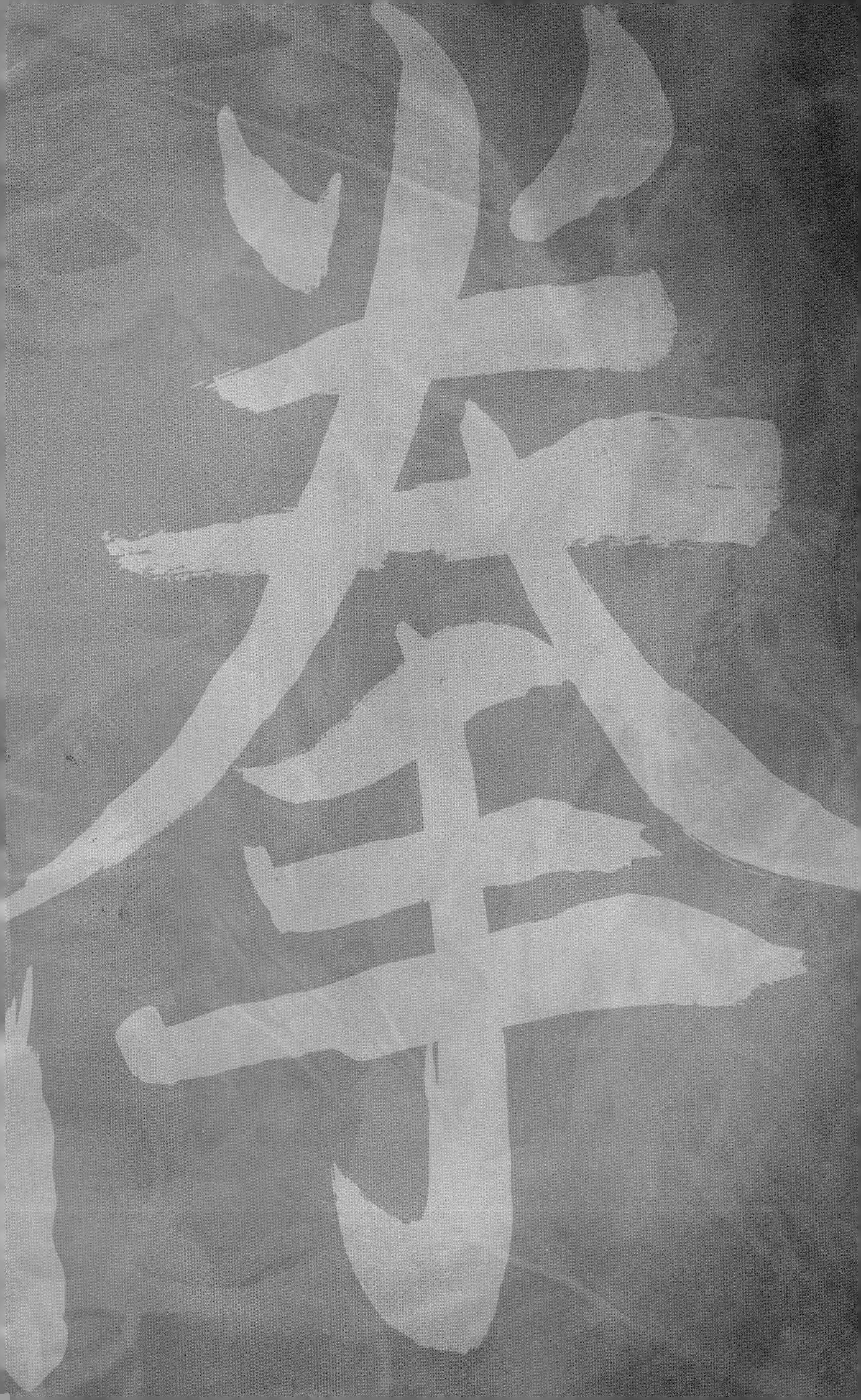
拳

Chapter 2:

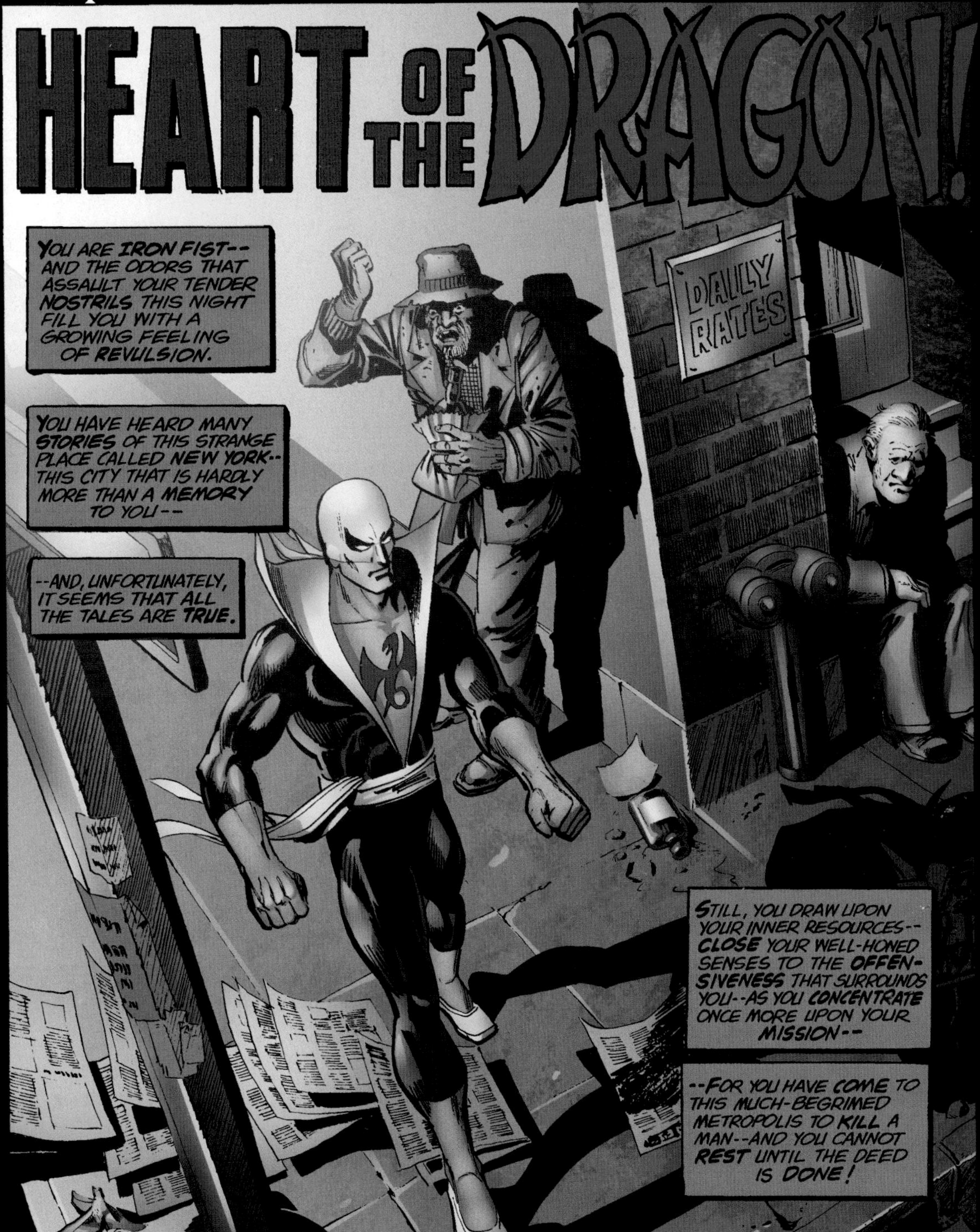
HEART OF THE DRAGON!
YOU ARE IRON FIST-- AND THE ODORS THAT ASSAULT YOUR TENDER NOSTRILS THIS NIGHT FILL YOU WITH A GROWING FEELING OF REVULSION.
YOU HAVE HEARD MANY STORIES OF THIS STRANGE PLACE CALLED NEW YORK-- THIS CITY THAT IS HARDLY MORE THAN A MEMORY TO YOU--
--AND, UNFORTUNATELY, IT SEEMS THAT ALL THE TALES ARE TRUE.
DAILY RATES
STILL, YOU DRAW UPON YOUR INNER RESOURCES-- CLOSE YOUR WELL-HONED SENSES TO THE OFFENSIVENESS THAT SURROUNDS YOU--AS YOU CONCENTRATE ONCE MORE UPON YOUR MISSION--
--FOR YOU HAVE COME TO THIS MUCH-BEGRIMED METROPOLIS TO KILL A MAN--AND YOU CANNOT REST UNTIL THE DEED IS DONE!

IN YOUR MIND'S EYE, YOU SEE HIS *FACE*--AND FURY GROWS WITHIN YOU AT THE *SIGHT* OF IT--

--BUT IT IS FURY CAST QUICKLY *ASIDE*--AS A *SOUND* INTERRUPTS YOUR GRIM REVERIE.

THE SOUND IS A *MOAN*--AND IT DRIFTS DESPERATELY FROM THE SHADOWS OF THIS ALLEYWAY.

SILENTLY, ALMOST CAT-LIKE, YOU STRIDE INTO THE DARKNESS, PURSUING THE ELUSIVE *WHISPER*.

A *DEAD-END* LOOMS BEFORE YOU--THE HACKLES RISE ABRUPTLY ON YOUR *NECK*--

--AND YOU CURSE YOURSELF FOR A *FOOL* TO HAVE WALKED SO WILLINGLY INTO A *TRAP!*

LOOKIN' FOR SOMETHING, *PAL?*

YOU HAVE SEEN THEIR TYPE *BEFORE*--THE LOW, SLOPING *BROWS*--THE CRUEL *TIGHTNESS* AT THE CORNERS OF THEIR EYES...

THEY ARE CONFIDENT--PERHAPS *TOO* CONFIDENT--AND THUS THEY ARE *VULNERABLE!*

STEP ASIDE AND LET ME *PASS,* PLEASE! YOU HAVE NO *BUSINESS* WITH ME!

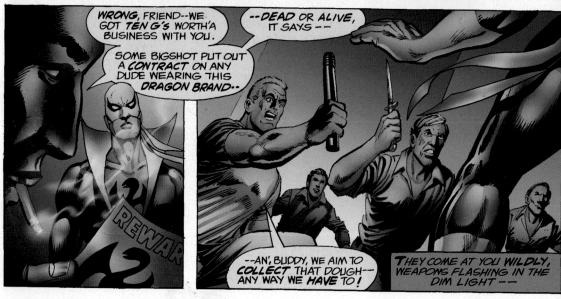

WRONG, FRIEND--WE GOT *TEN G'S* WORTH'A BUSINESS WITH YOU.

SOME BIGSHOT PUT OUT A *CONTRACT* ON ANY DUDE WEARING THIS *DRAGON BRAND*--

--*DEAD* OR ALIVE, IT SAYS--

--AN', BUDDY, WE AIM TO *COLLECT* THAT DOUGH-- ANY WAY WE *HAVE* TO!

THEY COME AT YOU *WILDLY,* WEAPONS FLASHING IN THE DIM LIGHT--

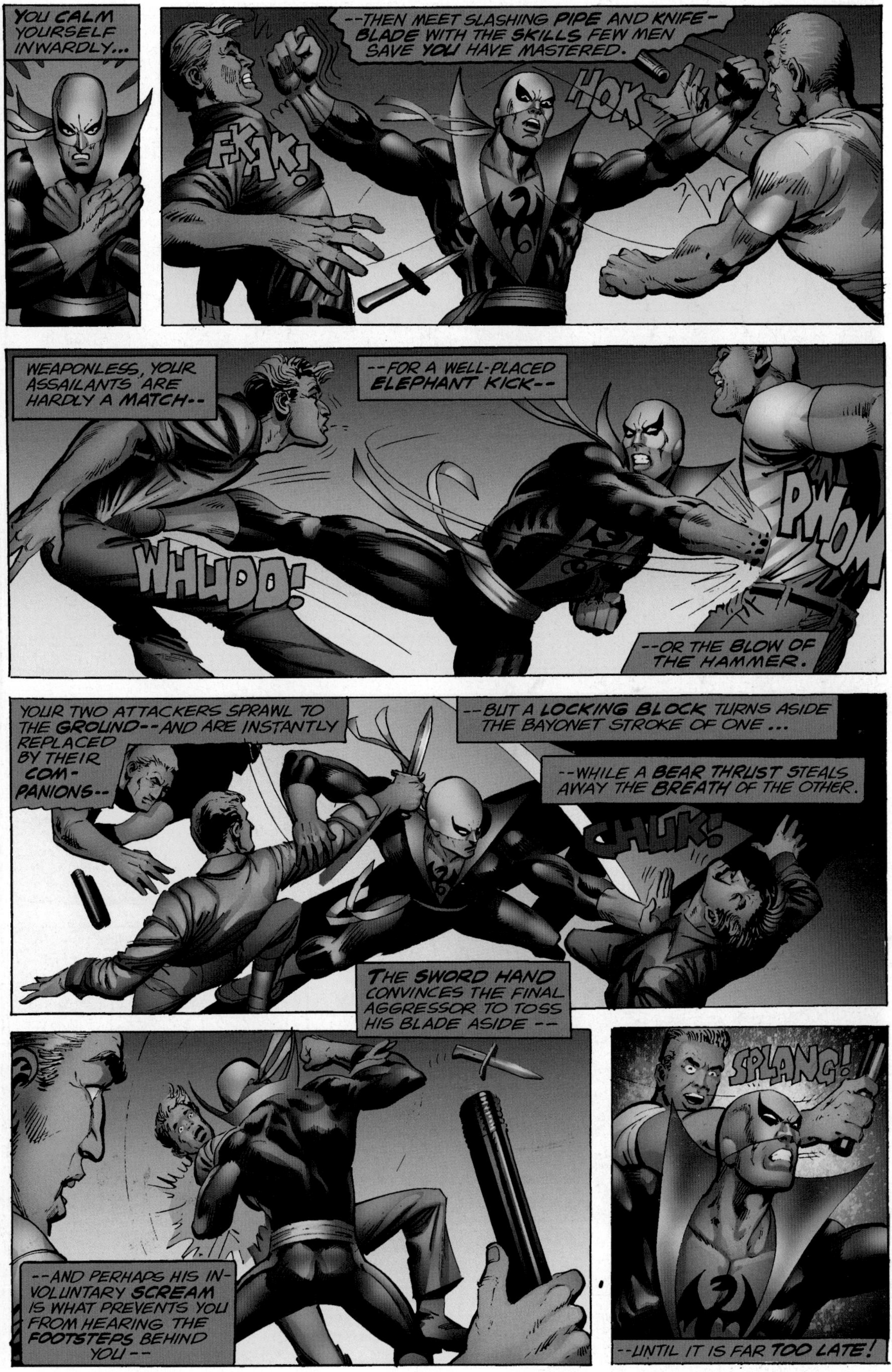
YOU CALM YOURSELF INWARDLY...
--THEN MEET SLASHING PIPE AND KNIFE-BLADE WITH THE SKILLS FEW MEN SAVE YOU HAVE MASTERED.
HOK
FKAK!
WEAPONLESS, YOUR ASSAILANTS ARE HARDLY A MATCH--
--FOR A WELL-PLACED ELEPHANT KICK--
WHUDD!
PWOM
--OR THE BLOW OF THE HAMMER.
YOUR TWO ATTACKERS SPRAWL TO THE GROUND--AND ARE INSTANTLY REPLACED BY THEIR COM-PANIONS--
--BUT A LOCKING BLOCK TURNS ASIDE THE BAYONET STROKE OF ONE ...
--WHILE A BEAR THRUST STEALS AWAY THE BREATH OF THE OTHER.
CHUK!
THE SWORD HAND CONVINCES THE FINAL AGGRESSOR TO TOSS HIS BLADE ASIDE --
--AND PERHAPS HIS INVOLUNTARY SCREAM IS WHAT PREVENTS YOU FROM HEARING THE FOOTSTEPS BEHIND YOU --
SPLANG!
--UNTIL IT IS FAR TOO LATE!

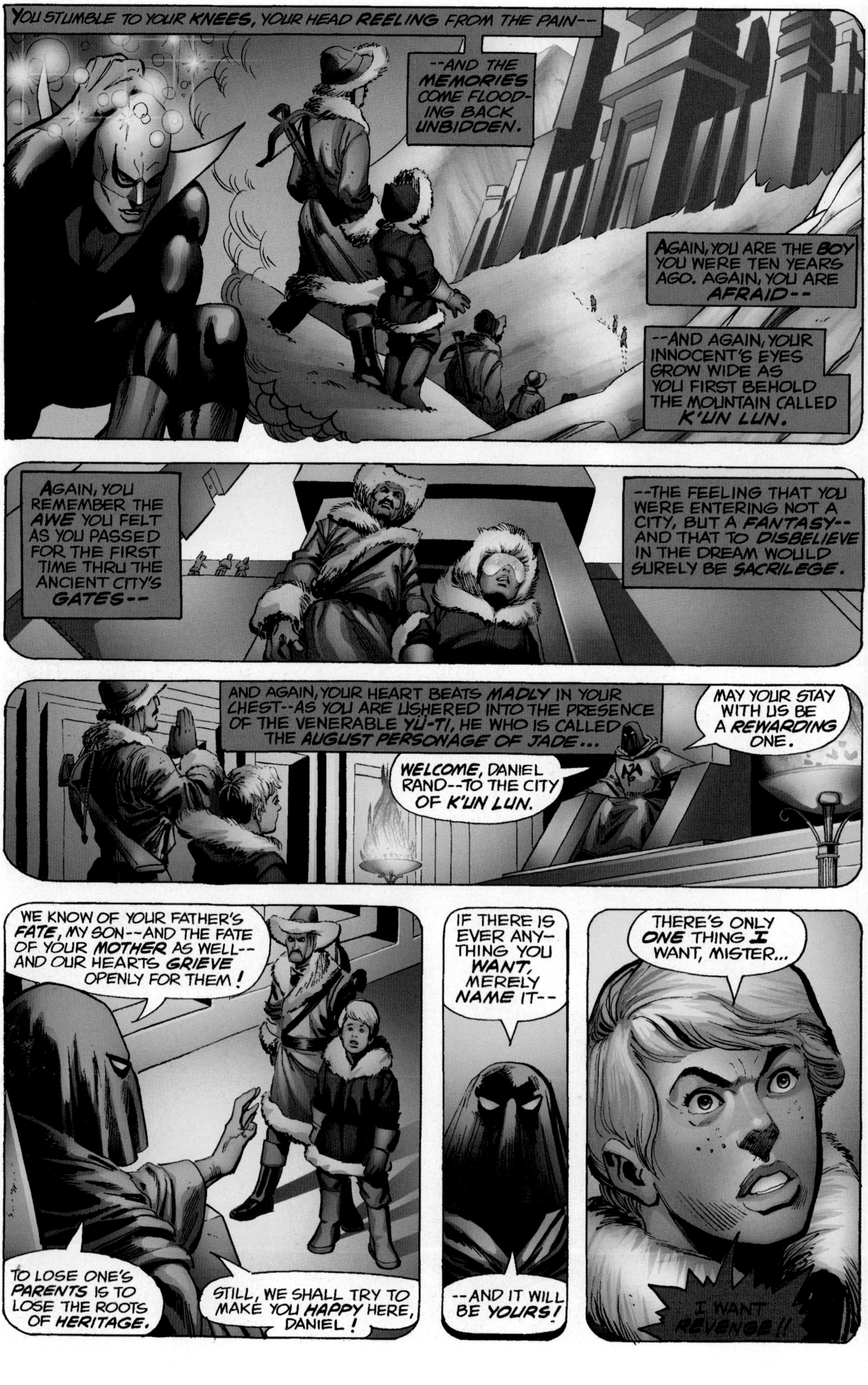

YOU STUMBLE TO YOUR KNEES, YOUR HEAD REELING FROM THE PAIN--
--AND THE MEMORIES COME FLOODING BACK UNBIDDEN.
AGAIN, YOU ARE THE BOY YOU WERE TEN YEARS AGO. AGAIN, YOU ARE AFRAID--
--AND AGAIN, YOUR INNOCENT'S EYES GROW WIDE AS YOU FIRST BEHOLD THE MOUNTAIN CALLED K'UN LUN.
AGAIN, YOU REMEMBER THE AWE YOU FELT AS YOU PASSED FOR THE FIRST TIME THRU THE ANCIENT CITY'S GATES--
--THE FEELING THAT YOU WERE ENTERING NOT A CITY, BUT A FANTASY--AND THAT TO DISBELIEVE IN THE DREAM WOULD SURELY BE SACRILEGE.
AND AGAIN, YOUR HEART BEATS MADLY IN YOUR CHEST--AS YOU ARE USHERED INTO THE PRESENCE OF THE VENERABLE YÜ-TI, HE WHO IS CALLED THE AUGUST PERSONAGE OF JADE...
WELCOME, DANIEL RAND--TO THE CITY OF K'UN LUN.
MAY YOUR STAY WITH US BE A REWARDING ONE.
WE KNOW OF YOUR FATHER'S FATE, MY SON--AND THE FATE OF YOUR MOTHER AS WELL--AND OUR HEARTS GRIEVE OPENLY FOR THEM!
TO LOSE ONE'S PARENTS IS TO LOSE THE ROOTS OF HERITAGE.
STILL, WE SHALL TRY TO MAKE YOU HAPPY HERE, DANIEL!
IF THERE IS EVER ANYTHING YOU WANT, MERELY NAME IT--
--AND IT WILL BE YOURS!
THERE'S ONLY ONE THING I WANT, MISTER...
I WANT REVENGE!!

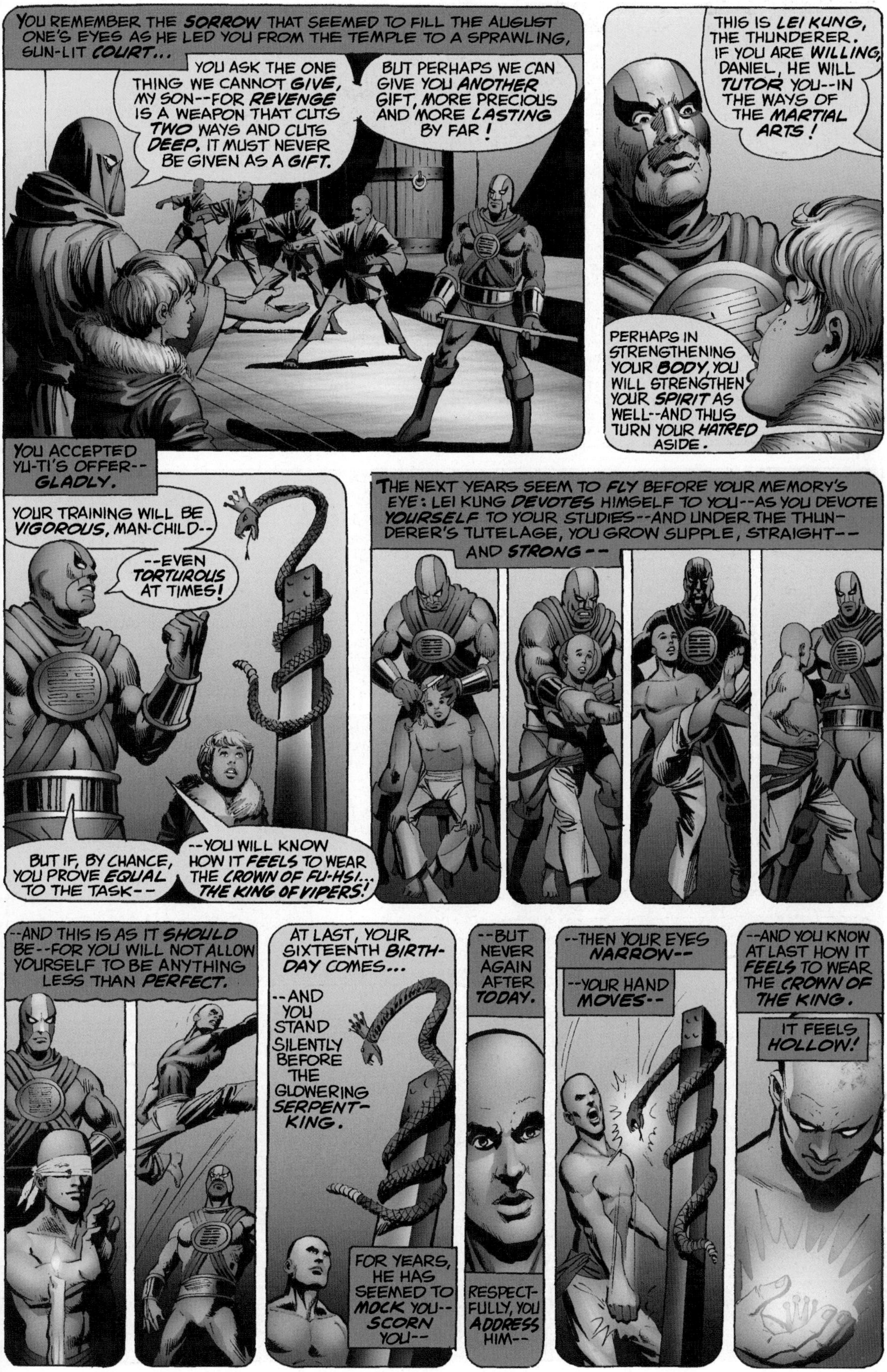
YOU REMEMBER THE SORROW THAT SEEMED TO FILL THE AUGUST ONE'S EYES AS HE LED YOU FROM THE TEMPLE TO A SPRAWLING, SUN-LIT COURT...
YOU ASK THE ONE THING WE CANNOT GIVE, MY SON--FOR REVENGE IS A WEAPON THAT CUTS TWO WAYS AND CUTS DEEP. IT MUST NEVER BE GIVEN AS A GIFT.
BUT PERHAPS WE CAN GIVE YOU ANOTHER GIFT, MORE PRECIOUS AND MORE LASTING BY FAR!
THIS IS LEI KUNG, THE THUNDERER. IF YOU ARE WILLING, DANIEL, HE WILL TUTOR YOU--IN THE WAYS OF THE MARTIAL ARTS!
PERHAPS IN STRENGTHENING YOUR BODY, YOU WILL STRENGTHEN YOUR SPIRIT AS WELL--AND THUS TURN YOUR HATRED ASIDE.
YOU ACCEPTED YU-TI'S OFFER--GLADLY.
YOUR TRAINING WILL BE VIGOROUS, MAN-CHILD--
--EVEN TORTUROUS AT TIMES!
BUT IF, BY CHANCE, YOU PROVE EQUAL TO THE TASK--
--YOU WILL KNOW HOW IT FEELS TO WEAR THE CROWN OF FU-HSI... THE KING OF VIPERS!
THE NEXT YEARS SEEM TO FLY BEFORE YOUR MEMORY'S EYE: LEI KUNG DEVOTES HIMSELF TO YOU--AS YOU DEVOTE YOURSELF TO YOUR STUDIES--AND UNDER THE THUNDERER'S TUTELAGE, YOU GROW SUPPLE, STRAIGHT--
--AND STRONG--
--AND THIS IS AS IT SHOULD BE--FOR YOU WILL NOT ALLOW YOURSELF TO BE ANYTHING LESS THAN PERFECT.
AT LAST, YOUR SIXTEENTH BIRTHDAY COMES...
--AND YOU STAND SILENTLY BEFORE THE GLOWERING SERPENT-KING.
FOR YEARS, HE HAS SEEMED TO MOCK YOU--SCORN YOU--
--BUT NEVER AGAIN AFTER TODAY.
RESPECTFULLY, YOU ADDRESS HIM--
--THEN YOUR EYES NARROW--
--YOUR HAND MOVES--
--AND YOU KNOW AT LAST HOW IT FEELS TO WEAR THE CROWN OF THE KING.
IT FEELS HOLLOW!

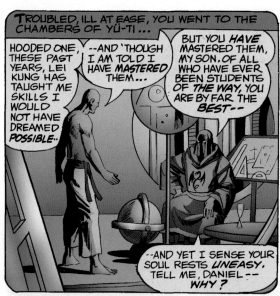

TROUBLED, ILL AT EASE, YOU WENT TO THE CHAMBERS OF YÜ-TI...

HOODED ONE, THESE PAST YEARS, LEI KUNG HAS TAUGHT ME SKILLS I WOULD NOT HAVE DREAMED POSSIBLE...

--AND 'THOUGH I AM TOLD I HAVE MASTERED THEM...

BUT YOU HAVE MASTERED THEM, MY SON. OF ALL WHO HAVE EVER BEEN STUDENTS OF THE WAY, YOU ARE BY FAR THE BEST--

--AND YET I SENSE YOUR SOUL RESTS UNEASY. TELL ME, DANIEL-- WHY?

AUGUST ONE, PLEASE--DO NOT THINK ME UNGRATEFUL FOR ALL YOU HAVE GIVEN ME--

--BUT IT IS NOT ENOUGH!

MEMORIES: FOR LESS THAN AN INSTANT YOUR MIND HAS WANDERED THRU THEM--

--BUT FOR ONE IN YOUR UNENVIABLE POSITION, EVEN SO BRIEF A DISTRACTION CAN PROVE QUITE FATAL.

THE ONE WHO STANDS BEHIND YOU CLENCHES HIS JAW-MUSCLES AS HE PREPARES TO DELIVER THE DEATH-BLOW--

--BUT THAT SPLIT-SECOND OF HESITATION IS AMPLE TIME FOR YOU TO REACT!

SPAK!

YOU WHIRL--A LIGHTNING KICK JARRING THE HEAVY BLUDGEON FROM HIS HAND--

--AND YOUR FOLLOW-THROUGH BRINGS YOU FACE-TO-FACE WITH YOUR ATTACKERS.

THEY'VE ALL REGAINED THEIR FOOTING AND STAND POISED TO RENEW THE ASSAULT--

--BUT YOUR SUDDEN RECOVERY HAS STARTLED THEM--

--AND THAT IS AN ADVANTAGE YOU QUICKLY PUT TO THE BEST OF USE!

CHUD!

PWOK!

YOUR ASSAILANTS ARE *NOT* INTELLIGENT MEN--BUT EVEN *THEY* QUICKLY REALIZE THAT NO REWARD IS WORTH SUCH SKILLFULLY-INFLICTED *PAIN.*

THEY *FLEE*--

OKAY, FREAK, SCORE ONE FER *YOU*--BUT YOU AIN'T HEARD THE *LAST* OF THIS!

AND YOU STAND, BATHED IN THE SWEAT OF YOUR *EXERTION,* WONDERING WHO COULD HAVE KNOWN OF YOUR *COMING*--

--AND PLACED SUCH A *PRICE* ON YOUR *HEAD.*

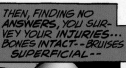

THEN, FINDING NO *ANSWERS,* YOU SURVEY YOUR INJURIES... BONES INTACT--BRUISES *SUPERFICIAL*--

--AND, ALMOST ACCIDENTALLY, YOUR FINGERS BRUSH THE DRAGON BRANDED ON YOUR CHEST-- THE DRAGON THAT MARKED YOU TO THESE MEN.

YOU *CONSIDER* THE DRAGON--THEN NOTICE YOUR WEAPON-*HANDS*--

...AND AGAIN THE *MEMORIES* COME...

YOUR HANDS: YOU WORKED DILIGENTLY TO *CONDITION* THEM AS LEI KUNG SAID YOU MUST--

--THRUSTING THEM CEASELESSLY INTO A DEEP TUB OF SAND--TO BUILD THE CALLUS AND DEADEN THE PAIN--

--AND, WHEN THE SAND WAS NO LONGER ENOUGH, INTO GRAVEL--

--AND, AT LAST, INTO BUCKETS OF *ROCK*--

--UNTIL YOUR HANDS *BECAME* AS THE ROCK--UNFEELING, IRRESISTIBLE--

HAI!

THRACK!

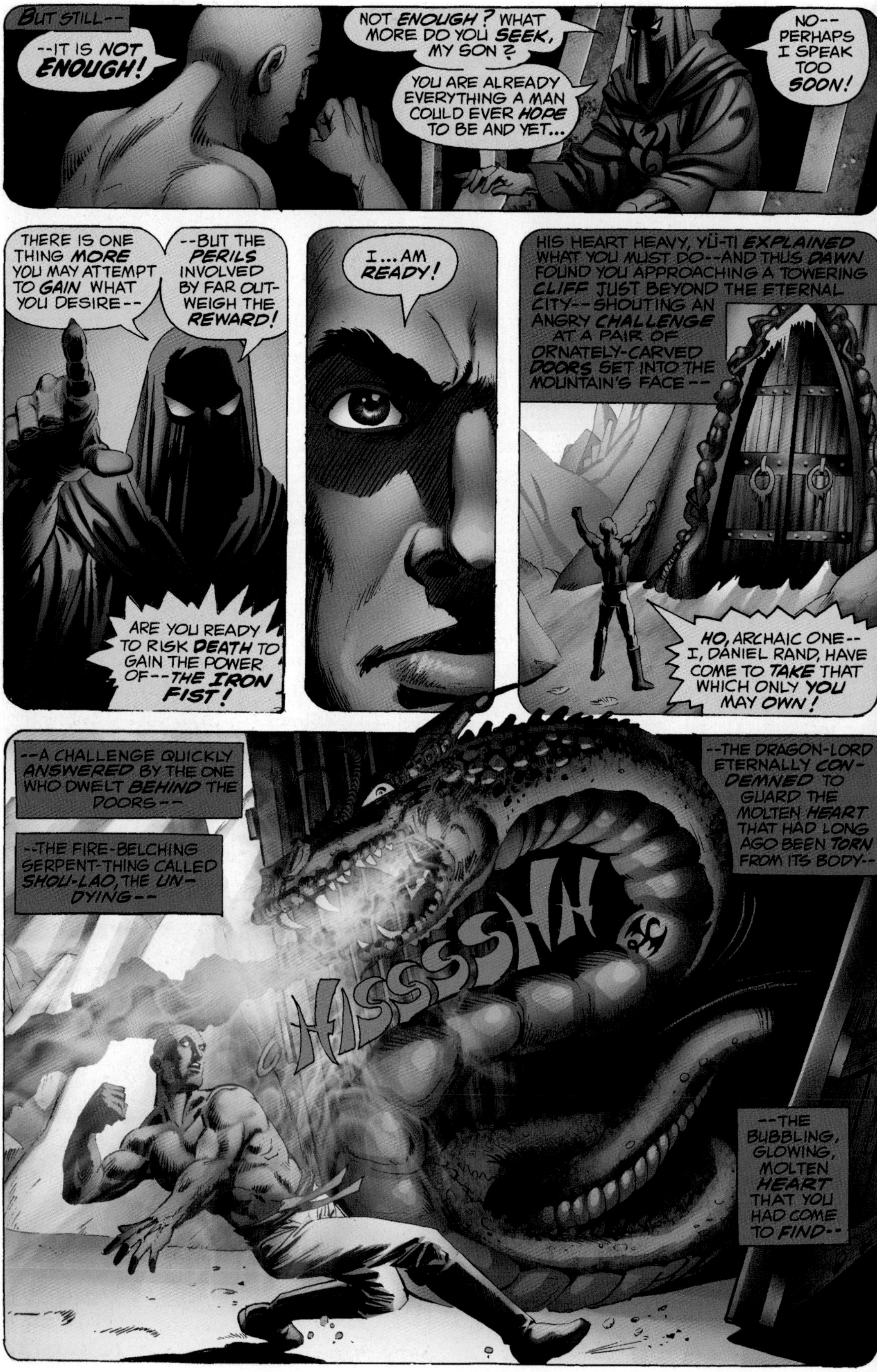
BUT STILL--
--IT IS NOT ENOUGH!
NOT ENOUGH? WHAT MORE DO YOU SEEK, MY SON?
YOU ARE ALREADY EVERYTHING A MAN COULD EVER HOPE TO BE AND YET...
NO--PERHAPS I SPEAK TOO SOON!
THERE IS ONE THING MORE YOU MAY ATTEMPT TO GAIN WHAT YOU DESIRE--
--BUT THE PERILS INVOLVED BY FAR OUTWEIGH THE REWARD!
ARE YOU READY TO RISK DEATH TO GAIN THE POWER OF--THE IRON FIST!
I...AM READY!
HIS HEART HEAVY, YÜ-TI EXPLAINED WHAT YOU MUST DO--AND THUS DAWN FOUND YOU APPROACHING A TOWERING CLIFF JUST BEYOND THE ETERNAL CITY--SHOUTING AN ANGRY CHALLENGE AT A PAIR OF ORNATELY-CARVED DOORS SET INTO THE MOUNTAIN'S FACE--
HO, ARCHAIC ONE--I, DANIEL RAND, HAVE COME TO TAKE THAT WHICH ONLY YOU MAY OWN!
--A CHALLENGE QUICKLY ANSWERED BY THE ONE WHO DWELT BEHIND THE DOORS--
--THE FIRE-BELCHING SERPENT-THING CALLED SHOU-LAO, THE UNDYING--
--THE DRAGON-LORD ETERNALLY CONDEMNED TO GUARD THE MOLTEN HEART THAT HAD LONG AGO BEEN TORN FROM ITS BODY--
HISSSSHH
--THE BUBBLING, GLOWING, MOLTEN HEART THAT YOU HAD COME TO FIND--

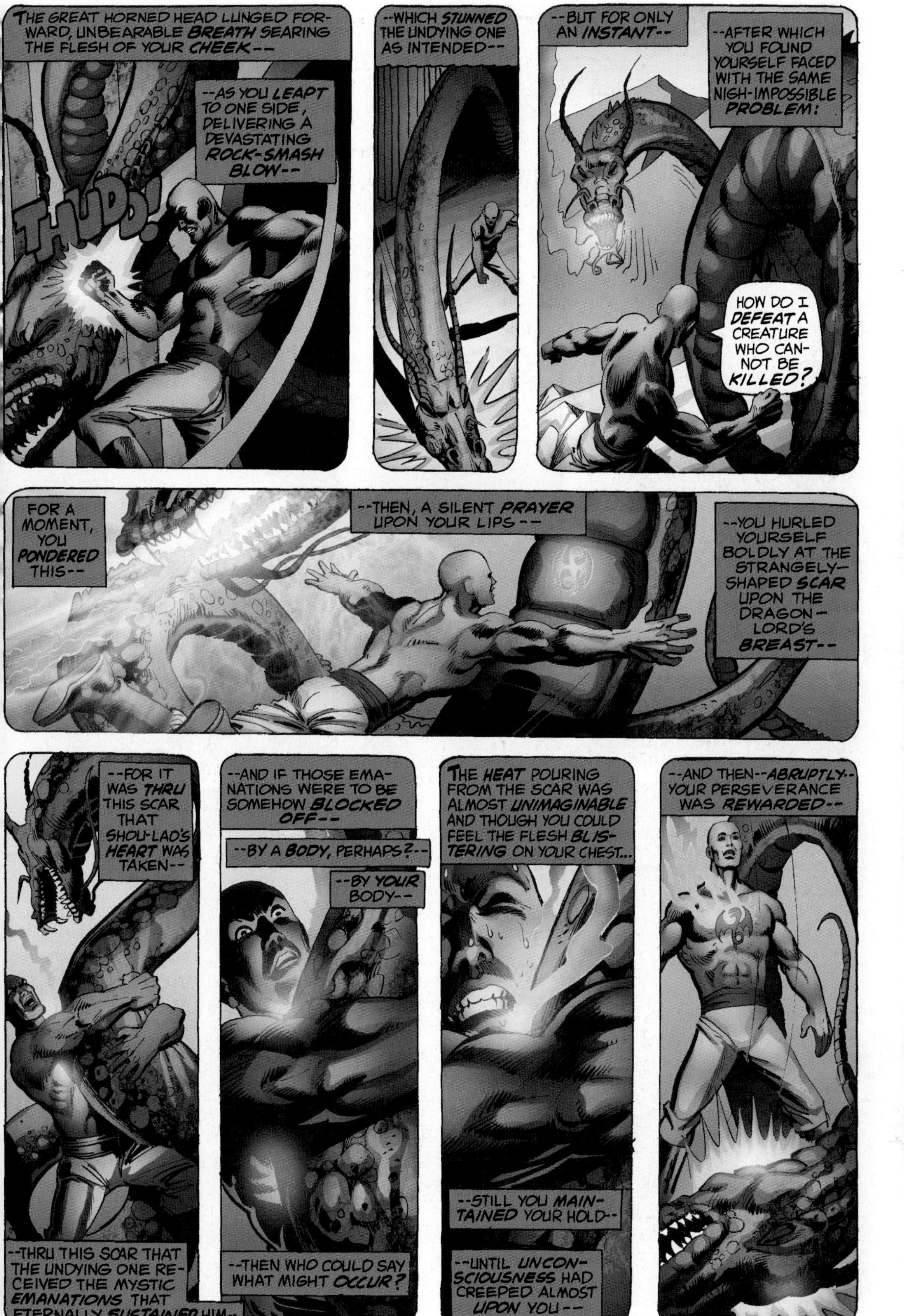
THE GREAT HORNED HEAD LUNGED FORWARD, UNBEARABLE BREATH SEARING THE FLESH OF YOUR CHEEK--
--AS YOU LEAPT TO ONE SIDE, DELIVERING A DEVASTATING ROCK-SMASH BLOW--
THUD!
--WHICH STUNNED THE UNDYING ONE AS INTENDED--
--BUT FOR ONLY AN INSTANT--
--AFTER WHICH YOU FOUND YOURSELF FACED WITH THE SAME NIGH-IMPOSSIBLE PROBLEM:
HOW DO I DEFEAT A CREATURE WHO CANNOT BE KILLED?
FOR A MOMENT, YOU PONDERED THIS--
--THEN, A SILENT PRAYER UPON YOUR LIPS--
--YOU HURLED YOURSELF BOLDLY AT THE STRANGELY-SHAPED SCAR UPON THE DRAGON-LORD'S BREAST--
--FOR IT WAS THRU THIS SCAR THAT SHOU-LAO'S HEART WAS TAKEN--
--THRU THIS SCAR THAT THE UNDYING ONE RECEIVED THE MYSTIC EMANATIONS THAT ETERNALLY SUSTAINED HIM--
--AND IF THOSE EMANATIONS WERE TO BE SOMEHOW BLOCKED OFF--
--BY A BODY, PERHAPS?--
--BY YOUR BODY--
--THEN WHO COULD SAY WHAT MIGHT OCCUR?
THE HEAT POURING FROM THE SCAR WAS ALMOST UNIMAGINABLE AND THOUGH YOU COULD FEEL THE FLESH BLISTERING ON YOUR CHEST...
--STILL YOU MAINTAINED YOUR HOLD--
--UNTIL UNCONSCIOUSNESS HAD CREEPED ALMOST UPON YOU--
--AND THEN--ABRUPTLY--YOUR PERSEVERANCE WAS REWARDED--

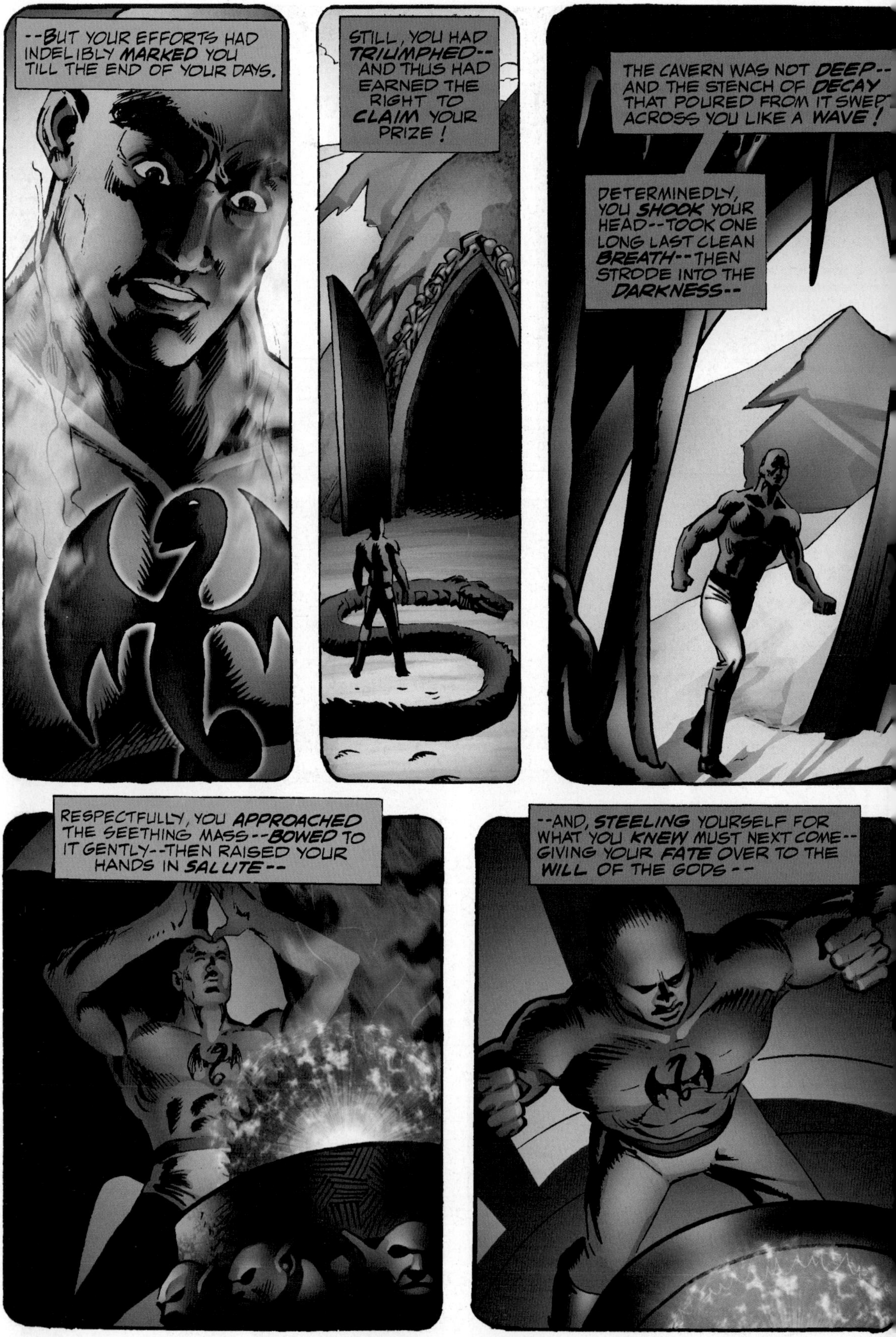

--BUT YOUR EFFORTS HAD INDELIBLY MARKED YOU TILL THE END OF YOUR DAYS.
STILL, YOU HAD TRIUMPHED-- AND THUS HAD EARNED THE RIGHT TO CLAIM YOUR PRIZE!
THE CAVERN WAS NOT DEEP-- AND THE STENCH OF DECAY THAT POURED FROM IT SWEPT ACROSS YOU LIKE A WAVE!
DETERMINEDLY, YOU SHOOK YOUR HEAD--TOOK ONE LONG LAST CLEAN BREATH--THEN STRODE INTO THE DARKNESS--
RESPECTFULLY, YOU APPROACHED THE SEETHING MASS--BOWED TO IT GENTLY--THEN RAISED YOUR HANDS IN SALUTE--
--AND, STEELING YOURSELF FOR WHAT YOU KNEW MUST NEXT COME--GIVING YOUR FATE OVER TO THE WILL OF THE GODS--

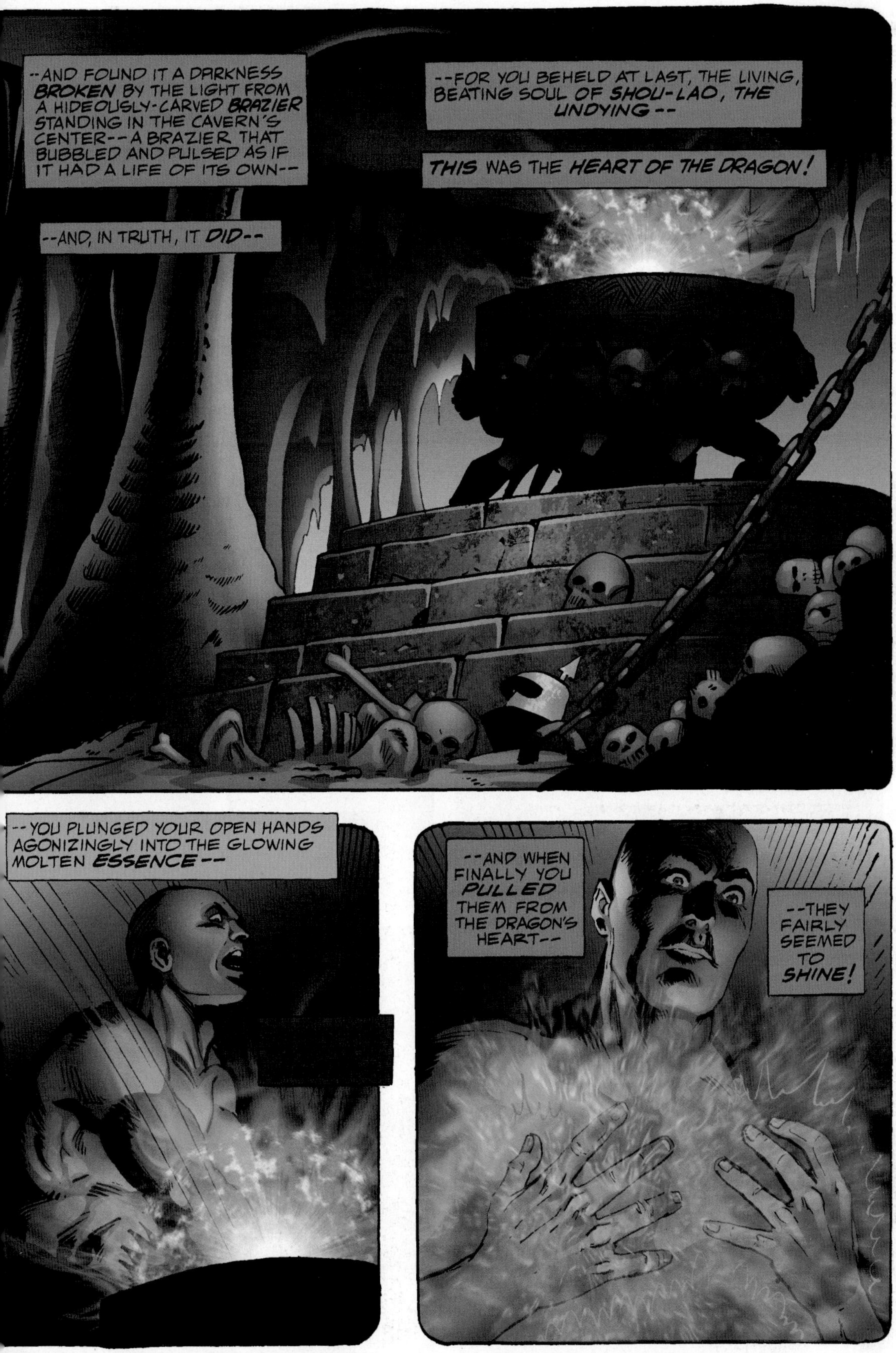
--AND FOUND IT A DARKNESS BROKEN BY THE LIGHT FROM A HIDEOUSLY-CARVED BRAZIER STANDING IN THE CAVERN'S CENTER--A BRAZIER THAT BUBBLED AND PULSED AS IF IT HAD A LIFE OF ITS OWN--
--AND, IN TRUTH, IT DID--
--FOR YOU BEHELD AT LAST, THE LIVING, BEATING SOUL OF SHOU-LAO, THE UNDYING--
THIS WAS THE HEART OF THE DRAGON!
--YOU PLUNGED YOUR OPEN HANDS AGONIZINGLY INTO THE GLOWING MOLTEN ESSENCE--
[redacted]
--AND WHEN FINALLY YOU PULLED THEM FROM THE DRAGON'S HEART--
--THEY FAIRLY SEEMED TO SHINE!

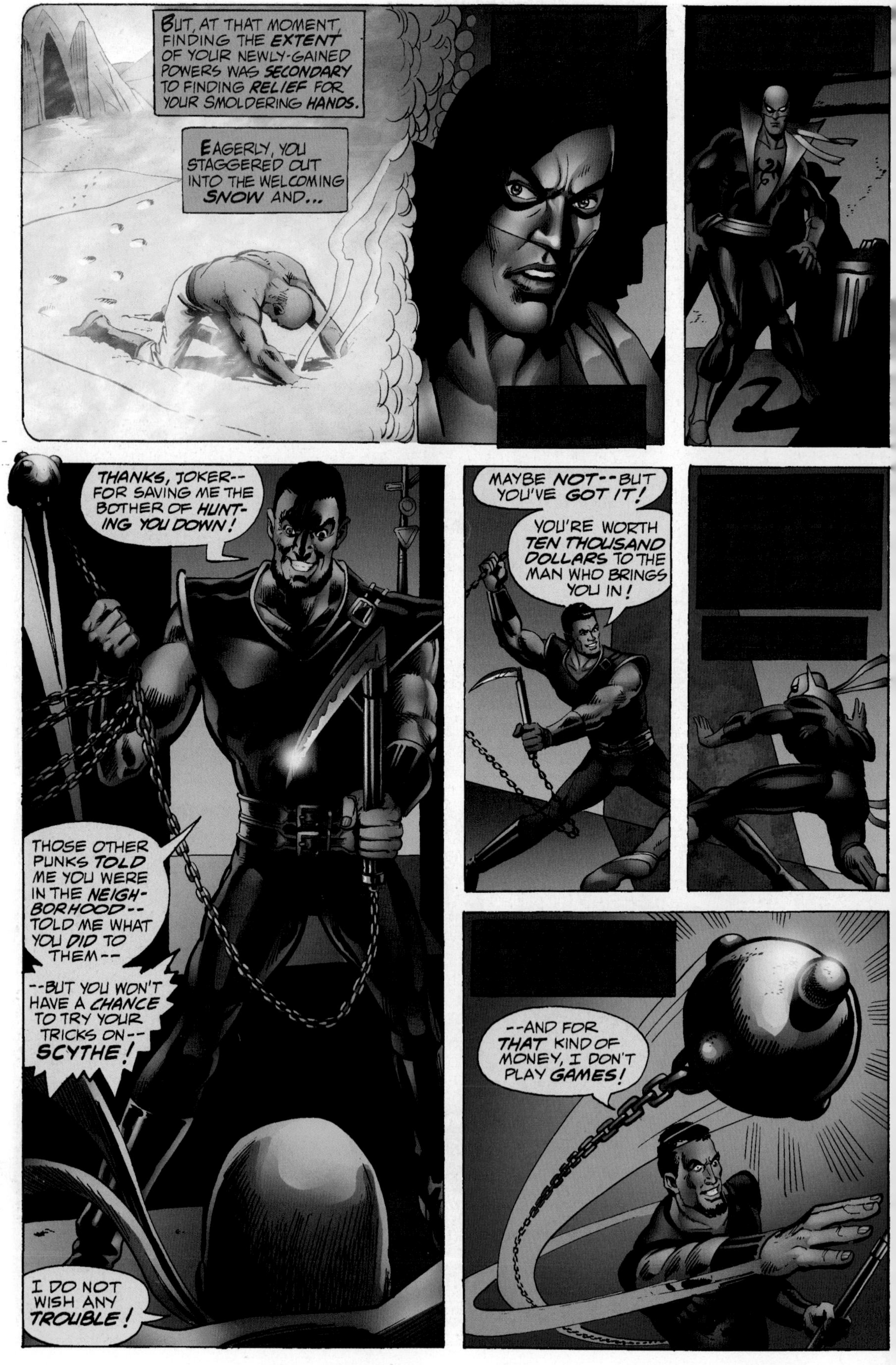
BUT, AT THAT MOMENT, FINDING THE EXTENT OF YOUR NEWLY-GAINED POWERS WAS SECONDARY TO FINDING RELIEF FOR YOUR SMOLDERING HANDS.
EAGERLY, YOU STAGGERED OUT INTO THE WELCOMING SNOW AND...
[redacted]
THANKS, JOKER-- FOR SAVING ME THE BOTHER OF HUNTING YOU DOWN!
THOSE OTHER PUNKS TOLD ME YOU WERE IN THE NEIGHBORHOOD-- TOLD ME WHAT YOU DID TO THEM--
--BUT YOU WON'T HAVE A CHANCE TO TRY YOUR TRICKS ON-- SCYTHE!
I DO NOT WISH ANY TROUBLE!
MAYBE NOT--BUT YOU'VE GOT IT!
YOU'RE WORTH TEN THOUSAND DOLLARS TO THE MAN WHO BRINGS YOU IN!
[redacted]
[redacted]
[redacted]
--AND FOR THAT KIND OF MONEY, I DON'T PLAY GAMES!

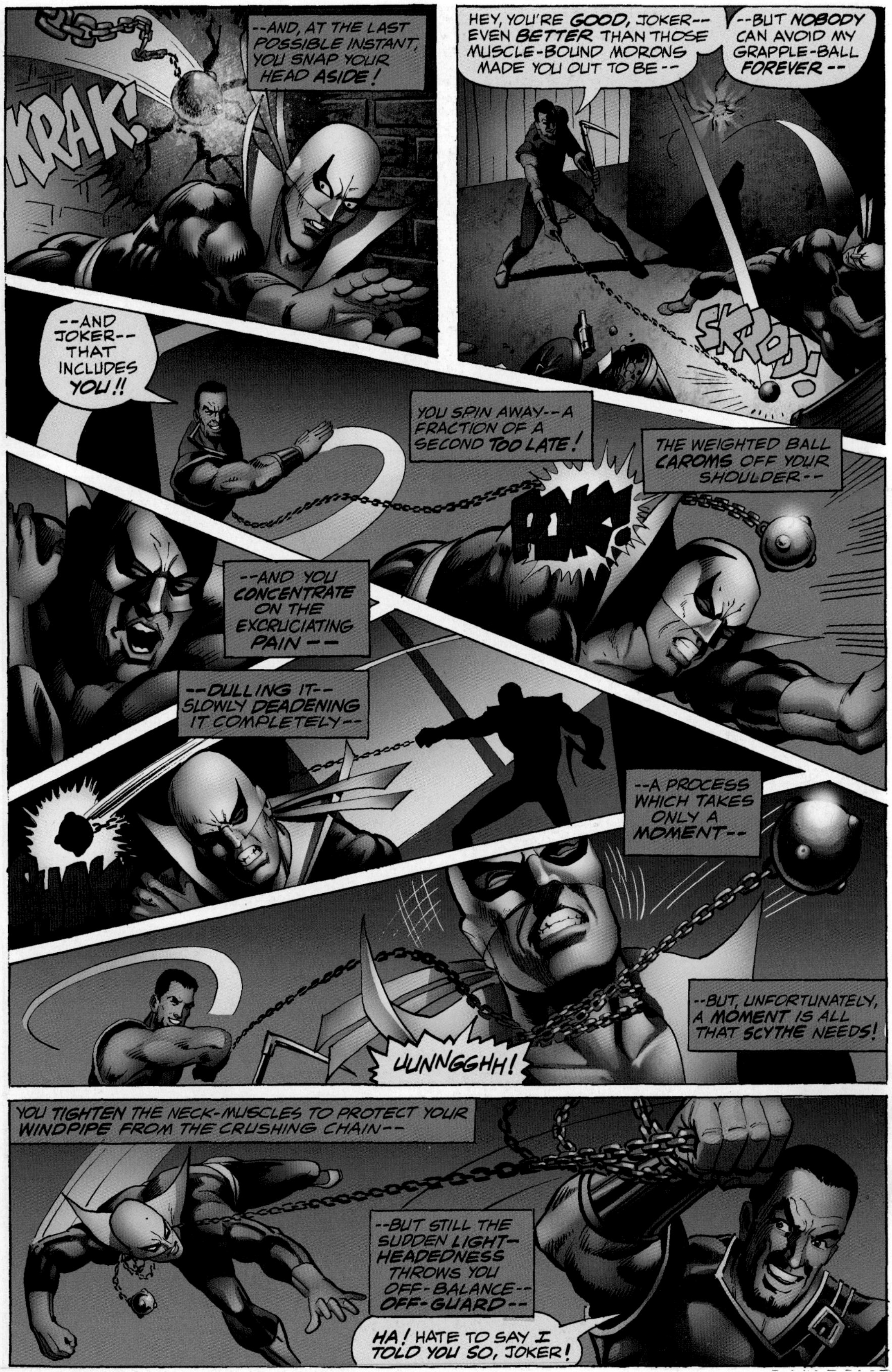
--AND, AT THE LAST POSSIBLE INSTANT, YOU SNAP YOUR HEAD ASIDE!
KRAK!
HEY, YOU'RE GOOD, JOKER-- EVEN BETTER THAN THOSE MUSCLE-BOUND MORONS MADE YOU OUT TO BE--
--BUT NOBODY CAN AVOID MY GRAPPLE-BALL FOREVER--
SKROD!
--AND JOKER-- THAT INCLUDES YOU!!
YOU SPIN AWAY--A FRACTION OF A SECOND TOO LATE!
THE WEIGHTED BALL CAROMS OFF YOUR SHOULDER--
--AND YOU CONCENTRATE ON THE EXCRUCIATING PAIN--
--DULLING IT-- SLOWLY DEADENING IT COMPLETELY--
--A PROCESS WHICH TAKES ONLY A MOMENT--
--BUT, UNFORTUNATELY, A MOMENT IS ALL THAT SCYTHE NEEDS!
UUNNGGHH!
YOU TIGHTEN THE NECK-MUSCLES TO PROTECT YOUR WINDPIPE FROM THE CRUSHING CHAIN--
--BUT STILL THE SUDDEN LIGHT-HEADEDNESS THROWS YOU OFF-BALANCE-- OFF-GUARD--
HA! HATE TO SAY I TOLD YOU SO, JOKER!

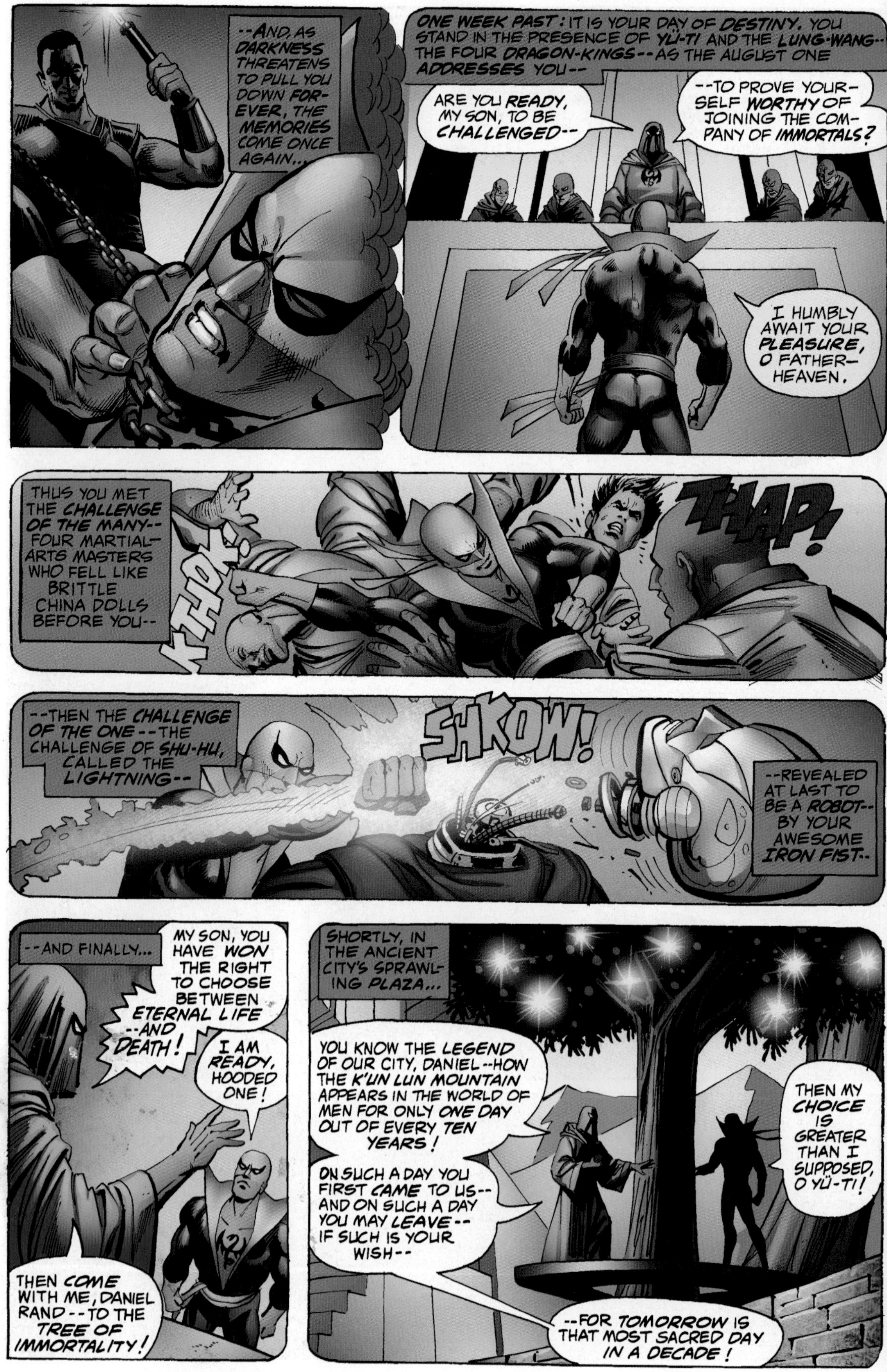
--AND, AS DARKNESS THREATENS TO PULL YOU DOWN FOR-EVER, THE MEMORIES COME ONCE AGAIN...
ONE WEEK PAST: IT IS YOUR DAY OF DESTINY. YOU STAND IN THE PRESENCE OF YÜ-TI AND THE LUNG-WANG--THE FOUR DRAGON-KINGS--AS THE AUGUST ONE ADDRESSES YOU--
ARE YOU READY, MY SON, TO BE CHALLENGED--
--TO PROVE YOUR-SELF WORTHY OF JOINING THE COM-PANY OF IMMORTALS?
I HUMBLY AWAIT YOUR PLEASURE, O FATHER-HEAVEN.
THUS YOU MET THE CHALLENGE OF THE MANY--FOUR MARTIAL-ARTS MASTERS WHO FELL LIKE BRITTLE CHINA DOLLS BEFORE YOU--
KTHOK
THAP!
--THEN THE CHALLENGE OF THE ONE--THE CHALLENGE OF SHU-HU, CALLED THE LIGHTNING--
SHKOW!
--REVEALED AT LAST TO BE A ROBOT--BY YOUR AWESOME IRON FIST--
--AND FINALLY...
MY SON, YOU HAVE WON THE RIGHT TO CHOOSE BETWEEN ETERNAL LIFE--AND DEATH!
I AM READY, HOODED ONE!
THEN COME WITH ME, DANIEL RAND--TO THE TREE OF IMMORTALITY!
SHORTLY, IN THE ANCIENT CITY'S SPRAWL-ING PLAZA...
YOU KNOW THE LEGEND OF OUR CITY, DANIEL--HOW THE K'UN LUN MOUNTAIN APPEARS IN THE WORLD OF MEN FOR ONLY ONE DAY OUT OF EVERY TEN YEARS!
ON SUCH A DAY YOU FIRST CAME TO US--AND ON SUCH A DAY YOU MAY LEAVE--IF SUCH IS YOUR WISH--
THEN MY CHOICE IS GREATER THAN I SUPPOSED, O YÜ-TI!
--FOR TOMORROW IS THAT MOST SACRED DAY IN A DECADE!

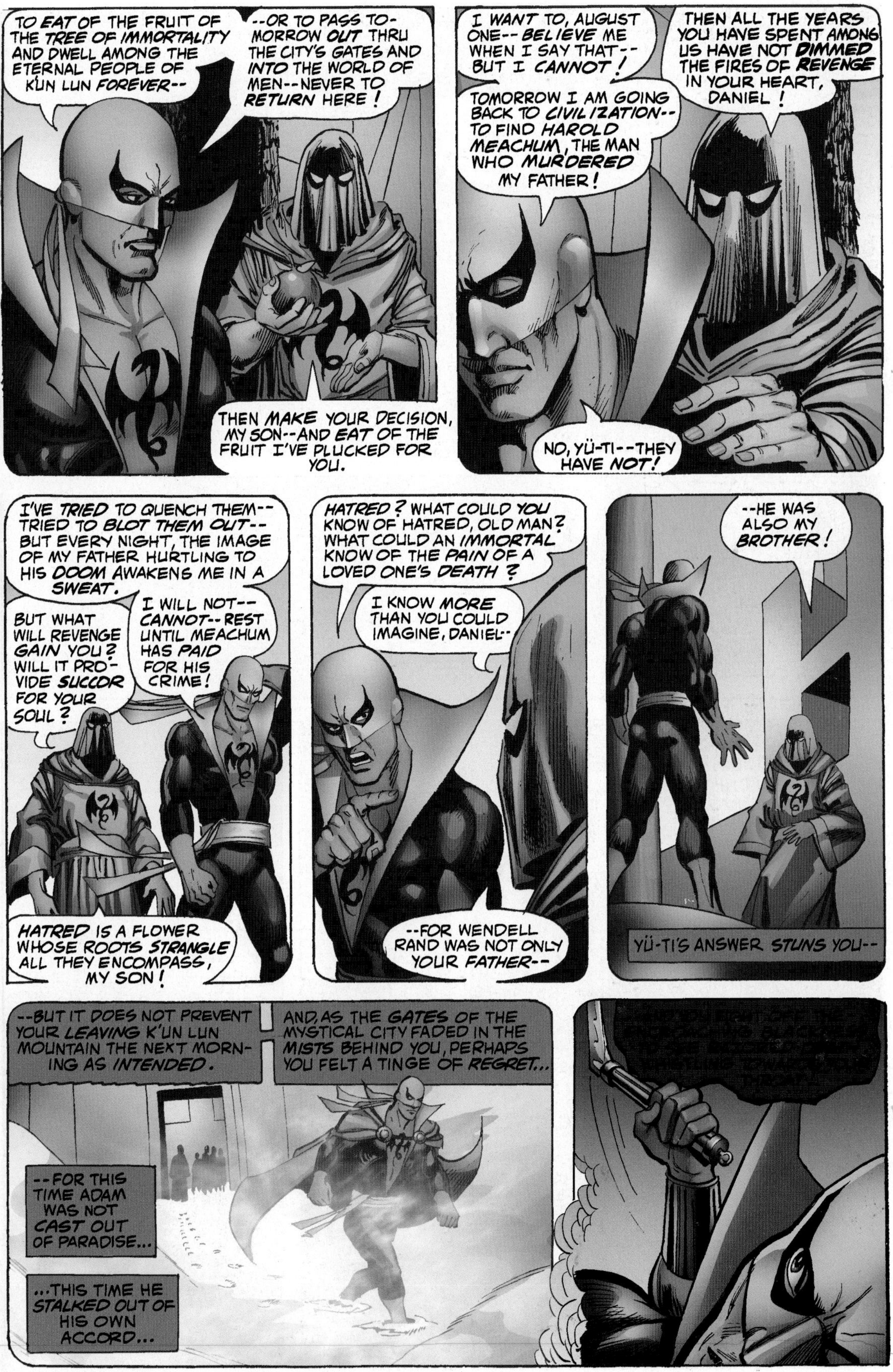

TO EAT OF THE FRUIT OF THE TREE OF IMMORTALITY AND DWELL AMONG THE ETERNAL PEOPLE OF K'UN LUN FOREVER--
--OR TO PASS TO-MORROW OUT THRU THE CITY'S GATES AND INTO THE WORLD OF MEN--NEVER TO RETURN HERE!
THEN MAKE YOUR DECISION, MY SON--AND EAT OF THE FRUIT I'VE PLUCKED FOR YOU.
I WANT TO, AUGUST ONE--BELIEVE ME WHEN I SAY THAT--BUT I CANNOT!
TOMORROW I AM GOING BACK TO CIVILIZATION--TO FIND HAROLD MEACHUM, THE MAN WHO MURDERED MY FATHER!
THEN ALL THE YEARS YOU HAVE SPENT AMONG US HAVE NOT DIMMED THE FIRES OF REVENGE IN YOUR HEART, DANIEL!
NO, YÜ-TI--THEY HAVE NOT!
I'VE TRIED TO QUENCH THEM--TRIED TO BLOT THEM OUT--BUT EVERY NIGHT, THE IMAGE OF MY FATHER HURTLING TO HIS DOOM AWAKENS ME IN A SWEAT.
BUT WHAT WILL REVENGE GAIN YOU? WILL IT PRO-VIDE SUCCOR FOR YOUR SOUL?
I WILL NOT--CANNOT--REST UNTIL MEACHUM HAS PAID FOR HIS CRIME!
HATRED IS A FLOWER WHOSE ROOTS STRANGLE ALL THEY ENCOMPASS, MY SON!
HATRED? WHAT COULD YOU KNOW OF HATRED, OLD MAN? WHAT COULD AN IMMORTAL KNOW OF THE PAIN OF A LOVED ONE'S DEATH?
I KNOW MORE THAN YOU COULD IMAGINE, DANIEL--
--FOR WENDELL RAND WAS NOT ONLY YOUR FATHER--
--HE WAS ALSO MY BROTHER!
YÜ-TI'S ANSWER STUNS YOU--
--BUT IT DOES NOT PREVENT YOUR LEAVING K'UN LUN MOUNTAIN THE NEXT MORNING AS INTENDED.
AND, AS THE GATES OF THE MYSTICAL CITY FADED IN THE MISTS BEHIND YOU, PERHAPS YOU FELT A TINGE OF REGRET...
--FOR THIS TIME ADAM WAS NOT CAST OUT OF PARADISE...
...THIS TIME HE STALKED OUT OF HIS OWN ACCORD...

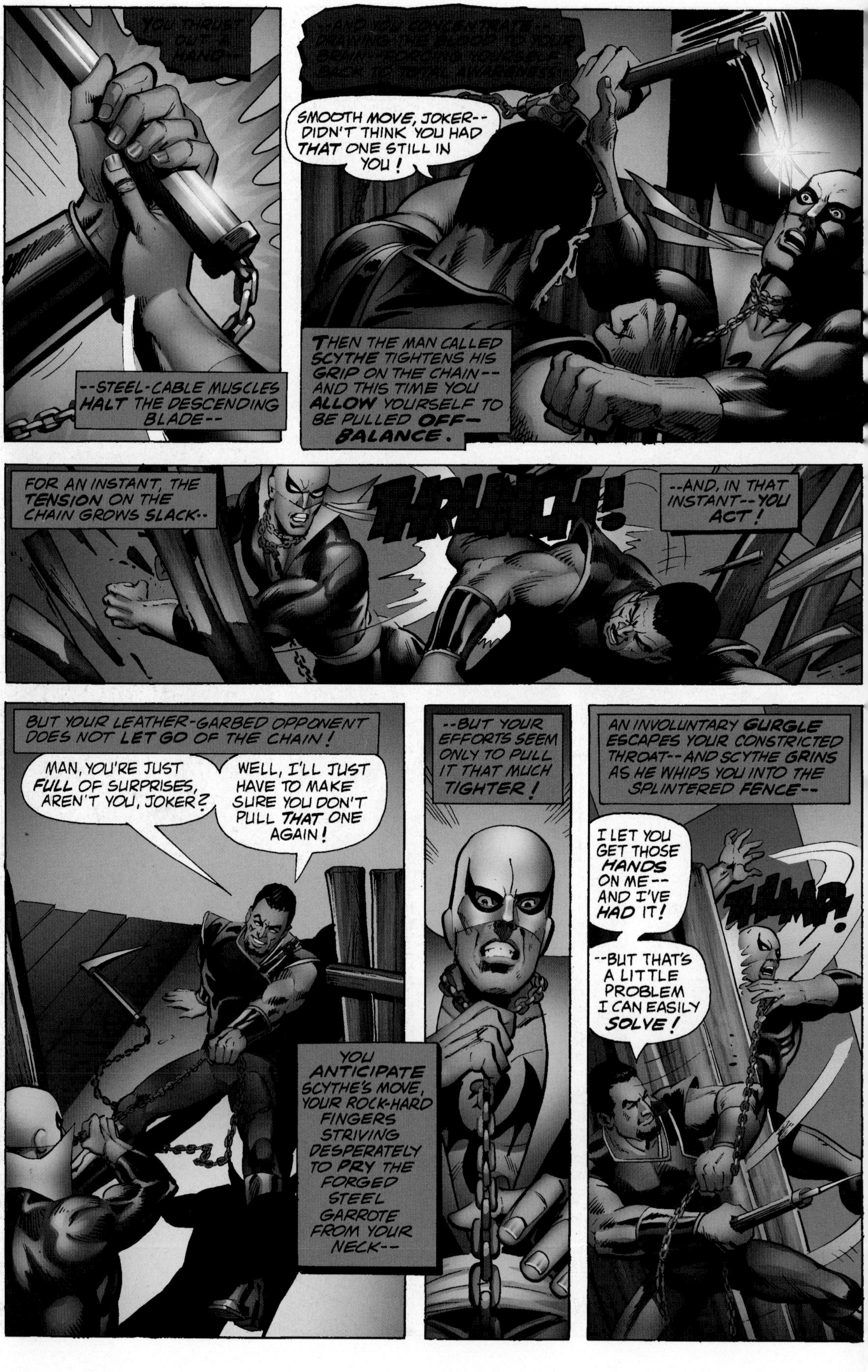

YOU THRUST OUT A HAND--
--STEEL-CABLE MUSCLES HALT THE DESCENDING BLADE--
--AND YOU CONCENTRATE--DRAWING THE BLOOD TO YOUR BRAIN--FORCING YOURSELF BACK TO TOTAL AWARENESS.
SMOOTH MOVE, JOKER--DIDN'T THINK YOU HAD THAT ONE STILL IN YOU!
THEN THE MAN CALLED SCYTHE TIGHTENS HIS GRIP ON THE CHAIN--AND THIS TIME YOU ALLOW YOURSELF TO BE PULLED OFF-BALANCE.
FOR AN INSTANT, THE TENSION ON THE CHAIN GROWS SLACK..
THRUNCH!
--AND, IN THAT INSTANT--YOU ACT!
BUT YOUR LEATHER-GARBED OPPONENT DOES NOT LET GO OF THE CHAIN!
MAN, YOU'RE JUST FULL OF SURPRISES, AREN'T YOU, JOKER?
WELL, I'LL JUST HAVE TO MAKE SURE YOU DON'T PULL THAT ONE AGAIN!
YOU ANTICIPATE SCYTHE'S MOVE, YOUR ROCK-HARD FINGERS STRIVING DESPERATELY TO PRY THE FORGED STEEL GARROTE FROM YOUR NECK--
--BUT YOUR EFFORTS SEEM ONLY TO PULL IT THAT MUCH TIGHTER!
AN INVOLUNTARY GURGLE ESCAPES YOUR CONSTRICTED THROAT--AND SCYTHE GRINS AS HE WHIPS YOU INTO THE SPLINTERED FENCE--
THUMP!
I LET YOU GET THOSE HANDS ON ME--AND I'VE HAD IT!
--BUT THAT'S A LITTLE PROBLEM I CAN EASILY SOLVE!

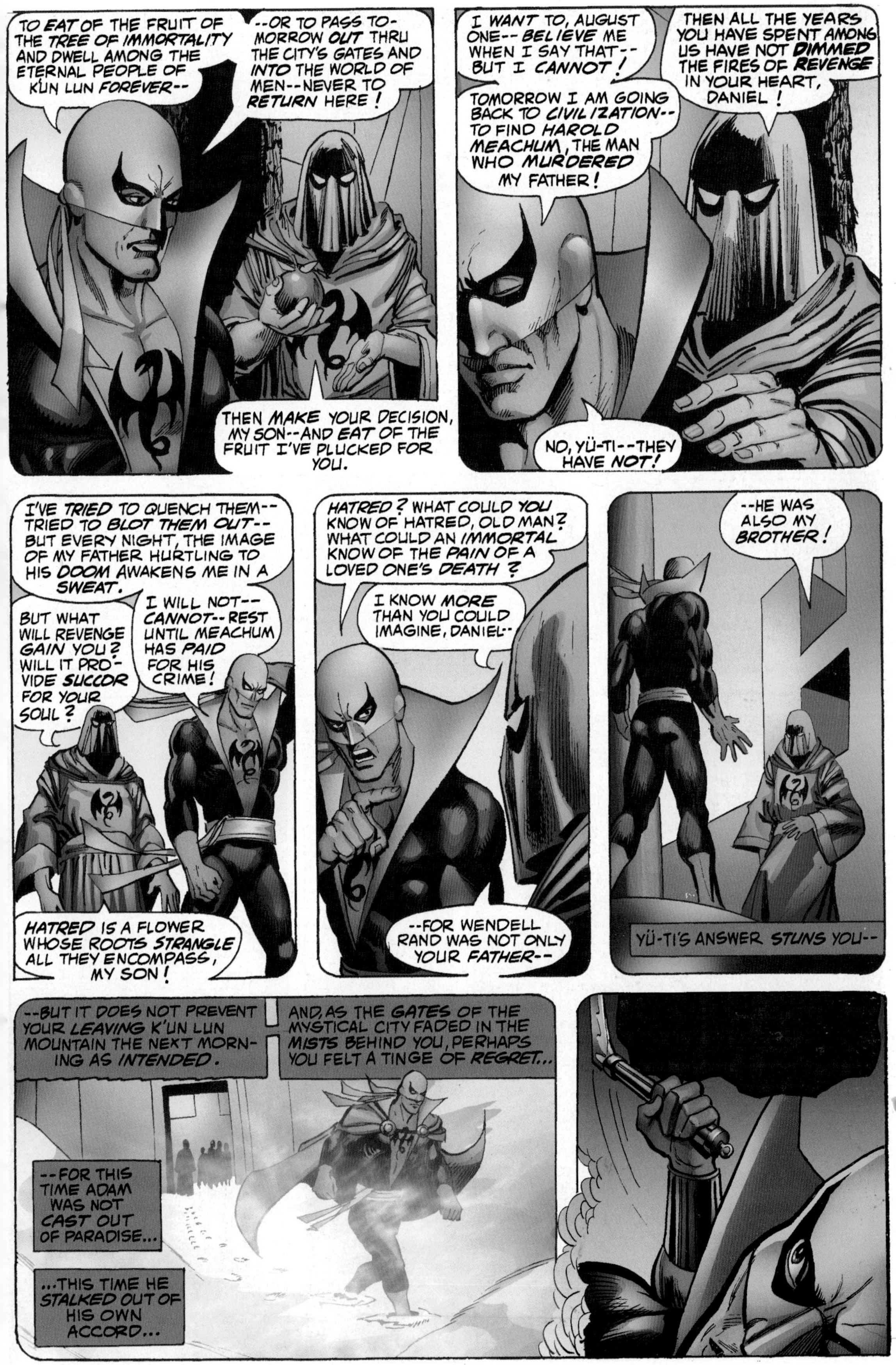
TO EAT OF THE FRUIT OF THE TREE OF IMMORTALITY AND DWELL AMONG THE ETERNAL PEOPLE OF K'UN LUN FOREVER--
--OR TO PASS TO-MORROW OUT THRU THE CITY'S GATES AND INTO THE WORLD OF MEN--NEVER TO RETURN HERE!
THEN MAKE YOUR DECISION, MY SON--AND EAT OF THE FRUIT I'VE PLUCKED FOR YOU.
I WANT TO, AUGUST ONE--BELIEVE ME WHEN I SAY THAT--BUT I CANNOT!
TOMORROW I AM GOING BACK TO CIVILIZATION--TO FIND HAROLD MEACHUM, THE MAN WHO MURDERED MY FATHER!
THEN ALL THE YEARS YOU HAVE SPENT AMONG US HAVE NOT DIMMED THE FIRES OF REVENGE IN YOUR HEART, DANIEL!
NO, YÜ-TI--THEY HAVE NOT!
I'VE TRIED TO QUENCH THEM--TRIED TO BLOT THEM OUT--BUT EVERY NIGHT, THE IMAGE OF MY FATHER HURTLING TO HIS DOOM AWAKENS ME IN A SWEAT.
BUT WHAT WILL REVENGE GAIN YOU? WILL IT PRO-VIDE SUCCOR FOR YOUR SOUL?
I WILL NOT--CANNOT--REST UNTIL MEACHUM HAS PAID FOR HIS CRIME!
HATRED IS A FLOWER WHOSE ROOTS STRANGLE ALL THEY ENCOMPASS, MY SON!
HATRED? WHAT COULD YOU KNOW OF HATRED, OLD MAN? WHAT COULD AN IMMORTAL KNOW OF THE PAIN OF A LOVED ONE'S DEATH?
I KNOW MORE THAN YOU COULD IMAGINE, DANIEL--
--FOR WENDELL RAND WAS NOT ONLY YOUR FATHER--
--HE WAS ALSO MY BROTHER!
YÜ-TI'S ANSWER STUNS YOU--
--BUT IT DOES NOT PREVENT YOUR LEAVING K'UN LUN MOUNTAIN THE NEXT MORN-ING AS INTENDED.
AND, AS THE GATES OF THE MYSTICAL CITY FADED IN THE MISTS BEHIND YOU, PERHAPS YOU FELT A TINGE OF REGRET...
--FOR THIS TIME ADAM WAS NOT CAST OUT OF PARADISE...
...THIS TIME HE STALKED OUT OF HIS OWN ACCORD...

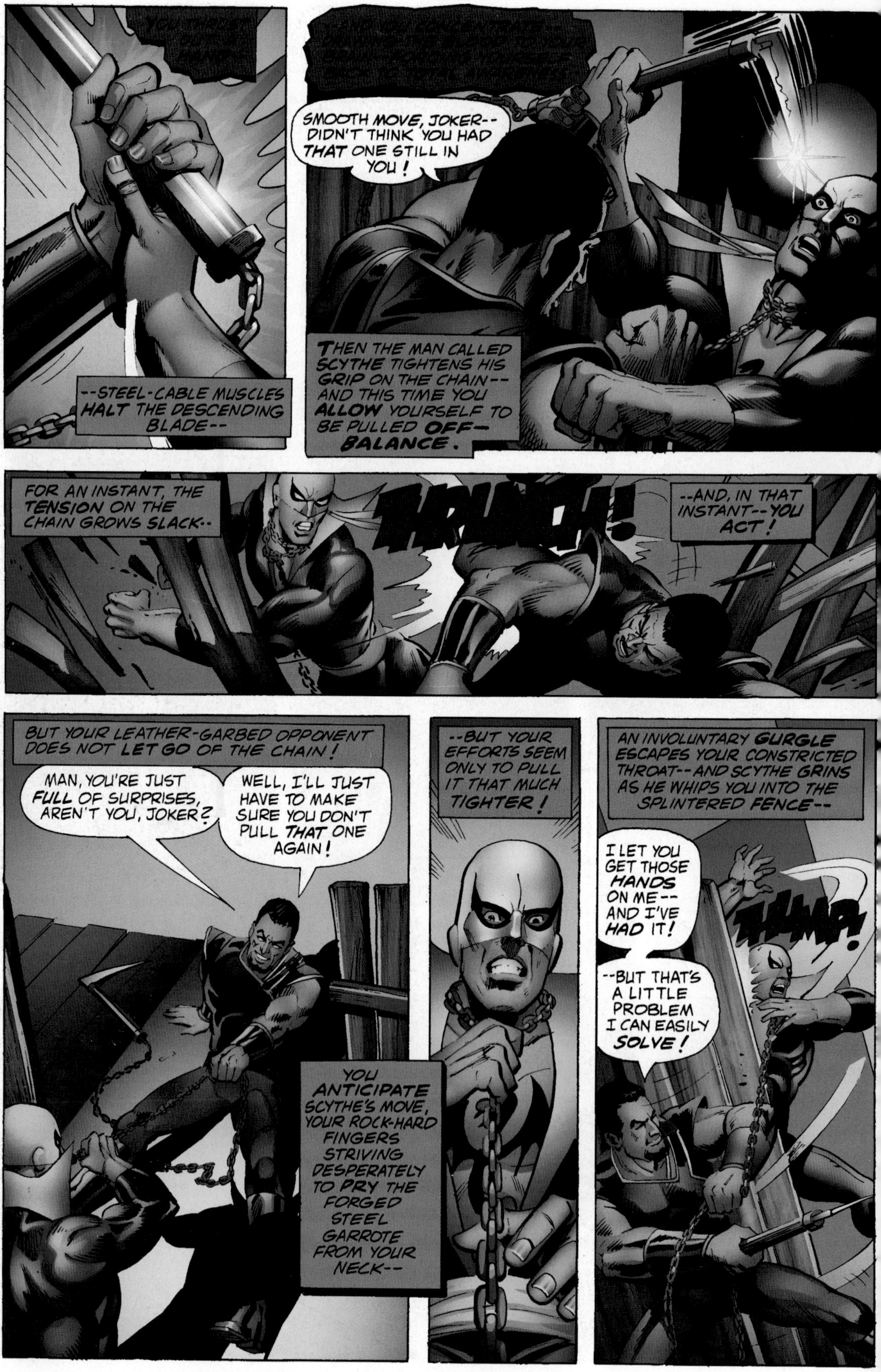
SMOOTH MOVE, JOKER-- DIDN'T THINK YOU HAD THAT ONE STILL IN YOU!
--STEEL-CABLE MUSCLES HALT THE DESCENDING BLADE--
THEN THE MAN CALLED SCYTHE TIGHTENS HIS GRIP ON THE CHAIN-- AND THIS TIME YOU ALLOW YOURSELF TO BE PULLED OFF-BALANCE.
FOR AN INSTANT, THE TENSION ON THE CHAIN GROWS SLACK--
THRUNCH!
--AND, IN THAT INSTANT--YOU ACT!
BUT YOUR LEATHER-GARBED OPPONENT DOES NOT LET GO OF THE CHAIN!
MAN, YOU'RE JUST FULL OF SURPRISES, AREN'T YOU, JOKER?
WELL, I'LL JUST HAVE TO MAKE SURE YOU DON'T PULL THAT ONE AGAIN!
YOU ANTICIPATE SCYTHE'S MOVE, YOUR ROCK-HARD FINGERS STRIVING DESPERATELY TO PRY THE FORGED STEEL GARROTE FROM YOUR NECK--
--BUT YOUR EFFORTS SEEM ONLY TO PULL IT THAT MUCH TIGHTER!
AN INVOLUNTARY GURGLE ESCAPES YOUR CONSTRICTED THROAT--AND SCYTHE GRINS AS HE WHIPS YOU INTO THE SPLINTERED FENCE--
I LET YOU GET THOSE HANDS ON ME-- AND I'VE HAD IT!
THAMP!
--BUT THAT'S A LITTLE PROBLEM I CAN EASILY SOLVE!

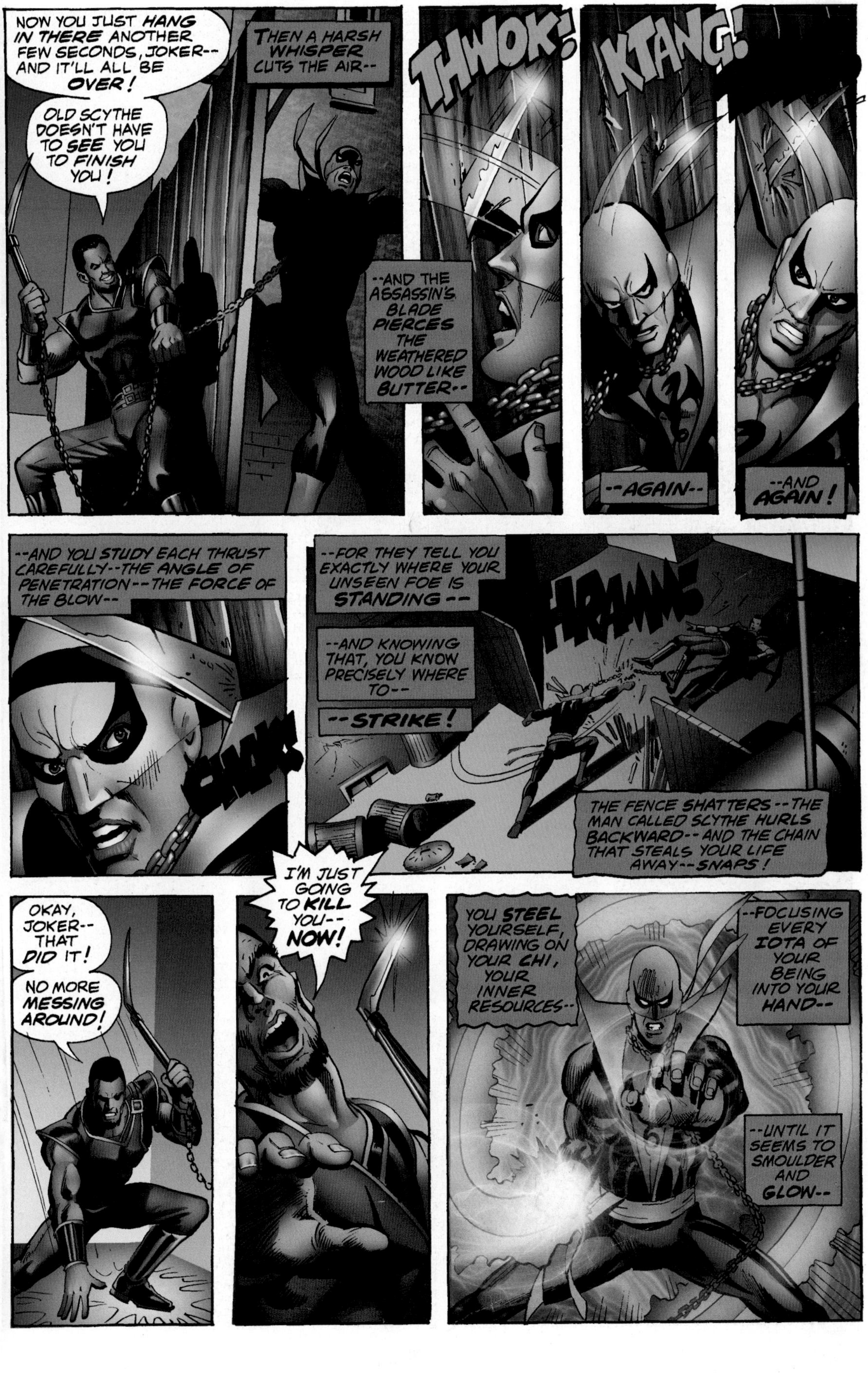
NOW YOU JUST HANG IN THERE ANOTHER FEW SECONDS, JOKER-- AND IT'LL ALL BE OVER!
OLD SCYTHE DOESN'T HAVE TO SEE YOU TO FINISH YOU!
THEN A HARSH WHISPER CUTS THE AIR--
THWOK!
KTANG!
--AND THE ASSASSIN'S BLADE PIERCES THE WEATHERED WOOD LIKE BUTTER--
--AGAIN--
--AND AGAIN!
--AND YOU STUDY EACH THRUST CAREFULLY--THE ANGLE OF PENETRATION--THE FORCE OF THE BLOW--
--FOR THEY TELL YOU EXACTLY WHERE YOUR UNSEEN FOE IS STANDING--
--AND KNOWING THAT, YOU KNOW PRECISELY WHERE TO--
--STRIKE!
THE FENCE SHATTERS--THE MAN CALLED SCYTHE HURLS BACKWARD--AND THE CHAIN THAT STEALS YOUR LIFE AWAY--SNAPS!
OKAY, JOKER-- THAT DID IT!
NO MORE MESSING AROUND!
I'M JUST GOING TO KILL YOU-- NOW!
YOU STEEL YOURSELF, DRAWING ON YOUR CHI, YOUR INNER RESOURCES--
--FOCUSING EVERY IOTA OF YOUR BEING INTO YOUR HAND--
--UNTIL IT SEEMS TO SMOULDER AND GLOW--

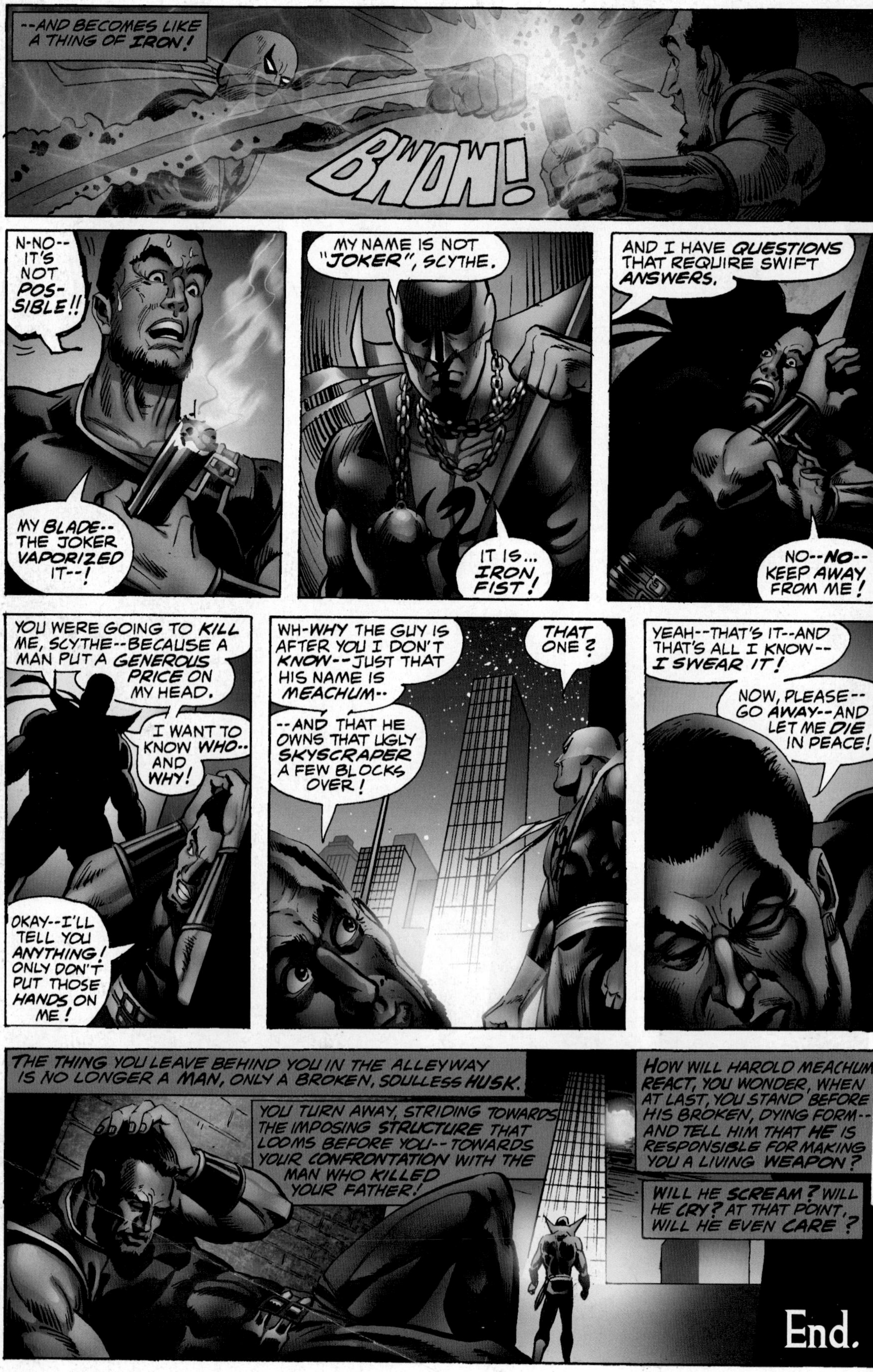
--AND BECOMES LIKE A THING OF IRON!
BWOW!
N-NO-- IT'S NOT POS-SIBLE!!
MY BLADE-- THE JOKER VAPORIZED IT--!
MY NAME IS NOT "JOKER", SCYTHE.
IT IS... IRON FIST!
AND I HAVE QUESTIONS THAT REQUIRE SWIFT ANSWERS.
NO--NO-- KEEP AWAY FROM ME!
YOU WERE GOING TO KILL ME, SCYTHE--BECAUSE A MAN PUT A GENEROUS PRICE ON MY HEAD.
I WANT TO KNOW WHO-- AND WHY!
OKAY--I'LL TELL YOU ANYTHING! ONLY DON'T PUT THOSE HANDS ON ME!
WH-WHY THE GUY IS AFTER YOU I DON'T KNOW--JUST THAT HIS NAME IS MEACHUM--
--AND THAT HE OWNS THAT UGLY SKYSCRAPER A FEW BLOCKS OVER!
THAT ONE?
YEAH--THAT'S IT--AND THAT'S ALL I KNOW-- I SWEAR IT!
NOW, PLEASE-- GO AWAY--AND LET ME DIE IN PEACE!
THE THING YOU LEAVE BEHIND YOU IN THE ALLEYWAY IS NO LONGER A MAN, ONLY A BROKEN, SOULLESS HUSK.
YOU TURN AWAY, STRIDING TOWARDS THE IMPOSING STRUCTURE THAT LOOMS BEFORE YOU--TOWARDS YOUR CONFRONTATION WITH THE MAN WHO KILLED YOUR FATHER!
HOW WILL HAROLD MEACHUM REACT, YOU WONDER, WHEN AT LAST, YOU STAND BEFORE HIS BROKEN, DYING FORM--AND TELL HIM THAT HE IS RESPONSIBLE FOR MAKING YOU A LIVING WEAPON?
WILL HE SCREAM? WILL HE CRY? AT THAT POINT, WILL HE EVEN CARE?
End.

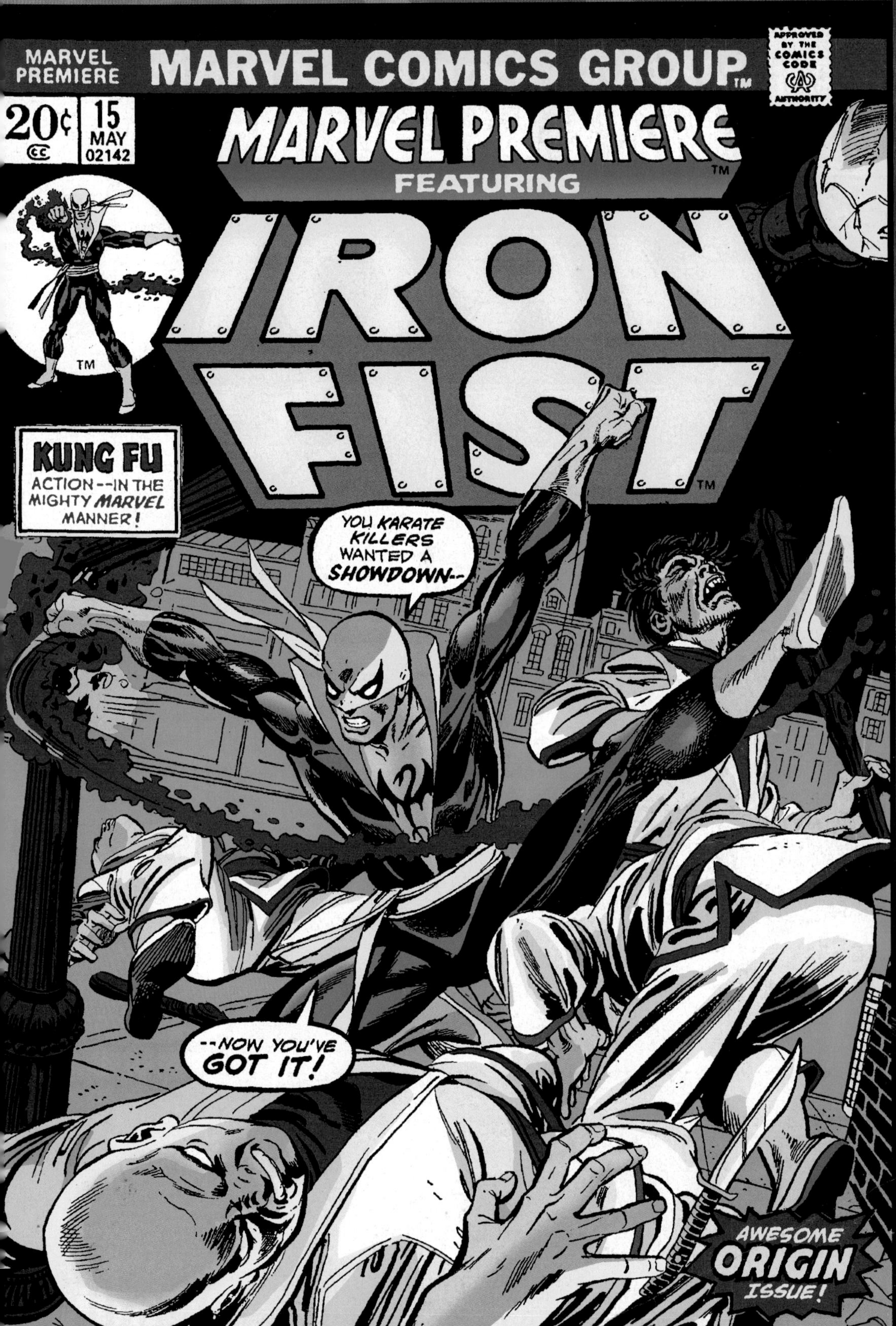
MARVEL PREMIERE
MARVEL COMICS GROUP
APPROVED BY THE COMICS CODE AUTHORITY
20¢
15 MAY 02142
MARVEL PREMIERE
FEATURING
IRON FIST
KUNG FU
ACTION--IN THE MIGHTY MARVEL MANNER!
YOU KARATE KILLERS WANTED A SHOWDOWN--
--NOW YOU'VE GOT IT!
AWESOME ORIGIN ISSUE!

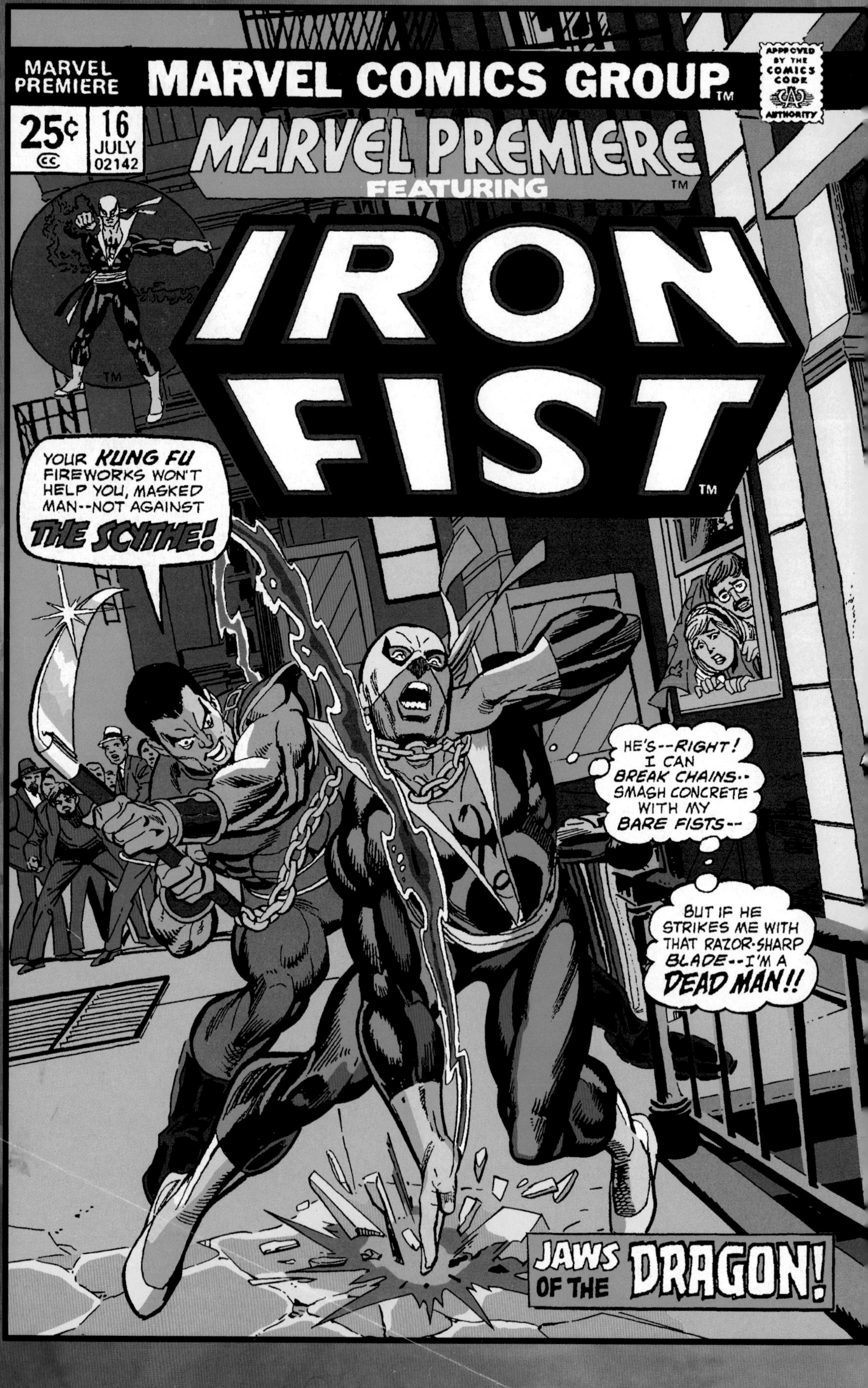
MARVEL PREMIERE
MARVEL COMICS GROUP
APPROVED BY THE COMICS CODE AUTHORITY
25¢ 16 JULY 02142
MARVEL PREMIERE FEATURING
IRON FIST
YOUR KUNG FU FIREWORKS WON'T HELP YOU, MASKED MAN--NOT AGAINST THE SCYTHE!
HE'S--RIGHT! I CAN BREAK CHAINS.. SMASH CONCRETE WITH MY BARE FISTS--
BUT IF HE STRIKES ME WITH THAT RAZOR-SHARP BLADE--I'M A DEAD MAN!!
JAWS OF THE DRAGON!

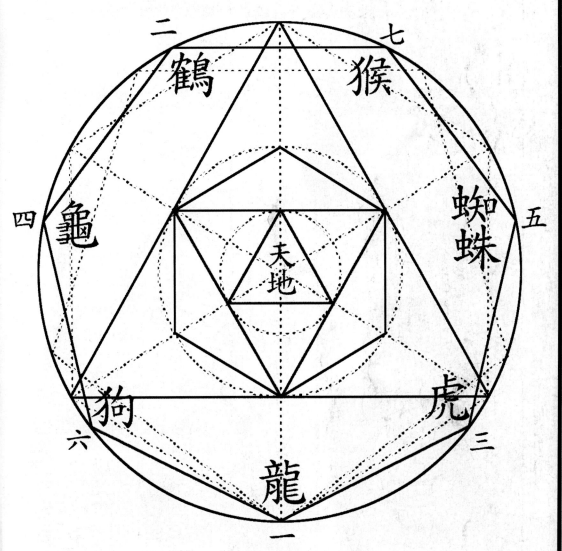

The Seven
Capital Cities
of Heaven

HEPTAGONAL MAP OF THE SEVEN CAPITAL CITIES OF HEAVEN
BY DAVID AJA

CHARACTER SKETCHES BY DAVID AJA

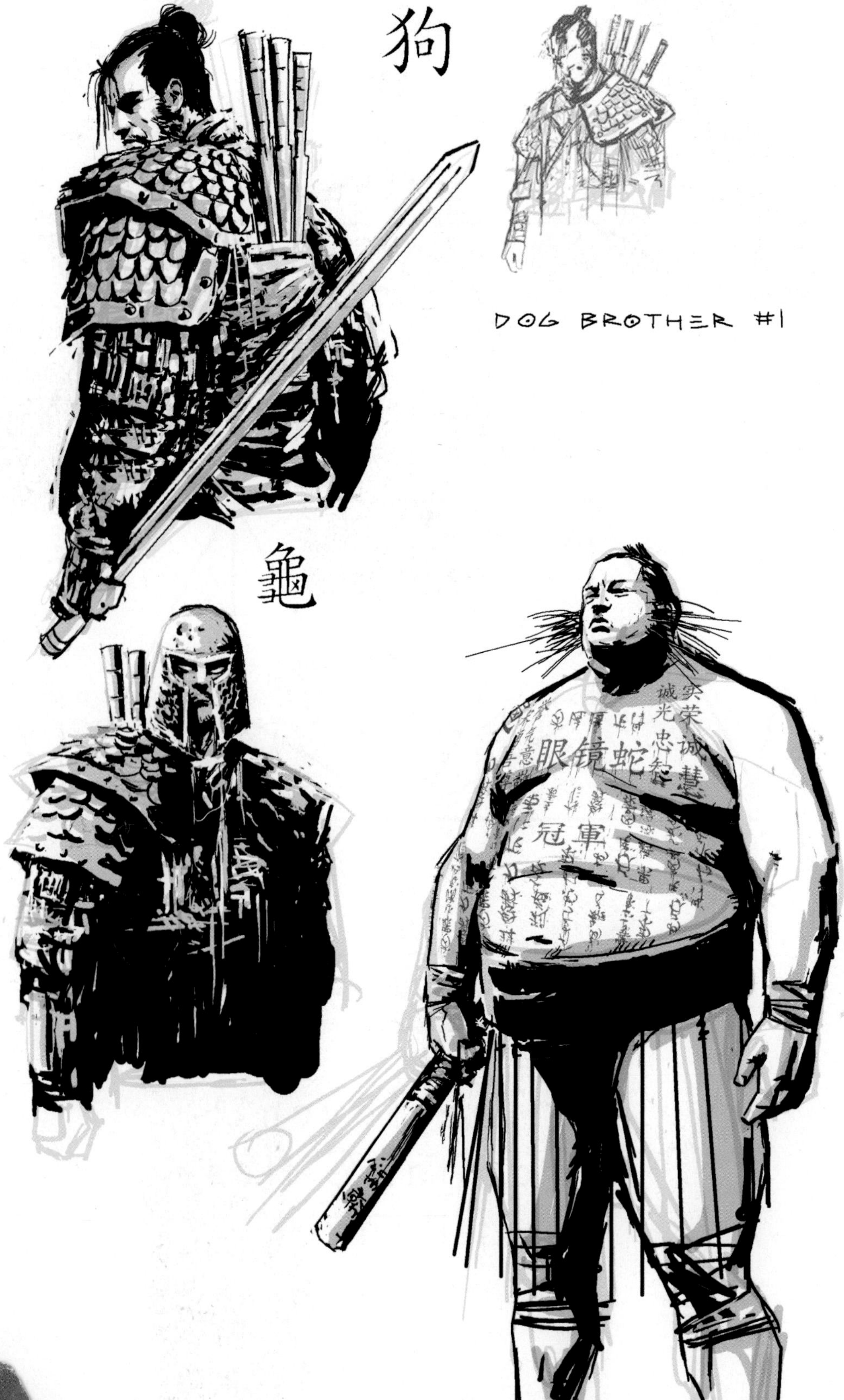

狗
DOG BROTHER #1
龜
眼鏡蛇
冠軍
FAT COBRA

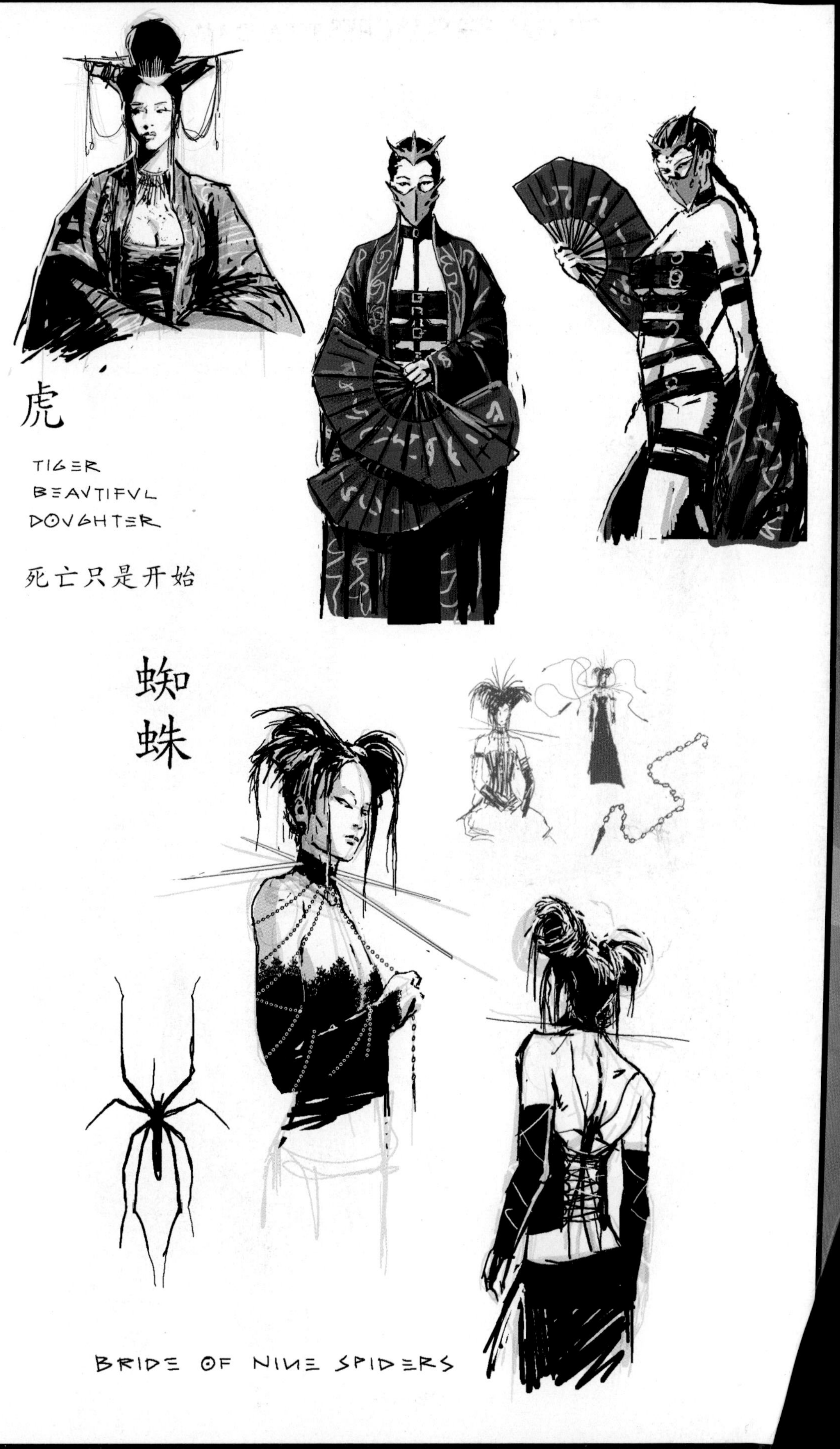
虎
TIGER
BEAUTIFUL
DOUGHTER
死亡只是开始
蜘蛛
BRIDE OF NINE SPIDERS

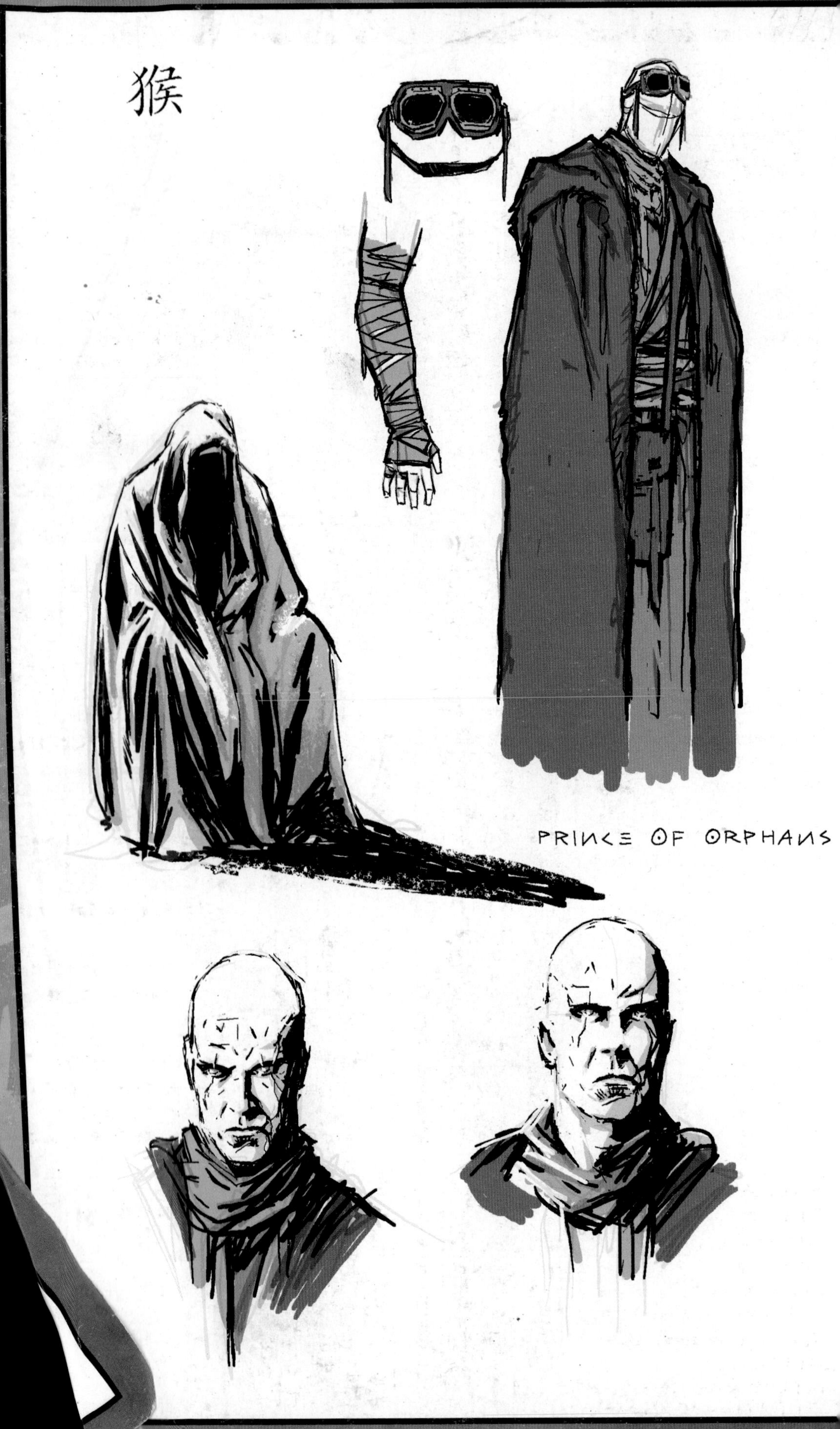
猴
PRINCE OF ORPHANS